★★★ THE STORY OF AMERICAN METHODISM

A History of the United Methodists and Their Relations

FREDERICK A. NORWOOD

ABINGDON
Nashville

THE STORY OF AMERICAN METHODISM

Copyright © 1974 by Abingdon Press

Fourth Printing 1981

Library of Congress Cataloging in Publication Data

NORWOOD, FREDERICK ABBOTT.
  The story of American Methodism.
  1. Methodist Church in the United States.   I. Title.
BX8235.N65   287'.673   74-10621

ISBN 0-687-39640-9
ISBN 0-687-39641-7 (pbk.)

MANUFACTURED BY THE PARTHENON PRESS AT
NASHVILLE, TENNESSEE, UNITED STATES OF AMERICA

To the ministering people of the
United Methodist Church of Mill Valley, California,
who provided spiritual nourishment
and the
Trinity Church of the North Shore, Wilmette, Illinois,
who provided both that and the other kind

CONTENTS

PREFACE

This is a kind of bicentennial book. It appears on the eve of a national remembering of revolutionary origins. This coincidence may serve as a reminder that the Wesleyan movement wrought another kind of revolution, at the same time it developed young sinews during the American Revolution. The book appears also between the bicentennial of the planting of the movement (1966) and that of the formation of the church (1984). The only significance of these is to indicate we are dealing with an organism two hundred years old. How long can a revolution last?

This question raises the more important one of perspective. Where does this book stand in its view? Or rather, where does its author stand? For a broad answer the reader is referred to my "Doing Denominational History for Landmarks and Liberation" in *The Christian Advocate,* August 31, 1972. The remembrance of things past always has therapeutic value. The record must be carefully and accurately kept and updated. Landmarks need to be sought out and recognized, and a new generation deserves to be freed from the false bonds and misconceptions of the past to move with understanding freedom into the future.

In the process of reinterpretation no historian can claim true objectivity. He is always, inevitably, writing about himself. I write of Methodism as a committed Methodist who belongs to the cultural mold of the later twentieth century in the United States. I offer no apology for this condition, only acknowledgment. At the same time no historian can escape the demands of his craft and profession. These include honest research, trained appraisal of sources, recognition of biases, consideration of failures as well as successes, conflicts as well as concords, and lucid written expression. I have tried to deal intelligently with ascertainable data. And I have tried to write well in the hope that the effect will be stimulating rather than soporific.

A particular sensitivity belongs to the more recent chapters which deal with issues yet unresolved and persons yet living. Henry Boehm, traveling companion of Bishop Francis Asbury, commenting on the publication of Jesse Lee's *A Short History of the Methodists* (1810, the first of many notable predecessors of the present volume), observed the new book "made the bishop nervous." I hope no bishops are made nervous by this writing. But I find support in a greater church historian than I, Thomas Fuller, whose seventeenth-century *Church History of England* approached his own times with the comment:

And now I perceive I must tread tenderly, because I go out, as before, on men's graves, but am ready to touch the quick of some yet alive. I know how dangerous it is to follow truth too near the heels, yet it is better that the teeth of the historian be struck out of his head for writing the Truth, than that they remain still and rot in his jaws by feeding too much on the sweetmeats of flattery.

A few mechanical matters require attention. I have tried to preserve consistency in the spelling of names (except as drawn from direct quotations), but the unconcern of some of our forefathers brings frustration. Nathan Bangs in his *A History of the Methodist Episcopal Church* (1839–41) put it well: "If anyone can untangle this tangled skain, and teach us how to spell every proper name correctly, he will perform a task for which I confess myself inadequate." In providing statistics I have rounded out most figures to the nearest hundred or thousand, because they read better that way and are based on imprecise estimates anyway. Footnotes have been reduced to the bare minimum in the interests of economy of production. If the author's word to the effect that thorough research underlies his whole writing is not sufficient, there is no help for it. On the other hand numerous notes of recommendation for further reading should be helpful to the student. They will be more helpful surely than a cumbersome general bibliography isolated from the pertinent reading matter. For the serious researcher I have only this word: I am sorry, but there is no quick easy way to instant footnotes. Major reading suggestions are indexed under *Bibliography*.

More important is the matter of balance. Methodists whose heart is in Epworth will perceive the short shrift given backgrounds in British Methodism, especially after Wesley. There are excellent books by Englishmen on that subject. Special attention has been given to many Methodist groups which are sometimes simply ignored. Likewise, an attempt has been made to recognize the diversity of Methodist witness in various minority forms which continue to insist, and properly so, on the integrity of their own identity. The cultural melting pot which dominated the age of William Warren Sweet, which would have made of America—and Methodism—a well-boiled homogenous stew, simply could not absorb the stubborn ingredients, white, black, red, German, Scandinavian, Hispanic, Oriental, and all the rest. A sad commentary on the male bias of most historians is the fact that about half the story, that part dealing with the women of Methodism, has been largely ignored and is only with great difficulty rediscovered. Something of the same thing could be said of the children. The time has come to begin to redress that balance.

PREFACE

In the long-term work of preparation an author becomes deeply indebted to many persons, some of them forever anonymous. First account must be taken of the sabbatical program of Garrett Theological Seminary, which made possible a year's freedom for the exclusive task of writing this book. Financial support, which made up for loss of income during one quarter, came from a generous contribution by Trinity Church of the North Shore, Wilmette, Illinois. In this way this local church has given witness to its involvement in the wider life of United Methodism and has in a significant way become a part of this history. Welcome encouragement came from a non-Methodist source in the invitation from the president and faculty of Golden Gate Baptist Theological Seminary, San Francisco, to settle for two quarters in accommodations on their spacious campus while engaged in writing. Many individuals have contributed through libraries and archives. Special thanks are due John H. Ness, Jr., Grant S. Shockley, and Philip S. Watson, who read extensive portions of the manuscript and made many helpful suggestions.

FREDERICK A. NORWOOD

ABBREVIATIONS

CA	*Christian Advocate* (New York)
CCA	*Central Christian Advocate*
CH	*Church History*
HAM	*History of American Methodism*
JGC	*Journal of the General Conference*
MH	*Methodist History*
MQR	*Methodist Quarterly Review* (and variant titles, see note 4, Ch. 19)
MQRS	*Methodist Quarterly Review* (and variant titles, M. E. Church, South)
NCA	*Nashville Christian Advocate*
NWCA	*Northwestern Christian Advocate*
WCA	*Western Christian Advocate*
ZH	*Zion's Herald*

INTRODUCTION

Reflection over a long time on a complicated series of events sometimes delineates trends, waves, courses which in turn give meaning to
otherwise unmanageable masses of information. Such is the intention
of this book, which proposes to bring together in one volume sufficient information on the history of United Methodism and related
movements to give meaning to the forces which have molded that
history. Is there any single force which gives direction to the entire
Methodist tradition? Probably not, considering the many complex
factors which enter into the making of so large a movement. Some
main lines, however, become clear as the pieces are sorted. These
lines will become the guiding channels for understanding this history.
Whether any one line becomes the determining channel for understanding the whole belongs properly to the conclusion, perhaps even
more properly to speculation about the course of the future.

Although the author's opinions undoubtedly affect the interpretations, a conscious effort has been made to avoid reading in a
philosophy of history which overrides the substance of the record.
The saying attributed to G. M. Trevelyan, "Philosophy is not something you take to the study of history, but something which you carry
away," applies to this approach. Nevertheless, some guidelines become apparent in the record itself.

In the first place, Methodism began as a revival, and its history has
been marked repeatedly by continuing revivals. From this point of
view the denominational story is part of a constant theme in the
history of Christianity in all times and places—continuing reformation. Inevitably, it seems, the church must go through such a process,
as strong institutions languish and traditions ossify. The history of
Methodism consistently demonstrates this theme. The Wesleyan
movement constitutes a major facet of the great Evangelical Revival
which poured over the churches on both sides of the Atlantic Ocean
in the eighteenth century. On the Continent, Pietism, which grew not
so much out of a languishing church as a languishing theology,
represents a similar movement. The early history of the Methodist
Episcopal Church illustrates almost without letup the spirit of
revival—Second Great Awakening, camp meeting, urban revival—all
stimulated by the evangelistic fervor of westward expansion. To the
circuit riders the whole country was a vast field ripe for the harvest of
souls. This is a continuing concern.

Second, American Methodists, and to a lesser extent United Brethren and Evangelicals, were caught up in the heady surge of the

westward movement. A couple of generations of historical scholars have attempted to disparage the hoary Turner thesis on the westward movement as the determinative factor in American History. But all they have been able to accomplish is to qualify it as one factor playing a part along with others. For Methodism this surge west determined at least the size and influence of the growing institution, and to some extent its quality and spirit. A church with an itinerant connectional system simply could not lose the battle for souls on the frontier. Infinitely adaptable and purposefully organized, bishops, traveling preachers, local preachers, exhorters, and class leaders went with the people through brooding wilderness, lush prairie, boundless plain, over shining mountains to the western sea. Like wing-born seeds on the wind they scattered, to put down little roots of sapling class meeting, growing wherever pioneers cleared little openings. What happened to the denomination in this process is food for thought.

Methodism was a social process as much as an ecclesiastical movement. In England the context was the Industrial Revolution. It is no coincidence that Wesley's societies sprang up first in the commercial entrepôt London, the new industrial cities of the Midlands, and the coal centers of Bristol and Newcastle. They got their start in iron mines and coal pits. Only half aware of what was going on, the People Called Methodists were thrown together in one of the greatest revolutions of history, the mechanization of power. In the United States the context was similar, but with an important addition: the political experiment of government by consent of the people in a representative democracy. Willy-nilly the churches were thrown into this political revolution, with all its uncertainties, contradictions, and possibilities. The first "classes" were formed as the clouds of taxation without representation and royal oppression gathered on the horizon, and the Methodist Episcopal Church was founded the year following the signing of the Treaty of Paris, which ended the War of the Revolution. It was born in the noisy cradle of the factory and nurtured in the nursery of democracy. Iron, coal, steam power, freedom, individualism, and the rights of man provided a heady brew for the feeding of an infant denomination. No wonder the baby experienced periods of colic and indigestion! Occasionally, it must be honestly admitted, she threw up.

This church possessed and expressed a metamorphosed theology not of her own original creation. John and Charles Wesley provided the basic ingredients and the special emphases: Catholic tradition, Reformation message, Anglican ecclesiology, Puritan discipline, and Pietist feeling. From many sources Wesley developed a theology of

the royal road of salvation which is best characterized as a *working* ✳
theology, designed to help persons on their way to heaven. The grace
of God was interpreted in various stages as enabling the fundamental
transformation of the individual through a conversion experience in
which God was the prime mover, Christ the mediator, and the individual a full participant as responder. The road led through the
perfecting of love to entire sanctification. This was "doing" theology
with a vengeance! Methodists have been doing their theology ever
since. Sometimes other Christians have looked on with disapproval as
they mistakenly thought Methodists were so busy doing things that
they had no time for theological understanding. What they didn't
realize was that the understanding was there all along in the doing.
You don't get far along Pilgrim's Progress without knowing your
direction. And that was what theology was all about. This Methodist
brand was so successfully peddled that it became a characteristic mark
of American Christians of all kinds. The question remains to be
discussed, whether this development was peculiarly Methodist or just
plain American. Even Calvinism, usually regarded in the early days as
the arch enemy, was deeply affected, to the detriment of the Eternal
Decrees.

Methodism became in many ways the most American of the
churches. Not only in its inception but throughout its development it
was most in tune with the American song. Does this mean that
America was Methodized or that Methodism was Americanized?
Probably some of both. But the degree of preponderance on the one
side or the other remains to be seen. Nevertheless, the formal visit
paid by Bishops Asbury and Coke on the new first President of the
United States, the deep involvement in the westward movement, the
friendship of Lincoln with Bishop Matthew Simpson, who preached
his funeral sermon in Springfield, the leadership in the temperance
movement, and the identification with ideas of American progress in
the early twentieth century, all point to a close and continuing love
affair, for better or worse, between the Methodist Church and the
United States. Who was the dominant partner?

The process of Americanizing and Methodizing brought on a tension which might be judged as the overriding theme of Methodist
history in America. This tension took the form of conflict between the
authoritarian tradition inherited from the Wesleyan movement in
Great Britain, as transplanted and developed by Thomas Rankin,
Francis Asbury, and strong bishops of later times, and the democratic
tradition implicit in the purely voluntary nature of the Wesleyan
societies from the beginning, as later expressed in the lay preachers

and class leaders, in the democratic processes of Annual and General Conference, and in the numerous pressures for reform which characterized legislation on presiding elders, lay representation, representation of women, and rights of minorities. If there is any constant flow from the days of the Fluvanna Conference of 1779 down through those recent days of Black Methodists for Church Renewal, this oscillation between authoritarian direction ("jesuitism") and democratic self-government ("congregationalism") marks the opposite banks of the channel. Sometimes, as with Joshua Soule, the course overflowed the right bank; other times, as with Nazarites, it overflowed the left bank. Always the tension, sometimes in balance, sometimes in conflict, but always the tension.

American Methodism, although it was born of the Evangelical Revival with its European base, became a distinctive entity, related to and indebted to its English progenitor, but independent almost from the start. One need only recall that the movement was planted in North America, not by Wesley's emissaries, but by freely operating lay preachers who had no license from Wesley at all. The first founders were Strawbridge and Heck and Webb, not Boardman, Pilmore, and Asbury. Moreover, Asbury himself, although deeply loyal to Wesley, was even more deeply committed to his special calling to spread scriptural holiness throughout his "circuit"—the entire eastern seaboard. If this meant operating an autonomous movement in a newly independent country, so be it. Old Daddy Wesley would simply have to adjust, in spite of his scruples over rebellion against divinely sanctioned (Hanoverian) order. Methodism in America thenceforth went its own way, bishops and all.

On the other hand, the distinctiveness of American Methodism ought not obscure the fundamental similarity of Christian movements, to say nothing of culture and civilization, on both sides of the Atlantic Ocean. In essays in *The Reinterpretation of American History* Winthrop Hudson and Martin Marty discuss the European roots of American Christianity, pointing out the continuing fruitful (sometimes baneful) interrelations of the Atlantic Community, a unitary and distinctive expression of Western civilization. The work of William W. Sweet and Sidney Mead and others in defining the distinctive features of the American side does not vitiate the fundamental unity. Time and time again influences whose origin was in Europe, as with the classic examples of Puritanism and Pietism, carried across the ocean to find root in America. Frequently these transplanted forces returned with new vigor in new guise to nourish the old country. The mutual exchanges of German Methodism offer instructive examples.

This history is not all of one piece. A sometimes overlooked diversity persists in spite of apparent connectional unity. Perhaps symbolic is the curious diversity of attitudes toward the use of tobacco and alcohol among Methodists in England, Germany, Australia, as well as northern and southern United States. There is a regional diversity in the old Methodist Episcopal tradition. Members in New England, still floating in a sea of Congregational-Unitarian establishmentarians, are quite different from Bible Belt members engaged in a still-running battle with Southern Baptists. ("Like ghosts they haunt us from place to place," complained Asbury.) Both groups are quite different from members in the broad Midwest, abundant as the grains of ripening wheat on the ample prairies, and from those of the Far West, "scarce as hen's teeth," confronting and sometimes communicating with the odd exotic creations of religion characteristic of the "California mentality."

The most serious neglect of this diversity, however, is the fault of the dominant branch, Episcopal Methodism, currently known as The United Methodist Church. At every turn one is faced with the easy assumption that the history of The United Methodist Church is the same as the history of American Methodism. It is apparent in the older textbooks, in the periodicals, in official pronouncements, in Simpson's *Cyclopedia,* and, in spite of sincere efforts to the contrary, in the new *Encyclopedia of World Methodism.* It will continue to be apparent in the present history through failure to provide equal time for all. But at least the diversity is recognized here, and an attempt is made to deal fairly with the many facets in the United States. This factor becomes especially important in relation to the racial and ethnic varieties, some of which represent significant strands of the story. If hundreds of thousands of black Americans are now members of Negro Methodist denominations which have broken off from the mainline parent body, the original responsibility for the break is not theirs. The validity and value of their traditions can be ignored only at the peril of future prospects for Methodism in America. The same can be said of the smaller movements associated with Spanish-speaking, Oriental, and Indian people. Other ethnic groups, which have been more or less assimilated, deserve at least to be remembered: the German, the Swedish, and the Norwegian-Danish.

Again, the diversity has been enriched by the continuation of the tradition of loyal but independent dissent begun by John and Charles Wesley as they sought to bring revival to the church they both loved. American Methodism has spawned a notable series of dissenters of many different kinds, but united in their common devotion to one or another struggle for reform, a struggle which some of them "lost" when they left the church they too loved, to begin what inevitably became another denomination. Robert Strawbridge was virtually uncontrollable, but escaped judgment because he was only an unofficial lay preacher while organization was still fluid. James O'Kelly excelled in maverick spirit and administrative ineptitude, and left his mark deep-notched to the present day, although he himself wandered off into inconsequential obscurity. A whole group of reformers of the 1820s, constituting an exceedingly talented gathering of strong-minded individuals, provided issues for debate down through the General Conference of 1972. And there followed Orange Scott, Gilbert Haven, B. T. Roberts, William Taylor, Phineas Bresee, Harry F. Ward, Harold Paul Sloan, to say nothing of the generous crop of more recent nonconformists spawned in the rich diffuse culture of the later twentieth century. These too deserve to be remembered and, more important, to be heard.

In conclusion of this statement of channels of understanding, we may return to the first emphasis, the inception and development of Methodism as a revival movement. John Wesley—much less Charles—had no intention of founding a denomination. "No separation." The Wesleys thought of their societies as the reviving leaven in the lump. John preached significantly on the "Catholic Spirit." When one of his enthusiastic followers complained that his definition of a true Methodist amounted to nothing more than the description of general Christian commitment, he calmly replied, "You have said, so I mean." The first point made by Joseph Pilmore in his public announcement at Philadelphia was "That the Methodist Society was never designed to make a Separation from the Church of England or be looked upon as a Church." [1] The descriptive term *connection,* once widely used of the movement, had to do with revival of spirit within the church by means of relatively small groups devoted to "scriptural holiness." Something of the same is denoted by the Evangelical term "association." *Connection* used to denote something quite different from the denominational, centrally organized "connectionalism" emphasized today. As the author of this history looks for meaning in the latter part of the twentieth century, the term *connection* takes on renewed pertinence in times which seem to witness the decline of the denomination and the increase of ecumenical form and spirit.

A document ("A Response and Greeting from 1966 to 1866 and 2066") prepared by the author of this book and approved by the Association of Methodist Historical Societies for inclusion in the

[1] Frederick E. Maser, ed., *The Journal of Joseph Pilmore* (1969), 29.

bicentennial capsule buried along with some famous bishops in Mt. Olivet Cemetery in Baltimore, states—after noting some distinctive contributions—that the people who open the capsule in the year 2066 with greater or less curiosity may or may not still be known as the People Called Methodists.

And last, we offer up our Methodist church in endowment of the highest dream of our generation—the achieving, at long last, of the fullness of unity with all our Christian brethren, confessing that we have "one Lord, one faith, one baptism, one God and Father of us all" (Ephesians 4:5).

This is our hope for you, Methodist brethren of 2066: That our common heritage in Wesley may, as he himself always recommended, be placed, in "catholic spirit," at the service of all Christians. If the Methodist Church in a hundred years matures into union with a larger ecumenical family, we rejoice in this fulfillment of our heritage. In this way the Wesleyan spirit shall enliven the whole.

Whether Methodists or not, if they are in connection with one another and with all other Christians in the work of reviving faithful witness as a leaven in whatever lump may then exist, they will still be spiritual children of John and Charles Wesley, United Methodists.

I. Ancestral Heritage
1725-1784

Chapter 1
The Wesleys

All the heirs of the Evangelical Revival, together with founders John and Charles Wesley, Philip William Otterbein, Jacob Albright, and others, drank deeply from many historical springs. Among them were the primitive church, the Reformation, Anglicanism, Puritanism, Pietism, and the Enlightenment. Out of the mingling of these springs in eighteenth-century Europe arose the Evangelical Revival, which in its English aspect is sometimes called the Wesleyan Revival.

Two points should be made. First, although it is virtually impossible to separate the men from the movement they founded, the lives of John and Charles Wesley deserve attention for their own worth. Second, one is ill advised, in treating of the revival, to dwell exclusively on the elder brother, leaving the younger to write hymns. Through good times and bad, they were in it together.

Youth

There weren't really so many children in Epworth rectory, not counting those who died young and those who, having grown up, had left home. Three brothers, seven sisters, no more, sometimes less.That left enough girls to get in the way, but the brothers were well-enough spaced. As usual in large families, the siblings grew up to diverse experiences of life. The sisters made more than their proportionate share of unhappy marriages, but the boys followed closely parallel paths, especially John and Charles. As children they had the common experience of the rectory home and the strict but well-organized upbringing under Susanna's tutelage.[1] They also shared the ambiguous influence of scholarly Samuel, the loyal Anglican (and Hanoverian) rector. The famous rectory fire left its mark on all, but especially on John, the "brand plucked from the burning." The theological influence of the mother was by no means insignificant, as she with assurance corresponded with her university-bred sons.

[1] See Susanna's famous letter to her son, 1732, which he included in his journal in 1742 upon the occasion of her death, N. Curnock, ed., *The Journal of the Rev. John Wesley* (1938), III, 34-39.

Homelife indubitably left its mark. Just what mark, and how deep, is subject to considerable debate. At least it may be said that the boys, as they went off to school, indelibly went as *Wesleys*.

Oxford University brought a parting of the ways for oldest brother Samuel, who now went his own way, not to be followed by the two younger brothers. On the other hand, the university brought John and Charles closer together, sharing as they did many intellectual discoveries and many personal experiences, not the least of which was the Holy Club. The four years difference in age was of little account. They were together, more or less, for the rest of their lives: in Oxford, in Georgia, with Peter Boehler, in their Aldersgate experiences, in relation to Moravians and Calvinists, in oversight of the societies, in loyalty to the Church of England, in publication of a remarkable series of hymnbooks (culminating in the Hymnbook of 1780), in their concern for the effects of the American Revolution, and in their deaths (Charles, 1788; John, 1791). They even married within two years of each other.

But that last event marks the first of the qualifications needed to line out their differences. Marriage for Charles led to many years of relatively serene contentment and a relaxation of the vigor of the itinerant life. Quite the opposite for John on both points. They diverged on the issue of ordinations, and on several other occasions Charles was disturbed at his brother's penchant for finding solutions to problems and devising explanations for them later. But Charles was always the more impetuous and the more artistic. And John *was* the older brother. Nevertheless, one is driven all the way back to biblical precedents for such teamwork as those two maintained till they died. For convenience we usually mean John when we say "Wesley." More often than not, however, Charles is there too, although invisible. Most of the time we should be justified in using the plural.

The university opened up the world of the intellect, great books, and manifold spiritual influences. Although Oxford was not at its best in the early eighteenth century, it offered rich fare to those willing to seek it. Over a ten-year period the reading of John Wesley is only to be described as omnivorous.[2] A few books among the multitude stood out clearly from the rest, as he later attested. Three authors in particular brought him to understand Christianity as complete dedication of the whole life to love of God and man: Jeremy Taylor, *Rules and Exercises of Holy Living;* Thomas a Kempis, *The Christian Pattern;* and William Law, *Christian Perfection* and *A Serious Call to a Devout and*

[2] See the immense list in an appendix of V. H. H. Green, *The Young Mr. Wesley* (1961), 305-19.

Holy Life.[3] Here was a very real "conversion" of a young university student. But it was to be only the beginning of a series of spiritual developments.

Running parallel with the intellectual experience was the practical experience of the Holy Club, that famous small and ill-assorted group of young men of serious religious intention for Bible study, prayer, conversation, and Christian service, especially to those in trouble or distress. Now already began that form of social witness common to later Methodism: witnessing to individuals in a social context, with powerful consequences both to the individual and to society. The fact that the social consequences were for the most part unintended does not detract from their significance.

Out of the university came a highly educated, seriously intent, somewhat stuffy young man ordained to the Anglican priesthood in 1728. Something of the same thing, with variations, could be said of Charles. After some unimportant ventures the two brothers volunteered to join the colony being developed by General Oglethorpe in Georgia. The purposes John offered were both unrealistic: to save his own soul and to convert the Indians. Of course he also undertook the responsibilities for which he was being paid, to serve as chaplain to the infant colony. Charles went as Oglethorpe's secretary. For both the experience was unmitigated disaster. Had they not been *Wesleys,* their careers might well have dissolved then and there. The disaster was shared by both, but the details were different. In admirable but naïve candor John reported the whole—or almost the whole—story in his journal. Charles learned about jealousy and rumor-mongering—or backbiting as the term went. John learned about Indians, about colonists, about the wrong ways of maintaining discipline, and above all, about women. On the latter, it must be sadly reported, he did not learn enough. His love affair with Sophy Hopkey, into which he stumbled unwilling to admit that was what it was, ended when the pretty young girl grew impatient and married another. Worse, confounding the unhappy outcome, the Rev. Mr. Wesley refused to admit the new Mrs. Williamson to the Lord's Supper on grounds of ecclesiastical discipline. A civil suit for damages was the result. For six excruciating months the case dragged on, until finally in disgust and despair John fled away and sailed to England. Charles had preceded

---

[3] *Journal,* I, 466-67; *A Plain Account of Christian Perfection* (in *Works,* XI, 366-67). All the biographies deal with this development, but see especially Green, *The Young Mr. Wesley,* and Martin Schmidt, *John Wesley,* Vol. I. By far the most thorough study is that of John S. Simon, whose five volumes with different titles (1921–1934) are a standard reference. Also useful for reference is Luke Tyerman, *Life and Times of Rev. John Wesley* (3 vols. 1870).

him homeward bound. A more positive encounter was with the Moravians, whose courage on shipboard and whose wisdom, as expressed by their leader August Spangenberg, tremendously impressed Wesley.

Discovery

John Wesley arrived in England, February 1, 1738. That single fact should suffice, at least for anyone who has been in London in midwinter, to describe not only the atmosphere of his homecoming but also the condition of his spirit. As he approached the familiar shores he reflected that he, "who went to America to convert others, was never myself converted to God." The next four months were a time of trouble, of deep spiritual struggle and searching. Charles also was afflicted, and in addition, with serious pleurisy. Under these gloomy surroundings (outward and inward) the Wesleys felt their way from uncertain hope to assured faith. They were not to arrive, as some would like to interpret the Aldersgate experience, all in one sudden jump. Rather, the process was much more complex and involved a series of steps. Appropriately for a life-long itinerant, those experiences for John took the form of a series of journeys, short or long. There was, first of all, a *voyage* to Georgia, then a *visit* with Boehler, a *walk* to church, an evening *stroll* in Aldersgate, a *tour* of Herrnhut, a *hike* to Oxford, and an *expedition* to Bristol.

Essential to the rest was the mainly negative experience in Georgia. From there the only way was up. Peter Boehler, whom Wesley had met already February 7, was able to point the way. Frequently Wesley visited with him in London, and one time the two went together to Oxford where they visited Charles. When John thought of ceasing his preaching because of his own lack of faith, Boehler encouraged him, "Preach faith *till* you have it; and then, *because* you have it, you *will* preach faith." [4] The helpful Moravian gave both brothers more hope of faith.

As spring came on more brightly, the spiritual seeking continued unabated, sometimes in hope, sometimes in near despair. On May 17 Charles, who had been suffering from pleurisy, was sufficiently recovered to read in Martin Luther's *Commentary on Galatians* about the gift of faith through the free grace of God. As Luther wrote about Galatians 2:20 ("the Son of God who loved me and gave himself for me"):

This he did of inestimable love; for Paul says, "who loved me." For he delivered neither sheep, ox, gold, nor silver, but even God himself

[4] *Journal,* I, 442; cf. 447, 457.

entirely and wholly "for me, even for me.". . . Read therefore with great emphasis these words "me" and "for me," and so inwardly practise with yourself, that you with a sure faith may conceive and print this "me" in your heart and apply it to yourself.

He had made the great discovery.

At last came the day which John thought best in his journal "to relate at large" with a preface eight pages long. The day began with opening the Bible to two passages which gave promise: "Exceeding great and precious promises" and "Thou art not far from the kingdom." In the afternoon he went to St. Paul's Church. There, in the vast space of the Wren masterpiece, he was deeply impressed by the service, which included the anthem "Out of the depths have I called unto thee, O Lord." In stark contrast was the meeting that evening in Aldersgate Street, at which, as someone was reading part of Luther's Preface to Romans, Wesley's "heart [was] strangely warmed." [5] With joy he joined his brother in their mutual discovery of faith. Presently he reported in a letter to brother Samuel: "By a Christian I mean one who so believes in Christ as that sin hath no more dominion over him; and in this obvious sense of the word I was not a Christian till May the 24th last past." But contrast to this his judgment, made early the next year, "I am not a Christian now." [6]

It was not quite so simple. For all the significance of that evening meeting his journey toward abiding faith was not complete. He continued to have troubles of spirit and doubts. Following the stroll in Aldersgate came the tour to the Moravian "capital," Herrnhut. His experience there was mixed. Although he found much to admire and later incorporate in the Wesleyan movement, he was disturbed by other aspects and not convinced that the Moravians had all the answers. The summer tour of the Continent left him still uneasy in spirit, not yet in full command of his own potential. Two more developments were needed.

The one occurred on a hike to Oxford from London.[7] As was sometimes his habit, he improved the walking time by reading. His choice was *A Faithful Narrative of the Surprising Work of God in the Conversion of Many Hundred Souls in Northampton,* published in Boston in 1738 by Jonathan Edwards. The journal account leaves no doubt of the powerful effect this description of the New England revival on Wesley's thinking. Later he would publish extracts not only of this tract but also of Edwards' *Treatise Concerning the Religious Affections.* "It

---

[5] *Journal,* I, 472-76.
[6] John Telford, ed., *The Letters of the Rev. John Wesley* (1931), I, 262; *Journal,* II, 125.
[7] *Journal,* II, 83-84, 88-91; cf. Albert Outler, *John Wesley* (1964), 16.

is not too much to say," concludes Albert Outler, "that one of the effectual causes of the Wesleyan Revival in England was the Great Awakening in New England."

Wesley's religious experience, and his theological understanding along with it, had now been formed. But it was not yet fixed as an effective force in his life. It took an expedition to Bristol to accomplish that. Acceding unwillingly to the urging of George Whitefield that he come to help out the work in Bristol, he found himself burdened with the responsibility of carrying on a revival he had not started and whose procedures he did not understand. Whitefield "the ebullient," fresh from huge success in America, lit the fires in Bristol with his famous outdoor preaching, and then characteristically dashed on to other victories. Wesley hesitated. However blessed outdoor nature may have been through God's creation, it was not consecrated. How could one preach out of doors, open to the sky and God knows what unleashed evils? It was indecent. Nevertheless, on Monday, April 2, 1739, "I submitted to be more vile, and proclaimed in the highways the glad tidings of salvation, speaking from a little eminence in a ground adjoining to the city, to about three thousand people." [8] Shortly after he preached in a meadow at Baptist Mills and on top of Hanham Mount, Kingswood. All around he witnessed the actualization of the descriptions he had read in Edwards' report. And more: to his own and Whitefield's amazement, the effects of his preaching were more lively even than those of Whitefield's more exciting proclamation. How could the waves of response to the appeals of this scholarly Oxonian be explained as other than the work of the Holy Spirit? The Wesleyan Revival was under way, and John Wesley at long last has not only faith but assurance. And Charles joined in the work.

Maturity

The rest of the story is all of one piece—a very large piece. For over fifty years John and Charles labored, each in his own way, with the Wesleyan facet of the Evangelical Revival. Although the younger brother settled more or less in Bristol after 1749 and in London after 1771, he never wavered in his commitment to the revival. As he wrote to James Hutton, "I am fixed, resolved, determined, sworn to stay by the Methodists and my brother through thick and thin." The only real difference was that while John was still the indefatigable itinerant,

[8] *Journal*, II, 172-73.

Charles had "located." He became a sort of senior pastor for the Methodists of Bristol and London, and they loved him. He sang his way into the hearts of all Methodists with his hymns.

John, however, maintained an almost unbelievable pace, blessed with the overflowing energy which is a gift to very few humans. In 1759 he confided, after preaching morning and evening at the foundry in Norwich, "How pleasing would it be to flesh and blood to remain in this little quiet place, where we have at length weathered the storm! Nay, I am not to consult my own ease, but the advancing of the kingdom of God."

And in 1788, only three years before his death, "Thence we went to Raithby; an earthly paradise! How gladly would I rest here a few days: but it is not my place! I am to be a wanderer upon earth. Only let me find rest in a better world!"[9]

Both of the Wesleys continued in their leadership of the societies, although in different forms of ministry. Both married, Charles in 1749, John in 1751, the one happily, the other quite unsatisfactorily. Sophy Hopkey might just possibly have drawn John from his destiny. Grace Murray might possibly have kept the pace and strengthened him. Mrs. Vazeille became a ball and chain. John Berridge, writing to Lady Huntingdon in 1770, took a jaundiced view of clerical marriage in general: "No trap so mischievous to the field preacher as wedlock. Matrimony has quite maimed poor Charles, and might have spoiled John and George [Whitefield] if a wise Master had not graciously sent them a brace of ferrets."[10]

The rest of the story is inseparable from the development of the Wesleyan movement. Between 1738 and 1744 most of the features of the United Societies of the People Called Methodists came into being; bands, classes, societies, select bands, love feasts, watch nights, and the British Conference. The Wesleys weathered the storms of the controversies with the Moravians and the Calvinists. Methodism spread into the urban centers, particularly those affected by the Industrial Revolution. Through it all the Wesleys, basing their work in the three points of the "Methodist triangle," London, Bristol, and Newcastle, moved with determination, organizational skill, and utter commitment. The movement *was* their life, although for Charles, more quietly.

The early struggles and conflicts with opponents within the Established Church, with political interests, with mob prejudice and violence, gave way gradually to acceptance, tolerance, and even

---

[9] *Journal*, IV, 301; VII, 412.

[10] Quoted in Luke Tyerman, *The Life and Times of John Wesley* (1871), II, 270.

broadly based approbation. Before he died John Wesley had himself become an English institution. The controversies of the early years contributed largely to the Wesley image, which threatened finally to become the Wesley legend. His courageous confrontation of rioters bent on doing violence to Methodist leaders, including himself, made him something of a hero.[11] The episode in which he deflated Beau Nash at fashionable Bath, with the help of an old woman, brought many a good-natured chuckle. Above all, he became the archetype of the Methodist circuit rider, ceaselessly going the rounds of the societies on horseback, and in old age by carriage.

Towering symbol though he finally became, there burned to the last in that slight figure a very real and human personality. A little over one year before his death (March 2, 1791) he wrote in his journal, "I am now an old man, decayed from head to foot. My eyes are dim; my right hand shakes much; my mouth is hot and dry every morning; I have a lingering fever almost every day; my motion is weak and slow. However, blessed be God, I do not slack my labour. I can preach and write still." [12] Charles had died three years before in 1788. By this time both their careers had been swallowed up in the worldwide movement which is ineradicably imprinted with their name, to which they gave their lives, and which has now outlived them by almost two hundred years.

---

[11] Cf. especially the Wednesbury mob, *Journal,* III, 98-102; II, 211; VII, 35.
[12] *Journal,* VIII, 35.

Chapter 2
The Wesleyan Movement

Many illustrations may be cited to prove the frequency with which religious leaders have been swallowed up in the movements they started, even during their own lifetimes. Francis of Assisi, Luther, and Calvin come to mind. The more successful the action, the more likely the submergence of the individual. Of the Wesleys this may be said to be true only in very limited degree. Mr. Wesley maintained an exceedingly firm control over the revival which carries his name. Nevertheless, it went through three distinct stages which pointed eventually toward the end against which both Wesleys fought to the end of their days—a separate denomination, a new "church." First was the movement, spontaneous and diverse, full of energy and aspiration, but almost bereft of organization, except for the bare voluntary association of those desiring "to flee the wrath to come," under the undefined leadership of two young Oxonians. The second stage began with the identification, still firmly within the structure of the Church of England, of a *connection* (or as the English will have it a "connexion"). The members of the United Societies of the People Called Methodists could still regard themselves as good Anglicans—indeed were urged so to view themselves. But they belonged to a visible network held together by an amazing plan of itinerant ministry centered in a conference of preachers. This would be the classic stage of the Wesleyan Revival. The third stage, or final product was, in 1784 in America and much later in England, the embodiment of an independent denomination, to all intents and purposes similar to other "dissenting" denominations. Perhaps the process was inevitable. The Wesleys were not willing to accept it on that account.

For the roots we go back briefly to mention two episodes in their careers: Oxford and Georgia. These constituted, as Wesley never wearied of stating, the first rise and the second rise of Methodism. In summer 1729 Charles had started at the university the little study group which came to be known as the Holy Club. It was also called a "little society" or "religious society," terms which fitted the concept of the later movement. Again, in Savannah, as Wesley's journal records, "We agreed (1) to advise the more serious among them to form themselves into a sort of little society, and to meet once or twice a week, in order to reprove, instruct, and exhort one another. (2) To select out of these a smaller number for a more intimate union with each other." [1] This was the second rise. The description fits perfectly, although the experiment was so remote and so impermanent as to have no direct effect on the later revival except through the persons of the Wesleys. The *idea* was there, however, in Oxford and Savannah, biding the times until its day came.

The Formative Period, 1738–44

Whatever one's final judgment may be of the significance of Aldersgate for the spiritual development of Charles and John Wesley, the year 1738 marks a real beginning for the Wesleyan movement. Although there is evidence of bands and societies before that time, the show got on the road in the six-year period down to 1744, culminating in the meeting of the British Conference. John Wesley was much impressed with the Moravians' experience with small groups, especially their concept of *collegia pietatis,* seen as *ecclesiola in ecclesia*—that is, the little circle of serious Christians existing within the large church. These had long existed in the Church of England as religious societies, nothing really new in an Anglicanism tinctured with Puritanism. But the life of Herrnhut gave new perspective. Beyond that, the even smaller bands into which these groups were divided also appealed. Wesley as usual adapted what he found, combined features of the Moravians' bands and "choirs," and introduced them in his movement.

The third rise of Methodism, then, was the organization of a society of Wesley's followers in London. Even earlier the same year the Bristol Society was organized. The story is told by Wesley himself, who is at pains to explain that there was no advance plan, but rather "everything arose just as the occasion offered." This procedure was to become a sort of hallmark of Methodism. Without intending it so, he goes on, the work was found to agree with common sense and Scripture, "though they generally found, in looking back, something in Christian antiquity likewise, very nearly parallel thereto."

About ten years ago [he wrote in 1748] my brother and I were desired to preach in many parts of London. We had no view therein, but, so far as we were able . . . to convince those who would hear what true Christianity was, and to persuade them to embrace it.
    The points we chiefly insisted upon were four: first, that orthodoxy, or right opinions, is, at best, but a very slender part of religion . . . ; sec-

[1] *Journal,* I, 197-202.

ondly, that the only way under heaven to this religion is to "repent and believe the gospel . . ."; thirdly, that by this faith, "he that worketh not, but believeth on him that justifieth the ungodly, is justified freely by his grace, through the redemption which is in Jesus Christ"; and lastly that, "being justified by faith," we taste of the heaven to which we are going; we are holy and happy.[2]

Profiting from the experience with the Moravians, the Wesleys undertook pastoral oversight of these small groups by providing rules of discipline, worship, and conduct, which by 1743 had been fixed as "The Nature, Design, and General Rules of the United Societies in London, Bristol, Kingswood, Newcastle-upon-Tyne, &c." Further, some were brought together in even more intimate relationship in the bands, which were primarily designed to serve particular needs of selected groups distinguished by age, sex, and spiritual level. Not until 1742 was the different plan introduced of organizing the entire society into essentially neighborhood groups called "classes." The difference may be visualized by seeing the society-band structure like a slice of swiss cheese, the holes being bands within the society, and the society-class like a round pie sliced into segments for serving. In the latter, therefore, everyone in a society was also in a class. A class ticket meant membership also in a society, and was indeed the only formal evidence. The "Plain Account" explains the evolution of the class system from the original device for raising funds begun in Bristol into the efficient means of spiritual and moral oversight and mutual sharing which became the chief mark of early Methodism. Bands continued, at least in the larger societies; but increasingly, the classes tended to replace them.

Except for the circuit system and the organization of preachers in the British Conference, the basic structure of early Methodism was complete. Mention of "tickets," however, suggests several practices which also were widely accepted. In 1741, in order that the membership in the society in Bristol might be controlled, Wesley gave out tickets which indicated membership in good standing. They were simply little cards, clearly marked for the effective quarter, on which were inscribed the name of the holder and the signature of the preacher in charge, at first Wesley himself. Possession meant much —so much that a veritable doctrine of the church is implied. No one received a card who had not been examined quarterly as to his Christian life and faith and had given evidence that he was following

---

[2] Thomas Jackson, ed., *The Works of John Wesley* (1829–31), VIII, 248–68. The slight chronological precedence of Bristol apparently was not considered of any importance.

the General Rules and seeking to grow in faith. He might still be a full member of the church, meaning in most cases the Church of England—that would not be affected. But active membership in the Wesleyan movement—in the society—required qualification for a quarterly ticket. Some implications are discussed in a later chapter.

The Wesleys tried many experiments in worship and life together. By 1748 watch nights had been established. At first they were observed on the eve of the new year, usually for one or two hours before midnight, devoted to preaching, prayer, and singing. At the stroke of midnight the group would sing one of the hymns Charles composed especially for that occasion. John found precedent for these affairs in the vigils of the early church. Another experiment was the "letter day." John began regular reading in meetings of correspondence he had received which bore useful testimony of God's work. And then came the love feast, another practice which Wesley had learned from the Moravians. It had two distinctive features: (1) distribution of bread and water to a select group, (2) spiritual testimony. Wesley found precedent here in the Agape or common meal of the primitive Christians. He always considered it comparable to a fellowship meal and not to the sacrament of the Lord's Supper.

As the movement grew it took on more and more the features of a worshiping community. That is, the preaching service brought together the members of the classes for informal worship. On one matter the Wesleys were quite clear: these gatherings to hear preaching were not to be seen as substitutes for the liturgical services of the church. Sunday worship, morning and evening prayer, ought to continue unabated, including especially frequent Communion. There the priestly function was supreme. Among the Methodists, however, the prophetic function of preaching was central. It is important to make this distinction, because it helps define the nature of Methodist ministry. Apart from his brother and a few sympathetic clergymen, Wesley had only "preachers." Whether they were identified as "assistants" (preachers-in-charge) or "helpers" (assistants), they were all preachers and nothing else. Of course they could not help being pastors also in such intimate associations as bands and classes. Since they were always on an unending round of itineration, however, they could not do much in the way of planned pastoral care. Class leaders, however, were informal pastors.

Hence the Methodist services consisted of preaching, aided by Bible, prayer, and hymn-singing. Although he regarded highly the *Book of Common Prayer*,[3] in both substance and form, he was not above

[3] See his preface to the *Sunday Service*, 1784.

34

revising it to suit the needs of Methodists. Nor did it restrain him from lively innovations in worship. He could not accept the strict interpretation placed on the Liturgy, so strong, he thought, the terms could scarcely be applied even to the Bible. "Neither dare I confine myself wholly to forms of prayer, not even in the church." [4] He favored extempore prayer as a supplement. As for the singing, the contributions of Charles are justly famous. But this does not mean that Methodist services were one long gospel hymn-sing. The tunes were rather dignified, certainly not the popular ditties of the day, and the emphasis was on the theological content, not on emotional response. When one remembers that the most characteristic Methodist service was morning preaching at five A.M., the figment of sawdust-trail revivalism fades rapidly.

This is not to say that emotion was absent, or even frowned on. All effort was directed toward commitment of the entire person in all aspects of his life. Such response was bound to carry deep emotion. Occasionally, especially during the early years, as with the outdoor preaching at Bristol, Wesley was embarrassed by what appeared to be excess of emotion. He was concerned, he was intrigued, but not repelled. Edwards had dealt with similar manifestations in his *Treatise on the Religious Affections*.

The buildings were never churches, rarely chapels, generally "preaching houses," a term which says much. The main directive was functional. A proper place of worship for Methodists (except sacramental occasions) would be a plain, well-aired structure suitable for preaching. But almost anything would do under necessity, including the run-down old foundry which became the headquarters of Methodism in London until the construction of Wesley's Chapel. Sometimes a hole would be cut through the ceiling in order that the preacher, standing on a table with his head in the opening, might preach to the men above and the women below.

Tying the whole together was the network of circuits served by Wesley's lay preachers. The basic grid was the sturdy triangle which marked the leader's own regular itineration: London, Bristol, Newcastle-on-Tyne. Within this triangle most of the Methodist work was concentrated, partly because the burgeoning cities of the Midlands fell within it. Until the end of his life John Wesley rode the rounds of the cities, with occasional expeditions to Scotland, Ireland, and corners of England not yet touched. There remained large areas scarcely influenced by Methodism at all. Since most of the work was centered in the cities, much of the countryside was unaffected. With

[4] To Samuel Walker, 20 Nov. 1758, *Letters*, III, 152. Walker was Vicar of Truro.

him to give guidance were his brother and a small handful of sympathetic clergymen of the Established Church. As to the rest, they were all lay preachers without ordination or much formal training.

Wesley's letter to Samuel Walker, Vicar of Truro, underlines the central importance of these lay preachers to the polity of Methodism. Speaking of the issue of separation from the church, which many urged, he admitted the strength of the arguments, and stated further that ultimately, "If we cannot stop a separation without stopping lay preachers, the case is clear—we cannot stop it at all." [5]

They varied from rough-hewn, Yorkshireman John Nelson to the more sophisticated Christopher Hopper, a well-educated family man, who preached all over the British Isles for fifty years. These men were preachers, not priests or pastors. They were, one and all, under the iron will of the founder of the movement, Mr. Wesley.

Not all the preachers traveled circuits. Some worked locally. Among these were women, who confronted Wesley with a special problem. He had had his scruples about lay *men* preaching—but *women?* Again his mother had to show him the way. On her own she began holding groups for Bible study at Epworth. Should she preach? Well, she could "testify," meaning she might "preach," but without a formal text. Now, later, appeared Sarah Crosby, who became in fact an itinerant field preacher. Beginning in about 1761 she met with twenty-seven persons in class. When two hundred people showed up the next week, she had to lead the whole group and in effect preach to them. Troubled, she wrote to Wesley, and he replied that she had done right under the circumstances of necessity. What his advice amounted to was: preach if you must, but don't call it that.[6] She took full advantage of the opportunity in a long and fruitful ministry, which included much personal counselling. As an old but very active woman she wrote, "I find my last days are my best days."

Outstanding among the other women was Mary Bosanquet, who in 1781 married John Fletcher, Wesley's able ordained Anglican lieutenant and theological spokesman. In spite of difficulties at home over her independent spirit and intention to convert her own family, she took her own apartment (almost unheard of in the eighteenth century) and entered on an active career of Methodist ministry, especially in establishing an orphan home. Later, back near home, and both before and after she married Fletcher, she led a large class and engaged widely in preaching, sometimes in the open.

---

[5] To Samuel Walker, 24 Sept. 1755, *Letters*, III, 146.

[6] To Sarah Crosby, in *Letters*, IV, 133. Cf. V, 130, 257. An excellent study of Sarah and other women preachers is Thomas M. Morrow, *Early Methodist Women* (1967).

The Conference marks the completion of the early organization of Methodism in 1744. They met first at the Foundry in London in a gathering attended by six Anglican clergymen including John Wesley and his brother and four lay preachers. Over several days both theological and organizational matters were discussed. The laymen were present on invitation, it being understood that they did not have automatic right of participation. This continued to be Wesley's practice. In 1785, when there were about two hundred preachers in active service, he wrote: "Our Conference began, at which about seventy preachers were present, whom I had invited by name. One consequence of this was, that we had no contention or altercation at all; but everything proposed was calmly considered, and determined as we judged would be most for the glory of God." [7] After open discussion, the final decision was usually made by Wesley himself. Hence there existed a sort of "apostolic" ministry among the Methodists, based on the extraordinary call of John Wesley. Even Charles acquiesced in this priority of call and authority.

The Definitive Period

The Methodist movement had taken form. It was now in the process of becoming a "connection." It was still within the Established Church and, outwardly at least, would remain so until John Wesley's death. Very little new would be added after 1744. It would be a period of definition, of organization, and of expansion.

Two conflicts within the movement had already taken place and a third begun—with the Moravians, the Calvinists, and the Anglicans. All helped in self-understanding. They carried an important freight of theology which is discussed later. Wesley and Boehler had cooperated in starting the Fetter Lane Society, at a time when apparently the former thought of blending his movement with those of the Moravians and the Anglican societies. But quickly enough tensions were rising. Wesley, though impressed with many features of Moravian life, features of Pietism of which he could approve, disagreed on the degrees of faith and the use of the means of grace. Especially did he reject that form known as "quietism," which insisted that to seek faith or use the means of grace before faith was granted was worse than useless.[8] The outcome was the departure of Wesley and his followers from the Fetter Lane Society. They now joined with the new Foundry

[7] *Journal*, VII, 100-101.
[8] See the long discussions in the *Journal*, II, 1739-41; also in Outler, *John Wesley*, 353-76, in more convenient form. See also Edward Langton, *History of the Moravian Church* (1956); Charles W. Towlson, *Moravian and Methodist* (1957). The departure: *Journal*, II, 370.

Society. Henceforth Moravians and Methodists went separate ways.

The controversy with the Calvinists was more complex, involved issues more theological than functional, and brought about personal rifts with George Whitefield and John Cennick, to mention only two. At this point we are concerned about the effects on the Methodist movement. The issues centered mainly on two points: the grace of God offered to all men through the Atonement, and the falsity of predestination. God's grace is "free"—that is, freely offered through an Atonement not limited to any "elect." Man is not "predestined" from all time through divine fiat. Rather, through the grace he already has he may "work out his own salvation." These views brought an alienation from John Cennick and his group at Bristol. It also temporarily separated the otherwise good friends and co-workers in the Evangelical Revival, Wesley and Whitefield. In Bristol in 1739 Wesley finally brought their disagreement into the open with his sermon, "Free Grace": "I declared the free grace of God to about four thousand people from those words, 'He that spared not His own Son, but delivered Him up for us all, how shall He not with Him also freely give us all things?' " [9]

Although Wesley refrained from publishing the sermon until Whitefield was out of the country, a rift developed which, though the principals were finally reconciled, brought a separation of the "Calvinistic Methodists" from the Wesleyan Methodists, the so-called Countess of Huntingdon Connection. Especially in Wales did this division have long-lasting effects. This theological debate continued without let-up. One effect of these divisions was the tightening of discipline. Against the Moravian quietists the General Rules insisted on regular attendance on the means of grace. Against the Calvinists came strictures against divisive doctrines. The objection Wesley had to Calvinists was not so much their doctrine as their disputatious spirit which led to disruptions. For example, at Alnwick in 1753:

> I spoke severally to those of the society, and found they had been harassed above measure by a few violent Predestinarians, who had at length separated themselves from us. It was well they saved me the trouble, for I can have no connexion with those who will be contentious. These I reject, not for their opinion, but for their sin; for their unchristian temper and unchristian practice; for being haters of reproof, haters of peace, haters of their brethren, and, consequently, of God. [10]

Hence two forces were at work in the settling of discipline among the Methodists. On the one hand, the societies, and more especially

[9] *Journal,* II, 185.
[10] *Journal,* IV, 64-65.

the classes and bands, were bound together in strong bonds of mutual discipline, each member correcting the others at the same time he sought to grow strong in faith himself. On the other hand, we begin to hear more and more of large Sunday preaching services attended by throngs who did not belong to either society or class and hence had no tickets. More and more these also were Methodists, but they were not the same breed as first gathered under Wesley's wing. As more and more became Methodists there were proportionately fewer and fewer to provide a smaller and smaller leaven in the lump. Such, it might be said, is the price of success. Wesley never gave up the struggle to maintain high standards, and sometimes his quarterly visitations left societies in shambles. But the time was long since gone when he could hope to look after all the societies himself.

Although the numbers who thronged to hear the Methodists created problems of discipline, these standards were progressively defined both for people and preachers. The General Rules became a sort of symbolic goal for all members of the movement. Acceptance of the General Rules (which specifically excluded any doctrinal requirement other than the famous "desire to flee from the wrath to come and to be saved from their sins") was required of would-be-members. Their regular reading before the societies was insisted upon.

As the connection developed the regulations were collected and codified in what came to be called the "Large Minutes" (that is, the minutes of legislation of the successive conferences). In Wesley's lifetime the final form was that of 1789. Here the form of organization was spelled out, and the standards of discipline for both people and preachers were defined. These Large Minutes (edition of 1780) became the basis for the first Discipline of the Methodist Episcopal Church, published in 1785. Here was to be found that most original definition of the purpose of the revival: "to reform the nation and to spread scriptural holiness over the land." Here were the standards for membership and growth. Here appeared first that remarkable Question 14: "How shall we prevent improper persons from insinuating themselves into the society?" The answer was to give tickets to no one not recommended by a leader, and not on trial for two months, to accept no one unless "recommended by one you know" or till they had been three or four times in class, and to distribute to them the rules on the first opportunity.

Here especially were the marks of excellence for the itinerant preachers. They were to be regarded as "extraordinary messengers," not to run competition with the regular clergy but to serve the needs of the revival (together with the hope that the regular clergy would be stimulated by example to do likewise). The preachers' duties were stated in the "Twelve Rules of a Helper."

> You have nothing to do but to save souls. Therefore spend and be spent in this work. . . . And remember! A Methodist Preacher is to mind every point, great and small, in the Methodist discipline! . . . Act in all things, not according to your own will, but as a son in the Gospel. As such, it is your part to employ your time in the manner which we direct. . . . Above all, if you labour with us in our Lord's vineyard, it is needful that you should do that part of the work which we advise, at those times and places which we judge most for his glory.[11]

No wonder that some Roman Catholics, enthralled at the discipline and devotion of the little army of Wesley's preachers, should have compared this movement to the Society of Jesus and its founder to Ignatius Loyola!

It was this structure of authority which distinguished early Methodism. It was clearly not democratic. The extraordinary calling precluded any compromise on that principle. And what applied to ministers also applied to people: "As long as I live the people shall have no share in choosing either stewards or leaders among the Methodists. We have not and never had any such custom. We are no republicans, and never intend to be." [12]

The question would be raised many times in the future history of the movement, whether this strict concentration of authority could in any sense outlive the founder. Was his authority, as some later reformers would argue, unique, never to be perpetuated? All the more impressive is the charismatic appeal which led strong-willed men to submit to such unlimited exercise of power. To say that such degree of power, to succeed, must be balanced by love says much about the character of John Wesley. Even democratically minded reformers among the Methodists have generally conceded that Wesley's authority was justified by his extraordinary call. As Edward Drinkhouse interpreted his position, he balanced paternalistic power with parental affection.[13] But, as with the unique authority of the Apostles, this authority ought not endure beyond the lifetime of the founder. Grudgingly, Drinkhouse was willing to grant to Francis Asbury some degree of this unique authority, but with the same lifetime limitation. No wonder Wesley had trouble in selecting and establishing a successor, and at last had to settle the power in a body of the ministers to be

---

[11] "Minutes of Several Conversations" (1789), in *Works,* VIII, 310.
[12] 13 Jan. 1790; *Letters,* VIII, 196.
[13] Edward Drinkhouse, *History of Methodist Reform,* I, 5.

known as the Legal Hundred. The Deed of Declaration (1784) was as definitive for English Methodism as the ordinations of the same year and their consequences were for American Methodism. Although that deed and its aftereffects were fateful for English Methodism, the concern of this history with Methodism in the British Isles stops at that point. There remained, of course, the development of the third stage in the evolution of Methodism from a movement through a connection to an independent denomination. This occurred on both sides of the Atlantic Ocean, but in the one case, only as a result of that "very uncommon train of providences," and in the other, only gradually after the death of the founder.

Chapter 3
Roots and Structure of Wesley's Theology

At first sight it would appear that John Wesley had more theological legs to stand on than he really needed. Various studies of his thought have been made,[1] and it seems each scholar has found a different leg on which the venerable founder was said to be standing theologically. They are all right—in part. Wesley's thought had many roots, and he would be the first to acknowledge it. He would prefer, however, to say his understanding of the Christian faith was based on the three traditional sources of religious knowledge: the Bible, reason, and experience.

Roots

It is helpful, in describing the roots of Wesley's thought, to establish three layers or floors. The bottom floor would be his Catholic heritage, the second floor the Reformation, and the third "our" own doctrines. Much he inherited through his Anglican tradition, more he learned by his own investigation. He gave testimony to the early influence of such classics as Thomas a Kempis' *The Christian Pattern*. He was intrigued through his life by many of the Catholic mystics, although he claimed to avoid mysticism himself. He reacted strongly against the negative other-worldly aspects.[2] In many ways the reformers, Wesley included, shared with Augustine a common understanding on matters of faith and grace. It was, as so frequently, more a matter of emphasis. The Apostles' and Nicene Creeds were shared by all.

Most significant, however, was Wesley's high regard for the norma-

---

[1] Among those which emphasize a particular facet of his theological sources are: Maximin Piette (Roman Catholic), *John Wesley in the Evolution of Protestantism* (1937); J. E. Rattenbury (Anglican), *The Eucharistic Hymns of John and Charles Wesley* (1948); Robert C. Monk, *John Wesley, His Puritan Heritage* (1966); Franz Hildebrandt, *From Luther to Wesley* (1951); George Croft Cell (Calvinist), *The Rediscovery of John Wesley* (1935); Umphrey Lee (Enlightenment), *John Wesley and Modern Religion* (1936); Martin Schmidt (Pietist), *John Wesley* (3v. 1953-73). Other recent works attempt a more balanced interpretation: William R. Cannon, *The Theology of John Wesley* (1946); Colin W. Williams, *John Wesley's Theology Today* (1960); Albert C. Outler, ed., *John Wesley* (1964); Philip S. Watson, ed., *The Message of the Wesleys* (1964).

[2] Cf. To Susanna Wesley, 28 May 1725, *Letters*, I, 15-16.

tive authority of the early church. Discovery of the strict discipline of devotion among the early Christians was one of the prime motivations for the Holy Club. So, throughout his life, he hopefully sought precedent in the early church for the "innovations" of the Evangelical Revival. Even in pioneer Georgia he spent long hours on the extensive collection of ancient Eastern texts in William Beveridge's *Pandectae*, published in 1672. He accepted at full value the ecumenical Rule of St. Vincent of Lérins—that belief and practice which has been observed by all men in all places at all times is apostolic and therefore true and authoritative.[3] This, at least, was the significance Wesley placed on the cherished rule. Until scholars raised doubts about their authenticity, he was deeply interested in the *Apostolic Constitutions*, which were thought to reflect genuine primitive practice in worship. He summarized his priorities of authority succinctly in "Farther Thoughts on Separation from the Church": "From a child I was taught to love and reverence the Scripture, the oracles of God; and, next to these, to esteem the primitive Fathers, the writers of the three first centuries. Next after the primitive church, I esteemed our own, the Church of England, as the most scriptural national Church in the world."[4]

Of more direct bearing on the content rather than the authentication of Wesleyan theology is the contribution of the Eastern Fathers, particularly Macarius the Egyptian and Ephraem Syrus. When it is realized that Macarius was actually a Syrian monk who was directly indebted to Gregory of Nyssa for his thought and some of his text, then the importance of the relation between this ancient Eastern Father and teacher of the doctrine of Christian perfection through devotion and this English preacher of revival who regarded the "going on to perfection" as one of "our" special emphases becomes clear. A sermon included in the Jackson edition of Wesley's works carries the title "On the Holy Spirit." It is full of early Eastern emphasis on participation in the divine Spirit. But it is not a sermon by Wesley. Rather, as analysis of the original manuscript reveals, it derives from a noted scholar who had special interest in Eastern patristics and who had great influence on Wesley. It is thus another piece of evidence on Wesley's wide-ranging interest in the Eastern Fathers. Therefore, Wesley's Catholic rootage is not only ancient but Eastern. It is also very, very Anglican.

Wesley's roots in the Continental Reformation are well symbolized

[3] See discussion and references in Outler, *John Wesley*, 8-10, 45-46, and Frank Baker, *John Wesley and the Church of England* (1970), 32-34. I am indebted to Albert Outler for data on "On the Holy Spirit," below.

[4] *Works*, XIII, 272.

by the active presence of Martin Luther (through his *Commentary on Galatians* and *Preface to Romans*) in the spiritual conversions of both Charles and John. At a crucial moment justification by faith, hallmark of the Reformation, entered both the life and the thought of both men. No mere coincidence led John Wesley to take as the theme of his first sermon after Aldersgate, "Justification by Faith." [5] Although Wesley was irritated at Luther's intransigence and exaggeration, and although he never really understood the theology of Luther, he knew he stood in the main line evangelical tradition of which Luther was the prime fountainhead. The case with Calvin is more complex. In one context Wesley could denounce Calvinism and all its works, even if it meant a break with his good friend and associate in revival, George Whitefield. In another context he could say the Methodists in their theology had come to the very edge of Calvinism, within a hairsbreadth. In the first instance Wesley really means the doctrine of predestination and the corollaries of limited atonement, irresistibility of grace, and perseverance of the saints. No! "Free Grace," offered to all men who can be saved if they will turn! In the second instance the meaning of Calvinism is much more accurate. Here the chief points of reference are the absolute sovereignty of God and the utter need of man. On these fundamentals Calvin and Wesley were one. Spin-offs of these doctrinal emphases were carried down into Puritan writings, once again to mark deeply Wesley's theological development.

Above all, even though Wesley was a Catholic *and* a "great voice of the Reformation," he was an Anglican. It was the English expression of the Reformation which was centrally his. That means, to begin with, that this Reformation was least of all a rejection of the Catholic heritage. The genius of Anglicanism has been its retention of what it fondly regards as the best of both. There is so much of Bishop John Jewel and his *Apology for the Church of England* in Wesley, so much of Thomas Cranmer and the *Book of Common Prayer*. He was steeped in them and other exponents of the Anglican tradition. His parents laid a firm Anglican foundation for the spiritual nurture of their children. At times he could be rather high church—even stiffly so. At other times he reflected the broader perspectives of low church, to say nothing of those determined Anglican purifiers, the Puritans.

Robert Monk[6] has no difficulty in establishing the importance of Puritan writers represented in Wesley's great *A Christian Library,* in which the scholarly founder of Methodism sought to bring together

---

[5] *Standard Sermons* (1951), I, 37-52; cf. to Dr. Horne, 10 Mar. 1762, *Letters*, IV, 173.
[6] Robert C. Monk, *John Wesley, His Puritan Heritage* (1966), especially Appendix I, 256-62.

for the edification of his followers the greatest classics of Christian devotion. With characteristic self-assurance Wesley abridged these authors, some of whom were strongly tinctured with the Calvinist doctrine of election. But he went out of his way in providing an introduction to this section of the *Library*:

> After an account of the lives, sufferings, and deaths of those holy men [Puritan martyrs], who sealed the ancient religion with their blood, I believe nothing would either be more agreeable or more profitable to the serious reader, than some extracts from the writings of those who sprung up, as it were, out of their ashes. These breathe the same spirit, and were, in a lower degree, partakers of the same sufferings. Many of them took joyfully the spoiling of their goods, and all had their names cast out as evil; being branded with the nickname of Puritans, and thereby made a byeword and a proverb of reproach. I have endeavored to rescue from obscurity a few of the most eminent of these. . . . I have therefore selected what I conceived would be of most general use, and most proper to form a complete body of Practical Divinity.[7]

Although it is noteworthy that all four of the Wesley's grandparents were of Puritan conviction, it would appear that neither brother knew much of this family heritage until he was a grown man. The influence on Wesley was more direct through the writings, the bulk of which he manfully plowed through, and assimilated that which he found useful.

But John Wesley was a child of his age. What was that?—the Age of Reason, of Enlightenment. At last, educated men said, human beings are being freed from the superstitions of the past. At last they have discovered the power of the mind to understand and, to some extent, to mold the forces of nature. In religious terms this was spelled out in attempts to prove "the reasonableness of Christianity." One chief expression was Deism. Up to a point Wesley shared this respect for the uses of reason. He too thought Christianity reasonable. He even engaged in scientific experiments, usually those which might offer some practical benefit, such as better health. He was intrigued by the machine which produced static electricity, one of the marvels of the age. Up to a point he was an English Benjamin Franklin. Hence he was concerned about the charges leveled against him of "enthusiasm," which was a label used in those days as a weapon to discredit one whose belief and practices were thought to be irrational or overly emotional. He most certainly did not want to be known as an enthusiast, because he too was a man of reason. But he would not settle for cold rationalism or Deism, which he was sure took the heart out of the gospel. He had a place for the warm heart, after all, which could

---

[7] *A Christian Library,* IV, 107.

be understood and interpreted by a clear mind.[8] He had a modern view of human nature as involving the whole person, the emotional as well as the intellectual.

Among the more direct roots of Wesley's thought was that of Pietism. Since this influence has already been discussed in several contexts, little more than reference to it is needed here. One ought not conclude, from his criticisms of the Moravians in Herrnhut, and especially in London, that that influence was negative. Both for his personal spiritual life and for his theology, Pietism was a major factor. Perhaps it would be accurate to say that this theological influence found its most effective expression in the institutional forms to which it helped give rise; the societies, bands, classes, and all those devices of Wesley for the spiritual nourishment of whole persons in every aspect of their lives. Other forces, especially Puritanism, shared in this development.

How many theological legs did Wesley have? We may say they were numerous, they were varied, they were all important. We may say further that Wesley took them all without being dominated by any and reforged them, metamorphosed them, into a theological structure, which, if it was not "systematic" nor "original," nevertheless served well the needs of Christians wending their way along the royal road of salvation.

Structure

Someone acquainted with a certain spectrum of Methodist literature may ask at the very outset: why this attention to Wesley's theology? Did he not state, as the first of the points of Wesleyan teaching in "A Plain Account of the People Called Methodists," that "orthodoxy or right opinions is at best but a very slender part of religion"? Did he not emphasize in the General Rules that "there is only one condition previously required" for admission to the society, namely, "a desire to flee from the wrath to come, to be saved from their sins"? Did he not, in his famous sermon, "Catholic Spirit," taking his text from II Kings 10:15, reject doctrinal difference in the greater unity, "If thy heart is as my heart, give me thy hand"? Yes, if by theology is meant narrow confessional orthodoxy ("right opinions"), Wesley would have no part of it.

But that is not what he meant by theology. The context of all those references shows clearly that theology was at the very center of the Evangelical Revival. To use a contemporary phrase, Wesley assuredly

[8] Cf. for example his warnings in *Journal*, II, 130, and IV, 486.

did theology. One must get away from the concept of theology as a set of systematic propositions purporting to define the truth of the Christian faith. For Wesley, from beginning to end, theology was *experienced* along the royal road of salvation. It was a sort of survival kit for pilgrims and refugees.

In *The Message of the Wesleys* Philip Watson has summarized the Wesleyan message as follows: "All men need to be saved; all men can be saved; all men can know they are saved; all men can be saved to the uttermost." That is what Wesley had in mind when he discussed "our doctrines," that is, those theological emphases which have a special place in the Methodist understanding of Christian faith.

Wesley shared with all of his theological sources a biblically based conviction of the sinfulness of the human race. Paul put it succinctly: "All have sinned and fall short of the glory of God." Hence, all men need to be saved because they need to be released from the sin that binds them. That is what is meant in the gospel, "You shall know the truth and the truth shall make you free." Freedom from sin is the first section of the journey toward salvation. One of Wesley's more bulky treatises is a full exposition of the doctrine of original sin.[9] He made this part of the Christian tradition his own. But with characteristic independence of mind he entered some specific qualifications that avoid the extreme "miserable worm" interpretation. The moral law of the universe—natural conscience—always offers some guidance, even to the most sinful. God gave us minds to think with, and the processes of reason are effective still, even in a sinful world. In some mysterious way man, though bound in sin, still possesses an ineradicable measure of freedom—at least enough to respond to the proffered grace of God. Conversion as a meaningful response of man thus becomes possible.

In his theological struggle to understand this latter point Wesley developed the concept of prevenient grace, or "preventing grace," that which "comes before." That is what he is talking about in the sermon with so peculiar a title, "Working Out Your Own Salvation." Even in a state of sin every man possesses some spark of original grace, sufficient to enable him to turn. It is by the grace of God that he turns, but *he turns.* Charles Wesley's hymns are full of "our doctrines" of the road of salvation:

> Sinners, turn; why will ye die?
> God, your Maker, asks you why;
> God, who did your being give,

[9] "The Doctrine of Original Sin, according to Scripture, Reason, and Experience," *Works,* IX, 196-464.

> Made you with himself to live;
> He the fatal cause demands,
> Asks the work of his own hands:
> Why, ye thankless creatures, why
> Will ye cross his love, and die? [10]

Thus the first step is acknowledgment of need. The second step is acceptance of the promise that man can be saved. This is why the doctrine of grace is at the center of Wesley's theology. The first sermon in the *Standard Sermons* begins: "All the blessings which God hath bestowed upon man are of His mere grace, bounty, or favour; His free, undeserved favour; favour altogether undeserved; man having no claim to the least of His mercies." [11]

That grace begins its work *before,* through the grace already in man enabling him first to turn to God. Saving grace comes through faith, which is a free gift of God. One who trusts that God can save by his grace has faith. There are—contrary to what the Moravians were saying—degrees of faith, all the way from materialists and Deists on to Evangelical Christians going on to perfection. The sacraments of baptism and the Lord's Supper are marks or channels of the grace of God through Christ. They are also themselves "converting ordinances," which suggests that would-be Christians ought to attend all the means of grace, because putting oneself in the way of God's mercy is one step in the right direction. When one has turned to God and received the gift of faith, he is justified. That is, "pardoned and received into God's favour and into such a state that, if we continue therein, we shall be finally saved." [12]

Another particular emphasis made by Wesley, one which he always regarded as one of "our doctrines," was assurance. When one is forgiven his sins, justified before God, and on the road to salvation, he can *know* it. Wesley's sermons on the witness of the Spirit make plain that God's grace produces a conviction within ourselves:

> How can a sinner know
> His sins on earth forgiven?
> How can my gracious Savior show
> My name inscribed in heaven?
>
> What we have felt and seen
> With confidence we tell;
> And publish to the sons of men
> The signs infallible.

[10] *Hymns on God's Everlasting Love,* 1741.
[11] *Standard Sermons,* I, 37.
[12] Minutes of Annual Conference, 1744; Outler, *John Wesley,* 137.

His Spirit to us he gave,
And dwells in us we know;
The witness in ourselves we have,
And all its fruits we show.[13]

He recognized that some persons may be justified without clear assurance. Bunyan named one of his noblest pilgrims Mr. Fearing.

That Wesley was concerned about assurance of forgiveness very early is indicated by a reference to Taylor's *Holy Living and Dying* in a letter of 1725, in which he takes issue with the man who had so much influence on his early thought. Whereas Taylor had been insisting that one must cling to faith in spite of never knowing one's condition, Wesley commented that such a position would appear to contradict what Taylor himself had said about the work of the Holy Spirit. "Now, surely these graces are not of so little force, that we can't perceive whether we have them or no." [14] At that time he associated this assurance with meaningful participation in the Lord's Supper. In later years he broadened and emphasized this doctrine of assurance as a special witness of the Methodists.

The final step toward salvation Wesley identified with the going on to perfection, that is, the overflowing of the love of God into the life of man so as to eradicate even the roots of original sin. The first blessing of saving grace may be compared to spraying a clump of poison ivy with weed killer: it is destroyed for a season, but the roots remain, always capable of bursting forth in new growth. Only a *rooting out* will utterly wipe out the dangerous weed. Wesley believed that the very roots of sinful disposition can be destroyed and replaced by "perfect love." This can be a second blessing instantaneously received and known, but it is always a lifelong process and hence, also gradual. It can happen any time after justification, up to the point of death. It should be sought all the time. And always there is the possibility of backsliding.

He tried to be plain-spoken on what he meant by this teaching to which he gave so much attention. On one occasion he wrote in his journal: "Constant communion with God the Father and the Son fills their hearts with humble love. Now this is what I always did, and do now, mean by perfection." He cited illustrations of how this found expression, in one case by testimony that "I search my heart again and again, and I can find nothing but love there." [15]

---

[13] *The Methodist Hymnal* (1964), 114.

[14] *Letters*, I, 19-20, cf. I, 255, 263; VII, 57. *The Rule and Exercise of Holy Living* (1650), . . . *of Holy Dying* (1651).

[15] *Journal*, IV, 369-70; cf. V, 324-25; *Letters*, IV, 206.

Repeatedly Wesley identified this going on to perfection as the fundamental emphasis which distinguished Methodists.[16] His motivation was clearly rooted in an awareness of how easily a Christian could slide into self-satisfied complacency and spiritual stagnation. The road of salvation is a long one which runs through a lifetime. He was also reacting against the quietism and antinomianism which he found among Moravians and Calvinists. In a sense the quest for perfect love in this life served as a substitute for the Catholic doctrine of purgatory.

As over against the reformers, particularly Luther, Wesley understood perfection not as absolute (which made impossible for Luther its realization in this life of ineradicable bent toward sin) but as relative. It is relative on the one hand to the incompleteness of the lifelong process, the always *going on,* and to the continuing possibility of backsliding, and on the other hand to the only absolute perfection, that of God's love. It is the love of God in man that is perfect, not anything that is man's own achievement. Wesley did come close to righteousness by works in his concern for perfection. To Miss Furly he set a tight tension, even paradox: "All who expect to be sanctified at all, expect to be sancified by faith. But meantime they know that faith will not be given but to them that obey. Remotely, therefore, the blessing depends on our works, although immediately, on simple faith.[17]

Wesley's insistence, perhaps too strongly, that his teaching on perfect love never changed indicates the seriousness with which he approached a difficult doctrine. For all its imperfections his teaching on perfection stands as a distinctive emphasis of the Wesleyan Revival. It expresses the central doctrine, held in common with the Protestant Reformation, of the grace of God in Jesus Christ as the source of salvation. It underlines the teaching that all true Christian religion is social religion, to be expressed through Christian love. It breaks over the barriers of creed and confession to bring men of faith together in an ecumenical fellowship. The original insistence of John Wesley that Methodists ought above all else to be people going on to perfection may have considerable value in a later day when little else besides Christian love is left to keep men of faith together.

---

[16] Cf. for example, *Journal,* IV, 529; *Letters,* IV, 110; VII, 102-3.
[17] 19 August 1759, *Letters,* IV, 71.

Chapter 4
Fruits of Wesley's Theology

> The most impossible of all
> Is that I e'er from sin should cease;
> Yet shall it be, I know it shall;
> Jesus, look to thy faithfulness;
> If nothing is too hard for Thee,
> All things are possible to me.

The first fruit of the royal road is a new person. The process of going on to perfection means a complete rebirth. What seems impossible to human nature becomes possible through grace. Whatever one may say regarding the relation and relative importance of individual and social religion, the latter is inconceivable without the former, and the former is incomplete without the latter. It is appropriate, therefore, in moving from Wesley's theology to its fruits, to begin where we left off—with reference to the doctrine of perfect love.

New Life

All other aspects of theology must give way to the first priority—the making of a new life. That is the reason why Wesley was so impatient with associates who involved themselves in secondary issues. For example, to one of his preachers he wrote: "I wish your zeal was better employed than in persuading men to be either dipped or sprinkled. I will employ mine by the grace of God in persuading them to love God with all their hearts and their neighbour as themselves." [1] That new life is marked by a new relation with fellow human beings. The best illustration is to be found in the General Rules, which from first to last describe the way in which a Christian lives with his fellows: doing no harm, doing good, attending on the "ordinances." These Rules have sometimes been misunderstood as setting rigid patterns of don'ts and do's. That is to overlook the important phrase, "such as." The main content is simply examples of how holy living may find expression in daily life.

Of course, one cannot deny elements of legalism and au-

[1] To Gilbert Boyce, 22 May 1750, *Letters,* III, 37.

51

thoritarianism in Wesley's work. Repeatedly he complained that people were giving up early morning preaching—as a result of which "Methodism too will degenerate into a mere sect." [2] He was always urgent on the necessity of following the regular discipline. In a hitherto unpublished letter he emphasized that, in the specific matter of bankruptcy, the discipline of the societies must be maintained, even though the failing brother is a leading member.

The apparently rigid discipline, however, was tempered by moderation. Nothing should be attempted to excess, lest the means interfere with the end—holy living. This advice applied even to preaching, the grand calling of Methodist ministers: "Our preachers have as great need of temperance in preaching as in eating or drinking." The rigor had a basic purpose: the strengthening of body, mind, and soul for the love of God and the service of man. This discipline was reflected even in the architecture of the preaching places. To Mary Bishop, Wesley wrote that the new building should have side aisles, no backs on the benches, and a rail down the middle to separate men from women. [3] The Methodists would indeed be a "society of Jesus."

New Church

As we have seen, the Wesleys stood firm in loyalty to the Church of England, which defined the church in the Thirty-Nine Articles (Article 19) as "a congregation of faithful men in which the pure word of God is preached and the sacraments be duly administered according to Christ's ordinance in all those things that of necessity are requisite to the same." One of the crucial questions was the necessity of bishops in direct historical succession from the apostles, which led to investigation of the precedent of the early church. The high regard Wesley had for primitive precedent has already been noted. Much of his struggle to provide necessary pastoral leadership for the People Called Methodists involved an attempt to understand the principles and practice of the early church. Finally, in 1784, armed with (1) a case of necessity consequent on the American Revolution, (2) research on the office of bishop in antiquity, and (3) some equivocal judgment in the Anglican tradition, he acted to ordain ministers for service in America. One of his main points was evocation of primitive precedent.

When he began to organize his followers into societies and classes,

---

[2] *Journal:* VI, 484-85. Cf. *ibid.*, 492-93. The unpublished letter is in Frank Baker "John Wesley and Miss Mary Clark," *MH,* 10 (Jan., 1972): 49-50.
[3] 27 Nov. 1770, *Letters,* V, 209.

again (characteristically after the event rather than before), he called
on the practice of the early church for justification:

> Upon reflection, I could not but observe, This is the very thing which was
> from the beginning of Christianity. In the earliest times, those whom
> God had sent forth "preached the gospel to every creature." . . . But as
> soon as any of these were so convinced of the truth, as to forsake sin and
> seek the gospel salvation, they immediately joined them together, took an
> account of their names, advised them to watch over each other, and met
> these "catechumens" . . . apart from the great congregation, that they
> might instruct, rebuke, exhort, and pray with them, and for them,
> according to their several necessities.[4]

In other words, he discovered that the early Christians had done as he
was already doing. Hence, at the very foundation of the Methodist
conception of the church is an ecumenical, thoroughly catholic understanding which sees the true church rooted, not in any one historical or confessional form, but in the primitive tradition closely associated with the apostles. Thomas Coke (always Dr. Coke to the
American Methodists) followed the same line, as for example in his
discussion of Hoadley's *Treatise on Conformity and Episcopacy.*[5]

Nevertheless, the Wesleyan doctrine of the church was firmly identified with the Anglican (and Reformed) tradition. Wesley thought
the Established Church to be "the most Scriptural National Church in
the world." He knew of no liturgy more admirable than the *Book of
Common Prayer.* Although he would, upon occasion of necessity, depart from the form of that church, he always remained faithful, at
least in his own understanding, to the Anglican tradition. When he
spoke of the "church" in ordinary usage, he always meant the Church
of England, never the Roman Catholic, or the Congregational, much
less the Methodist Societies. In the Church of England he saw the
finest combination of the catholic and the reformed, the Body of
Christ and the Word, the *Ecumené* and the Reformation.

Wesley was adaptable to circumstances, not bound to formulations.
He was willing to admit that, in spite of the Anglican definition, there
might well be some true Christians in a genuine part of the church,
who preach *some* unscriptural doctrines or who unduly administer the
sacraments—provided the main direction was valid and their intentions good.[6] This adaptability permitted Wesley to construct a new
form of the church within the existing structure; the relatively small
societies of the People Called Methodists were then subdivided into

---

[4] *Works,* VIII, 250-51.
[5] Thomas Coke, *Journal* (1793), 11-12.
[6] *Works,* VI, 397.

more intimate bands and classes for spiritual oversight and mutual ministry one to the other. "Ye are a new phenomenon in the earth,—a body of people who, being of no sect or party, are friends to all parties, and endeavour to forward all in heart-religion, in the knowledge and love of God and man." [7] The formal church had failed to reach many of the people. There was a field ripe for harvest inside the Anglican establishment, to say nothing of many others who, being dissenters or wholly outside any church, stood in need of spiritual ministry. This explains the decision, taken first by Whitefield, to go to the people around Bristol *where they were*. As Wesley wrote in a letter, "To this people Mr. Whitefield last spring began to preach the gospel of Christ; and as there were thousands of them who went to no place of public worship, he went out into their own wilderness 'to seek and to save that which was lost.' " [8] As to the form of ministry the same principle prevailed—go to the people at their greatest need. The itinerant system of keeping the preachers always on the move best suited these changing needs. Of the excellence of itineracy Wesley had no doubts and never compromised: "As long as I am alive, the Methodist itinerant will itinerate." This principle also explains the iron hand with which the leader led. The conference of preachers was gathered to consult, advise, assist, and obey, not to legislate or make decisions. Preachers came at Wesley's invitation, not as a right, and normally they did not vote, except in advisory capacity by consensus. Every aspect of the new form of ministry was directed toward a single goal: to reach people who were not being reached, to proclaim to them a gospel they were not hearing, to win souls to Christ, and to encourage them on to perfect love. A sole devotion produced a spare and disciplined organization.

Like ministers, like people. The active development of the priesthood of all believers, the ministry of all Christians, required of all Methodists the same sole devotion, whether as local preachers, exhorters, class leaders ("the lowest wheel but one"), or ordinary members of societies. What the Large Minutes (the compilation of regulations of the annual conferences) did for the preachers, the General Rules and band and class rules did for members. Nowhere in Christian history has the priesthood of all believers been more fully expressed than in the early Methodist class meetings. "We will have a holy people or none," said Wesley.

[7] *Works*, VII, 280.

[8] To Nathanael Price, 6 Dec. 1739, *Letters*, I, 339. Cf. II, 15. On unusual preaching situations see *Letters*, II, 99; *Journal*, II, 167. On itineracy see *Journal*, VI, 42; *Letters*, III, 192; V, 63, 194; VI, 40, 117.

A distinctive doctrine of the church emerges from these prudential regulations. As noted above, Wesley accepted the tradition of the "holy Catholic church" of all ages and places. To a Baptist minister he wrote: "I do not think either the Church of England, or the People called Methodists, or any other particular Society under heaven to be *the True Church of Christ.* For that Church is but one, and contains all true believers on earth. But I conceive every society of true believers to be a branch of the one true Church of Christ." [9] Although the familiar passage "I look upon all the world as my parish," appears early and in context has more limited application, it fits the concept of church and ministry in the Methodist movement. Writing to Joseph Benson in 1773 with itinerant ministry in mind, he said, "We are debtors to all the world. We are called to warn every one, to exhort every one, if by any means we may save some." Wesley believed in the *catholic* church.

He also believed in the *communion of saints,* which found expression in the societies. If the sacraments were duly administered in the Anglican Church, the Word was truly preached in the societies. Moreover, here the saints were in fellowship, as Charles Wesley's hymns never wearied of reaffirming. This meant, among other things, the emotional as well as the intellectual involvement of the person. To experience conversion, to be reborn, to live the faith along the royal road of salvation meant feeling as well as thinking, the heart as well as the mind. Such emphases inevitably brought tensions. The more staid Anglicans fretted much about Methodist *enthusiasm.* For example, William Warburton, commenting specifically on Whitefield, but by implication on the whole Wesleyan revival, thought that famous preacher "quite mad" in his "ridiculous expressions": "I tell you what I think would be the best way of exposing these idle Fanatics —the presenting of passages out of George Fox's Journal [founder of the Quakers], and Ignatius Loyola, and Whitefield's Journals in parallel columns. Their conformity in folly is amazing." Edmund Gibson, Bishop of London, asked

> Whether it does not savour of Self-sufficiency and Presumption, when a few young Heads, without any Colour of a Divine Commission, set up their own Schemes, as the great Standard of Christianity: And, How it can be reconciled to Christian Humility, Prudence, or Charity, to indulge their own Notions to such a Degree, as to perplex, unhinge, terrify and distract the Minds of Multitudes of People, who have lived from their Infancy under a Gospel Ministry, and in the regular Exercise of a Gospel Worship; and all this, by persuading them, that they have never yet

[9] To Gilbert Boyce, 22 May 1750, *Letters,* III, 35. Cf. I, 286; VI, 3.

heard the true Gospel, nor been instructed in the true Way of Salvation before; and that they neither are, nor can be true Christians, but by adhering to *their* Doctrins and Disciplin [sic], and embracing Christianity upon *their* Schemes: All the while, for the Sake of those Schemes, and in Pursuance of them, violating the wholsom Rules, which the Powers Spiritual and Temporal have wisely and piously established, for the Preservation of Peace and Order in the Church.[10]

Tensions were inevitable, and did not fail to develop, in a church which shared such disparate roots. But this again was Wesley's genius, that he could draw upon such rich sources and make them his own in a new and distinctive expression. Thus, along with the catholic sense of the universal church of all ages as the vessel of sacramental grace, Wesley brought in the Reformation doctrines of the Word of God and the priesthood of all believers, and also the emphasis of the Radical Reformation and Pietism on discipleship and whole commitment. The church thus becomes not only a vessel of salvation but also a way of life. In John Wesley's doctrine of the church there is room for the catholic church as the vessel of objective grace, the reformed church as the pulpit of the confessional Word, and the radical church as the way of committed discipleship. The really unique feature is the distinctive combination in which these all found expression in the societies without breaking from the Church of England. When Methodism did finally break—suddenly in America, gradually in England—something essential was lost.

New Society

One must distinguish clearly between Wesley's intentions and the effects of his theology. One must also distinguish between the purposes of the societies and the effects of the movement. It has been correctly pointed out that the social views of John Calvin were quite conservative, whereas the effects of the Calvinistic reform were revolutionary. The same may be said of Wesley. To be blunt, he was a Tory, politically and socially, but for a theological reason: governments are instituted by God. Yet, the influence of Methodism on the political status of ordinary people and on their role in social life was in many respects revolutionary. Of both Calvin and Wesley it may prop-

[10] Quoted in M. Lawrence Snow, "Methodist Enthusiasm, Warburton Letters 1738–40," *MH*, 10 (Apr., 1972): 30-47, pp. 38, 44. Gibson in *Observations upon the Conduct and Behaviour of a Certain Sect. Usually Distinguished by the Name of Methodists* (1740?), in *English Historical Documents* (London: Eyre & Spottiswoode, 1957), X, 389-90.

erly be said that they would have been horrified at some of the ideas to which their movements gave rise.[11]

Hence, when one discusses Wesley's political views, his own conservative stance becomes obvious. "We are no republicans and never intend to be." Or, as he put it in "Observations on Liberty," "The greater the share the people have in government, the less liberty, civil or religious, does a nation enjoy. Accordingly, there is most liberty in a limited Monarchy, less under an Aristocracy, and least under a Democracy." Governments are instituted by God, not by the will of the people. The common man does not have enough sense to participate in making public decisions, and, on account of his sin, cannot use what little he has. Even titled noblemen waste their talents and cannot be trusted. On the other hand, kings are by God appointed. Wesley stopped short of the divine right of kings. It should come as no surprise, then, that he stood strong against the revolution by the British colonists in America. His "Calm Address" was only one of several tracts written to counsel submission to royal authority. When one considers that democracy was almost unheard of in the eighteenth century and was proposed chiefly by irreligious men like Thomas Paine, one can understand, in the context of his own times, why he should have been so conservative.

But all this is to ignore the implications of his theology from beginning to end; that is, from original sin to perfect love. Both doctrinal emphases worked powerfully toward recognition of the fundamental equality of all men. Kings are subject, as are all men, to the bonds of sin and equal before the judgment seat of God. By like token, even the most miserable sinner, the lowest dregs of humanity, may by the grace of God be raised to that level of Christian perfection in which he is, at last, a free man. The notion of freedom from sin carries over very easily into freedom from oppression, political equality. Wesley was no reformer and had little understanding of the political trends forecasting the future. But his teaching and his movement provided an arena favorable to the development of just those democratic ideas which were beginning to flourish among the radicals of the day. Ordinary Methodist laymen had no part in the government of the societies, but they did have ample opportunity to exercise their talents at the local level, as preachers and class leaders, trustees and stewards. Wesley raised up a whole generation of En-

---

[11] Among the books dealing with the social influence of Methodism are F. R. Wearmouth, *Methodism and the Common People in the Eighteenth Century* (1945); Wellman J. Warner, *The Wesleyan Movement in the Industrial Revolution* (1930); Maldwyn Edwards, *John Wesley and the Eighteenth Century* (1933); E. R. Taylor, *Methodism and Politics* (1935); S. Paul Schilling, *Methodism and Society in Theological Perspective* (1960).

glishmen (including some women) capable of thinking for themselves, disciplining their wayward inclinations, and speaking out on important matters. Here was political democracy at work, all unbeknownst to the leader. Some of his spiritual children proved more perceptive than the parent.

Only upon rare occasions did Wesley take a position outside the traditional stance of Tory conservative. A noble exception, to which he was forced by his own doctrine of man, was the evil of the slave trade. He was with William Wilberforce in active promotion of the abolition of the slave trade in the British Empire. In this he was, unfortunately, well in advance of some of his children, especially in the United States. Dr. Coke was of the same mind as Wesley in this matter.

It would be too much to expect that Wesley would have been able to perceive the full significance of the Industrial Revolution and the factory system, which was just beginning to spread portentously over the very trails he had followed all his life. He was well aware of the changes. The main lines of his itineration mark out accurately the main centers of the Industrial Revolution—the entrepôt London, commercial and mining Bristol, coal-begrimed Newcastle, the iron-mining and manufacturing Midlands. Methodist societies sprang up in those very places which were first marked—branded—by the Industrial Revolution. London is a case in point. A demographic charting of societies demonstrates that there were none located in the city of London itself (the small political core), or the city of Westminster —that is, in the central areas dominated by the middle class, which was Anglican. Rather, the societies flourished in the outer areas, industrial communities where poor workers lived.[12] Until the end of Wesley's life the larger part of the Methodist constituency came, not from the agrarian yeomen-farmers nor from the rising middle class, but from the working people, those most immediately influenced by the new factory system.

One might expect, therefore, that Wesley would be in sympathy with movements designed to restructure society and provide a rightful place for the working man. Such is not the case, but there are some particular qualifications. He was no socialist, but neither was he a devotee of *laissez-faire*, the free enterprise system. In some of his writings he would appear to lean toward individualism in economic matters. But in others, he clearly advocated government controls. His "Thoughts Upon the Present Scarcity of Provisions" (1773) makes a

---

[12] I am indebted to Albert Outler, personal conversation, for this data.

place for government initiative in regulating economic activity.[13] On the whole he was no social reformer, any more than he was a political reformer.

But two points must be made on the other side. In the first place, the implications of his theology carried powerful influences on the lives of his followers. This is to be seen, on the one hand, in the indirect effects of the Wesleyan message of redemption, and on the other, in the prudential ethics which Wesley inculcated. The new man, the reborn Christian, was changed in his entire being, including his social relations. All the way from his daily habits of cleanliness to his highest career aspirations, he was changed. He might be headed toward heaven, but on the way he would act like the sober, diligent, purposeful, disciplined person he had become. Benefiting from the useful education which Wesley always encouraged, he would understand more of the world and of life, would direct his activities in more intelligent channels, would invest his efforts and funds more wisely, and eventually would reap the harvest of industry. In fact, this is precisely what happened. More and more Methodists, honestly following the General Rules, were becoming more and more prosperous—much to Wesley's dismay. As he grew older he devoted more and more time to advice on meeting the challenges and temptations of worldly prosperity. "Gain all you can," he advised, "save all you can—and give all you can." The new man of the Wesleyan Revival was not, perhaps, creating a new society, but he certainly was profiting from it.

In the long run, the influence of the Wesleyan movement was to the good, as the evil as well as beneficial potentials of the Industrial Revolution became obvious. Whatever Wesley's own intentions may have been—and they were no better or worse than those of his well-intentioned contemporaries—the net effects on society were favorable to the changes which brought in what we call the modern industrial world. Together with those other influences which worked toward broader democracy and human rights, the new birth of individuals contributed mightily to the birth of a new society. The manner in which these contributions were sullied and compromised in the next century is part of a later story.

In the second place, the whole Methodist movement was laced with activities designed to relieve suffering and need. Philanthropy is a work which comes naturally to Methodists, if only because of the varied participation of Wesley himself. He was always concerned, in a

[13] See Robert M. Kingdon, "Laissez-Faire or Government Control: A Problem for John Wesley," *CH*, 26 (1957): 342-54.

century famous for callousness, with human welfare. He supported many philanthropic causes and started many himself. He was always urging members of the societies to make regular contributions to the needy, both inside and outside the societies themselves. The Wesleys set an example by regular visitation of the sick, the needy, and the imprisoned. The primary purpose was always spiritual ministration, but care of bodily needs was understood to be part of it. The history of Methodist social service goes back directly to the fountainhead.

It would be a mistake to try to claim Wesley as a forerunner of the "social gospel." It would be equally a mistake to conclude, on the basis of his own conservative views, that either he or his movement was a negative factor in social change. In the end it must be said that his theology was better than his politics and his economics and overrode both.

Chapter 5
Lay Beginnings

One of the mysteries of Methodist church history is the fate of the groups gathered together by John and Charles Wesley in Georgia. Another mystery is the organized consequences, if any, of the several preaching missions of George Whitefield in the 1740s and 1750s. In neither case is there any clear evidence that the movement had any more than a temporary organized expression. No society is known to have descended from the work of these men. Wesley did form a society in Savannah, and did employ at least one lay preacher, Charles Delamotte, who kept the society going at least a half year after John left for England.[1] Possibly some of those who were caught up in Whitefield's revival preaching continued, at least as indivduals, to join in the early societies of the 1760s. The most direct evidence is in Philadelphia and in Lewes, Delaware. The English evangelist formed a society in Philadelphia, and later Joseph Pilmore referred to one in that society who had "stood fast in the faith thirty years." William Warren Sweet speculates that he may have left some persevering Methodists in Williamsburg after three visits between 1739 and 1755. But in all this, as with so much of history, the snows of yesteryear have quite vanished.

The American Religious Situation

The actual beginnings of Methodism in America, those with demonstrable historical consequences, date from the 1760s. At that time Protestant Christianity had been growing in the English colonies for nearly one hundred fifty years. Methodists were preceded by Congregationalists, Anglicans, Baptists, Dutch and German Reformed, Lutherans, Presbyterians, Quakers, and numerous other small groups. They had been on the scene for a long time already, and in some colonies had preempted the ground as established churches, protected and fostered by the government through tax revenues and legal preference. Thus the Congregationalists were established in

[1] Frank Baker, "The Lay Pioneers of American Methodism," *Forever Beginning* (1967) 169-77. William Warren Sweet, *Virginia Methodism* (1955), 30.

New England (except for Rhode Island) and the Anglicans in Virginia and the Carolinas. Although the Roman Catholics had begun a unique experiment in Maryland, they had been displaced by the Anglicans.[2]

All these denominations had their origin in Europe, most of them in Great Britain. All the early roots of American religion run deep into European history. In this sense the Methodist movement is no exception. Denominationalism had a distinctive and spectacular development in America, but it got its start in Europe. Almost everything in American life at this early period got its start in Europe.

On the other hand, new forces were already at work. For example, mainline churches, such as the Congregationalists of New England and the Anglicans of the southern colonies, were strongly affected by the pressures for lay participation—if not control—and for local autonomy in opposition to centralized authority. In New England the Congregationalists failed to achieve an overall synodical unity; in Virginia and the Carolinas lay vestries succeeded in wresting power over parishes from clerical control and for long opposed the introduction of episcopal authority. A bishop in London was quite close enough. The same trend is seen among Presbyterians with the vigorous rise of local presbyteries opposed to centralizing synod and assembly.

But the most important feature of colonial religion was the most obvious—diversity. Already, long before the arrival of Methodists, the religious situation was one of unresolved variety. It was clear that no one religious establishment could hope to dominate the English seaboard. Even colonies with established churches had to connive with the diverse forces to the extent of permitting, with varying degrees of reluctance, other forms of religious expression. No "Elizabethan Settlement," no German territorialism (Peace of Augsburg 1555), no Edict of Nantes (1598) or its revocation (1685), would suffice for the ebullient populations of the more or less friendly, but competing, colonies which owed allegiance to his English royal majesty.

Hence, when Methodists began to spread from their early centers, they encountered quite different situations in different colonies. In New England, they found a Congregational church firmly planted on

[2] Among the many introductions to American church history the following are both recent and reliable: Winthrop Hudson, *Religion in America* (1965); H. Shelton Smith, Robert T. Handy, and L. A. Loetscher, *American Christianity, An Historical Interpretation with Representative Documents* (2 vols. 1960); William Warren Sweet, *Religion in Colonial America* (1942); Perry Miller, *Orthodoxy in Massachusetts* (1933); L. J. Trinterud, *The Forming of an American Tradition* (1949); Sydney E. Ahlstrom, *A Religious History of the American People* (1972).

each village green, with no other allowed on the common land. In Virginia, they found a parish system in operation similar, at least in principle, to the Anglican network in England. Wherever they went, they were in somebody's parish. That was tolerable, so long as Methodists regarded themselves as Anglicans. Some rectors, like Devereux Jarratt, would welcome a spiritually stimulating itinerant evangelist. In Pennsylvania, they found a confusing variety of churches and sects living together in generally agreeable satisfaction. Quaker control of the colony founded by William Penn, himself of the Friends, had been given up about the time of the French and Indian War. Law-abiding, religious groups were welcomed if they agreed to the tolerant terms of settlement.

About 1740 a few small brush fires of spiritual revival burst out into a general conflagration which has come under the name *Great Awakening*. No churches were unaffected, and some were veritably transformed. American religion after the Great Awakening would never be the same. One more distinctive factor had been added to those differences which, although they arose from a common source, marked the special character of religion in America. The Awakening brought in powerful religious influences which greatly strengthened the churches. It also brought in tensions which resulted in divisions, a rise of new sects, and opposition from intellectual forces of the Enlightenment. In this case, at least, growth brought stress.

Before the fire broke out, there were stirrings in particular areas. In the Dutch Reformed Church in New Jersey, Theodore Frelinghuysen led a revival in the 1720s. William and Gilbert Tennant led a similar revival among the Presbyterians. Then, in Massachusetts Jonathan Edwards began a series of doctrinal sermons in the 1730s, which brought strong results in Northampton. His report on the revival in *A Faithful Narrative of the Surprising Work of God* (London, 1737; Boston, 1738) made a deep impression on John Wesley. Edwards' incisive attempt to understand the meaning of revival has become a classic: *A Treatise Concerning Religious Affections* (1746). In it he explained, "'Tis a hard Thing to be a hearty zealous Friend of what has been good and glorious, in the late extraordinary Appearances, and to rejoice much in it; and at the same Time, to see the Evil and pernicious Tendency of what has been bad, and earnestly to oppose that."

Persons inclined to the providential interpretation of history would no doubt explain that the appearance of George Whitefield on the American scene in Philadelphia, November 2, 1739, was ordained by God. Certainly no evangelical leader made his appearance at a more dramatic moment. The little fires which had smoldered locally for years now suddenly burst forth in the general conflagration of the Great Awakening. Whitefield, more than any other single person, was responsible for bringing the whole stirring together. Edwards and the Tennants were caught up with the enthusiasm. Gilbert Tennant delivered a controversial sermon on "The Danger of an Unconverted Ministry" in which he declared, "From what has been said we may learn, That such who are contented under a dead Ministry have not in them the temper of that Saviour they profess. It's an awful Sign that they are as blind as Moles, and as dead as Stones, without any spiritual Taste and Relish." Even Harvard and Yale opened their doors to the spirit of revival. That is, they did at first. On later visits the reception was definitely cool. Then the Harvard faculty, seconded by Yale, condemned him for "enthusiasm . . . sudden impulses . . . distemper of the mind . . . pernicious reflections upon the ministers . . . deluder of the people . . . extempore manner of preaching . . . itinerant way . . . always fraught with enthusiasm."

Naturally, so strong a movement brought a force of opposition. It came especially from those persons under the philosophical influence of the Enlightenment. They were offended by the extreme forms of emotional revivalism displayed by such enthusiasts as James Davenport. Charles Chauncy of Boston led the reaction with a sermon on "Enthusiasm Described and Cautioned Against," followed by a book on *Seasonable Thoughts on the State of Religion in New England.* Congregationalists divided into New Lights and Old Lights. Likewise, the Presbyterians split (temporarily) into new side and old side. Extreme proponents founded revivalist sects, and extreme opponents founded rationalist movements.

Among the positive effects of the Great Awakening were the developments of missionary spirit and educational concern. Several colleges, such as William Tennant's "Log College," the College of New Jersey (Princeton), and the College of Rhode Island (Brown), were sparked by the revival fires. Moreover, the theological emphases of the revival, although they did bring about institutional schisms, nevertheless proved in the long run a unifying force in American religion. From now on all the churches, whatever factors still held them apart, had something important in common, a sense of having lived through deep movings of the Holy Spirit, which brought about amazing transformations and conversions. This common experience contributed strongly to the form of the church distinctive of American Christianity—the denomination, a church composed of many parts or forms, in which each recognized the common Christian faith of the others. Finally, this pervasive religious influence had its political consequences in the closer association of the colonies as the powerful revival crossed boundaries and brought men of distant regions into contact with one another. The Great Awakening may not have planted the seeds of the American Revolution, but it plowed the ground and fitted it for new things.

The Planting of Methodism

It is worthy of note that the three volume *History of American Methodism* (1964) devotes only six pages to the beginnings of Methodism in North America carried on by independent laymen. The simplest explanation for this brevity is the paucity of firm information. On the other hand, whole books have been written in analysis of the circumstantial evidence which has been painstakingly winnowed out.[3] Another possible factor is an ingrained tendency to overlook the work of unauthorized laymen. Almost the sole influence motivating the book writers has been an intense desire to prove the priority of one beginning against other claimants. The real significance of the theme—the clear priority of lay initiative in the planting of Methodism in America—has been lost in the struggle to prove who was first.

These earliest planters were certainly unauthorized. They had no warrant from anyone. John Wesley in England did not even know what they were up to, until he had a letter in 1768 asking for help.

The weight of available evidence would appear to favor Maryland as the scene of first plantings. Although one can date the society in New York from 1766, the evidence for an organization in Maryland at least a half year earlier is almost as specific.[4] The key figure is

[3] See John Bowen, *The Rise and Progress of Methodism on Sam's and Pipe Creek, Maryland, from the Year 1764* (1856); John Lednum, *History of the Rise of Methodism in America* (1859); Mrs. Arthur B. Bibbins, *The Beginnings of American Methodism: Robert Strawbridge, Founder* (1916); *idem, How Methodism Came: The Beginnings of Methodism in England and America* (1945). All the above argue for Maryland priority. Defending New York as first are J. B. Wakeley, *Lost Chapters Recovered from the Early History of American Methodism* (1858); Samuel Seaman, *Annals of New York Methodism* (1892); H. K. Carroll, *The First Methodist Society in America* (1916). Most recent, and probably definitive for the Maryland case is the chapter by Edwin Schell in Gordon Pratt Baker, ed., *Those Incredible Methodists* (1972), a history of the Baltimore Annual Conference. The partisanship of many of these works renders their enthusiasm if not their accuracy suspect.

[4] See Edwin Schell in *Those Incredible Methodists;* also his article in *MH,* 9 (Apr., 1971): 62-64. Robert Strawbridge may well have carried on organized work in the early 1760s. One of the members of the class was John England, a former Quaker who became a Methodist some time before June, 1766. This evidence, which dates England's departure from the Quaker meeting, "for the first time documents from an independent

from Md.

Robert Strawbridge, the first of a long line of Methodist mavericks who grazed in fenced pastures very unwillingly. No one knows when he came from Ireland to the New World. No one knows when he began his preaching ministry. What we do know is that he had already begun preaching as a Methodist in Ireland, and that he began the same activity soon after arrival in Maryland. He settled in the northern part of that colony near Sam's Creek, where he built a substantial log house (near New Windsor, now preserved, with alterations, as a historical shrine). Quite possibly he formed the first Methodist class in this house. Francis Asbury later recorded that "Here Mr. Strawbridge formed the first society in Maryland—and *America*." [5] More specific evidence indicates that for some time before the spring of 1766 Strawbridge's group was active. Possibly as early as 1764, he built a log meeting house, which would be the first Methodist church building.

This first Methodist preacher in America was a strong-willed Irishman who saw no reason to ask permission to carry on his ministry. He began preaching on his own, because he recognized a need. For the same need, he began presently to administer the sacraments of baptism and the Lord's Supper. This practice raised an important issue which, by the time of the Revolution, almost caused a schism. Even Francis Asbury and that arch-disciplinarian, Thomas Rankin, found him very difficult to handle. The first conference of preachers in 1773 decreed that no one should administer the sacraments, and, Asbury was constrained to add in his journal, "except Mr. Strawbridge, and he under the particular direction of the assistant." At Rankin's direction, Asbury held a quarterly meeting in Maryland, and "I read a part of our minutes, to see if brother Strawbridge would conform; but he appeared to be inflexible. He would not administer the ordinances under our direction at all." No wonder that, when this unsubmissive Irishman died in 1781, Asbury commented, "He is now no more: upon the whole, I am inclined to think the Lord took him away in judgment, because he was in a way to do hurt to his cause." [6]

For all his recalcitrance, Strawbridge stood way out front as an early planter of Methodism, not only along Sam's Creek, but also throughout Maryland and in Virginia as well. He left his mark wherever he went, and some of the most important native leaders of the Methodist

source the assertion of Bishop Asbury that Strawbridge formed the first Society in Maryland and America." If anyone around at that time wants to plan for the tricentennial, he may well fix on the traditional 2066 for the main beginnings anywhere, but impatient souls may argue for an earlier date.

[5] Clark, E. T., ed., *The Journal and Letters of Francis Asbury* (1958), II, 294.

[6] Asbury, *Journal*, I, 85, 88, 411.

Episcopal Church first heard a call to Christ and to the ministry under his preaching. Among them were William Watters and Freeborn Garrettson. The main point, however, is that *all* the early beginnings, including Virginia and Pennsylvania as well as New York, were by laymen, generally operating under the designation of "local preacher." Of course, they were not ordained. They were not even under the regular appointment as traveling preacher. What they did, they did on their own initiative, or that of their friends who urged them on. The planting of Methodism in America was a lay movement.

About the same time, Methodists were getting together in New York. The society there, which became the John Street Methodist Episcopal Church, was definitely founded in 1766 in the fall. Among those most active were Barbara Heck and Philip Embury. If Straw-bridge, along with Embury and Thomas Webb, represents the initiative of lay men, Barbara Heck stands for the enduring influence of lay women in Methodism. She was born Barbara Ruckle in Ireland, part of a colony of German refugees from the Palatinate. In 1760, she married Paul Heck and with him, Embury, and others migrated to New York. There, in 1766, she stirred up her cousin, Philip Embury, to recover his role as class leader and local preacher and to organize the Methodists there into a class. The story may well be true that she disrupted a card game which included Philip and her brother. This early class included Paul and Barbara Heck, John Lawrence, a hired man, and Betty, a slave. As the little society grew, larger quarters were needed. For a time a former rigging loft was used (located on Cart and Horse Street, later William Street). Here a new recruit, Captain Thomas Webb, preached, attired in his military uniform which attracted even more hearers. He had come to America in 1758 on military service, had returned to England, and then come again in 1766. He was active in lay preaching in New York, Long Island, Philadelphia, and other centers. On April 11, 1768, one of the members in New York, Thomas Taylor, wrote a letter to John Wesley, which reported the progress of the little society in building a new chapel (Wesley Chapel on John Street). The main point of the letter, however, was an appeal for more experienced leadership. "There is a real work in many hearts, by the preaching of Mr. Webb and Mr. Embury; but although they are both useful, and their hearts in the work, they want many qualifications necessary for such an undertaking where they have none to direct them." [7] As a direct result of this appeal, Wesley, in 1769, appointed the first of a series of official missionary preachers to give direction to the struggling little societies

[7] Quoted in Wade Barclay, *History of Methodist Missions* (1949), I, 15-17.

in America. Nathan Bangs is one of the several influential writers who have claimed priority for New York, "where the seeds of Methodism were first planted in American soil." [8] Although this claim cannot technically be sustained, New York is entitled to equal share with Maryland in "firsts." New York saw the first active leadership on the part of women. It also was one of the first centers for participation of black Methodists. The reference to the slave girl Betty brings to mind the effective local service of Peter Williams, who was an able and active member, long filling the office of sexton. He played host to all the traveling preachers as they came in and out of New York. For seven years he and his wife lived in the old parsonage. He obtained his freedom when the church bought'him from his master and set him free. He insisted on paying back this loan to the church, as the old records attest. Only later did the elements of discrimination worsen and becloud the relations in John Street Church.

The old church on John Street, nestled among the skyscrapers of the Wall Street financial area, witness to the daily migrations of bankers and market people, is a warm reminder of the early history of Methodism. The present building dates from 1841, the third on the same site. The first Wesley Chapel, built in 1768, was the result of efforts by Thomas Webb, Thomas Taylor and others, who found the rigging loft cramped. It was a plain structure, forty by sixty feet, equipped with a large candelabra for light and a corner fireplace for heat. It was dedicated by Philip Embury on the last Sunday of October, 1768. From that time to the present a Methodist society has worshiped here.

Elsewhere on the eastern seaboard Methodism had an early start. No clear evidence is available to date the actual beginnings of the church in Virginia.[9] Certainly Leesburg was early, probably in 1766. An original deed indicates Methodist ownership in that year, although not specifically a society. By 1768 a building had been erected, and Leesburg became an important center for Methodism in Virginia.

Captain Thomas Webb is associated with the beginnings of Methodism on Long Island and in Philadelphia, as well as other places. He was living on Long Island while he preached to the Embury group in 1767 with such success that they had to move to the rigging loft. He helped organize the society in Philadelphia in 1767 and preached in St. George's Church on November 26, 1769, two days after the congregation had moved into the spacious brick colo-

---

[8] Nathan Bangs, *History of the Methodist Episcopal Church* (1838), I, 59.
[9] See William Warren Sweet, *Virginia Methodism* (1955), 46-48.

nial church, which they had acquired from a Dutch Reformed group. This building has remained in unbroken use as a Methodist church and is justly famous as a historical shrine. Webb also preached the first sermon in Lovely Lane Chapel in Baltimore. John Adams, second president of the United States, heard him in 1774 in Philadelphia and remarked, "He is one of the most fluent, eloquent men I ever heard. He reaches the Imagination and touches the Passions very well, and expresses himself with great Propriety." [10] Thomas Webb shares with Strawbridge the honor of planting Methodism in America.

Of all the historic shrines of Methodism, Old St. George's is perhaps the most attractive, partly because of its authenticity and partly because of its excellent state of restoration. The fine brick colonial structure was erected in 1763 by a German Reformed group, who were unable to complete it after barely roofing it. Philadelphia Methodists, who had been worshiping in crowded private quarters, bought the shell for a bargain and completed the work. Webb and Joseph Pilmore, one of the first two Wesleyan missionaries, were active in leadership of the rapidly growing society. All the early itinerants preached from the high pulpit to congregations ranged, much the same as today, in neat, white colonial pews on main floor and balcony. As part of the Independence Hall complex designated as a national historical park, Old St. George's plays a remarkable role in symbolism of the twin growth of church and state—an association of considerable significance for the future development of Methodism in America.

These, then, were the small but sturdy saplings planted in American soil in the 1760s. All of it was accomplished by lay men and women who recognized a need and responded to it. When Wesley's appointed missionaries appeared in 1769, they found a movement already under way and strongly growing. The lay people were there first. That is a story many times to be repeated in this history.

---

[10] Quoted in Frank Baker, "Captain Thomas Webb, Pioneer of American Methodism," *Religion in Life,* 34 (1965): 417.

Chapter 6
The American Mission

Unofficial beginnings of Methodism were carried on by laymen, who at least by 1766, probably earlier, had organized groups in operation. That was the first step. It lasted until 1769, when the first two of John Wesley's appointed preachers arrived. These Wesleyan missionaries conducted the American work until the Christmas Conference of 1784. During this time, in terms of structure, three periods may be discerned: (1) 1769–73, the Quarterly Conference system, (2) 1773–79, the Annual Conference system, and (3) 1779–84, the dual and then multiple session, or "Baltimore Conference" system. In the context of American history, however, there are only two periods: (1) colonial, (2) revolutionary.

Wesley's Missionaries

Wade Barclay is entirely justified in developing the history of Methodist missions in the early period as a total history involving every aspect of the life of the church in America.[1] Wesley's preachers on this continent were in every sense of the term missionaries. The history of American Methodism, at least down to 1784, is nothing but the history of missionary enterprise. The development of indigenous leadership was a part of that mission.

Hence, the arrival of Richard Boardman and Joseph Pilmore in Philadelphia on October 22, 1769[2] marks a new era. They were the first two of a series of pairs of preachers appointed by Wesley to the American circuit. In response to Thomas Taylor's letter, these two had been selected, had been appointed at the Conference of 1769, and had sailed from England on August 21. Boardman, the senior partner, was thirty-one years old, but already suffered periodically from poor health. For this and other reasons, he spent most of his time in New York. He made an unsuccessful foray into New England

[1] Wade C. Barclay, *History of Methodist Missions* (3 Vols., 1949–1957)

[2] The editors of *The Journal of Joseph Pilmore* (1969) infer, p. 23, n. 20, that the date of arrival was the 22nd, a Sunday, although Pilmore himself records the event under the 21st. Historians have usually said the 24th, which is certainly incorrect.

and apparently urged regular exchange with Pilmore, who began his work in Philadelphia. He returned to the Bristish Isles in 1774 and continued his ministry in Ireland.

Joseph Pilmore, who was thirty years old on his arrival, was much more aggressive and effective. His ministry in Philadelphia was quite successful. Moreover, he did much to expand the field, not only in the immediate environs, but in the course of a very important expedition into the South in 1772.[3] His journal is full of frustrated remarks on the limitations which attended his relations with Boardman. Pilmore, even less than Boardman, was no friend of endless itineration. He frankly favored city life with its conveniences and more ample opportunities to preach to easily assembled groups. He was an intelligent and relatively cultured person who appreciated the beauty of nature and some of the finer things of life. He shared some of the romanticism of the era, as revealed in his delight at the fireflies in the evening "darting though the air, and sparkling with their little lights as if they would shew forth the praise of him."

These interests in civilization, however, did not deter him from the chief business to which he had been appointed. At the very outset he organized his thoughts as to his purpose in coming to America, and shared them with the people:

1. That the Methodist Society was never designed to make a Separation from the Church of England or be looked upon as a Church.

2. That it was at first and is still intended for the benefit of all those of every Denomination who being truely convinced of sin, and the danger they are exposed to, earestly desire to flee from the wrath to come.

3. That any person who is so convinced, and desires admittance into the Society, will readily be received as a *probationer*

4. That those who walk according to the Oracles of God, and thereby give proof (of) their sincerity, will readily be admitted into full connexion with the Methodists

5. That if any person or persons in the Society, walk *disorderly,* and transgress the holy Laws of God, we will admonish him of his error—we will strive to restore him in the spirit of meekness—we will bear with him for a time, but if he remains incorrigable and impenitent, we must then of necessity inform him, he is no longer a member of the Society

6. That the Church now purchased, is for the use of this Society, for the Public Worship of Almighty God

7. That a subscription will immediately be set on foot to defray the Debt upon the said Church—and an exact acct. kept of all the Benefactions given for that purpose

8. That the Deeds of settlement shall be made as soon as convenient, exactly according to the Plan of the settlement of all the Methodist Chapels in England, Scotland, and Ireland.

[3] Related in Pilmore, *Journal,* 135-203.

> I then told the people, we left our native land, not with a design to make divisions among them or promote a Schism but to gather together in one the people of God that are scattered abroad, and revive *spiritual religion*. This is our one point, Christ that died for us, to live *in* us and reign over us in all things.[4]

His rejection of separation from the Church of England and his acceptance of the new denominational concept of the church are characteristic. He hated bigotry and the narrow sectarian outlook. Rather he favored "Christian moderation," which would allow people of different churches to respect one another.[5] As the clouds of the American Revolution gathered, he returnèd with Boardman to England in 1774, and later retured to America to become a clergyman of the Protestant Episcopal Church. He never lost his Methodist orientation, however.

Boardman and Pilmore shared to the full the concept of ministry which grew out of the Great Awakening. They also knew the dangers of an "unconverted minister." Their activity marks a contrast to the sometimes easy-going careers of the colonial clergy.[6] Pilmore kept his days—and sometimes nights—full of preaching and organizing, disciplining and counseling. In New York he began Wednesday evening "lectures" on I John: "The *novelty* of the thing brought a great multitude to the Chapel." Again, he did another Wednesday series on the Lord's Prayer. Always he tried to "*speak all the truth* without giving offence," and yet, "I would not for ten thousand worlds be guilty of flattering men to the destruction of their souls." [7]

The next two belong together, because, although they did obtain a preacher's license, they came to America on their own volition without an appointment from Wesley. Robert Williams arrived shortly before Boardman and Pilmore, and John King shortly after. If they were counted, they would make four of Wesley's preachers, along with Francis Asbury and James Dempster, who stayed in America during the Revolution. Only Asbury, however, remained active in the traveling connection. Both Williams and King married and "located," that is, settled on farms and became local preachers without full Conference relation. Pilmore was quite explicit in his judgments on these men. For Williams he writes, "His gifts are but small, yet he may be useful to the Country people." He dismisses King, remarking that, "Altho he is by no means fit for the City, he is well qualified to do good in the Country." It is interesting to compare these comments

---

[4] Pilmore, *Journal*, 49-50; 29.
[5] E.g., Pilmore, *Journal*, 103, 110, 112.
[6] See Martin Marty, *Righteous Empire* (1970), 74.
[7] Pilmore, *Journal*, 67, 92.

with Pilmore's judgment of Webb: "His preaching, though incorrect and irregular, is attended with wonderful power." [8]

In 1771 two more appointees arrived, one destined to become the veritable father of American Methodism—Francis Asbury and Richard Wright. Asbury, who was all of twenty-four, so dominates the story for a generation that he need not be discussed here. Wright was a virtual nonentity of whom almost nothing is known.

In 1773 the next two came, Thomas Rankin and George Shadford. Rankin was a ripe thirty-five years old and eager to demonstrate his maturity as the newly appointed "general assistant" for America. Asbury, who had a brief tenure, was obliged to play second fiddle to the strictest disciplinarian this side of the Atlantic Ocean. Asbury's judgment hit the bull's-eye: "He will not be admired as a preacher. But as a disciplinarian he will fill his place." [9] These two strong-minded leaders shared a grudging mutual respect, but each was critical of the other. Both Rankin and Asbury were men of authority who naturally assumed the reins of leadership. Neither, however, had any success in whipping Strawbridge into line. Rankin, a Wesley man, was constrained to return to England in 1778.

Quite in contrast to the controversial Rankin was well-beloved George Shadford, to whom Wesley wrote as he appointed him, "I let you loose, George, on the great continent of America." [10] Wherever he went he demonstrated his pastoral gifts. Especially spectacular was his work on the Brunswick circuit in Virginia in 1775–76, where the revival associated with Anglican Devereux Jarratt brought an amazing upsurge of religious devotion. Early in 1778 Shadford felt bound to return to England. He and Asbury, who had become good friends, had a sad parting, which Asbury wrote was like Jonathan and David.

Of the last pair, James Dempster and Martin Rodda, who arrived in 1774, little need be said, for they made very little contribution. Dempster retained Presbyterian predilections which led him back to that church. Rodda was so confirmed a royalist that his ill-advised activities gave the Methodists a poor reputation among the supporters of the Continental Congress. He left the country in 1777.

Such were the emissaries sent by Wesley to serve the Methodists across the Atlantic Ocean. They did their work well for the most part. But, when the Revolution showed signs of succeeding, none was left in active service except Francis Asbury, and he chafed under severe limitations.

---

[8] Pilmore, *Journal,* 25, 58, 30.
[9] Asbury, *Journal,* I, 80.
[10] Wesley, *Letters,* VI, 23.

Development of the Movement

Before the Revolution, Methodism had spread along the eastern seaboard, but the movement was not even and balanced. Rather, it was irregular and sporadic. There were Methodists in almost all of Maryland, except the western neck. They were numerous in New Jersey and eastern Pennsylvania, and were spreading south through Virginia toward the Carolinas at a rapid rate. There was a strong center in New York city, but not many upstate. Least of all did Methodism spread into New England. There were some circuits which probed westward, but not west of the Alleghenies until after the war.

In 1769 the total number in societies would approximate six hundred. The minutes of 1773, which give the first firm statistics, reported as follows: Maryland, 500; New Jersey, 200; New York, 180; Philadelphia, 180; Virginia, 100. The total was 1,160. Hence, Maryland and Virginia had more than half the total membership. During the Revolution the membership declined in New York, Pennsylvania, and New Jersey; but it increased in Maryland, Delaware, Virginia, and North Carolina—spectacularly in the last three. The total in 1779 was 8,673. By 1784 the membership was almost 15,000. The members were distributed as follows: Maryland, 4,578; Virginia, 3,721; the Carolinas, 3,271; Delaware, 1,712; New Jersey, 963; Pennsylvania, 560; Georgia, 99; New York, 84. They were served by 83 traveling preachers, plus many more local preachers. There were 46 circuits. Again, over half of the membership lived in Maryland and Virginia.

Several comments will help explain this peculiar pattern of growth. First, the population was growing in the colonies: in 1770 there were about 2,205,000 people; in 1780, 2,781,000; in 1790, 3,929,214 (the first official census). Second, the Revolution disrupted church life in some areas more than others. New York suffered most as far as Methodist work was concerned, on account of the British occupation. Development was exceedingly slow toward the northeast, because in New England the churches of the established order (Congregational) enjoyed a virtual monopoly and already had a long and distinguished history. Competition with the Presbyterians created difficulties in Pennsylvania. In the South, where Anglicanism was not firmly established, the fields were ripe and open. Until 1784, it must be remembered, the Methodist movement was generally understood by both members and outsiders to be taking place within the Anglican Church. In Maryland, Robert Strawbridge had given an early and vigorous push. In Virginia, the early friendly relations with Anglican rector Devereux Jarratt encouraged the spread. Nothing except time and manpower stood in the way of further expansion south. The remarkable southern expedition of Joseph Pilmore, which brought organized societies to Norfolk and elsewhere, demonstrated the opportunities ready for the taking. As he summed up in his journal:

> It is now above a year since I left this City: I set out with a consciousness of *duty,* and was determined to *obey* what to me was a Call from above. I was totally unacquainted with the people, the road, and everything else, only I knew there were multitudes of souls scattered through a vast extent of country and was willing to encounter any difficulty, and undergo the greatest hard ships so I might win them to Christ. My plan was to following the leadings of Providence, and go wherever the "tutelary cloud" should direct. With this view I turned my face to the South and went forward above a thousand miles through the Provinces, visited most of the Towns between Philadelphia and Savannah in Georgia, where I have preached the Gospel of Christ.[11]

To the west, Methodism was caught up in the complex factors which determined American movement until after the Revolutionary War. Wilderness, Indians, and the French and British conflict conspired to limit the pressures of expansion, which nevertheless built up, ready for explosion after 1783. Before the organization of the Methodist Episcopal Church in 1784, only two circuits, both of them only a year old, had been established beyond the Allegheny barrier: Holston, along the headwaters of the Tennessee River, and Redstone, at the head of the Ohio River.

Regionally, the development was spotty. In New York the membership was concentrated around New York city and Westchester County. West Jersey was more widely occupied than East Jersey. In Pennsylvania the spread was in the east and south, out from Philadelphia, into Bucks and Montgomery counties and along the southern border near Maryland, just penetrating the Juniata River valley. Methodists were all over Maryland and Delaware, and in eastern Virginia (with an out-point in Holston country). There was a thin net of circuits in North Carolina, few in South Carolina.

The strongest factors which influenced this early growth were: (1) the presence of the Anglican Church, which favored; (2) the presence of the Congregational and Presbyterian churches, which hindered; (3) the Revolutionary War, which worked a complex pattern; (4) the sociological makeup of the population. Data on this last factor as an influence on Methodism are scarce and insufficient for generalizations.

[11] Pilmore, *Journal,* 202.

The structure of the movement kept pace with the growth. Quarterly conferences of a sort were already in operation. Rankin, seeking means of strengthening discipline, called the preachers together for a conference, which met in Philadelphia at St. George's Church in July, 1773. Ten persons were invited, or at least ten came. Besides Rankin there were George Shadford, who had come with Rankin under Wesley's appointment, and a local preacher, Joseph Yearbry, who had also tagged along; Asbury and his traveling colleague, Richard Wright; the original pair, Boardman and Pilmore; John King, who had come on his own in 1770; Thomas Webb, who antedated them all and was the chief unauthorized lay Methodist attending; and Abraham Whitworth. They were all English-born and, except for Webb, young. The minutes of the three-day meeting occupy not quite two pages as printed. When they were done, they had reaffirmed the obedience of American Methodists to the founder, John Wesley, and to the doctrines and discipline of the Large Minutes; they had prohibited administration of the sacraments by lay preachers (which all of them were); they had identified the Wesleyan movement in America with the mother church of England; they had regularized the processes for religious publishing by Robert Williams, a first step in formation of The Methodist Publishing House; and they had begun the practice of keeping track of everything in reports and records. The two persons most affected by the legislation, Strawbridge on the sacraments and Williams on printing, were not in attendance. Were they not invited? Nor were any of the young native American preachers there. From 1773 on, Annual Conferences have been held without a break. Regular Annual Conferences were held, though with difficulty, even during the War. Quarterly conferences were already in operation, and these were more or less regularly conducted by the "assistants." Societies and classes were organized in accordance with the rules, which were vigorously promoted by both Rankin and Asbury. After 1779 we note the beginnings of a multiple conference system in place of the single Annual Conference—that is another story. By that time "Annual Conference" had come to mean a geographical area as well as an annual meeting. In sum, the Methodists, along with most other Americans—except for General Washington's army and the direct adherents of the Continental Congress —conducted business as usual during the long struggle for independence, although not always "as usual." By the time the war was over, Methodists discovered that they, as well as the colonies, were free and independent. Even John Wesley, puzzled though he was at the strange vagaries of Providence, had to recognize this indisputable fact.

Issues

Growth usually brings growing pains. It did now. The problems are all well illustrated by that important early document, the journal of Joseph Pilmore.

There was, to begin with, the issue of itineracy. Francis Asbury was quite content to continue and, indeed, emphasize Wesley's grand principle of keeping the preachers moving. Asbury would show them the way. Pilmore was not so convinced. "Frequent changes amongst gospel preachers, may keep up the spirits of some kinds of people, but is never likely to promote the spirit of the Gospel nor increase true religion." He regularly complained about the insistence of Boardman that they exchange stations in New York and Philadelphia quarterly. "This is rather trying, not to leave this Place, but to leave the Work at this time when God is so manifestly Working by me." [12] The history of itineracy in America is long, and the tensions between traveling circuit and stationed pastorate are not yet resolved.[13]

More immediately important for the development of the American mission was the question of Wesley's authority. No one dreamed of repudiating the old man. Boardman and Pilmore and the other preachers did their best to transplant the Wesleyan movement without loss of principle or leadership. This is amply evident from the statement of principles made by Pilmore in Philadelphia. Although he was unusually ecumenical in his relations with other churches, he nevertheless insisted on the Methodist plan for the societies. At the same time he experienced difficulties in relations with the English leader. Rankin's arrival brought these comments: "For more than two years Mr. Wesley, who should have been as a compassionate father to us, has treated us in a manner, not to be mentioned. . . . I was greatly amazed that Mr. Wesley should treat me as if I had been the foulest offender and an enemy to God and Mankind!"[14] The problem of Wesley's authority would crop up with increased tension after the formation of the Methodist Episcopal Church. Asbury also faced the question of Wesley's relationship to the American movement. In fact, until the old man's death in 1791, the problem would continue to trouble all the leaders, including Rankin in his brief tenure. His journal, however, reveals unswerving loyalty to the English founder. It was not that the others were disloyal; rather, in their loyalty they were troubled by conflict with the best interests of the American work.

[12] Pilmore, *Journal*, 163, 112; cf. 79, 111.
[13] See Frederick A. Norwood, "The Americanization of the Wesleyan Itinerant," in Gerald O. McCulloh, ed., *The Ministry in the Methodist Heritage* (1960).
[14] Pilmore, *Journal*, 206; cf. 43, 60, 92.

Pilmore demonstrates most clearly the relation of the Methodist movement to the other colonial churches, especially the Church of England. At the outset he worked both in and out of his own church. For example, in Philadelphia he preached to the society and then later went to St. Paul's Church, and there he took the sacrament of the Lord's Supper. He did the same in New York. His openness extended to all denominations. "Sects and Parties are nothing to me, as I heartily love all the lovers of Jesus." He was willing to visit a Roman Catholic service, although he found it "disgusting." In New York he visited a synagogue in friendly spirit. Another important contact was made, not by Pilmore, but by Robert Williams, who first cooperated with Devereux Jarratt, the rector of Bath Parish in Dinwiddie County, Virginia.[15] Jarratt wrote joyfully to Wesley and others describing the revival in Virginia and his happy relations with the Methodists. If these relations had prevailed, the future history of the Methodist Episcopal Church and the Protestant Episcopal Church might have been quite different. Unfortunately, rectors like Jarratt were very rare, and even this connection soured when the Methodists formed an independent church. Before that, tension had risen over the issue of slavery. Jarratt was unwilling to denounce the institution as unequivocally as the Methodists. One is pleased to report that the break was healed by 1790, as Asbury commented in his journal: "Mr. Jarratt preached for us; friends at first are friends again at last." [16]

A continuing issue which caused repeated tension was that of discipline. Here Rankin is the best example. Wesley sent him with the explicit assignment of tightening discipline: "There has been good, much good done in America, and would have been abundantly more had Brother Boardman and Pilmoor continued genuine Methodists both in doctrine and discipline. It is *your* part to supply what was wanting in them. Therefore are you sent." [17]

That Rankin took his assignment seriously is well demonstrated by the first conference held in 1773. That and all the other conferences he held were in strict accordance with the English plan. In 1774 he recorded in his journal:

I met all the societies as I rode along, and found many truly alive to God. Nevertheless, I saw the necessity of enforcing our discipline strongly wherever I came. I found a degree of slackness in this respect in almost every society. I am more and more convinced that unless the whole plan

[15] William Warren Sweet, Virginia Methodism (1955), 60, 65-66; Pilmore, *Journal*, 73, 81, 122.
[16] Asbury, *Journal*, I, 642.
[17] Wesley, *Letters*, VI, 57, (4 Dec. 1773).

of our discipline is closely attended to we can never see that work, nor the fruits of our labours, as we would desire.[18]

Rankin expected the preachers to maintain the Wesleyan standards among the people, but he also imposed stricter standards on the preachers themselves. The result was, on the one hand, a remarkably committed body of men who spent their lives in uttermost service of their ministry, and on the other hand, a large erosion of the forces, which took many out who could not stand the pace. Between 1773 and 1778, of sixty traveling preachers listed, only twenty-eight were left, including ten admitted that year. "Location" continued to be a major problem in ministerial supply.

Asbury was as firm on discipline as Rankin, but his tactics were better designed to gain willing support. In identifying himself more completely with the American cause—both politically and ecclesiastically—he was able to show them the way, asking no more of anyone than he demanded of himself. Even so, his rigor was too much for Pilmore, who complained that the strictness of discipline was damaging the work at St. George's in Philadelphia.[19]

Another point of tension developed between the English missionaries and the new native preachers like William Watters, Philip Gatch, and Freeborn Garrettson. Watters was from Maryland and had been influenced toward the ministry by Strawbridge, King, and Williams. He was already in itinerant service in 1772 at the age of twenty-one, and continued till he located in 1786 because of poor health. He returned to the traveling ministry for a few years after 1801, and died in 1827. Gatch also came from Maryland and began his preaching career in 1773 at twenty-two. He worked in New Jersey, Pennsylvania, and Maryland before he located in 1778 on account of poor health. He married and settled in Virginia and later moved to Ohio. Certainly, the most competent native preacher was Freeborn Garrettson, who was born in 1752 in Maryland. He became a Methodist under Strawbridge and began itinerating in 1776. He was much troubled by persecution during the Revolution. He stood with Asbury during the difficulties surrounding the Fluvanna Conference, and was one of the most influential leaders at the time of the Christmas Conference.

These men, native Americans all, viewed the Methodist movement from a different perspective. They certainly were not caught up in Tory loyalties. The whole issue of authority looked different to them. Moreover, being bred in a revivalistic religious scene, they were freer

[18] *MS Journal* (Garrett Theological Seminary), 29 July 1774.
[19] Pilmore, *Journal,* 134.

in their attitudes toward formally organized ecclesiastical bodies. Not surprisingly, these differences created considerable tension from time to time.[20]

Finally, several problems of a social nature began to complicate life for those who wanted to bring men to Christ. These, for the most part, remained of secondary concern during the early period and became major issues only later. But they were present from the start. They need only be enumerated here.

Social consciousness found expression more in attacks on specific sins, such as intemperance and pew rentals, rather than in support of major social changes. Methodists were not unique in this respect. Few persons in colonial America understood the processes of society sufficiently well to foresee the possibility of social reform. On the other hand, because the preachers went everywhere, they saw much of the suffering and squalor of life among the poor and lowly. Most of the concern was with those who were low in the economic scale—although many exceptions to this may be noted. Hence the preachers became aware of specific evils and specific needs. Drunkenness was an evil, the effects of which they repeatedly observed. No wonder they became staunch advocates of temperance! Illiteracy was another widespread evil against which the early Sunday schools set themselves to struggle.

Many social issues appeared early because of the strong current of democratic thought among both preachers and people. However authoritarian the structure of the societies may have been, the members and leaders were united in opposing the pretensions of rank and class and wealth. Every man had worth before God. Most of the activity, however, was directed not at changing the system but in helping its victims. This would be true of alcoholism, of poverty, of prisons, of slavery, and the rest. Considering the limited perspective of colonial people, it is amazing how much Methodists spoke out against the whole evil institution of slavery. The legislation of the Christmas Conference was no new thing. Much sympathy was expressed for "the poor Affricans" as Pilmore called them. For a while, apparently, little or no segregation on the basis of race was practiced. Pilmore and others devoted much time to visiting poorhouses and prisons—not to protest the conditions, although they did note and protest the worst—but to help the inmates.[21] Preaching at an execution and praying for a condemned criminal were terrifying experi-

[20] See Frank Baker, "Wesley's Early Preachers in America," *The Duke Divinity School Review*, 34 (1969): 143-62.

[21] See, in Pilmore's *Journal*, 26-27, 38-39, 45, 69, 75, 96, 102, 120, 122.

ences, but amply rewarding if attended by the conversion of participants or audience.

The day of broad social concern, to say nothing of social gospel, was
not yet. But the day of small beginnings in social witness was evident
as Methodist preachers traveled unwearyingly among the people in
common life, wherever they might be.

Chapter 7
Methodism in the American Revolution

In 1835 a perceptive French traveler, Alexis de Tocqueville, published in Brussels a classic interpretation of American civilization, *Democracy in America*. He wrote,

> On my arrival in the United States the religious aspect of the country was the first thing that struck my attention; and the longer I stayed there, the more I perceived the great political consequences resulting from this new state of things. In France I had almost always seen the spirit of religion and the spirit of freedom marching in opposite directions. But in America I found they were intimately united and that they reigned in common over the same country.[1]

The Setting

Was there really such a close connection in America between the spirit of religion and the spirit of freedom? A less sophisticated version of the same view was expressed by a Hessian captain in 1778: "Call this war by whatever name you may, only call it not an American rebellion; it is nothing more or less than a Scotch Irish Presbyterian rebellion." [2] Now, it would be ridiculous to describe the Revolution as a religious, much less an ecclesiastical, affair. It was primarily a political and secondarily a social upheaval. William A. Williams and Richard B. Morris and others are correct in emphasizing the social as well as the political aspects.[3]

Nevertheless, there is a religious perspective on the Revolution. Sidney Mead has written a perceptive essay in which he argues that the religious forces of Pietism and the Enlightenment (Evangelical Revival and rational philosophy) joined forces in the later colonial period to bring about a new relation between church and state which

---

[1] Alexis de Tocqueville, *Democracy in America* (1948), I, 308.

[2] Quoted in James G. Leyburn, "The Scotch-Irish," *American Heritage,* 22 (Dec., 1970): 31.

[3] William A. Williams, *The Contours of American History* (1961, 1966); Richard B. Morris, *The American Revolution Reconsidered* (1967). The latter points out, for example, that the number of white indentured servants (that is, "term slaves") was highest on the eve of the Revolution, and that southern planters gave active support to the Continental Congress when the British appealed to slaves for support in return for the promise of freedom (pp. 71, 74).

resulted in religious freedom.[4] For a season both heart and reason
agreed that religion was a personal matter, and that there was no
place for ecclesiastical establishments. The final result, although this
was not consciously intended by either party, was religious pluralism,
which required not only toleration but full religious freedom. The
large number of independent religious movements prevented the
victory of any one. By necessity and not by choice, argues Mead,
Americans stumbled into a new concept of the church: the denomination, one of many autonomous groups, each entitled to cherish and
propagate its form of faith within the bounds of the common society.
The seeds of this new concept, it should be noted, had been planted
by Puritans in England. The Revolution marked the parting of the
ways for Pietism and Rationalism, beginning with Joseph Priestley's
moderate *History of the Corruptions of Christianity* (1782) and ending
with Thomas Paine's radical *Age of Reason* (1794).

One is justified, I think, in agreeing with de Tocqueville that religion and politics in America have stood in close mutual relationship,
and that the development of each has affected the other. One is
further justified in viewing the religious involvement in the Revolution in two phases, the Evangelical-Calvinist and the Rationalist. Some
New England revolutionaries illustrate the former, and the Virginia
statesmen, along with Benjamin Franklin, the other. In most cases
both forces were at work. As far as churchmen are concerned, they
fall into the same categories as the general population: ardent supporters of the Revolution, lukewarm adherents, those politically but
not socially motivated (and vice versa), neutralists, the disaffected,
and ardent opponents. Devereux Jarratt, that slave-holding Virginian, Anglican rector, was among those who fall somewhere in the
middle. H was not opposed to the Revolution, and his concern for
individuals encouraged the concept of human rights. But, as he
mused after it was over:

> In our high *republican times*, there is more *levelling* than ought to be,
> consistent with good government. I have as little notion of oppression
> and tyranny as any man, but a due subordination is essentially requisite
> in every government. At present, there is too little regard and reverence
> paid to magistrates and persons in public office; and whence do this
> disregard and irreverence originate but from the notion and practice of
> levelling?[5]

Some churchmen, like the redoubtable pastors, sons of Lutheran

---

[4] Sidney Mead, *The Lively Experiment* (1963), 36. Cf. H. Shelton Smith, *et al., American
Christianity* (1960), I, 421.

[5] *The Life of the Reverend Devereux Jarratt, . . . Written by Himself* (1806), 14-15, quoted
in Smith, *et al., American Christianity*, I, 424.

founder Henry Melchoir Mühlenberg, entered actively into the military and diplomatic service of the Continental Congress. Others, like their old father, retired into isolated neutrality. Still others, like many Anglican ministers who took seriously their oaths to the establishment, opposed the Revolution and either returned to England or fled to Canada.

Certainly, whatever may have been the views of clergymen, the yeast of Puritanism, religious pluralism, and the Great Awakening, along with the rights-of-man outlook attendant upon the Enlightenment, worked to provide an environment, unintended and unanticipated but potent and pregnant, which induced a turning point in the history of the human race.

Development of Methodism

Although the Revolution brought on powerful challenges to all the churches, it would be a mistake to conclude that all the leaders and ministers, as well as members of the Methodist movement, were obsessed with political and moral issues connected with the war and were distracted from their chief business—to preach the gospel and spread scriptural holiness through the land. As already indicated, the movement continued to grow and was adversely affected only in particular places, such as British-occupied New York. The diaries of the traveling preachers continue to be dominated by accounts of individual spiritual experiences and successful revivals. In some cases one would not suspect a war was going on.

Nevertheless, the challenges and problems of the Revolution gave a special character to the history of the Methodist movement in the years 1775 through 1783. It was a crucial coincidence for both church and state: the third Annual Conference occurred at the same time and place (May, 1775, in Philadelphia) as the Second Continental Congress. The particular situation of the Methodists was determined by the Wesleys, especially John, whose deliverances on the subject of rebellion against legitimate monarchy were clear. His early sympathy with the grievances of the colonists was changed by the reading of Samuel Johnson's "Taxation No Tyranny," which he proceeded to republish with changes to suit himself as "A Calm Address to our American Colonies." He stood on a firm Tory foundation—which means, in terms of English history, adherence to the governmental system under the Hanoverian kings and resistance to Whiggish reforms. For him it meant obedience to the divine governance of God. It obviously did not make much sense to American colonists, whether they were Methodist or not. From the wide distribution of Wesley's tract, Methodists were suspected throughout the Revolution of following the Tory prejudices of their English leader.

And he kept at it, and so did Charles. The elder brother delivered a sermon in 1777, "For the Benefit of the Widows and Orphans of the Soldiers Who Lately Fell, near Boston, in New England." Charles was even more incapable of understanding the situation in America, and for many years continued to inveigh against the rebellion.

> Ye vipers who your Parent tear,
> With evil all our good requite.

And after the Treaty of Paris, 1783, he mused in verse,

> Where is old England's glory fled,
> Which shone so bright in ages past?
> Virtue with our forefathers dead,
> And public faith have breath'd their last
> And men who falsified their trust
> Have laid our honor in the dust.[6]

Wesley did not escape without censure for his strong Tory position. Presently there appeared a "Cool Reply to a Calm Address," followed by a virulent diatribe, "A Wolf in Sheep's Clothing, or an Old Jesuit Unmasked," which recommended for the Methodist leader a "hempen neckcloth." Augustus Toplady, of "Rock of Ages" fame, got into the act with "An Old Fox Tarred and Feathered." Unlike Charles, John was constrained at last to acknowledge God's strange providences and let what must be, be. As he wrote to Edward Dromgoole in America in 1783, "It is well you "agree to disagree" in your opinions concerning Public Affairs. There is no end of disputing about these matters. Let everyone enjoy his own persuasion. Let us leave God to govern the world: and He will be sure to do all things well. And all will work together for His glory, and for the good of them that love Him." [7] The tone is reminiscent of the famous letter Wesley sent to the preachers in America as he provided ordination for administration of the sacraments in 1784.

Obviously Wesley's appointed missionaries were forced to a difficult decision as the Revolution gave evidence of continuing and even succeeding. Asbury was the only one in active service who remained in America. All the rest returned to England or went to Canada.

---

[6] Quoted in Donald Baker, "Charles Wesley and the American War of Independence," *MH*, 5 (Oct., 1966): 16, 37.

[7] Quoted in Sweet, *Virginia Methodism*, 97, from manuscript letter in Dromgoole collection, University of North Carolina. Petition in *ibid.*, 76-77.

While Shadford was still in the country, he took action in Virginia, which clearly defined the self-understanding of the Methodists as a movement within the Church of England. In 1776 he prepared a petition to the General Convention meeting in Williamsburg, which sought to counteract the pressures by Baptists for disestablishment of the Anglican Church. Methodists, he explained, were against the Baptist drive, because "we beg leave to set forth that we are not Dissenters, but a Religious Society in communion with the Church of England." Hence, the Methodists desired to retain the establishment.

But, soon he and all the rest were gone. Some left behind evidence of Tory inclinations, which made the lot of Methodists even harder. Especially reprehensible was the propaganda of Martin Rodda, who gave all the followers of Wesley a bad name, and then left them the burden of his actions. No wonder those who were left encountered prejudice and persecution.[8] Rankin, for all his hard-headedness, was more moderate in his attitude. He would in no case give aid and support to the Revolution; yet, he did not want to hurt the Americans. "How difficult to stand in such a situation, and not to be blamed by violent men on both sides?"[9] Rankin left with Rodda and Shadford in 1778.

Who was left? Asbury and a group of young American-born preachers. Williams was dead and King located in 1778. Asbury, who now was acting head of the movement ("general assistant"), found the work of leadership increasingly difficult as the governments of the former colonies imposed greater restrictions. Especialy oppressive were the oaths of loyalty designed to assure support of the revolution. The colonies varied in the form of oath used. In Maryland, which used an especially rigid form requiring military support, Asbury faced a moral decision as a Christian minister opposed to the use of violence in war. Hence, he moved into Delaware, where the oath was much more liberal and relaxed. He was able to settle in the home of a good Methodist, Judge Thomas White of Kent County, where he remained for the better part of two years from 1778. George Roberts, in a manuscript reminiscence of Asbury, emphasized the Anglophobia occasioned by the tracts of John Wesley on the Revolution, and particularly, the difficulties they caused Asbury. Yet, Roberts continued:

The lord raised up for him a fast friend and protector in Mr. White of Delaware in whose house he found an asylum during the storm. Mr. White was a magistrate and a gentleman of influence and he did every-

[8] Jesse Lee, *Short History* (1810), 55-56.
[9] Rankin, "Journal," 19 Sept. 1773, 20 Sept. 1775.

thing to make his life comfortable. Here he was hid like the prophet of Israel and he pour[ed] out his soul to God for the prosperity of Zion, and the peace of the world—and looked with solicitude for the time when he could go forth unrestrained and öffer once more salvation upon the whole of the Gospel. [10]

The worst time came in the spring of 1778, when Judge White himself was arrested, apparently on suspicion of being a Methodist with connections with Asbury. Asbury for a brief while hid in a swamp, but later returned to White's, where he remained until spring of 1780. In this way the English-born preacher avoided an open confrontation with the authorities, yet did not oppose the movement of the colonies for independence. Ezekiel Cooper, one of his close friends and fellow preachers, put the delicate balance this way: "His prudence and caution as a man and a citizen, his pious and correct deportment as a Christian and a minister, were such as to put at defiance the suspicious mind and the tongue of slander. They were never able to substantiate any allegation, or the appearance of a charge against him, that was incompatible with the character of a citizen, a Christian, or a faithful minister of the Gospel." [11]

Against his will, therefore, Asbury had to curtail his work drastically during the middle of the revolutionary period. Although he was the acting general assistant, the actual direction of the day-to-day responsibility lay in the hands of the native preachers. This became clear at the Annual Conference of 1777, the record of which is significantly deficient in the printed minutes. Fortunately, Philip Gatch kept a fuller record, which was subsequently printed in the *Western Christian Advocate*. Question 11 read:

Can any thing be done in order to lay a foundation for a future union, supposing the old preachers should be, by the times, constrained to return to Great Britain? Would it not be well for all who are willing, to sign some articles of agreement, and strictly adhere to the same, till other preachers are sent by Mr. Wesley, and the brethren in conference? A. We will do it.

Thereupon a document was drawn up and signed by twenty-five preachers, which read as follows:

We, whose names are underwritten, being thoroughly convinced of the necessity of a close union between those whom God hath used as instruments in his glorious work, in order to preserve this union, are resolved,

[10] Robert Bull, "George Roberts' Reminiscences of Francis Asbury," *MH*, 5 (July, 1967): 28-29.

[11] Quoted in Abel Stevens, *History of the Methodist Episcopal Church in the United States of America* (1864–67), I, 279.

God being our helper, 1. To devote ourselves to God, taking up our cross daily, steadily aiming at this one thing, to save our souls and them that hear us. 2. To preach the old Methodist doctrine, and no other, as contained in the Minutes. 3. To observe and enforce the whole Methodist Discipline, as laid down in the said Minutes. 4. To choose a committee of assistants to transact the business that is now done by the general assistants, and the old preachers who come from Britain.[12]

Then Question 12 listed the members of the committee: Daniel Ruff, William Watters, Philip Gatch, Edward Dromgoole, William Glendenning. All these arrangements were later omitted from the printed minutes, presumably on the ground that they were *ad hoc* decisions arrived at as a counsel of necessity and not intended for permanent institution. It is noteworthy that, although Asbury was among the signers of the document, his name is not among those on the committee. It is further noteworthy that in 1778, Asbury, now in virtual retirement in Delaware, was not listed as an assistant and was not given an appointment.

What was going on? All the officially appointed English preachers were now out of circulation, including, temporarily, Asbury. The American preachers entered the vacuum of power and took over. The question then becomes: Will they willingly relinquish the power they have thus taken? Part of the answer to that one is given in the crisis of 1779, which is discussed below. For the time being it is clear that Methodism had become a thoroughly American movement as a result of the necessities imposed by revolutionary conditions.

Problems

Even the American-born preachers, to say nothing of lay people, did not escape various forms of persecution as a result of the suspicion, arising from the Anglican connection of the Methodist movement and from the unwise utterances of such persons as Rodda, that Methodists were Tories opposed to the revolutionary efforts of the Continental Congress and its supporting governments. Many stories have survived of painful and dangerous experiences. Freeborn Garrettson had repeated difficulties, although he was certainly in sympathy with the Revolution and had influential connections through his wife. His trouble arose chiefly from the conscientious objection to war which he maintained throughout. Rumors charged him with being a British spy. In Virginia he had to defy authorities who were about to break up a service he was conducting because he would not

[12] *WCA*, 4 (26 May 1837): 18.

take the oath. He refused to stop, was threatened with jail, but eventually was allowed to work. He had more trouble in Maryland and Delaware, where he was beaten almost to death and later imprisoned. Although released after a hard month, he continued to encounter opposition till the end of the war. Philip Gatch was tarred and feathered by a crowd of vigilantes. Unfounded suspicions (plus those founded on Wesley's tracts and on the activities of outspoken Tories like Rodda) continued to plague the Methodists until 1781.

Related to these difficulties was the moral problem of patriotism and pacifism. Jesse Lee is a good example. He certainly was loyal to the American cause and even allowed himself to be drafted into the military services of North Carolina, but he refused when ordered to train with a gun and was jailed for a time.[13] He earned the respect of his fellows during this hard experience because of his courageous stand on Christian pacifism as a minister of the gospel. Both he and a Baptist preacher under similar compulsion agreed to noncombatant service such as wagon-driving. Watters had views similar to those of Lee. When the Methodists were criticized by a minister as disloyal Tories, he replied that they were not Tories, that the preachers do not emphasize "passive obedience and non-resistance," and that they seek to stay out of politics as much as possible.

> I concluded by observing that though I did not think politics ought to be introduced into the sacred pulpit on any occasion; yet I did most seriously deny that there was one drop of Tory blood flowing through my veins. I firmly believed my business was to preach the Gospel, and not to meddle with those public affairs, which were in much better hands, and in my opinion was unbecoming men of my profession.[14]

Thomas Ware, on the other hand, was actively involved in military operations. He volunteered and served at Perth Amboy, but had to drop out on account of illness. He was not a pacifist and believed in the principles of liberty at stake in the Revolution.

> Others pleaded conscientious scruples against bearing arms, and were excused on that account, though their property was laid under requisition to support the war. Having now abjured my king, and taken up arms against him, I had time to think and reason with myself on the part I had taken in this great national conflict; and some of my reflections I can never forget while memory lasts.

Among his questions were the chances of success and the consequences for continued tyranny in the event of failure. "Yet, with the views I entertained of the justness of our cause in the sight of

[13] Lee, *Short History*, 372.
[14] William Watters, *A Short Account* (1806), 51-52.

Heaven, I could not doubt, and resolved for one on liberty or death." [15]

Even more outspoken was John Littlejohn, who, observing the peril of British advance toward Baltimore, concluded that Christians may properly bear arms in a just cause.[16] Of course, many lay persons of Methodist persuasion were active in the political and military aspects of the Revolution.

But other leading ministers, like Garrettson and Jesse Lee, were committed to the pacifist principle. Lee's statement, which he made at the time he refused to take up a gun in military service, will suffice. "I weighed the matter over and over again, but my mind was settled; as a Christian, and as a preacher of the gospel I could not fight. I could not reconcile it to myself to bear arms, or to kill one of my fellow-creatures; however I determined to go, and to trust in the Lord; and accordingly prepared for my journey." [17]

Perhaps more poignant is the poem William Duke was moved to write in 1775 in his journal:

> What sound is this that strikes mine ear
> Of terror and the rage of war
> Commotions bloodshed and distress
> The bane of harmony & peace
> The nations to the battle haste . . . .
>
> Oh what shocking bloody scene
> Such woe as this had never been
> If man had not been spoiled by sin
> But O thou Father of Mankind
> Change and renew the carnal mind
> True peace and love to each restore
> And so shall we learn war no more.[18]

The greatest problem of the Methodists during the Revolution had nothing to do with politics—unless they were ecclesiastical politics: the issue of the ordinances, which brought on the crisis of 1779.

The Crisis over the Ordinances

The Revolution provided a setting in which the crisis of 1779 was made more likely. For one thing, Asbury was in enforced retirement

[15] Thomas Ware, *Sketches of the Life and Travels of Rev. Thomas Ware* (1842), 29-30.
[16] See his journal, 6 July, 20 Aug., 1777, quoted in Gordon Pratt Baker, ed., *Those Incredible Methodists,* 50.
[17] His own account is given in Minton Thrift, *Memoir of The Rev. Jesse Lee* (1823), 26-35, and in Leroy Lee, *The Life and Times of The Rev. Jesse Lee* (1860), 88-91.
[18] Mimeograph copy of journal, courtesy of Edwin Schell, entry for 18 Nov. 1775.

in Delaware. For another, the Anglican Church was in a crisis itself, having lost its source of establishment. If Methodist preachers were suspect of being Tories, Anglican clergymen were, people thought, almost sure to be. The ties with English authority were being surely broken, and Methodists could think of themselves as twice orphaned; once by John Wesley's stand against the Revolution, again by the collapse of the Church of England. Most especially, the question of provision for the sacraments of baptism and the Lord's Supper now became acute. No longer could one easily say Methodists should repair to the Anglican churches for the sacraments. No longer did it seem possible that Wesley would succeed in making some arrangement. The Methodists of America were on their own.

In this situation two groups began to form. The one advised that, until political affairs became more settled, nothing should be changed until Wesley could act. The other insisted that in the critical circumstances American Methodists should take action themselves to provide sacramental ordinances. But what action? In 1779, at the regular Annual Conference of the preachers held at Broken Back Church in Fluvanna County, Virginia, the southern preachers (the only ones who attended) decided to act. Prior to this gathering a "preparatory conference" was held at Judge White's house in Delaware, Asbury being present and leading. There, the northern preachers agreed to postpone any action till next year, confirmed Asbury as leader, and then proceeded to fill their own appointments. Nathan Bangs, Methodist historian of the early nineteenth century, considered this the regular conference because Asbury was there.[19]

In fact, the early meeting was irregular and was called because the exigencies of war prevented Asbury and many of the preachers in the North from going to Virginia. The occasion of the Fluvanna Conference was regular; its *action* was highly irregular.

As it turned out the crisis involved not only the sacraments, but also the relation of Methodists to the Church of England and the authority of Asbury as general assistant—to say nothing of the authority of Wesley in England, at this time almost totally out of touch with his American followers. Three weeks after the meeting in Delaware, the southern brethren met, with Philip Gatch prominent in leadership. William Watters served as observer from the northern group. After discussion, the decision was made by majority vote to set up a presbytery of four ministers who should ordain each other, and then in turn

[19] Bangs, *History of the Methodist Episcopal Church,* I, 128-35. But Lee, *Short History,* 61-63, honestly calls it a "preparatory conference." For varying interpretations see Abel Stevens, *History,* II, 56-66; Edward Drinkhouse, *History of Methodist Reform,* I, 214-15; also the more nearly contemporary views of James O'Kelly and Nicholas Snethen.

they should ordain as many other preachers as desired to administer the sacraments. Of the three possible broad choices before them—to seek ordination through regular channels of another denomination, to put to effect the doctrine of the priesthood of all believers and administer sacraments as laymen, or to ordain themselves—they chose the last. This kind of ordination was not episcopal, nor was it presbyterian or congregational. Perhaps the closest parallel would be the self-baptisms of the Anabaptists of Zurich in the sixteenth century.

At any rate the deed was done. Asbury's plea by letter not to act was rejected. The northern preachers, with the general assistant, went one way on a fundamental issue; the southern preachers went the other. That is the way schisms are made. At this early juncture, when the Methodist movement was still in infancy, not yet even an organized church, a division was taking place which might be irreparable. In the process, the authority of the general assistant, and of Wesley himself, was brought into question. The northern minutes not only recognized Asbury as general assistant but extended specifically to him the extraordinary power exercised by Wesley in England:

Question 13. How far shall his power extend?

Answer. On hearing every preacher for and against what is in debate, the right of determination shall rest with him according to the Minutes.

The southern conference ignored Asbury and proceeded to arrange for the sacraments in a manner precisely contrary to the will of both Wesley and Asbury.

How could so deep a schism, already a fact, be healed? For a year nothing was done except letter-writing and wringing of hands. The next May the northern branch met again, denounced what the southern preachers had done, and refused to call them Methodists "till they come back." A committee composed of Garrettson and Watters, along with Asbury, was sent to declare the northern position. Although at first reconciliation seemed impossible, a last minute compromise was agreed to by the skin of the teeth. The plan for administering the sacraments would be deferred for a year until Wesley could be consulted. A letter went to him, and he replied with strong support for the position of Asbury. In the meantime the war itself was winding toward its end, and all men could see a new day was at hand for a new nation. This new day would have tremendous implications for the church as well. Also, this year Asbury made a broad peacemaking itineration of the southern parts of the Methodist work. By conference time in 1781 the worst was over.

Nevertheless, the issues were still alive. The immediate one, administration of sacraments, had been discussed ever since the active days of Strawbridge, who had his own one-man plan of lay administration. It had brewed throughout the connection for some ten years before the crisis of 1779. It continued much alive right down to the Christmas Conference, which provided a solution bearing the Wesleyan stamp.

Other issues were stewing under the surface and occasionally above. Everyone understood that Asbury's authority, and behind him that of Wesley, hung in the balance. It was a tribute to his political sagacity that he was able to weather the storm. It certainly says something striking about the strength of character in the American leader. Even further below the surface was another issue which would not go away, indeed, would cause crises of its own in 1792 and 1820: the relation of the preachers to the bishop. As yet there was neither bishop nor presiding elder, but the core of trouble was stirring. At the bottom was an issue which apparently bore only peripheral relation to the matter of sacraments—slavery. At the Conference of 1780 in Baltimore the northern preachers went out of their way to require preachers who held slaves to free them and then answered in the affirmative the questions:

> Does this conference acknowledge that slavery is contrary to the laws of God, man, and nature, and hurtful to society, contrary to the dictates of conscience and pure religion, and doing that which we would not others should do to us and ours?—Do we pass our disapprobation on all our friends who keep slaves, and advise their freedom?

Chapter 8
From Society to Church

The president of Yale in 1783, Ezra Stiles, made a prediction regarding the future of religion in America. He averred that the country would be about equally divided among Congregationalists, Episcopalians, and Presbyterians.[1] As with most predictions his also was wrong, owing to faulty data. No account was taken of the Baptists, who were really in third place. Second, that worthy college president could not have anticipated the phenomenal growth of one of the inconsequential movements which began to take form in the course of the Revolution—those "enthusiastic" Methodists. If Stiles' perspective had not been foreshortened a few miles west of New Haven, he might have taken into consideration the experience of religious pluralism in a nation whose western door was just opening for one of the greatest explosions of space in human history.

The Situation

Sidney Mead has offered a stimulating revision of the frontier theme in his suggestion that in American history space has played the same role as time has in European history. Whereas in the old countries a long history reaching to antiquity has provided "room" for development and change, in America time has been of the essence, that is, in short supply. Rather, space—wide-open space to the West—has provided the room for development and change.[2] This factor has left its mark as a continuing thread. Not the least of the numerous consequences has been the unparalleled spread of religious denominations and movements in such manner as to fix religious pluralism as a distinguishing mark.

Proponents of the providential view of history will again take note of the interesting combination of circumstances which led to the formation of the Methodist Episcopal Church. The war was over and the Articles of Confederation loosely bound the former colonies into a new nation. On September 3, 1783 the final Treaty of Paris was signed. In the year of the Christmas Conference, the state of Franklin

---

[1] Noted in Marty, *Righteous Empire*, 19.
[2] Sidney Mead, *The Lively Experiment* (1963), esp. 19-20, 33-36.

was organized in the watershed of the Tennessee River, and by the Treaty of Fort Stanwix (October 22), the six nations of the Iroquois Federation ceded to the United States all claims to the lands of the Old Northwest. About five months after the Christmas Conference, the Land Ordinance of 1785 established the range and township system of surveying western lands on a six-mile-square grid. A little over a year after the Christmas Conference (January 16, 1786), the statute for establishing religious freedom, devised by Thomas Jefferson, was adopted by the legislature of Virginia. In 1787 the Northwest Ordinance (July 13) provided provisional government for the Old Northwest, specifically excluding slavery from the territory. On September 17, the delegates to the Constitutional Convention signed the document which would become, when ratified, the Constitution of the United States. Within a few years there were fundamental changes in the social structure. Laws of primogeniture were abolished, restrictive social regulations such as indentured service and slavery were resisted, and farmers and laborers in Massachusetts joined Shays's Rebellion to protest their economic servitude to the merchants and lawyers of Boston and other coastal cities. Even a few black men, such as Peter Williams and Richard Allen, were able to grasp something of this new spirit. In such a heady environment the Methodist Episcopal Church was born.

Wesley's Solution for the Ordinances

Frank Baker is correct in suggesting that, although John Wesley, in his relations with his church, the Church of England, "was not Mr. Facing-Both-Ways, but he came uncomfortably close to it." [3] Generally he spoke with considerable assurance on his position and the reasons for it. But in a letter to Samuel Walker in 1755 he frankly admitted that, though he would not separate, he could not refute the arguments urging separation. "I will freely acknowledge that I cannot answer these arguments to my own satisfaction. So that my conclusion (which I cannot yet give up), that it is lawful to continue in the Church, stands, I know not how, almost without any premises that are able to bear its weight." [4]

[3] Frank Baker, *John Wesley and the Church of England* (1970), 2. For those who are interested, the major documents on the question of ordinations are: Wesley, *Journal,* III, 232; VII, 15-16, 101, 192, 389; Wesley, *Letters,* III, 182; VII, 20, 30, 191, 238-39, 262, 284; Luke Tyerman, *The Life and Times of the Rev. John Wesley,* M.A. (1870–71), III, 428-29, 439, 443; Asbury, *Journal,* I, 471, 473-74; Thomas Coke, "Ordination Sermon" (1785), in Frank Baker, 269; *Minutes of the Methodist Conferences,* I, 189-91; Thomas Jackson, *Life of the Rev. Charles Wesley* (1841), II, 396-98.

[4] *Letters,* III, 145.

Over many years Wesley had given much thought to the broad question of his authority as leader of the People Called Methodists and to the specific question of administration of sacraments by his preachers. These questions came to a head in the ordinations which he performed in 1784 in response to the new situation in America. It is not necessary here to recount the long process in which his thought developed. It has been analyzed many times from various points of view. Certain salient factors, however, ought to be called to attention at this crucial juncture. Wesley had already thought out the historical, theological, and ecclesiastical issues and now was confronted with the argument of necessity. He *had* to do something about the provision of sacraments for American Methodists. Since he was opposed to lay administration, this meant providing some form of ordination.

Hence, he now acted in accordance with his understanding of his position as an ordained minister of the Church of England and as the superintendent of the People Called Methodists. This position, in his view, coincided with the position of the bishops of the primitive church as he found it in the New Testament and the writings of the early Fathers. A bishop, he concluded, was a presbyter who exercised authority over a diocese or segment of the church. More particularly, he saw himself as comparable to the itinerant bishop, the *chorepiscopos.* He was a presbyter in apostolic succession. He was also an administrator of a large movement. This made him a "scriptural episcopos," as he put it. The influence of Lord Peter King and Bishop Edward Stillingfleet had drawn him to these conclusions.

All these points he made briefly in his famous "By a very uncommon train of providences" letter (September 10, 1784) to the preachers in America, sent as part of a package of documents with Dr. Coke who arrived in the fall of 1784. Wesley had avoided acting on his authority as long as possible, but the problem was now acute. "Here, therefore, my scruples are at an end; and I conceive myself at full liberty."

Thus came about the ordination of Whatcoat and Vesey and the "setting apart" of Dr. Thomas Coke to be a "general superintendent" of the American Methodists. Thus, armed with ordination, these three would be able to provide relief from the long-standing problem of administering the sacraments. The solution was not that of Strawbridge, who opted for lay administration. Nor was it that of the self-ordained rebels of 1779. It was, in the English leader's view, a proper procedure based on scriptural and historical warrant, carried through decently and in good order by the laying on of hands by ordained clergymen of the Church of England. To the arguments against it, including the polity of the church and the refusal of the Bishop of London to ordain Methodist preachers, he was prepared to set the argument of necessity. He *had* avoided acting until necessity required it.

Several secondary questions persist. One has to do with the ambition of Dr. Coke to receive the kind of authority he now enjoyed. Did he exert undue pressure on a senile man? He was ambitious—of that there is no doubt. Perhaps he was importunate. But Wesley was not senile, and he knew precisely what he was doing. Another question has to do with Wesley's reluctance to take brother Charles into his confidence. This was one of the few occasions in which the brothers stood at odds. John knew Charles's views and to avoid unnecessary conflict presented him with a *fait accompli.* Charles's reaction is well known. He was appalled, shocked, and deeply hurt at his brother's lack of candor. He tore off a hymn which didn't get into the *Hymnbook:*

> So easily are Bishops made
> By man's, or woman's whim?
> W——— his hands on C——— hath laid,
> But who laid hands on Him?
>
> Hands on himself he laid, and *took*
> An Apostolic Chair:
> And then ordain'd his Creature C———
> His Heir and Successor.
>
> Episcopalians, now no more
> With Presbyterians fight,
> But give your needless Contest o're,
> 'Whose Ordination's right?'
>
> It matter not, if Both are One,
> Or different in degree,
> For lo! ye see contain'd in John
> The whole Presbytery! [5]

Still another question has to do with the appointment of Coke. He was already ordained in the same succession as Wesley himself. The ordination certificate states he was "set apart" to be a "superintendent." But Wesley's diary simply records, "Ordained Coke." What occurs when hands are laid on one who is already ordained? Methodists in America have not worried overmuch about it, but they have never quite reconciled themselves to a clear interpretation. Here beginneth the definition—or lack thereof—of the office of bishop in

---

[5] Frank Baker, *Representative Verse of Charles Wesley* (1962), 368.

the Methodist Episcopal tradition. A subsidiary question revolves around the mysterious figure of a "Bishop Erasmus," who was in England and in touch with Wesley. This person, if he had any valid episcopal position at all, was an Eastern bishop. It has been claimed, on unconvincing grounds, that Wesley obtained episcopal consecration at Erasmus' hands.[6] The matter is curious but has little bearing on the subsequent history in the United States.

The main point is that Wesley had answered the great need to which Joseph Pilmore had given expression in 1770, when he wrote, "The Chief difficulty we labour under is the want of ordination." [7] From the very beginning, when Wesley began to use lay preachers in England, and from the beginnings in America with greater urgency, the question of the administration of sacraments in the societies was of increasing concern. It had almost caused a schism during the American Revolution. Now, as the Methodists faced the new day of an independent nation and an orphaned church, once again the issue came to the fore. Can the preacher be priestly? Can he also proclaim the Word in the sacraments? Is that an option in spreading scriptural holiness? At long last, Wesley answered yes, and the Christmas Conference ensued.

The Christmas Conference

The formation of the Methodist Episcopal Church is inseparably connected with three famous old buildings, two of them still standing: Barratt's Chapel in Delaware, Perry Hall near Baltimore, and Lovely Lane Meeting House in downtown Baltimore. The third, in which the organizing conference took place, is long since gone, its location marked by a bronze plaque fixed on a modern business wall. Barratt's Chapel was the scene of the historic meeting of Thomas Coke and Francis Asbury shortly after the former arrived in America. The fine brick building takes its name from Philip Barrett, who gave the land and, with the help of Waitman Sipple, built it in 1780.

Dr. Coke had arrived in New York with Richard Whatcoat and Thomas Vasey on November 3. After their progress through Philadelphia, Vasey left and Coke went with Whatcoat on to Barratt's Chapel, where on Sunday, November 14, 1784, Coke led the worship service, preached, administered the Lord's Supper "to five or six hundred communicants," and held a love feast. "After the sermon,"

[6] See a letter published in *Discovery*, Northeastern Jurisdictional Association of Methodist Historical Societies, Jan., 1964, 6-8.
[7] Printed in *MH*, 10 (Apr., 1972): 56-58.

he recounted in his journal, "a plain, robust man came up to me in the pulpit, and kissed me: I thought it could be no other than Mr. *Asbury,* and I was not deceived." [8] Asbury for his part professed surprise at the turn of events.

> I came to Barratt's chapel: here, to my great joy, I met these dear men of God, Dr. Coke, and Richard Whatcoat, we were greatly comforted together. . . . I was greatly surprised to see brother Whatcoat assist by taking the cup in the administration of the sacrament. I was shocked when first informed of the intention of these my brethren in coming to this country: it may be of God. My answer then was, if the preachers unanimously choose me, I shall not act in the capacity I have hitherto done by Mr. Wesley's appointment.[9]

Asbury informed Coke that he had brought a number of preachers together for consultation on the desirability of calling a conference of all the preachers. This was agreed to, and Freeborn Garrettson was sent off "like an arrow" to spread tidings of the assembly set for December 24 in Baltimore. "Mr. Asbury," Coke added, "has also drawn up for me a route of about a thousand miles in the meantime." It didn't take him long to discover Asbury's ordering of priorities.

After everyone had taken his share of itinerating, several preachers along with Coke and Asbury gathered in the new mansion of Harry Dorsey Gough, Perry Hall, a little out of Baltimore. Coke reported it was "reckoned one of the most elegant in the thirteen states." It was the scene not only of the meetings preliminary to the Christmas Conference, but of innumerable other visits and events. There the men worked over plans and worried about what best to do. No one was really sure what was in store. The tone and main direction were set at these preliminary consultations.[10]

If the new church was born in the Lovely Lane Meeting House, it was conceived in Perry Hall. Coke had brought several documents from Wesley: an abridged Articles of Religion taken from the Thirty-Nine Articles of the Church of England; a revised Sunday Service based on the *Book of Common Prayer;* ordination certificates authenticating Wesley's actions with regard to Coke, Whatcoat, and Vasey; and a general letter to the preachers in America. They also had at hand the Large Minutes, that book of discipline and polity which governed Methodists on both sides of the Atlantic Ocean. As to

---

[8] Thomas Coke, *Extracts of the Journals of the Rev. Dr. Coke's Five Visits to America,* (1793), 15-16.

[9] Asbury, *Journal,* I, 471, 14 Nov. 1784.

[10] There is no evidence for the "plotting" which Edward J. Drinkhouse, always sensitive about episcopal motives, suspected. (*History of Methodist Reform* (1899)), *passim.*

the rest, Wesley must perforce leave his far-flung children free: "They are now at full liberty simply to follow the Scriptures and the Primitive Church. And we judge it best that they should stand fast in that liberty wherewith God has so strangely made them free." [11] Considering his habit of arranging divine providences to suit himself, Wesley was in this case remarkably restrained. The Americans were not left without guidance and advice, but they were free to decide what they would do with them. The main decision was to hold that famous conference of preachers for consultation and decision on the best direction.

And so, at last, on Christmas Eve, those preachers who had received the notice gathered in the little chapel on Lovely Lane in Baltimore. Coke recorded: "On Christmas-Eve we opened our Conference, which has continued ten days. I admire the American Preachers. We had near sixty of them present. The whole number is eighty-one. They are indeed a body of devoted, disinterested men, but most of them young." [12] Founding fathers are generally thought of as elder statesmen. Thomas Coke Ruckle's painting depicting the conference, an engraving of which has survived, does nothing to dispel the tradition. As a matter of fact, this was a meeting of vigorous young men, some of whom, like Thomas Ware and Thomas Haskins, were acutely conscious of their lack of experience and accordingly cautious. What transpired we know only from the journals of such men as these, together with those of Coke and Asbury and the *Discipline* which embodied the decisions, published in 1785. No official minutes have survived. The place was a small stone building which had been erected in 1774 and stood until destroyed by fire in 1786. It had two simple entrances in front and was lighted by arched windows.

Wesley's documents were received, and it was decided to form a Methodist Episcopal Church to carry his provisions into effect. As Asbury had insisted from the beginning, his position as general superintendent was confirmed by election by the members of the conference. Apparently, no one was fooled by the term. Ware recalled that "the plan of general superintendence, which had been adopted, was a species of episcopacy." [13] On three successive days Asbury was ordained deacon, elder, and superintendent, with participation of Philip William Otterbein, a German Reformed pastor. The rest of the time was spent in organizing the work, with special attention to ordinations of twelve (or thirteen—the exact number is

---

[11] Wesley, *Letters,* VII, 239.
[12] Coke, *Journal,* 23.
[13] Ware, *Life and Travels,* 106.

uncertain) elders. That, we must remember, was the original reason for the whole proceeding. On the first day of the new year, the conference was sufficiently advanced to consider a project already proposed, the establishment of a college at Abingdon, Maryland (near Baltimore), to be named Cokesbury in honor of the two superintendents. This action later gave Wesley occasion to excoriate both leaders for their presumption.

Asbury was typically laconic in his report of these significant events: "We spent the whole week in conference, debating freely, and determining all things by a majority of votes. . . . We were in great haste, and did much business in a little time." [14]

Finding the Way to Church

If Sidney Mead is correct in his judgment that American Christians more or less stumbled upon the concept of the church which provided for religious liberty and the idea of the denomination, so it may be said that Methodists stumbled their way from society to church. As I have written elsewhere:

The church had been created, but it was almost without form. Its great need was to be raised up in the ways of being a church, not a "society." One is amazed to discover how very little Methodism in America after the organizing conference differed from its former state. The form of discipline, based on the Large Minutes of Wesley's British Methodism, remained virtually unchanged. From habit the societies were still called societies, as if nothing had happened in 1784. The cumbersome multiple-conference system of government, which had evolved by trial and error in the 1780's, continued as the practical form for several years. Thomas Coke and Francis Asbury continued their customary forms of activity in leadership. Itinerants attended the same Annual Conferences and answered the same disciplinary questions. People attended the same meetings and worshiped in the same way. Certain changes which in principle should mark a thorough transformation, especially the introduction of the rite of ordination and the observance of the Lord's Supper, were received with scarcely a ripple of significance. Almost everything remained as it had been. Separated from its historical context, 1784 was a date, nothing more.

Only gradually, like a conservative man trying to adjust to a sudden and unexpected change of fortune, did American Methodists begin to realize that a society was not yet a church. The story of the transformation of the Wesleyan "connection" into an institution capable of sharing in the life of the universal church of the ages identifies a major theme in the history of American Methodism. In many ways that history has been

[14] Asbury, *Journal,* I, 476.

marked by the struggle of an erstwhile sect for self-understanding as a church. [In many ways that same tension between the little that was and the great that is to be continues to provide fuel for controversy and energy for lively growth.] One comes close to the heart of the unique witness of Methodism as a church when he studies the process of shaping, defining, specifying, enlarging, clarifying, and nurturing that dominates the period with which we are now concerned.[15]

This process, which has brought its share of confusion to the ecclesiastical and theological counsels of Methodism, is not out of keeping with what Wesley would have wished. It is significant, as Norman Spellmann has noted,[16] that Wesley omitted in his service book any form for reception into church membership, that is, a confirmation service. Instead he relied entirely on the strong ecclesiastical implications of the service of baptism. This was understood to be the means for entrance of all individuals into the church *universal*—not a particular denomination or sect. That is the way, he thought, it should be. From first to last Wesley's doctrine of the church envisaged this universal aspect which transcended any temporal or spatial limitations. Within this great church persons should be drawn together, as in societies, for closer ministry.

And yet there was now the Methodist Episcopal Church. That was the rub! The shaping of this institution was a long process. In some ways Methodists have not yet decided whether to be a church or a society.

[15] *HAM*, I, 419-20 (text slightly altered).
[16] *Ibid.*, 217-23.

Chapter 9
Origins of the United Brethren

One may say that the Methodist Episcopal Church was founded in 1784. For centennial and similar observances that suffices. But it is not quite accurate, because the church was in the *process* of beginning all the way, say, from 1766 to 1808. Institutions do not spring full grown like Venus from the sea. If this qualification on origins must be stated for Methodism, all the more does it apply to United Brethren and Evangelicals. Both of these denominations were exceedingly reluctant to admit that what they were about was the foundation of a new church. Neither was at all sure what it wanted to call itself for a long time. Hence, assignment of a specific date for the foundation of either one is quite difficult. The traditional dates will do, but they don't really tell us much about the *process*. Both went through a prolonged and troubled infancy before they decided who they were.

In this chapter we deal with the United Brethren. In the next we cover the Evangelical Association and discuss the concept of the church which both groups exemplified.

Early Stirrings

Although Philip William Otterbein (usually called by his second name) cannot be designated without qualification the founder of the Church of the United Brethren in Christ, his name is indissolubly connected with that denomination.[1] The central role he played and the distinguished position he held as pastor of the German Evangeli-

---

[1] No comprehensive history of the Evangelical United Brethren exists at this writing. There is a useful handbook by Paul H. Eller, *These Evangelical United Brethren* (1950). For the United Brethren an older book, A. W. Drury, *History of the Church of the United Brethren in Christ* (1924), though long out of print and dated, is quite useful. The older histories serve as useful compendia and occasionally as a primary source for their own times. Otterbein's writings have been edited by Arthur C. Core in *Philip William Otterbein, Pastor, Ecumenist* (1968). J. Steven O'Malley, *Pilgrimage of Faith: the Legacy of the Otterbeins* (1973), gives theological roots. Christian Newcomer's journal, published in English as *Life and Journal of Rev. Christian Newcomer* (1834), tr. by John Hildt, is a prime source. An *Index* to it has been prepared by Homer D. Kendall. The publishing history of both denominations is the subject of a definitive monograph by John H. Ness, Jr., *One Hundred Fifty Years, A History of Publishing in the Evangelical United Brethren Church* (1966).

cal Reformed Church in Baltimore make him a key figure, although his relationship to the nascent denomination was equivocal. As a young minister he had come to America in 1752 in response to a call from the German Reformed leader, Michael Schlatter, in Pennsylvania. His education and ministerial training were thoroughly Reformed in the spirit of the Heidelberg Catechism. After a few years service in Lancaster, York, and elsewhere, in 1774 he became pastor of the church in Baltimore which bears his name and in which he remained till his death in 1813. Such, outwardly, was the life history of the man crucially responsible for the rise of the United Brethren.

But that formal ministry overlooks a major facet—his strong evangelical spirit. His contacts went far beyond his local congregation and the Reformed Church. And that congregation, although it was considered Reformed, was independently chartered and called itself evangelical. If it was Reformed, it was deeply rooted in German pietism. Its charter also gave it autonomy among the United Brethren until 1949. This was one of the main sources for the United Brethren.

Pietism is the designation of a movement which had its rise in Europe in the seventeenth century and was associated especially with two Lutheran pastors, Philip Spener and August Francke. Although these men were in the Lutheran tradition, they challenged the direction of the church of their day in Germany. They believed that doctrinal definition and refinement had gone to the point of obscuring the main message of the gospel. Far from being antitheological or nonconfessional, they wished to bring the church and its theology back to the main channel, which was redemption through faith in Jesus Christ. The most important doctrinal features were those which emphasized the Christian experience of salvation. Hence, they tended to insist on the necessity of personal experience of religion and a living of the faith in daily activity. Doctrinal correctness was less important than personal commitment. As a result these "pietists," as they came to be called, cherished the expressions of spirituality seen in devotion and prayer, testimony of faith, Bible study, conversation on religion in small groups, and works of love such as care of the orphaned, aged, ailing, crippled. One knows Christians by their love for one another and their ministry to the needy.

Such was the spirit which motivated William Otterbein as he came to America and undertook the ministry of the German *Evangelical* Reformed Church in Baltimore. Inevitably, the nonpietist elements among the Reformed forces were critical and suspicious of what went on in Baltimore. But Otterbein never came to an open break with his confessional heritage. Whatever else he was, he remained a reformed pastor till he died. But this evangelical, pietist spirit brought him and his congregations to other, broader relationships. One of these, and as it turned out, a crucial one, was the encounter with Martin Boehm at a "great meeting" in Isaac Long's barn, probably in 1767. It could later be seen as the first in the series of events which marked the rise of the United Brethren as a denomination. Not far from Lancaster and twenty-five miles from York, where Otterbein was at that time pastor, the meeting took place on the farm of a diligent Mennonite, Isaac Long. Since it was a special revival gathering, people came from considerable distance. Although most were Mennonites, a people who dominated the rural population of that part of eastern Pennsylvania, a scattering of Lutherans and Reformed also came.

Martin Boehm was a Mennonite preacher born in Lancaster County in 1725, whose parents were Swiss Mennonite immigrants. They belonged to that movement of the Continental Reformation of the sixteenth century called the left wing or Radical Reformation. Its members carried further than the major reformers their insistence on the Bible as a guide to faith and life and their belief that the Christian life was one of discipleship. Many of them also believed that the proper biblical understanding of baptism should apply only to adult believers. Hence, they were called Anabaptists. Among their descendants were the Mennonites and Amish.

That day in Long's barn Boehm preached, and Otterbein was one of the listeners in the congregation. After the service he came forward and greeted the preacher with the words which have become classic in United Brethren tradition: *"Wir sind Brüder"* ("We are brothers"). They were an interesting pair: Otterbein the stately university-trained minister and Boehm the Mennonite farmer with a full beard. From that day the destinies of Otterbein and Boehm were intertwined. Both men were deeply influenced by the pietist tradition. Both highly valued personal religious experience. This was a second main source of the United Brethren.

The third main influence was Methodism, which had begun in America almost at the same time as the encounter in Long's barn. The contact between Otterbein and Francis Asbury came at the moment the former took up his work as minister in Baltimore. That the two should meet is not surprising, because the Methodists were already well established in the city, and much of the Wesleyan Revival would find ready response among the followers of Otterbein and Boehm. Asbury entered a typical comment in his journal: "Had a friendly intercourse with Mr. Otterbein and Mr. Schwope, the German ministers, respecting the plan of church discipline on which they intended

to proceed. They agreed to imitate our methods as near as possible."
As it turned out Otterbein's eagerness for imitation was not quite so
great as Asbury's. Nevertheless, the continuing and increasing contacts between the leaders of both movements were fruitful and significant. Asbury later wrote, "There are few with whom I can find so
much unity and freedom in conversation." It was no accident that
brought William Otterbein to lay hands of ordination on Asbury's
head that day at the end of December, 1784, when the Methodist
Episcopal Church was born.

Martin Boehm also came early under the influence of the Wesleyan
movement. He studied diligently Wesley's works, which he read in his
fluent English. This was one of the forces which led him to break
from the more rigid pattern of the Mennonites and accept the spirit
of the Evangelical Revival. About 1775 he was excommunicated for
infractions of the discipline of the Mennonite Church. On the other
hand, in 1791 Martin, through his son Jacob, provided the Methodists
with an acre plot for building a chapel. Through this connection the
elder Boehm, and even more his son Henry, identified themselves
with the Methodist Episcopal Church.

Two meetings which took place in 1789 and 1791 mark another
step toward the rise of the United Brethren. These were preliminary
conferences, which, although they do not constitute anything like
organization of a church or look like annual conferences, indicate that
there was a movement on foot. The only record of what was done is
contained in one statement: "After mature deliberation how they
might labor most usefully in the vineyard of the Lord, they again
appointed such as fellow laborers, of whom they had cause to believe
that they had experienced true religion in their souls." Not much can
be made of that. A record of those who attended one or both meetings, however, was kept. Of the twenty-two, ten, including Otterbein,
George A. Geeting, and Benedict Shwope, were Reformed; six, including Martin Boehm, Christian Newcomer, and John Neidig, were
Mennonites; one was Amish and another Moravian. The three Reformed listed were ordained members of the Coetus. Newcomer
became the most influential leader in the development of the new
denomination after its formation. His journal, which he began in
1795, thus becomes a prime source for United Brethren history.

Formation of a Church

On September 25, 1800, a group of fourteen German ministers met
in the home of Peter Kemp, a little way outside Frederick, Maryland.

Among them were Otterbein, Martin and Henry Boehm, Newcomer, and Geeting, who was chosen secretary. Minutes were kept and have been preserved. From this conference began the series of annual conferences of the United Brethren, a major step in the rise of the denomination. The central decision was that each year a conference of these *unparteiisch* ("unsectarian") ministers should be held. The use of that term is significant. It reveals an obvious connection with a famous book written in 1699 by Gottfried Arnold, a continental scholar who differed from the standard Lutheran and Reformed church historians and defended what later were called the "free churches," that is, churches not established by political authority. He entitled his great work *Unparteiische Kirchen- und Ketzer Historie*. It is the same word—unsectarian. Heretics, he averred, are not heretics by virtue of their identification as such by formally established opponents. "Those who make heretics are the real heretics, and those who are called heretics are the truly pious."

So it was in 1800. Those men were not about to establish a new church or denomination. By the curious operations of Providnce, that is precisely what they did. That unsectarian spirit, however, blurred the course of events for many years and led many United Brethren to ignore or deny what was actually happening. A new concept of the church was struggling for recognition, but its birth was a hard one. Although the minutes do not record the action, both Otterbein and Boehm were chosen as leaders and given the designation *eltesten* (properly *Ältesten*), "elders." The term meant they were given administrative authority over the movement. In that sense they became bishops, although that term was not officially used until 1813.

In his English *Reminiscences* Henry Boehm stated that the Conference of 1800 formed "The Church of the United Brethren in Christ." Those who attended that meeting would not have used the word church, which first appears in the minutes of the Miami Conference of 1814: *Kirche*. Geeting used the expression *Die Vereinigte Brüderschaft in Christo* ("The United Brotherhood in Christ"), but the manuscript shows *schaft* crossed out, thus leaving the name as United Brethren in Christ. Alternatively, they used the terms *Gemeinde* ("society"), *Gesellschaft* ("association"), and *Gemeindschaft* ("fellowship"). *Not* church *(Kirche)*. This word-game reveals a very important struggle for identity. Boehm further recorded another action not included in the formal minutes: "Father Otterbein made a move to get the Methodist Discipline translated. They all agreed to it. Praise the Lord. It appeared to me as if the Lord was pleased with it."

Otterbein, who was growing old, attended annual conferences only until 1805. The elder Boehm stopped in 1809. Already, the first generation was passing from the scene, and new leaders were stepping forth. Among them was Christian Newcomer, who was elected bishop in 1813 upon Otterbein's death. He was vigorous, in his early sixties, an able administrator, and a friend of the Methodist system. He came from a family of Swiss Mennonites, and as a young man he had joined the Mennonite Church. Under the influence of Otterbein, he began preaching and attended the conference of 1789 and 1791. He was a consummate circuit rider, ceaselessly wending his way from his home in Maryland into Pennsylvania west of the Susquehanna River, back east toward Baltimore, south along the Shenandoah Valley of Virginia. By the end of the century he was traveling in western Pennsylvania, and in 1810 he entered Ohio to organize the first annual conference in the state near Chillicothe. In many ways he was the William McKendree of the United Brethren. Ironically, he who loved horses was killed in 1830 at the age of 81 as a result of a fall from a horse. No man has left a larger mark on the United Brethren than Christian Newcomer.

The final step in organization came in 1815, when the first general conference was held June 6-10 in a schoolhouse near Mt. Pleasant, Pennsylvania. Of the twenty delegates elected, fourteen attended. The members spent most of their time working on a proposed discipline. The minutes of this five-day conference, which are extant, fill three-quarters of one manuscript page. Such brevity does not reveal the strong tension which must have permeated the sessions. Some members were uneasy about any form of organization beyond what was thought to be provided in the Bible and about any form of discipline other than New Testament teachings. Quite likely some Mennonite participants were against the ideas of organization and formal discipline.

Nevertheless, it was done, and a discipline was prepared for publication the following year. The headings of the sections demonstrate the direct influence of the Methodist *Discipline:* of general and annual conferences, election and ordination of bishops, their office and duties, presiding elders and elders, method of receiving preachers, trials of preachers, members. The first section was devoted to a confession of faith couched in traditional language drawn from the ancient creeds and Reformation emphases, with some Mennonite influence as seen in recommendation of foot-washing—but not in any particular doctrine of baptism. This may have been another cause of discontent among the Mennonite members. As early as 1789 the "united ministers," who met in conference with Otterbein, accepted his draft of a brief confession which was the basis for the later official statement. The force of the confession was uncertain; some regarding it as advisory only, others declaring it was authoritative and could not be changed even by a general conference. Bishops were to be elected for a term of four years, yet were to be ordained—thus introducing some confusion in understanding the office of bishop and the meaning of ordination. The latter was rescinded in 1825. Presiding elders were to be chosen by the annual conference from a list of elders submitted by the bishop. Both traveling and local preachers had voting rights in annual conferences.

Two main points indicate special features of the United Brethren Discipline: (1) as distinct from the Methodists, bishops were elected for four-year terms; (2) as distinct from the "Albright People," both traveling and local preachers had voting rights in annual conferences. These differences would play a part in preventing union with either of the other denominations until the twentieth century. In all this the hand of Newcomer is visible. He was repeatedly subject to criticism as domineering or seeking to turn everyone into Methodists. What had been implicit in the careers of Otterbein and Boehm, Newcomer frankly sought to make explicit. In large measure he succeeded.

In the following decades the new church—for such it was —continued to expand geographically into the Midwest and to grow in size. A second general conference was held in 1817, and thereafter regularly every four years until 1945. The first two of these were held in eastern Pennsylvania, and the next six in Ohio. This suggests that the center of activity was moving west, and such is the case. An Indiana Conference was formed in 1830. The total membership grew from about 10,000 in 1813 to about 47,000 in 1850, and stood at over 61,000 in 1857, the year of the first statistical report. In the later decades the huge flow of immigration from Germany inevitably brought a strong challenge. By 1860, 1,380,000 Germans had settled in the United States. More continued to come, although proportionately the immigration from southern Europe increased faster. A constitution was formally established in 1841, which, because of some ambiguities, provided occasion for a schism in 1889. How, for example, would one legally interpret "by request of two-thirds of the whole society" as a basis for changing the constitution, which included also a provision that neither the Confession of Faith nor the itinerant plan should be changed? The arguments would come later.

Quite early the United Brethren began to move out of the cocoon of German language and culture. Both preachers and people were in close contact with English language and culture, and the young people were increasingly oriented toward things American. In 1821 the Miami Conference (Ohio) chose two secretaries, one to keep minutes in German, the other in English. By 1837 English was commonly used in general conferences, and the United Brethren *Discipline* was ordered printed in six thousand English and two thousand German copies. German, however, continued in use as a minority language until 1930.

As a small, somewhat isolated group, the United Brethren tended to avoid involvement in controversial political and social issues. An inescapable issue, however, was slavery. Although a few members were slaveholders, United Brethren were in general relatively free of entanglement with the cotton South and its peculiar institution. In 1821 a vigorous regulation was passed prohibiting contact of members with slavery, it being understood that some state laws forbade manumission. In the 1830s the prohibition was made stronger, and a violent debate broke out in the *Religious Telescope* between abolitionists and moderate antislavery spokesmen. For four years the *Telescope* was under a gag rule which excluded discussion of the controversial issue.

Generally, however, the United Brethren in their social witness took the sect-type approach of inculcating personal morality. The church, considering its strongly German origin, took a surprisingly strong stand against liquor, following much the same lines as the Methodist churches. Two points of special and unique emphasis were observance of the sabbath and avoidance of secret societies, especially the Masonic Order. In 1829 any connection with freemasonry was explicitly forbidden all members.

By the time of the Civil War the United Brethren had dug in strongly in Pennsylvania and the Ohio Valley. They had developed a vigorous and centralized government. Yet, even in 1890, when they had a membership of two hundred thousand, they were still *United Brethren*, very uneasy in the use of the term church as applied to themselves. They had come a long way and had built a meaningful tradition witnessed by the existence in print of several denominational histories. Although they shared a common German cultural heritage with the Evangelical Association and a common discipline with the Methodists, all efforts directed toward union failed. They finally fell into unhappy division over constitutional issues. Healing and union, and even that imperfect, would have to wait until the next century.

Chapter 10
Origins of the Evangelical Association

Still another European religious influence entered the broad background of The United Methodist Church with the rise of "Albright's People" in the early nineteenth century in Pennsylvania. Jacob Albright was of Lutheran background in the Rhineland region known as the Palatinate, from which his family migrated in the eighteenth century. This Lutheran influence, however, was strained through the sieve of Pietism, and hence expressed much the same approach to faith as did the Reformed of the Schlatter-Otterbein tradition. Both groups grew from German communities in eastern Pennsylvania, Maryland, and Virginia. Both had been critical of the state churches from which they had come. From both groups sprang natural leaders: Albright was the counterpart to Otterbein.

On the other hand, the long preparation, step by step, by which the United Brethren came into being was compressed into a decade and a half with the Evangelical Association. At least four influential ministers gave many years service preceding the United Brethren organization—Otterbein, Geeting, Boehm, Newcomer. Albright was almost alone and preached only for nine years before he died. John Walter, George Miller, and John Dreisbach did not come on the scene till he was almost gone. Curiously, while all the United Brethren leaders mentioned lived to an advanced old age, only Dreisbach among the Evangelicals lived past forty-nine and was active well after the Civil War.

Small Beginnings

Jacob Albright, at first, was all there was of the Albright Movement. The beginnings of the Evangelical Association are concentrated in his personal career.[1] He was born in 1759 in Montgomery County, Penyslvania, where he joined the Lutheran Church. He received an elementary education, primarily in the German language, but he was

[1] An excellent, though somewhat outmoded history of the Evangelical Church is Raymond W. Albright, *A History of the Evangelical Church* (1942). Earlier histories by W. W. Orwig and Reuben Yeakel, written in German, provide much source material. A prime source is the unpublished journal of John Dreisbach, which covers the years 1813 to 1818, (available in typescript, Comm. Archives and History, Dayton, Ohio).

able to learn some English also. At the age of sixteen he served in the American Revolution as a drummer boy with the Pennsylvania militia. Subsequently, he settled on a farm in Lancaster County. There he suffered a shock through the deaths of at least three of his children in an epidemic of dysentery. The next year, under the influence of a Reformed minister, a Methodist local preacher, and a lay preacher with the Otterbein Movement, he was converted and joined a Methodist class meeting which was nearby. He was strongly attracted to the spiritual atmosphere of this class meeting and was also favorably impressed by the Methodist organization. Soon, he had an exhorter's license and began preaching in 1796.

He was largely self-taught, like Francis Asbury, and had very little contact with the world of eighteenth-century culture except those bucolic aspects which filtered into the farm life of colonial Pennsylvania. But, he immersed himself in Bible study and became proficient in the practical work of the ministry. He was of severely ascetic temperament and spent long periods in prayer, fasting, and other works of self-denial. In his preaching, he itinerated widely in eastern Pennsylvania, parts of Maryland, and the Shenandoah Valley. By 1800 he had organized three small, independent classes with a total membership of about twenty, plus a large number of constituents. These little groups were new in the sense that, unlike most of those formed by Otterbein, they were not formed within existing congregations.

Three years later, Albright gathered his helpers together at the home of Samuel Liesser in Berks County for a two-day meeting during which a new religious movement began to take shape. Albright's People declared themselves a society under his direction, and proceeded to ordain him as their minister.

> From the Elders and Brethren of His Society of Evangelical Friends: We the undersigned Evangelical and Christian friends, declare and recognize Jacob Albright as a genuine (Wahrhaftigen) Evangelical preacher in word and deed, and a believer in the Universal Christian Church and the communion of saints. This testify we as brethren and elders of his Society (Gemeinde). Given in the State of Pennsylvania, November 5, 1803.[2]

Five classes were reported in existence with forty members. Two men, John Walter and Abraham Liesser, were chosen as ministerial helpers to Albright.

That conference marks the organized beginning of the Evangelical Association, comparable to the Conference of 1800 among the United

[2] Albright, *History,* 66.

Brethren. Taking the Bible as authority, they formed an evangelical group which acknowledged Albright their leader. Significantly, they took the dual definition of the church from the Apostles' Creed: "The Universal Christian Church and the communion of saints." From the start they wanted to identify themselves with the true church of all times and places and avoid narrow sectarianism. At the same time, they understood the church to be a community of saints. The later strong emphasis of the Evangelical Association on sanctification, or holiness, derives from this understanding of the Christian community as a select group going on to perfection.

The next step came with the institution of "regular" annual conferences in 1807. The first such meeting took place November 13–15 in the home of Samuel Becker near Kleinfeltersville, Pennsylvania, with twenty-eight persons in attendance, including Albright, John Walter and George Miller (traveling preachers), and Jacob Fry and John Dreisbach (on trial). Two hundred twenty members were reported. The work was organized and regularized with a decision to prepare a discipline based on the Methodist *Discipline*. The group found a new name as the "Newly-Formed Methodist Conference," a designation which suggests a favorable disposition to things Methodistic, but does not imply association with the Methodist Episcopal Church. It also suggests that Albright's People were not ready to think of themselves as an independent denomination. But they were on the way. Albright himself was elected bishop, a title which he held until his death a few months later, May 18, 1808.

The Evangelical Association

By this time the movement had spread into several counties of eastern Pennsylvania on both sides of the Susquehanna River. New Berlin was already a recognized center which in a few years would see the first Evangelical church building, the first publishing house, the first magazine, *Der Christliche Botschafter,* the first missionary society, and the first school, Union Seminary. Whether the conference or the people realized it or not, they were headed toward denomination-hood. After the death of their leader the work was carried on by a second generation composed of George Miller, who died in 1810; John Walter, who died in 1818; and John Dreisbach, who died in 1871(!). Miller was responsible for preparing the first *Discipline* (1809). He also wrote the first biography of Albright,[3] a little pamphlet

---

[3] Reprinted 1959 in English translation by the Historical Society of the E.U.B. Church.

published in 1811 Dreisbach, who was only seventeen when he was granted a local preacher's license, was proficient in both German and English and educated himself in Protestant theology after the fashion of Francis Asbury. He was well acquainted with Wesley's sermons. His long career was filled with administrative achievement, writing, editing, pastoring, just about everything in spite of recurrent health problems. He attended every general conference between 1816 and 1867 and filled a role in his church similar to that of Christian Newcomer for the United Brethren.

The first general conference, when Albright's People brought into existence the Evangelical Association in name and in fact, met in 1816 at the home of Martin Dreisbach in Union County, Pennsylvania with twelve ministerial delegates. Although there was only one annual conference, it was thought a general conference of select leaders could act more expeditiously on matters of basic policy. John Dreisbach was chairman and Henry Neibel secretary. The new name indicates an increasing awareness of denominational entity, but a reluctance to use the word church persisted for a long time (until 1922). The printing establishment was organized, and consideration was given to a proposal for union with the United Brethren. Dreisbach and Newcomer had been working toward this end for some time. Nothing came of it, however, partly because the United Brethren had so few ordained ministers and thus gave much more responsibility to lay preachers. The membership at the outset of the general conference was about fifteen hundred. By 1839, the size had grown to almost eight thousand.

For several years the responsibilities of annual and general conferences were not clearly distinguished. All the ministers attended, although only the traveling preachers voted. In 1827, however, a Western Conference was established for the work in the Ohio Valley, and this conference remained subordinate to the Eastern Conference for ten years. General conferences met very irregularly, and there is some uncertainty about whether a particular meeting was a general conference or not. Sometimes general conferences met jointly with the Eastern Conference. Although the *Discipline* provided for the office of bishop, no bishop was elected between the death of Albright and the election of John Seybert in 1839. Curiously, during this long interregnum, the general conference legislated a change in the term of the nonexistent office, limiting any holder to two four-year terms. In the place of the bishop, a presiding elder gave leadership and presided at conferences.

The westward movement of the Evangelical Association was rather slow, as befits a small struggling denomination. By 1837, some Evangelical families settled near Chicago in Des Plaines and Naperville, which subsequently became strongholds of Evangelical influence in the Midwest.

In contrast to the United Brethren, the Evangelical Association clung firmly to the German language and tradition. The use of English was more common by the 1830s, but its minority status is illustrated by the expulsion of one minister for insisting too much on its use. A pro-German reaction set in which continued through the nineteenth century and into the difficult times of World War I.

At the seventh general conference in 1839, John Seybert, a bachelor minister who had served since 1821, was elected bishop, the first since Albright's brief episcopate in 1808. From then on the Evangelicals had episcopal supervision down to the time of union in 1946. The same general conference fixed the Articles of Faith, which had been adopted in 1816 and altered from time to time, and prohibited any further changes. The United Brethren had done this in 1833 and 1841. *Der Christliche Botschafter* appeared in publication in 1836, and *The Evangelical Messenger* began in 1848. The general conference also approved the organization of the Missionary Society of the Evangelical Association of North America, which antedated by a couple of years the missionary society of the United Brethren. William W. Orwig was the most influential proponent of missions among the Evangelicals.

As to the slavery controversy, the Evangelical Association, partly because it was very small and therefore intimate, but principally because it had few members in the South, escaped violent conflict. In 1847 the General Conference stated concisely, "None of our members shall be permitted to hold slaves or traffic in them under any pretext whatever." The church papers were strongly abolitionist.

Bishop Seybert continued until his death in 1860 to be the chief figure. His Lutheran pietist background gave him a strong traditionalist understanding of Christianity, which was tempered by his modest and moderate personality. He was an inveterate traveler and visited all the centers of work in the church, always on horseback. He took special interest in the western work, and bought a home and farm near Freeport, Illinois. He was plain in dress and deportment and spoke critically of any show of comfort or ease. He was quite strict on such matters as dress, adornments, amusements, beverages, and tobacco. The denomination continued to grow, although rather slowly, until in 1900 it counted over 166,000 members (compared with the United Brethren's 241,000). Unfortunately, before the end of the century both denominations were rent by bitter controversy and schism. Those stories are part of the process which led to ultimate unification in the Evangelical United Brethren Church.

The Church Is People

Underlying the concept of the church in both the forerunners of the Evangelical United Brethren is an idea strongly rooted in the Pietism of the previous century: the *ecclesiola in ecclesia,* the little church within the church. Originally, this meant the nurture of small informal groups within the structure of the state church (Lutheran or Reformed in Continental countries). Although formal membership remained in the official structure, spiritual fellowship was found in the small groups, the "little churches," within the great church (the established institution). In this way a dual membership existed; one formally in the state church, the other informally in the "society," the *Gemeinde* composed of those persons who *experienced* divine saving grace in their own lives and who were at least seeking to go on to perfect love and sanctification.

A very important mechanical fact must be noted here: membership in the state church was not dependent on membership in the society. One could be born into the former, baptized as a baby, trained (after a fashion), and confirmed in membership without much more being required than bodily presence. As long as the movement for small societies remained within the official ecclesiastical structure, all members of societies were members of the church. One could thus drop out of—or be expelled from—a society without thereby forfeiting church membership. In the same manner, as John Wesley could visit the English Methodist societies and sometimes drop as many as half the members from a given roll without thereby dropping *anyone* from the Church of England; so in Pietist societies, sometimes called *collegia pietatis,* members could be held to strict standards without affecting their official church relationship.

That original notion of dual membership is important to remember, because in the United States these little groups were placed in an entirely different situation. After the abolition of any form of established religion in the federal constitution (a provision carried into the Northwest Ordinance of 1787 and, after some foot-dragging, into the older states), no denomination could aspire to formal privileged status in the new nation or any of its parts. The general consequence was that membership in hitherto informal small groups within a state church became identified with membership in one or another denomination. To be in a Methodist society was to be a member of the Methodist Episcopal Church. To be a member of the United Brethren or Albright's People was to be a member of—what? That was the big question with which these two groups struggled.

One thing was pretty clear: they did not want to call themselves a *church*. They would be a *Vereinigte Brüderschaft*, "a United Brotherhood," or *Vereinigte Brüder*, "United Brethren." They were willing to refer to their groups as *Gemeinde*, "society," *Gesellschaft*, "association," *Gemeindschaft*, "fellowship." The others were willing to call themselves Albright's People, the Newly Formed Methodist Conference, and eventually the Evangelical Association. But not *church*, not yet church. United Brethren afterwhile got used to the Church of the United Brethren in Christ, but the Evangelical Association clung to that name until 1922.

Why this reluctance to become a church in the American sense, a denomination, a visible ecclesiastical entity? One central reason lies in the Pietist background with its concept of *ecclesiola in ecclesia*. Otterbein symbolizes the abiding loyalty to the Reformed tradition. Many of Albright's followers were reluctant to depart from their Lutheran heritage. Some Mennonites tried to remain good Mennonites while yet gathering together with other evangelical Christians who were not under Mennonite discipline. A very complex skein of intertwined relationships and loyalties characterizes the early development of both United Brethren and Evangelicals. Undoubtedly for some, the reluctance to burn bridges unnecessarily was a factor. This same maintenance of dual loyalty and membership was to be found among early Methodists, who liked to think of themselves as a kind of leaven in the lump for the edification of all Christians.

Inevitably, sooner or later, a moment to decide arrived. It came sooner with the Methodists, whose connectional system was already strong as a legacy from Wesley. Long lingering usage of terms like "society" could not disguise the reality of a very visible denomination. United Brethren were more resistant, not only in the choice of a name but also in such matters as ordination, executive administration, and ritual. The Evangelical Association, although it willingly accepted Methodist standards of discipline, long rejected the idea of a new church. After Albright, there was no bishop for decades, until at long last Seybert was pressed forward.

This uncertainty about self-image may have played a large part in the successive failures to effect mergers, either between United Brethren and Evangelicals or between either of them and the Methodists. It is, perhaps, significant that Newcomer was more enthusiastic about union with the Methodist Episcopal Church than was Otterbein. However many features they might have in common, however great advantage might be found in union; none was ready to acknowledge the ecclesiastical character of his movement, at least sufficiently to make a conscious merger. That would mean a new denomination. *Unparteiische* movements ("unsectarian," to use Gottfried Arnold's term) would have no need for mergers, unions, or any other form of church. Hence, the suggestion for union of the United Brethren with the Methodists, which had been made by Newcomer in 1809, fell through. The fact that he had been attending Methodist annual conferences for six years carried no institutional implications. The same thing can be said for the friendship of Martin Boehm with Asbury and his membership in a Methodist class meeting, as explained by his son, Henry, who did become a Methodist.[4] The father, one of the founders of the United Brethren, could join a Methodist class meeting without "becoming a Methodist." As to Otterbein, his interest in Methodism lay chiefly in his friendship with Francis Asbury, whom he admired greatly.[5] Whereas the Methodist leader was urgent on the necessity of proper organization and discipline for his friend's movement, Otterbein resisted closer religious ties.

The fact that Otterbein's groups were organized within congregations—at least at the start, while Albright's were not related to a church structure, helps explain why these two movements had difficulty getting together. Perhaps for this same reason, the United Brethren, although more numerous, had fewer ordained ministers than the Evangelicals. Aside from these differences, however, the very reluctance of both movements to identify themselves as denominations or churches operated to discourage any action that would inevitably mean denominational development. After some decades had gone by, of course, both settled for denominational structure as urged by men like Dreisbach and Newcomer. By that time they had become so successfully "denominationalized" that they could no longer come together if they wanted to. Many more decades would have to go by and a new world would have to be born in the twentieth century before these two so-similar churches, like the three branches of Methodism, could become one as the Evangelical United Brethren.

[4] See his *Reminiscences* (1865), 377-86. Also Paul Blankenship in *MH,* 4 (Apr., 1966); 5-13.

[5] See Paul Eller, "Francis Asbury and Phillip William Otterbein," *Forever Beginning* (1967), 3-13. Also Edwin Schell, "Early Methodist-United Brethren Relationships in Maryland," private paper (1964).

II. Pioneer Development 1784-1860

Chapter 11
The Shape of the Church

At the three sessions of the Annual Conference of 1785, held between April 29 and June 15, the action taken by the Constitutional Convention at Baltimore at the end of 1784 was confirmed. The printed minutes, which include a copy of Wesley's letter to the preachers, then continue: "Therefore, at this conference we formed ourselves into an Independent Church: and following the counsel of Mr. John Wesley, who recommended the Episcopal mode of church government, we thought it best to become an Episcopal church, making the Episcopal office elective, and the elected superintendent or bishop, amenable to the body of ministers and preachers."

Something new has been added. The first three disciplinary questions deal with superintendents, elders, and deacons; categories not heard of hitherto. Twenty elders are listed along with four deacons. Then follows the customary series of topics, including "How are the preachers stationed this year?" New, also, is the grouping of these appointments under the elders who now become presiding elders in all but name. This is the origin of the district superintendent. Except for a reference to Cokesbury College and the minute on slavery, all the rest is the same. Even the old terminology remains: "What members are in society?" (18,000).

Something Old, Something New

The word *society* is crucial. If one understands the specific meaning of the term in the Wesleyan Revival, the self-understanding of American Methodists after 1784 becomes clear. They had become a church and were independent, but they were still *in society*. While continuing to think of themselves as members in a voluntary association *within the church*—which is the original meaning of *society*, they were now going about the business of organizing those societies as if they were a church. Here, then, was a church which kept on being a society. This lack of resolution between two related, but not identical, concepts has left a permanent mark on the Methodist tradition and has placed that denomination in a peculiar position with regard to the Ecumenical Movement. That position has been a source of confusion, but it has also been a source of strength.

Whatever this new thing was, it was growing. In five years before 1790 the membership had risen to 57,631. Since the minutes already were dividing the figures into white and black, we know that 11,682 members, 20 percent of the total, were black. Fifteen years later, in 1805, almost 120,000 members were reported. The minutes, which for 1773 occupy two pages and for 1785 six pages (not counting Wesley's letter), for 1805 fill thirty-one pages and include obituaries of preachers. Before the Christmas Conference, all the circuits and stations except two (Redstone and Holston) were east of the Allegheny Mountains. By the turn of the century, Methodists were pouring westward by the thousands, and a whole new annual conference, the Western, was formed.

Indicative of a new self-consciousness are the two interviews by Bishops Coke and Asbury with George Washington. The Christmas Conference, sensitive to the equivocal position of Methodists during the Revolution, had inserted a twenty-fifth article to the twenty-four Wesley had supplied: "Of the Rulers of the United States of America." More significant are these formal visits by the bishops. On May 26, 1785 they journeyed to Mount Vernon and were well received by the general, who responded favorably to the business they brought on this occasion, the abolition of slavery in Virginia. On a second occasion, a month after Washington's inauguration as president of the United States, Coke and Asbury, accompanied by Thomas Morrell and John Dickins, paid a formal visit in the capital, New York city, probably on June 2,[1] and submitted a greeting and congratulations on his inauguration. In establishing a Methodist stance in the new republic, this event has considerable significance. It did not, as sometimes claimed, set a precedent for other denominations to follow. Almost everybody was congratulating the president, who was already on his way to the adulatory pedestal of patriotic tradition. Even the best public relations, however, sometimes backfire. Certain persons wondered in public why Bishop Coke, a British subject, should presume to take so direct a part, and how "Dr. Coke and Mr. Asbury" got their episcopal consecration.

The making of the new church meant a parting from the old, and partings can be painful. During the Christmas Conference, probably on the last day of December, two Episcopal rectors, John Andrews of the parishes of St. Thomas and St. James and William West of St. Paul's, had Coke and Asbury to tea. They argued against separation and suggested that special bishops might be provided for the

---

[1] The exact date is not clear. See Richard M. Cameron in *HAM*, I, 248. See Bangs, *History*, I, 280-86, for documents.

Methodists. The former Anglicans were themselves throughout the 1780s in the protracted and difficult process of forming a new Protestant Episcopal Church in the United States. A movement led by William White, outstanding rector of Christ Church, Philadelphia, brought about a national organization which provided, significantly, for equal clerical and lay representation in its governing body. An autonomous movement, led by Samuel Seabury in Connecticut, was brought into this national body by the end of the decade.

The tea in Baltimore changed nobody's mind. It was already too late. Coke was not allured by the prospect of becoming a special bishop, nor was Asbury attracted to the rectorship of an Episcopal church. Yet, the process by which two American denominations were being formed raised similar problems for both. William White had written an influential pamphlet (1782), "The Case of the Episcopal Church Considered," in which he suggested that, on grounds of necessity (shades of Wesley!), the American church be organized without formally consecrated bishops. This would serve, he argued, as a justified, though temporary, procedure. He was developing ideas similar to those earlier argued by King and Stillingfleet and used by Wesley. Although it would not be accurate to equate White's views with Wesley's, it is remarkable how the counsels of necessity brought the two men together in their thinking.

Later, in 1787, White sought to talk with John and Charles Wesley about the issue and did have conversations with Charles, but nothing came of these efforts. The same unsuccessful outcome attended the approach made by Coke in 1791 to White and Seabury, by then bishops of the Protestant Episcopal Church, in which he proposed reunion on the basis of episcopal ordination for himself and Asbury. Unfortunately, his first letter to White, dated April 24, 1791, prevented his receiving a reply before he heard (April 29) of Wesley's death and hurriedly sailed for England. He also wrote (May 14, 1791) to Seabury. Asbury was furious with his episcopal colleague when he discovered the correspondence. Coke was acting from complex motives, among which were his changing views of relations with the Anglican Church,[2] a controversy centering on James O'Kelly, and his own deeply held ecumenical spirit. In any event, this approach failed. Equally unsuccessful was the attempt made by Episcopal Bishop James Madison of Virginia in 1792 to form a basis for union. His plan was rejected by the lower house of the general convention.

[2] See John Vickers, *Thomas Coke, Apostle of Methodism* (1969), 176. See also Paul Blankenship, "History of Negotiations for Union between Methodists and Non-Methodists in the United States," (Diss., Northwestern, 1965).

Did separation of Anglicans and Methodists thus take place by the skin of the teeth? Probably the division was inevitable in spite of possible delays and compromises. The forces at work in American Christianity were such as to push the two groups, for the time being, farther apart. The equivocal position of John Wesley, the unwillingness of Anglican authorities to act, the impatience of American leaders, the powerful forces of revivalism, and the pressures toward pluralism in American religion conspired to separate the Methodists and the Episcopalians. The forces, perhaps ultimately more deeply rooted, which would tend to bring them together were for the time being submerged. Curiously, two of the principal Methodist actors already mentioned received Episcopal ordination and served as rectors of parishes—Joseph Pilmore (ordained by Seabury) and Thomas Vasey (ordained by White). To these should be added Absalom Jones, black friend of Richard Allen and a founder of the African Methodist Episcopal Church.

Emerging Structure

A series of administrative problems brought about changes and improvements in the structure of the Methodist Episcopal Church.[3] In every case the problems centered on the double-deck issue of authority: bishops in relation to the whole body of itinerant preachers, and preachers in relation to the general membership —complicated by the interests of those neither-fish-nor-fowl local preachers and exhorters. As the new denomination came into being, the bishops continued their administration through meetings held at different places and at different times. The annual conference, in this early period, consisted of all the meetings and recorded minutes over a one-year period or between general conferences. This increasingly cumbersome system brought pressures for streamlining the structure. There was no geographical delineation of annual conference until 1796.

Before this, however, a more fundamental issue of authority had to be faced. John Wesley had undertaken in 1786 to send Coke back from one of his periodic visits to England with instructions for the American Methodists to gather in conference the following May and to receive the appointment of Richard Whatcoat as a third superintendent. There were two things wrong with these instructions. First, the meeting times for the annual conference had already been set the

[3] For further information on these developments, briefly summarized in this section, see *HAM*, I, Chaps. 6 and 9.

previous year, and second, the American Methodists were not ready to accept a bishop on the basis of Wesley's appointment. On the first issue, the meeting was held over the protests of those who through previous engagement could not come. On the second, Whatcoat was passed over and no new bishop selected at all. In reaction, the conference refused to abide by the "binding minute" of the Christmas Conference by which the preachers agreed to remain under the direction of Wesley. Thomas Ware gave a lucid and measured explanation of what was going on:

> Mr. Wesley had been in the habit of calling his preachers together, not to legislate, but to confer. Many of them he found to be excellent counsellors, and he heard them respectfully on the weighty matters which were brought before them; but the right to *decide* all questions he reserved to himself. This he deemed the more excellent way; and as we had volunteered and pledged ourselves to obey, he instructed the doctor, conformably to his own usage, to put as few questions to vote as possible, saying, "If you, brother Asbury, and brother Whatcoat are agreed, it is enough." To place the power of deciding all questions discussed, or nearly all, in the hands of the superintendents, was what could never be introduced among us—a fact which we thought Mr. Wesley could not but have known, had he known us as well as we ought to have been known by Dr. Coke. After all, we had none to blame so much as ourselves. In the first effusion of our zeal we had adopted a rule binding ourselves to obey Mr. Wesley; and this rule must be rescinded, or we must be content, not only to receive Mr. Whatcoat as one of our superintendents, but also, as our brethren of the Bristish conference, with barely discussing subjects, and leaving the decision of them to two or three individuals. This was the chief cause of our rescinding the rule. All, however, did not vote to rescind it. Some thought it would be time enough to do so when our superintendents should claim to decide questions independently of the conference, which, it was confidently believed, they never would do.[4]

After two years this breach, which pained Wesley, was healed with the restoration of his name in the minutes. This was accomplished in a typically Methodistic fashion. Instead of one disciplinary question about authority, there were two:

Quest. 1. Who are the persons that exercise the episcopal office in the Methodist Church in Europe and America?

Ans. John Wesley, Thomas Coke, Francis Asbury.

Quest. 2. Who have been elected by the unanimous suffrages of the General Conference to superintend the Methodist connection in America?

Ans. Thomas Coke, Francis Asbury.

[4] *Sketches of the Life and Travels of Rev. Thomas Ware* (1839), 130-31.

Coke got his fingers burned in this episode, because he had incautiously brought Wesley's instructions under the assumption that they would be followed explicitly. He was forced to agree that he would not attempt to administer American affairs as bishop when he was in Europe. By 1808 the estrangement had gone far, as recorded in the *Journal* of the General Conference, "Dr. Coke, at the request of the British Conference, and by the consent of our General Conference, resides in Europe. He is not to exercise the office of superintendent among us, in the United States, until he be recalled by the General Conference, or by all the Annual Conferences respectively." His missionary vision and, perhaps, his personal ambition as well were simply too large for the Atlantic community. He died, it may be noted here, in 1814 on a missionary voyage to India.

One of the most curious and little known episodes in the process of emerging structure was the attempt to form a council. There is no mention of it at all in official records, but it was established with Asbury's urging and had two formal meetings.[5] The details are of no importance, but the interest of Asbury is clear. He devised the plan of a council in order to forestall growing pressure for the establishment of regular general conferences. The plan carefully preserved his power in all affairs of the church. It was so poorly set up that it fell of its own weight after two years. Asbury abandoned it and reluctantly accepted the idea of a general conference.

He had good reason. The multiple session annual conference, which served the needs of both annual and general conferences as they later developed, was becoming so onerous that no one wanted to keep it up. Three persons in particular, each for his own reasons, were pressing strongly for a general conference: Bishop Coke favored it as a more efficient plan; Jesse Lee favored it in opposition to the council plan; James O'Kelly favored it as a means of restricting Asbury's authority. As a result, a call was sent out for a meeting of the traveling preachers in a general conference set for Baltimore, November 1, 1792, a year after the death of John Wesley. This, not the Christmas Conference, nor Wesley's "general conference" of 1787, was the first general conference. Until now all regular business had been transacted in multiple sessions of an annual conference as established by Thomas Rankin in 1773.

One reason for Asbury's foot-dragging came out on the second day. James O'Kelly made a motion: "After the bishop appoints the preachers at conference to their several circuits, if anyone thinks

---

[5] Minutes of these meetings were kept and printed. The brief pamphlets are very rare. Copies are in the library of Garrett Theological Seminary.

himself injured by the appointment, he shall have liberty to appeal to the conference and state his objections; and if the conference approve his objections, the bishop shall appoint him to another circuit." This famous motion for an appeal led to a long and sometimes acrimonious debate. The outcome was defeat for the motion and vindication of Asbury's power to appoint. Although Asbury absented himself from the floor and let Coke preside, there was never a doubt that this maneuver was directed against the almost unchallenged leader.

Two major results came from the General Conference of 1792. In the first place, the controversy over O'Kelly's motion caused the first notable schism in American Methodism. In the second place, the plan for a quadrennial general conference was approved. John Tigert defined this body in his *Constitutional History:* "As a mass convention of the entire traveling ministry its powers were general, supreme, and final." [6] Well might Asbury be uneasy about such unlimited powers. No one was about to depose him. In fact, he was able to surmount all the storms of controversy to remain the supreme power as long as he lived. But this was based on deference to the character of the man, not on any constitutional foundation. Until 1808, except for the existing totality of the general conference, there was no formal constitution.

The second General Conference of 1796 (the first of which we have actual journal record) strengthened the structure by establishing six geographically defined annual conferences, one of which was the open-ended Western Conference. The *Discipline* begins to reflect increasing legislative activity. The original, rather simple and unorganized Discipline of 1785 was by 1792 reorganized into three chapters: ministry, membership, and temporal economy. As a result of the O'Kelly schism, the General Conference of 1796 instructed the bishops to prepare explanatory notes replete with fortifying scriptural passages for the Discipline. This was incorporated in the edition of 1798, which thus becomes one of the prime sources of information on early American Methodism. The *Discipline* of 1808 records the plan for a *delegated* general conference with a constitutional basis of authority in the form of six restrictive rules, which prevail in the councils of United Methodism to this day.

By the turn of the century, the growth of the church was such that great disparities existed in the representation in the general conference. From the North, South, and West came increasingly bitter complaints that the distances were such as to disfranchise ministers. The combined power of the Baltimore and Philadelphia annual conferences, with their heavy attendance, was able to dominate legisla-

---

[6] *A Constitutional History of American Episcopal Methodism* (1916), 263.

tion. Hence, over considerable traditional opposition, the plan was accepted whereby each annual conference would be entitled to a proportional share of representation by ministers elected to that responsibility by each annual conference. From 1808 on up until the present time general conference has been composed of *delegated* members who represent particular regions and constituent groups.

The six restrictive rules, in the original form, follow:

1. The general conference shall not revoke, alter, or change our articles of religion, nor establish any new standards or rules of doctrine contrary to our present existing and established standards of doctrine.
2. They shall not allow of more than one representative for every five members of the annual conference, nor allow of a less number than one for every seven.
3. They shall not change or alter any part or rule of our government, so as to do away with Episcopacy or destroy the plan of our itinerant general superintendency.
4. They shall not revoke or change the general rules of the United Societies.
5. They shall not do away the privileges of our ministers or preachers of trial by a committee, and of an appeal: Neither shall they do away the privileges of our members of trial before the society or by a committee, and of an appeal.
6. They shall not appropriate the produce of the Book Concern, or of the Charter Fund, to any purpose other than for the benefit of the travelling, supernumerary, superannuated and worn-out preachers, their wives, widows and children.

Provided nevertheless, that upon the joint recommendation of all the annual conferences, then a majority of two-thirds of the general conference succeeding, shall suffice to alter any of the above restrictions.

Nicholas Snethen, who by the 1820s had become a reformer, described what he saw as a contrast between ecclesiastical authoritarianism and American democracy. "What scripture authority can you produce to authorise you to govern Americans otherwise than as free men?" His axiom was, "The religious liberty of a people should never be reduced in principle, below the standard of their civil liberty." [7] His able argument is weakened by his failure to take ac-

---

[7] Snethen, *Snethen on Lay Representation* (1835), 317, 319, reprinting an article in *Mutual Rights*, II (1826).

count of the discipline which may be expected of those who join *voluntary* associations like churches.

The O'Kelly Schism

In the evolution of early structure, the continuing theme of authority in relation to freedom found expression. Without the authority, as personified by Wesley originally and by Asbury, presumably, the amazing growth and spread of this church would have been impossible. It was the disciplined corps of preachers, sometimes almost like a Protestant society of Jesus, which gave Methodism its tremendous energy and efficiency on the frontier. The circuit rider fully deserves his proverbial fame. On the other hand, without the involvement of all the People Called Methodists in the life and work of the church, it would have been impossible to achieve the new community of faith which distinguished the Methodist Episcopal Church and all its related bodies. In short, without local preachers, exhorters and class leaders, the circuit rider's work would have been impossible. The two forces, for better or for worse, were destined to go together. The result was continual tension between authority and freedom, between centralization of leadership and democracy. It is of the very genius of Methodism. Without this tension it would not have fulfilled its destiny. The price was conflict.

That conflict broke out powerfully and tragically in the O'Kelly schism of the 1790s. It was a struggle marked by involvement of strong personalities. If great issues were at stake, forceful persons were fighting. The *dramatis personae* is impressive: Francis Asbury, Thomas Coke, James O'Kelly, Rice Haggard, Jesse Lee, Nicholas Snethen, and many others. O'Kelly's motion in the General Conference of 1792 started off the fireworks. His defeat resulted in a walkout of those who demanded reform. Jesse Lee mused, "I stood and looked after them as they went off, and observed to one of the preachers, that I was sorry to see the old man go off in that way, for I was persuaded he would not be quiet long; but he would try to be head of some party." With Rice Haggard and young William McKendree, who had served under him in Virginia, O'Kelly departed to form what was briefly known as the Republican Methodist Church and later as the Christian Church. Richard Whatcoat, who detested conflict among Christian brethren, recorded in his journal, "It was a trying time to Some, But we Concluded with Great Love and the Lord Gave us a Gratious Shower of Refreshing Grace." [8]

The effects can be measured in terms of loss of membership and of

[8] MS Journal, Garrett Theological Seminary, entry 11 Nov. 1792.

literary production. The church was especially hard hit in Virginia. Southern Virginia was O'Kelly's home ground, and he had succeeded in being reappointed regularly as presiding elder. The loss there amounted to 3,670 in 1795. Whatcoat mused, "I began to think wether my work was not finished in America if not in the world or wether I had not better return to England for I must be where the Living Streams flow." For leaders accustomed to amazing growth from revivals, such loss was hard to take. The experience was a shock to Asbury, even though he weathered the storm. His journal reveals repeatedly and indirectly the deep mark, almost a scar.

It was also painful for O'Kelly's friends. A former supporter reported: "Jehu had a mighty zeal, but what sort of a zeal was it? Exactly such a zeal in my humble opinion as poor old unhappy Dadda O'Kelly has." Some of O'Kelly's Christians survived to participate in the merger which formed the Congregational Christian Church in 1931. More interesting is the career of Rice Haggard, who brought some followers into the Disciples of Christ. According to Barton W. Stone, one of the founders, Haggard was one of three O'Kellyite elders who joined.[9] His "An Address to the Different Religious Societies on the Sacred Import of the Christian Name," which was long lost, was a prime basis for the principles of the Disciples of Christ.

One of the most remarkable results of the schism was the pamphlet war that went on into the next century. It began with O'Kelly's *The Author's Apology for Protesting Against the Methodist Episcopal Government* (1798).[10] Stalwartly he reviewed the long conflict, which he saw as an increasing drive for power by Asbury. Taking a pseudobiblical style, he attacked "Francis" and "Thomas" and all other aspirants to power. Much of his material is untrustworthy, but it gives a vivid presentation of many complaints against the sometimes high-handed administration of Francis Asbury. He proceeded finally to offer a brief sketch of the "Royal Standard," by which he meant a soundly scriptural plan of church government without denominational distinctions.

Two years later Nicholas Snethen, at that time an Asbury supporter, produced *A Reply to an Apology for Protesting Against the Methodist Episcopal Government* (1800). Devoting most of his space to refuting O'Kelly's allegations, he concluded, "All that we require of our brethren is, that they keep the unity of the spirit, in the bond of peace, and not take any step to sow discord among the brethren." Rather they

[9] Barton W. Stone, *History of the Christian Church in the West* (1956, originally 1804), 42. Haggard's Address was reprinted by the Disciples of Christ Historical Society (Nashville, 1954, 32 pp.).

[10] Published privately in Richmond, Virginia. Copies of the first three works are in Garrett Theological Seminary.

should abide by the will of the majority as all well-governed democracies do. But, what if the majority be wrong? Ah, there's the rub! O'Kelly had enough ammunition to return with *A Vindication of the Author's Apology with Reflections on the Reply* (1801). The last in the series was Snethen's *An Answer to James O'Kelly's Vindication of his Apology* (1802).

O'Kelly was a truly ecumenically minded Christian whose strong personality got in his own way. The result, instead of ecumenical progress, was rather the spawning of yet another denomination. In the process, all the main issues which were fought over during the reform decade of the 1820s were raised by O'Kelly. For all his limitations and frustrations, he belongs in the noteworthy company of Methodist mavericks, along with Robert Strawbridge, Alexander McCaine, Orange Scott, and a host of others.

Membership

The shape of the church became visible in formal structure. It developed sinews in controversy. It came alive in its membership. Wesley had already set the tone: "I was more convinced than ever that the preaching like an apostle, without joining together those that are awakened and training them up in the ways of God, is only begetting children for the murderer." Therefore, he brought his followers together "in order to pray together, to receive the word of exhortation, and to watch over one another in love, that they might help each other to work out their salvation." [11] When these little societies became awkwardly large, they were divided into various kinds of smaller groups, including the class meeting. This entire plan was transported to America and became the basis for church membership.

One of the cardinal principles was discipline. Membership in the societies in England and in the Methodist Episcopal Church in America was completely voluntary. That is, no one was ever forced to become a Methodist. Quite the contrary—a candidate had to prove himself worthy of membership. One of the most revealing questions to be found both in the English Large Minutes and the American *Discipline* was, "How shall we prevent improper persons from insinuating themselves into the Society?" The answer at first emphasized the general rules and the issuing of "tickets" of membership. In the American church, the question introduced the section on the class meeting. The point is that from the beginning strong emphasis was placed on the terms of membership. Although there was no

[11] Wesley, *Journal*, V, 26; *Works*, VIII, 250.

doctrinal barrier and nothing required but a "desire to flee from the wrath to come and be saved from their sins," entrance was not easily achieved.[12] A probationary period of two months was extended in 1788 to six months throughout the nineteenth century (till 1908 in the North, but 1866 in the South). Coke and Asbury in their Notes to the *Discipline* of 1798 underline the point: "It is manifestly our duty to fence in our society, and to preserve it from intruders; otherwise we should soon become a desolate waste." The purpose of the societies was "to raise a holy people . . . . We will have a holy people or none." And especially, "to admit frequently unawakened persons to our society-meetings and love-feasts, would be to throw a damp on those profitable assemblies, and cramp, if not entirely destroy that liberty of speech which is always made a peculiar blessing to earnest believers and sincere seekers of salvation."

That last emphasis comes close to the heart of the matter of membership in early Methodism. Always central was the idea of close personal fellowship which could be achieved only in a small group. This is where the class meeting comes in. If ever the society or local congregation became too unwieldy, at least in the small class meeting intimate community could be maintained. Ideally, no more than twelve would be together under a class leader to meet weekly for spiritual guidance, prayer, Bible study, individual witness, and discipline. Everyone would know, in close personal terms, everyone else. The class leader would be familiar with the personalities of each individual and his situation in life, including his family background and business relations. In the typical class, persons of different ages and stages would be together—old, young, men, women, beginners and those going on to perfection. Practice varied widely from place to place as to size and composition. Sometimes the sexes were separated, probably in carry-over from habits of worship. Maxwell Gaddis reported he was leader of "the female class" which met at William Neff's house.[13] James B. Finley has recorded in his autobiography a poignant account of his first exposure to a Methodist class meeting. He went very unwillingly with his wife to visit one and shocked the members by his presence, being at that time so notorious a sinner.

> The time having arrived for meeting to commence, it was opened by singing and prayer. I conformed to the rules, for I never was wicked enough, devil though I was, in the estimation of the people, to persecute

---

[12] For more detailed discussion see my *Church Membership in the Methodist Tradition* (1958), especially the chapter on "Getting In."

[13] Maxwell P. Gaddis, *Footprints of a Pioneer* (1855), 277.

the righteous, or show my ill-breeding and vulgarity by disturbing a worshiping assembly, nor would I suffer any one else to do it where I was without correcting them. After several prayers, the leader—Mr. Sullivan—rose and said, "We are now going to hold our class meeting, and all who have enjoyed this privilege twice or thrice will please retire, while those who have not and are desirous of being benefited by the exercises may remain." I was anxious to be benefited, and being favorably impressed, thus far, with the exercises, concluded to remain. My wife also kept her seat. The members of the class eyed me very closely, and I could easily tell by their furtive glances that my room would be better than my company. The leader, as is customary on such occasions, opened the speaking exercises by relating a portion of his own experience, in which he spoke feelingly of the goodness of God to his soul. After this he spoke to the rest in order, inquiring into their spiritual prosperity; addressing to them such language of instruction, encouragement, or reproof, as their spiritual states seemed to require. It was a time of profound and powerful feeling; every soul seemed to be engaged in the work of salvation. I was astonished beyond all expression. Instead of the ranting, incoherent declarations which I had been told they made on such occasions, I never heard more plain, simple, Scriptural, common-sense, yet eloquent views of Christian experience in my life. After all the members had been spoken to the leader came to me, and, in a courteous, Christian manner, inquired into my religious condition.[14]

The history of the Methodist class meeting has yet to be written. An abundant literature has appeared, starting with Wesley's writings and continuing with early English and American tracts describing and advocating it, and concluding with more tracts which decry its decline. Without realizing it, modern advocates of small group procedures are reviving an original emphasis of Methodism. During the first half of the nineteenth century, the class meeting was a thriving institution which gave a distinctive mark to the Methodist way. As Coke and Asbury summarized its significance in their notes to the *Discipline* of 1798, "In short, we can truly say, that through the grace of God our classes form the pillars of our work, and, as we have before observed, are in a considerable degree our universities for the ministry."

Around the middle of the century the class meeting went into decline. Evidence of this is clear in official records and personal recollection.[15] Those who had been nurtured in faith via class meeting felt a deep loss at the decline of interest. For several decades articles and pamphlets appeared regularly either bewailing the loss or

[14] James B. Finley, *Autobiography* (1853), 178.
[15] See for example *JGC*, 1848, p. 173; Moses M. Henkle, *Primary Platform of Methodism* (1851); Charles C. Keys, *The Class-Leader's Manual* (1851); John Miley, *Treatise on Class Meetings* (1851); W. J. Sasnett, "Theory of Methodist Class Meetings," *MQRS*, 5 (1851): 265-84; report on debate in General Conference, "Class Meetings," *MQRS*, 12 (1858): 507-35.

seeking for a remedy. The revision of the *Discipline* made in 1872 resulted in this new statement: "The primary object of distributing the members of the Church into classes is to secure the sub-pastoral oversight made necessary by our itinerant economy" (Par. 76).

There is the nub of the matter—the itinerant ministry. The high point of the class meeting coincides with the heyday of the circuit rider. Its decline dates from his dismounting. As long as the traveling preacher was on the go around his circuit and from appointment to appointment, the place of the class meeting was secure. The class leader was needed to perform those pastoral functions which are part of a balanced ministry. But when the preacher settled down in a parsonage as a stationed pastor, the class leader (and along with him the local preacher and exhorter) became, at least so it seemed, an unnecessary wheel. Inadvertently, because of the settling down of the traveling preacher, Methodism lost one of its strongest supports, the active *ministerial* participation of the lay people.

For that is what is involved in this story of membership in society and class. It is of the essence of the Methodist doctrine of the church. This is the priesthood of all believers, the ministry of all Christians, in operation. For a season American Methodism caught the vision of each person as minister to others, all "baked in one bread," as Luther put it. That was what went on in class meeting. That is what church membership meant. Originally with Wesley, this could all take place within the bosom of the church. With American Methodists the church had to be found here in society and class meeting—it could be nowhere else. Francis Asbury never realized how profoundly true was his comment in his "Valedictory" for McKendree in 1813: "We were a Church, and no Church." Ever since, Methodists have been trying to decide whether they would be a great church or a holy people.

Chapter 12
The Shape of the Ministry

In a perceptive essay, Bishop William R. Cannon has pointed out a fundamental "ambiguity between an ordained layman and an unordained clergyman" in the Methodist tradition.[1] As a result, Methodism has been incapable of distinguishing clearly between clergy and laity. Although this blurring has been ecclesiastically confusing, it has theological significance which has not always been recognized. Methodism began with and has never abandoned the principle of the priesthood of all believers.[2] In this context the office of "local preacher" takes on meaning, and the uncertainties about ordination fall into perspective.

The Local Ministry

From the beginning a functional distinction has been made between the traveling preacher, full member of an annual conference, and the local preacher, authorized to preach in the place where he resides, but not a member of an annual conference or entitled to a regular appointment. He was usually regarded as a lay preacher, but sometimes he was ordained. The position was usually a step toward the traveling ministry, which meant membership in the annual conference and ordination as deacon and elder. The confusion which arose from this position has been worse confounded by disciplinary regulations which have permitted, under specific conditions, unordained lay pastors to administer the sacraments. In the early days, however, the confusion was of no concern because the utility of the practice was apparent to all.

The General Conference of 1796 regularized the office by stipulating that a local preacher might be granted a license to preach if he had been (1) recommended by the society of which he was a member and (2) examined by the quarterly conference of the circuit. After

[1] William R. Cannon, "The Meaning of the Ministry in Methodism," *MH*, 8 (Oct., 1969): 3. Cf. A. B. Lawson, *John Wesley and the Christian Ministry* (1963).

[2] See the recent statement of British Methodism in *The Constitutional Practice and Discipline of the Methodist Church* (1951), 4.

four years, he might receive deacon's orders. Following an extended debate, the General Conference of 1812 authorized local elder's orders after four years of service as deacon. Nathan Bangs frankly stated that the whole issue was decided on the basis of "expediency and the probable utility of the measure." [3] Still unsettled were problems raised in a memorial to the next general conference regarding representation of local preachers in the general conference, participation in the administration of societies, and provision of salary. These issues spilled into the reform movement of the 1820s with considerable conflict of interest among the reformers.

The quality of the local preachers varied widely. Many of them were untrained and inexperienced members of local churches who had a call to preach, but could not or would not undertake the obligations of the traveling ministry. Some of them were well-educated professional persons whose leadership in the community commended them for religious responsibilities. Jacob Young, famous Ohio circuit rider, esteemed Captain Whitney, who, "although he always remained among the laity, he was, in a good degree, a bishop in the Methodist Church." [4] Even more influential was Edward Tiffin, first governor of Ohio, who had a call to preach, but never became a traveling preacher because of his family responsibilities. Ordained local deacon by Asbury, he retained his license to preach throughout his long career as public servant—member of the state constitutional convention, two terms as governor, and United States senator. Other local preachers were former traveling preachers who had located, that is, resigned from membership in the annual conference while yet retaining their orders as local preachers.

The local preacher was neither fish nor fowl, neither layman nor clergyman—or rather, he was something of both, a curious hybrid. O'Kelly had championed their cause without providing a solution. The reformers of the 1820s were sympathetic, but were more concerned with the issues of election of presiding elders (rights of traveling preachers) and lay representation (rights of laymen). Caught in the middle, local preachers lost out on both counts. Nevertheless, the ranks grew to amazing proportions, and the work of local preachers can scarcely be overestimated. In 1812, compared with seven hundred itinerants, there were two thousand locals. By 1854, local preachers numbered eighty-five hundred. A common experience of the circuit rider sent to organize a new circuit in the wilderness was to discover, upon his arrival, that a local preacher was already on the

[3] Bangs, *History*, II, 315.
[4] Jacob Young, *Autobiography of a Pioneer* (1857), 150.

scene and had a class meeting in operation. The story of the expansion of Methodism on the frontier cannot be told without due account of the persistent local preachers who sometimes outrode the circuit riders.

And they were not only out front; they were back behind. As the traveling preachers followed their appointed rounds, local preachers filled in during their long absences. William Watters, who had experience in both roles, argued that each was a necessary complement to the other:

> I have learned from experience that though a travelling preacher has, in most particulars, far the advantage of obtaining useful knowledge, and of being useful, yet, not so in all things. The travelling preacher that comes into, and passes through a neighbourhood, and especially in a time of revival, generally sees the best side of professors, but the local preacher who resides amongst them has an opportunity of taking into view the whole of their conduct, and from his more intimate knowledge (if a man of attention and observation), he can suit their particular cases beyond what any one can who wants such information. . . .
>
> I have found that a local preacher's sphere of action is much more extensive than I thought it was before I tried it. And though I must prefer that of a travelling preacher; yet I think the great thing is in either state to be instant in season, and out of season endeavouring to do all we possibly can in so good a cause, taking care not to pull down with one hand any part of what we build up with the other.[5]

Only when the circuit rider dismounted and settled in the community where the local preacher lived did the problem arise, as it did with the class leader, of what his role should be, especially in a community accustomed to a congenial combination of the two.

One aspect of the local ministry was negative: an embarrassingly large number of traveling preachers located. This was a persistent and nagging problem for Asbury and all the bishops. Time and again able preachers gave up their annual conference membership and located. This usually meant that they married and settled on a farm. They did not cease their ministry. They continued it on a local basis, sometimes quite actively. Nicholas Snethen continued to exert strong influence among the reformers years after his location.[6] Nevertheless, these men were considered to be second-string preachers whose usefulness was sadly limited. Although Asbury was critical of preachers who located, he continued to hold the office of local preacher in high regard.[7]

[5] William Watters, *A Short Account of the Christian Experience and Ministerial Labors* (1806?), 116-19.

[6] See his *Snethen on Lay Representation*, 184-93, 215, *et passim*.

[7] Asbury, *Journal and Letters*, III, 311.

The Traveling Ministry

Historically speaking, admission to membership in the annual conference as a traveling preacher had nothing to do with ordination. None of the early preachers, before 1784, was ordained. The annual conference and distinctive membership therein were firmly established eleven years before ordination became an identifying factor in the Methodist ministry. The introduction of ordination provided for the sacraments, but it made almost no difference in the nature of the ministry. From that day to this, the really important factor in definition of the Methodist minister has been membership in an annual conference, not ordination.

Alfred Brunson, writing in 1856, offered a helpful description of the ministry as he knew it. A traveling preacher should possess four cardinal characteristics: (1) conversion, (2) fruits, (3) calling of God, (4) seals from the church. He should demonstrate three types of qualifications: (1) natural characteristics, such as clear speech and common sense; (2) gracious gifts of the Holy Spirit in understanding and interpreting revelation; (3) acquired skills through training and preparation. Of the second he said, "It is this, above every other qualification, that renders the minister useful in his calling, and it must be acquired by faith in Him who has called to the work." [8] Brunson was one of the old school, a conservative who held all formal training under suspicion. Training comes *in* the ministry, not *for* it.

All the early preachers would have agreed with Brunson in his insistence on a spiritual calling. Benjamin Lakin is one of many illustrations.[9] The Episcopal Address of 1840 said this was "the true doctrine of Apostolic Succession," because Christ alone has the power to commission. The apostles themselves merely confirmed those whom God had chosen.

Ecclesiastical confirmation of the divine call to ministry was the point of coincidence of authority and freedom. That is, admission to the annual conference placed the preacher in that select body who possessed the entire power in the church. The whole body of elders (at first in multiple sessions of the annual conference, after 1792 in general conference, after 1808 in delegation) possessed the ultimate authority. *But:* no person has ever entered the ministry of The United Methodist Church or any of its antecedents except by the will of the people. He or she must first be raised up by the members gathered in quarterly conference. The steps, then, would follow: member, class

---

[8] Alfred Brunson, *The Gospel Ministry* (1856), 6 ff; 20.

[9] W. W. Sweet, *Religion on the American Frontier* (1946), Vol. IV, *The Methodists,* 247. *Episcopal Address* (pamphlet), 5.

leader, exhorter, local preacher, traveling preacher on trial, traveling deacon, finally traveling elder.

The term *traveling preacher* is both formal and descriptive. The heart was the itineracy. "Every thing is kept moving as far as possible," explain Coke and Asbury in the notes to the *Discipline* of 1798. Citing much scripture, they called it "the primitive and apostolic plan." They were unwilling to consider any change or novelty which might "run the least hazard of wounding that plan which God has so wonderfully owned." What they meant by itineracy was that plan of appointments by which ministers were kept moving twice-over. In the first place, each man had his appointment for a strictly limited time. With Boardman and Pilmore the change had come quarterly; then (1804) a two-year limit was established with the understanding that an annual change was normal; the limit became three years in 1864 in the Methodist Episcopal Church, four years in 1866 in the Methodist Episcopal Church, South. In the second place, every preacher kept on the move on his circuit, and this was true even of ministers appointed to city stations, for they had several outpoints. Thus the itinerant system went round and round, like a little hoop (the circuit) always turning around on a larger hoop (the annual conference), which itself was always in motion. In this way, some preachers were appointed to circuits in which they preached perhaps four times (once each quarter) in each of many preaching points, and then went off to the annual conference for appointment to a different circuit. Four powerful sermons, ringing the changes from conviction of sin all the way to perfect love, would take care of an entire year's preaching!

The emphases of Coke and Asbury were repeated like a litany during the first half of the nineteenth century. Loyal William Watters wrote, "I never moved from one Circuit to another, but what it reminded me that I was a Pilgrim—that here I had no continuing city—that I was a tenant at will, and ought to be always ready." Brunson echoed this praise of itineracy. He was opposed to the two-year time limit, not because it was too short a time, but because it was too long. Preachers who got a reappointment for a second year were criticized. "It was said of such that they had but half done their work the first year, and were returned to finish it." [10] Abel Stevens at mid-century, after reviewing the glorious history of the itinerant ministry and marshaling all the arguments in favor of the plan, asked, "Do we assert too much when we say, that for one hundred years the Methodist ministry, though mostly uneducated, have transcended in labors, in results, and in conservative adherence to their great princi-

[10] Watters, *Short Account* (1806), 43. Brunson, *A Western Pioneer*, I, 376.

ples, any other body of men engaged in moral labor on the earth?" [11]

But some of the men who had experienced this itinerant form of ministry were not so sure of its unalloyed perfection. Benjamin Lakin, in a poignant section of his partly published diary, recounts the profound struggles he and his wife had about moving from the local to the traveling ministry.

> I could not Beare the thought of traveling, my wife also made some objections to it. I laid the matter before the Lord by prayer and fasting. And took this for my direction, that if some difficulties were removed that appeared in the way and my wife gave her consent that it was the will of God that I should travel. My wife soon began to be much exercised about my traveling and soon not only gave her consent but also advised me to go. I still felt a reluctance to going, and my distresses ware such before I gave up to travel that I was for some time in continual fear of being murdered[.] my pain was great and all worldly comfort was entirely gone. At last being fully convinced it was the will of God I gave up to travel, accordingly I attended conference at Bethel on the first of October. 1800. and took an appointment in Limestone circuit.[12]

That the system of itinerant ministry was not universally popular is indicated by the increasing number of locations of men who for one reason or another simply couldn't take it any longer. A substantial report of the Committee on Ways and Means of the General Conference of 1816 dealt with the problem and recommended a series of improvements to render the plan more tolerable. Salaries (allowances) should be higher (though still very low); parsonages should be provided, along with fuel and food; provision should be made for support of retired preachers; and a plan for a course of study should be set up. Both Thomas Ware and Nicholas Snethen, committed preachers though they were, had their doubts about the itinerant plan. Ware later wrote,

> I thought our system too severe. It called us in youth to sacrifice all means of acquiring property, and threatened to leave us dependant on the cold hand of charity for our bread in old age. Some plead that we had no asylum for our sons, so that, while we were travelling and preaching to others, they had none to take care of them; and they said they must locate to preserve them from ignorance and crime. And the fact that there was no provision made for superannuated men, induced many to forsake the itinerant ranks in order to provide, while they had health and strength, against absolute want in time of infirmity and old age. And who could blame them? [13]

[11] Abel Stevens, *An Essay on Church Polity* (1853), 142; Cf. 139-47. Cf. Bangs, *History*, I, 362.

[12] Lakin diary, in Sweet, *Religion on the American Frontier*, IV, 220.

[13] Ware, *Sketches*, 214; Snethen, *On Lay Representation*, 164, 171-73.

Thus, it becomes clear that many objections to the itineracy derived from the practical arrangements—or rather lack thereof—which attended it. A portion of the blame rests with Francis Asbury, who throughout displayed a martyrlike spirit. He was content that preachers should receive extremely low allowances, for that would guarantee "involuntary celibacy." When the preachers complained they could not marry on such an income, Asbury's response was, "So much the better!" His views stand in strong contrast to the sensible moderation of Dr. Coke.

The strong emphasis on celibacy as a part of the early itineracy has not been widely recognized. It began with that prize celibate (even though he finally did marry), John Wesley. His alter ego in this respect was Francis Asbury. The contrary examples of happily married Charles Wesley and Thomas Coke were not sufficient to offset the prime images. Even Ware, who saw many limitations of the itinerant system, for long remained single as testimony of his commitment.[14] Asbury, although he generally was fair to married men, was impatient with the special problems they presented. He never ceased to pay tribute to the celibates among the itinerants. At the Virginia Annual Conference in 1809, when he discovered that of eighty-four men present, only three were married, he rejoiced.[15]

Inevitably, such stringent discipline took its toll. One correspondent of Edward Dromgoole wrote in 1788: "It is strange to me to see so few of my old acquaintances in the minutes. But you solve the difficulty at once. *'They are married,'* So there is an end of them." [16] Later on, William Taylor testified that if a young man married while on trial, he was not admitted. If he were admitted and married before the fourth year, he was appointed to "a very poor circuit, where he and his young wife would enjoy their honeymoon among the whippoorwills." [17]

One may ask whether, in the long run, the extreme privations endured by the early circuit riders were all necessary. It may offer some kind of inspiration to learn what they went through. But if, as Dr. Coke believed, they could do their work better and serve longer in effective ministry when their basic needs, natural concerns for normal family life, and support in old age were provided for; then, one may well question a policy which drove many of these brave men at a very early age either to location or to the grave. The celibate ministry of Methodism was on its way out by the time of Asbury's death in 1816.

[14] Ware, *Sketches,* 182.
[15] Asbury, *Journal,* II, 591.
[16] Dromgoole correspondence in Sweet, *Religion on the American Frontier,* IV, 136.
[17] William Taylor, *Story of my Life* (1896), 63.

The broader principle, the itineracy, endured throughout the century and, in theory, still remains effective today.

Wherever these traveling preachers served, once each year they enjoyed the rare pleasure of gathering together in the annual conference. It takes considerable imagination on the part of Methodists, accustomed to the large conference sessions of later years, dominated by well-digested agenda of business, to envisage an annual conference of the early nineteenth century. A few men, brought together over rough roads and trails from great distances, men who had not seen one another, or perhaps any fellow minister, for a year, now joined in singing hymns they all knew, praying and worshiping together in some ordinary house or perchance a small chapel. It was a rare time indeed! Let Thomas Ware tell about it:

> The annual meetings of the preachers, sent, as they hold themselves to be, to declare in the name of the Almighty Jesus terms of peace between the offended Majesty of heaven and guilty man, were to them occurrences of interesting import. The privilege of seeing each other, after labouring and suffering reproach in distant portions of the Lord's vineyard, and of hearing the glad tidings which they expected to hear on such occasions of what God was doing through their instrumentality, encouraged their hearts every step they took in their long and wearisome journeys, and served as a cordial to their spirits.[18]

At the end of the annual conference, in a final dramatic moment, the bishop read off the appointments of the preachers for the next year. Many, until this moment, had no idea where they would be sent. A preacher like William Milburn would never forget the experience:

> The last scene of the conference is one peculiarly touching and solemn. A hundred men, many of them married, have surrendered their right of choice, and placed their lives and fortunes, under God, at the disposal of a single man—the bishop. He, with the wisdom of an overseer, with the simplicity and sincerity that spring from the abiding consciousness that his motives and decisions are ever in the great Taskmaster's eye, and with all a father's tenderness for the preachers and the people intrusted to him—he has considered the claims of the men and of the work, and is now to read the weighty decision. At his word they are to go forth to their fields of duty and of danger, accepting his arbitrament as the interpretation of providence. Whither they are to go they know not, nor what shall betide them. . . . The prayer has been offered which commends them and their families to God and to the word of his grace, which is able to build them up and to give them "an inheritance among all them which are sanctified;" and in the midst of a profound silence the bishop reads out the appointments. A new year has begun, the week's holiday is over.

---

[18] Ware, *Sketches,* 103.

Hands are shaken, farewell is said, and ere an hour has passed most of the men are on the road to their new posts.[19]

The Superintending Ministry

Of all forms of Methodist ministry, the office of district superintendent has changed the most. In 1784, twelve (thirteen?) elders were ordained. In effect these became "presiding elders," the old term for district superintendent. From the first they were assigned a group of circuits over whose unordained preachers they assumed guidance. It was their special responsibility to take the sacraments to the people. This was, then, the first definition of the office of district superintendent or presiding elder: to provide the sacraments of baptism and the Lord's Supper to the People Called Methodists. Theirs was a priestly and pastoral office. They began to be called presiding elders in the Minutes of 1789. Coke's and Asbury's notes to the *Discipline* of 1798 list six advantages: the presiding elder strengthens the quarterly conference, helps change appointments between annual conferences, supplies vacancies, aids the bishop on his rounds, exercises emergency powers of suspension, and takes care of many administrative details. The list fails to mention a prime service performed by the early presiding elders—to provide young preachers with education and training.

Almost from the beginning, a difference of opinion arose over the relation of the presiding elder to the bishop. Was he to be regarded as the bishop's lieutenant in administration, or was he to be seen as the representative of his peers in the ministry in consultation with the bishop on policy? The issue was raised again and again until the crisis of the reform movement of the 1820s.[20] As it turned out, the presiding elders became a useful arm of the episcopate.

The office of bishop is inseparably connected with the personality of Francis Asbury. Although Dr. Coke was the first general superintendent in American Methodism, Asbury is the man who molded the office. In a manner of speaking, he lives today in the institution of episcopacy. Of medium height and slight build, he nevertheless cut an impressive figure with his fine head of flowing hair, which became a white mantle as he grew older. He dressed in plain traditional manner in blue or gray jacket and breeches. According to Thomas Ware, he was better at praying than preaching.[21] In his relations with his men

[19] William Milburn, *Ten Years of Preacher-Life* (1859), 79-80.

[20] Discussed in a later chapter. Bangs, *History* II, 338-43, gives a convenient summary of the debate, listing with fairness the arguments of both sides.

[21] Ware, *Sketches*, 84; L. C. Rudolph, *Francis Asbury* (1966), the most recent biography. For thorough, though different, interpretations of the office of bishop, see Jesse

he was a carbon copy of John Wesley, the firm, dominant, committed, and beloved patriarch. "He was beloved by the preachers as a father is by his children," said George Roberts, but "he did not temporize." He could be almost ruthless on occasion.

> In every case he could say I have labored more abundantly than you all—He would frequently be on horseback at sunrise travel fifteen or twenty miles to breakfast and not put up till nine and ten o-clock at night—He would of[ten] say to the preachers when complaining of their hardships, "You must have a stomach for every man's table and a back for every man's bed—that the cause was His who said to His disciples when He was with them in the flesh, *The foxes have holes and the birds of the air have nests but the Son of Man has not where to lay His head.*" [22]

This stern ascetic spirit, although much admired by some of his contemporaries, was sometimes overdone. His health suffered unduly, and frequently his friends had to step in to aid. There is a very fine line between reliance on Providence and improvidence.

He was the dominant—although not unquestioned—leader of the American Methodists. By whatever title he went, he was the top man. The episcopacy did not make Asbury; Asbury made the episcopacy. Until he died (March 31, 1816), he was *the* bishop. Coke and Whatcoat, whether they liked it or not, were assistant bishops. William McKendree, whose service in that office overlapped Asbury's by eight years, was too much like the prototype to be anybody's assistant. But, even he deferred to the patriarch as a matter of prudence.

Asbury's concept of his authority says much about his concept of the office. In 1805 he listed in his journal the sources of his authority: a divine call, seniority in America, election by the Christmas Conference, ordination by Coke and others, and "because the signs of an apostle have been seen in me." He had followed Wesley's reasoning about the office of bishop in the early church, and had read such books as William Cave, *Apostolici; or, History of the Apostles and Fathers* (1677), and Jean Ostervald, *The Grounds and Principles of the Christian Religion* (1704). A whole literature appeared defending the origins of Methodist episcopacy, typified by Nathan Bangs's compilation, *An Original Church of Christ; or, A Scriptural Vindication of the Orders and Powers of the Ministry of the Methodist Episcopal Church* (1837), and Ezekiel Cooper's unpublished notes on "Ordination and Succession."

Hamby Barton, "The Definition of the Episcopal Office in American Methodism," (Diss., Drew, 1960); Norman W. Spellman, "The General Superintendency in American Methodism, 1784–1870," (Diss., Yale, 1961); Gerald F. Moede, *The Office of Bishop in Methodism, Its History and Development* (1964).

[22] Robert Bull, "George Roberts' Reminiscences of Francis Asbury," *MH*, 5 (July, 1967): 25-35; esp. 30-31, 33.

Needless to say, critical responses from non-Methodist sources were not lacking.

The early disciplines listed the duties of these general superintendents as follows: fix the appointments; preside in conferences; change, receive, and suspend preachers; travel throughout the connection; oversee spiritual and temporal business; and ordain bishops, elders, and deacons. The chief point of significance is that the bishops symbolized the connectional system which bound Methodism together in a tightly disciplined unity. Bishops were *superintendents;* they were *general* superintendents; they were *itinerant* general superintendents. Coke's and Asbury's notes hit home: "It would be a disgrace to our episcopacy, to have bishops settled on their plantations here and there, evidencing to all the world, that instead of breathing the spirit of their office, they could, without remorse, *lay down their crown,* and bury the most important talents God has given to men!"[23]

Of Coke much has already been said. Although he was the senior bishop, his equivocal relation to American Methodism and his wide-ranging interests which included England, Ireland, the West Indies, and eventually India, prevented his full acceptance as leader. Whatcoat, the most unassuming bishop the church has ever seen, would rather have been a servant in the household of the Lord. In fact, that is how he viewed his office. Nicholas Snethen characterized him as follows:

> In his neat, plain, parson's grey, after returning from the devotions of the closet, a painter or a statuary might have taken him as a model for a representation of piety. The mild, the complacent, and the dignified, were so happily blended in his looks, as to fill the beholder with reverence and love. His speech was somewhat slow and drawling; but not disagreeable after a little; his excellent matter came so warm from the heart, that a genial spirit of devotion never failed to kindle and blaze afresh, under its sounds, his very appearance in the pulpit did his hearers good.[24]

Whatcoat's distaste for controversy has already been noted. It resulted in frequent periods of depression. "May God break the Snare of Satan," he wrote in his journal. The conditions of his election as bishop in 1800 pained him. The tie vote with Jesse Lee, the first in a long and distinguished line of "almost bishops," brought excruciating tension. Until he died (1806), he was quite willing to serve humbly as Asbury's assistant.

[23] *The Doctrines and Discipline of the Methodist Episcopal Church* (1798), 44.

[24] Snethen, *Lay Representation,* 81; Whatcoat, "Journal," 20 Nov. 1792.

It was quite different with William McKendree, tough home-spun product of the western frontier. Like Wesley, Rankin, and Asbury, he would play second fiddle to no one. We see him as a young man caught up in the O'Kelly movement and rescued by Asbury. We see him as spokesman for Western Methodism, taking the General Conference of 1808, which elected him bishop, by storm with a powerful sermon. If he made a few sophisticated easterners uneasy with his frontier ways, he embodied the growing power of the west in the affairs of both church and state. He is the bishop who introduced what later became the standard practice of cabinet consultation on ministerial appointments. He got around Asbury's objections to this innovation adroitly by explaining that, unlike his old father in the faith, he needed the help of the presiding elders. But, as his role in the reform movement of the 1820s amply illustrates, he was no democratic, reforming bishop.

With the death of Asbury, the office of bishop changed perceptibly. Enoch George and Robert R. Roberts were elected at the General Conference of 1816. A plan of episcopal supervision was arranged. Without exception, they adhered strictly to the Asburian ideal of an itinerant general superintendency. There was, as yet, nothing of diocesan episcopacy. The constitution of 1808 protected this institution from any tinkering by the general conference. In this context, then, the reform movement of the 1820s became a challenge to the Asburian concept of episcopacy as fixed in the constitution. The office of presiding elder became the focal point of the attack.

Chapter 13
Westward East

There is something powerfully symbolic about the little company of three men who laboriously crossed the Cumberland Gap in September, 1800. They were the Bishops Francis Asbury and Richard Whatcoat, accompanied by young William McKendree, newly appointed presiding elder of the Western District, the only district in the entire open-ended Western Conference. The historic Wilderness Road which they traversed had only recently been widened to accommodate wagons. The land was still almost entirely howling wilderness. They were on their way to the first session of the Western Conference, which convened in Bethel Academy, Jessamine County, Kentucky on October 6, ten preachers attending. Circuit rider Tobias Gibson, after a difficult trip to Cumberland country, embarked in a canoe on a seven-hundred-mile voyage down the Cumberland, Ohio, and Mississippi rivers to begin his work in Natchez. That same year, Johnny Appleseed began scattering tracts and apple seeds in the Ohio Valley, and the Public Land Act (Harrison Land Law) authorized the sale of 320-acre parcels at two dollars an acre.

The westward movement of Methodism cannot be viewed in proper perspective apart from the backdrop of national expansion. A systematic comparison between the two offers rich insight. A beginning may be made with the admission of states and the organization of annual conferences in the eastern part.

In most cases, the annual conference was organized between territorial status and statehood. In only seven cases was a state admitted before the conference was organized. Missouri forms a complete web: territory in 1812, Missouri Conference (original) in 1816, state in 1821, Missouri Conference (divided) in 1824. Above all in importance is the interrelationship between the Northwest Ordinance of 1787 and the Western Conference of 1796. A further web of relations is shown by comparing the organization of territories and the development of early circuits.

These exercises in the relationship of space and time provide a new method of placing the westward expansion of Methodism in proper context. In proceeding to a brief survey of that expansion, we are reminded that in this case, as in so many others, the history of Methodism is inextricably bound with the history of the United States. In this chapter we reach the Mississippi River.

The Other Side of the Alleghenies

Although there was no master plan for the westward expansion of Methodism, there seemed to be, because of the peculiar polity of the church. The effective combination of local preachers and traveling preachers was perfectly suited to the environment of the frontier. It was the *combination* of the two that worked the wonders. The famous circuit rider would have been severely limited without the able service of the local preacher, who was his complement. If the traveling preacher provided the necessary mobility, the local preacher provided the perseverance for survival. Frequently, the circuit rider penetrated a scattered wilderness community only to discover that a local preacher—or exhorter—or class leader—had already begun to organize a society. Nevertheless, the adaptability of the traveling form of ministry made possible the systematic pursuit of the frontier following the westward movement of the people. The growth of Methodism may best be observed in two specific cases, and the process was repeated endlessly in other frontier areas: Holston in eastern Tennessee and Redstone in western Pennsylvania.

The Holston River is one of several main sources of the Tennessee River. In a region dominated by mountain ridges running northeast and southwest, the French Broad cuts northwest through the Great Smoky Mountains from present-day Asheville to Knoxville as does the Nolichucky, its tributary. Flowing northwest, the Watauga River cuts through from the watershed of the Yadkin Valley to the Holston. The Holston, the Clinch, and the Powell run from the watershed of the New River southwest, joining the French Broad to form the Tennessee near Knoxville. The New and Yadkin provide access from the Shenandoah Valley and the southeast. Just across one more mountain ridge—Cumberland Mountain—via the renowned Cumberland Gap flow the upper reaches of the great Cumberland River. By this magnificent river system the way was open from the Shenandoah region of Virginia along the rivers and over the gaps to the seemingly endless wilderness of the Tennessee and Cumberland watersheds, which is to say, present-day Kentucky and Tennessee, with easy access across the Ohio to the northwest and to the gulf regions to the southwest. This river-mountain system is crucial for understanding movements west and especially for the beginnings of Methodism in Holston country.

This was the land of the Holston Circuit, one of the two in existence beyond the Alleghenies before the organization of the Methodist Episcopal Church in 1784. When it was first formed in 1783, the region had only recently been opened and was sparsely settled. Only a few years before, Daniel Boone had cut his narrow trace across Cumberland Gap into what Richard Whatcoat in his journal calls "Coontucky" or "Cantuck." Horsemen and hikers could follow his trail up the New River into the Holston Valley through Sapling Grove (Bristol), then either down the valley to the Tennessee or across Clinch Mountain via Moccasin Gap and on across the Cumberland Gap into Cumberland country. Not until 1796 was the Wilderness Road widened sufficiently to permit passage of wagons.

By 1787, the work was so well developed that a division was made, in which the Holston became two circuits, Holston and Nolichucky, each centered in its own river valley. Already Acuff's Chapel (near Blountville, a Methodist historical shrine) and a few other buildings for worship were in use. This division, amoeba-like, is typical of one of the two chief methods of Methodist expansion. It would be repeated thousands of times westward. The Holston-Nolichucky division thus becomes a classic prototype. John Smith and Thomas Ware were among the early circuit riders.[1] The former was more closely associated with the early Greenbriar Circuit just north of Holston. He records how, in 1786, he penetrated into the mountains beyond the Potomac, along the "Little Yaw" (Casselman Creek) and the "Big Yaw" (Youghiogheny River), where he obtained a fine view to the west, "which put me in mind of Moses's Vewing the Land of Canian from Pisgahs top." Ware's autobiography is full of poignant descriptions of the rigors of circuit rider life. In 1787 on the Nolichucky Circuit, he remarked on the problems of overnight accommodation which forced him "to lodge in open log-cabins, with light bed-clothing, and frequently with several children in the same bed." One of the better cabins was that of Edward Cox, who was one of the first Methodists in Holston country. A handsome two-story double log cabin with a central "dog trot" (breezeway), it still stands near Bluff City as a Methodist historical shrine. Cox entertained the preachers whenever they passed on their rounds.

[1] Both wrote accounts. Smith's has been published in part by Lawrence Sherwood in the *Journal of the Greenbriar Historical Society,* 1 (Oct., 1966): 12-41. The original is in Garrett Theological Seminary. Ware wrote *Sketches of the Life and Travels of Rev. Thomas Ware* (1842). The quotes are from Smith, 14, and Ware, 135; cf. 132-50.

Associated with, but not a division of, Holston was the Greenbriar Circuit, the farthest north, in New River country (West Virginia), formed in 1787 by Smith. Another historical shrine, Rehoboth Chapel, lies in this area, near Union. Farthest south was the French Broad Circuit, laid out by Ware in 1788. The same year, the New River Circuit was formed from the eastern end of the Holston Circuit. This grand assembly of five wilderness circuits led Francis Asbury to hold the first ✳ session of an annual conference west of the Alleghenies, May 13, 1788 in the home of Stephen Keywood. Asbury commented, "The weather was cold; the room without fire, and otherwise uncomfortable. We nevertheless made out to keep our seats, until we had finished the essential parts of our business." [2] Apart from a few changes (divisions and mergers), the Methodist work in Holston country was stabilized for the rest of the century.

A second major method of expansion is also illustrated by Holston. In 1786, a Kentucky Circuit was established. This was the result of planned development along the Wilderness Road, using Holston Circuit as a point of departure. Ware's work in setting up the French Broad Circuit is much the same thing. Thus, as established circuits multiplied themselves like amoebas by division, runners went out into new areas, like creeping ground plants, putting down new roots in virgin land. Detailed geographical case studies, such as Holston and Redstone, are highly instructive on the manner of the spread of Methodism over thousands of miles, although the prototypes become less typical in the complex developments beyond the Mississippi River.

The other major nucleus of Methodism west of the Alleghenies before 1784 was the Redstone Circuit, formed that year. Western Pennsylvania, like eastern Tennessee, was dependent for its development on a system of rivers. Access was either overland or along valleys via the Potomac to Fort Cumberland, then up Wills Creek and over the watershed to Casselman Creek, and down the Youghiogheny River to the Monongahela (the present route of the Baltimore and Ohio Railroad). Thomas Cresap and Christopher Gist had done around the mid-eighteenth century what Boone did for the Wilderness Road. Their traces preceded the famous Braddock's and Forbes's roads which were hewn during the French and Indian War. They were still stump-strewn trails when the end of the Revolution signaled the beginning of the great push west. Once over the mountains, however, the way west was open via one of the finest highways nature ever provided—*La Belle Rivière* as the French *voyageurs* called it, the Ohio

[2] *Journal*, I, 572 (May, 1788).

River. Formed by the junction of Allegheny and Monongahela rivers at Fort Pitt, the mighty stream swept around a vast curve northwest before coursing along its southwestward way to form the southern borders of Ohio country. At convenient intervals, large rivers—the Beaver, Muskingum, Scioto, Miami, Wabash—provided open access to the lands of the great Northwest Territory, organized in 1787, just three years after the formation of the Redstone Circuit in southwestern Pennsylvania. Kentucky was available on the other side.

While Redstone was going through the same process of division and expansion seen in Holston, western lands were being surveyed and opened by a combination of governmental and private enterprise. By 1790, the Ohio country was already divided into publicly held areas (the Seven Ranges, the Virginia Military Reserve, and the Western Reserve) and huge tracts held for private development (the Ohio Company, the Scioto Company, and Symmes Purchase). In 1796, Ebenezer Zane cut the trace that bears his name from Wheeling to Maysville. On April 16, 1811, work began on the congressionally authorized national road designed to run graded without stumps all the way from Cumberland to St. Louis. By 1818, it was open to Wheeling, by 1837 to the Indiana line. Another federal road was planned to run to Natchez and New Orleans. Least used by Methodists was the remaining great route to the west, the Great Genesee Road across New York state.

Redstone Circuit was the original base for Methodism in the area. It ran over an immense region on both sides of the Monongahela River, and stretched at points as far west as the Ohio River and thirty miles south into (West) Virginia.[3] For three years it remained a single circuit. Then in 1787, as a result of growth many times over and the increasing significance of the area for the entire westward movement, it was divided into three: Ohio, the portion to the northwest and reaching across the river around Beaver Creek; Clarksburg, to the southwest up the Monongahela; and Redstone. In 1788, surprisingly delayed, perhaps, because the Presbyterians had preempted the region, came the Pittsburgh Circuit, formed by Robert R. Roberts, later bishop. A fifth circuit, Randolph, was the "hard-luck" circuit located in the mountains east of the Clarksburg Circuit. It lasted only three years. In 1793, came the Washington (Greenfield) Circuit in the far southwest corner of Pennsylvania. All these circuits developed from a combination of division and new expansion. These five circuits settled the

[3] See map in Wallace Guy Smeltzer, *Methodism on the Headwaters of the Ohio* (1951), 50. This excellent conference history provides full information on the development of the church in western Pennsylvania and nearby regions.

organization of Methodism in the area for the rest of the century.

From 1799 on, new circuits sprang up from Redstone in hopscotch fashion on both sides of the Ohio River and northward to Lake Erie: Little Kanawha (West Viriginia), 1799; Muskingum, 1799; West Wheeling, 1802; Hockhocking (southern Ohio), 1803; Guyandotte (Sandy River, West Virginia, and Kentucky), 1804; and northward, Shenango, 1800; Erie, 1801; Deerfield (Ohio), 1803. At this stage the expansion via Holston and Redstone met. In 1799, the Scioto Circuit was formed by expansion north from Kentucky. Northern Kentucky, southern Ohio and southern Indiana were the merging areas. But, the dominant force was the Ohio River, which inexorably drew the connectional arms of Methodism downstream toward confluence with the Mississippi River at Cairo.

On to the Mississippi

The first notable visit by Methodists to Ohio country had been recorded by John Smith in his journal. On June, 26, 1786, he "crost the great Ohio over into the Indian Contry in company with Mr. Asbury[,] Henry[,] and several others. This river runs into the Missesippy bordering upon south Amarica inhabited by the Spanyards."[4] After sporadic visitation and preaching, Francis McCormick, a local preacher from Kentucky, formed the first class north of the Ohio in 1797. John Kobler was the circuit rider who regularized a circuit up and down the Big and Little Miami rivers above Losantiville (Cincinnati). This circuit, together with Scioto and those spawned from Redstone, provided a vigorous start for Ohio Methodism. The movement there was certainly not harmed by the fact that the first governor of the state, Edward Tiffin, was an active Methodist local preacher. A society in Marietta, then the seat of provincial government for the Northwest Territory, was formed in 1799 by Robert Manley. Benjamin Young, Elisha Bowman, James Quinn, John Sale, and Shadrach Bostwick, a physician and local preacher around Deerfield, were among the early founders. Similar development took place farther down the Ohio. In 1803, Benjamin Young was appointed "a Mitionary to the Illinoies" from the Western Conference. His severe difficulties were not a propitious beginning in the great Methodist state of Illinois. Finally, Joseph Oglesby stretched his Illinois Circuit across the Mississippi River in 1804 to visit Missouri, which became a formal circuit in 1807.

[4] "Journal," in *Journal of the Greenbriar Historical Society,* 1 (Oct., 1966): 15. Kobler's MS Journal is in Lovely Lane Museum and is partly printed in Gaddis, *Footprints,* 504-11.

The spread of Methodism into the rest of the Northwest Territory followed in order—except for Michigan, which received its beginnings from Canada after the War of 1812. The career of Alfred Brunson, the long-lived curmudgeon of the old northwest frontier, covers the development of Methodism during this stage. When he was sent to Detroit, he wondered why he, with a large family, was sent to so forsaken a circuit (fourteen members in the city and a hundred thirty on the whole circuit). He speculated that the purpose was "to try me, and decide whether I would obey the appointing power." [5] His circuit included the entire territory except Sault St. Marie, and counted preaching places in Pontiac and along rivers like Clinton and Rouge and Raisin, down to the Maumee, and back along the lake road fifty-eight miles to Detroit. It took a month to get around the twelve preaching appointments. In the 1830s, he was busy on the Wisconsin frontier, using Prairie du Chien as a center. There he organized a class of ten persons, the first "north and west of the Wisconsin River."

Inevitably, he came into confrontation with that other lion of the frontier, Peter Cartwright. At the Illinois Conference of 1836, he got into a fiery debate with the hero of Illinois, which bade fair once again to set the irresistible force against the immovable object. According to his own testimony, a crisis was avoided only when he realized that a personal struggle for power was developing. The figure of Cartwright is so familiar that nothing need be said of him here, except to indicate his role as one of many who struggled not so much to plant Methodism as to make it grow. Methodism had started early in southern Illinois, but was slower in reaching the northern parts, which belonged to the frontier region of Michigan and Wisconsin. The first preacher who worked in the area of the Rock River Conference was one John Dew, who was sent under Presiding Elder Cartwright in 1828 to Galena in the far northwest corner of the state, where lead mining had drawn several hundred people, and a local preacher had already formed a class meeting. He beat the Presbyterians by one year, but both denominations cooperated.[6] These two groups, along with the Baptists, arrived in Chicago only a year after James Thomson platted the city. Jesse Walker began preaching, but a society was first organized the next year by S. R. Beggs. Walker was always more interested in Indian missions. The first session of the Rock River Conference took place in 1840, when the Illinois Conference was divided.

[5] Brunson, *A Western Pioneer* I, 265; II, 63.

[6] See A. D. Field, *Memorials of Methodism in the Bounds of Rock River Conference* (1886), 26, 29; 49, 66, 69, 196-97. See also G. Gordon Melton, *Log Cabins to Steeples* (1974).

In this way Methodism made the Old Northwest her homeland. Almost every town and village, even crossroads, from Pittsburgh to Prairie du Chien, had its little Methodist church. The man who had originally put the whole thing together was William McKendree. In 1800 he had come full of vigor across the Cumberland Gap to take charge of the Western District. His election as bishop in 1808 did not change his way of life or his commitment to the work in the west. No man more completely personified the westward movement of Methodism, at least west to the Mississippi.[7] He grew up with the Western Conference, which began with one "Kentucky District" with the entire operation under his presiding eldership. Henry Boehm has left a warm description of the Western Conference of 1808, which took place at Liberty Hill, a little west of Nashville. They met in the house of Green Hill, the same local preacher who had housed the first annual conference after the Christmas Conference in North Carolina, 1785. This was the first annual conference McKendree attended as bishop. The eighty ministers ate and slept in tents, which were conveniently close to the lively camp meeting grounds. Boehm met the presiding elders, Learner Blackman, William Burke, John Sale, Jacob Young, and James Ward. He also met Jesse Walker and Peter Cartwright. But, apart from the venerable Asbury, the dominant figure, new to the episcopal chair, was McKendree. Like Asbury, he left an indelible mark on Methodism, but in the west.

All the while, the same process was going on all over the Old Southwest. Kentucky was occupied by circuits based on the Wilderness Road to Harrodsburg and Boonesborough. Francis Poythress, from 1788 until his mental health broke, was the dominant figure. Cumberland, in central Tennessee, became another center from which circuits were spawned. In 1787, Benjamin Ogden formed a circuit which ran up and down the river around present-day Nashville. In the fall of 1800 Tobias Gibson made his famous canoe trip down the Mississippi to Natchez, holding his appointment from the South Carolina Conference! A year later the circuit became part of the Western Conference. When Gibson died in 1804, he was followed in the slow, uphill struggle in that area by Learner Blackman and Nathan Barnes.

Holland McTyeire struck home with his comment on the unique challenge of planting Methodism in lands long occupied by Spaniards and French. He noted that the gospel plowshare never struck into harder soil than in Louisiana. "Elsewhere in the Valley of the Missis-

[7] Albea Godbold, "Bishop William McKendree and His Contribution to Methodism," *MH*, 8 (Apr., 1970): 3-12. Henry Boehm, *Reminiscences* (1865), 206-7.

sippi the itinerant preacher sowed the seed of the gospel in virgin soil; but in Louisiana tares had been long and plentifully scattered and cultivated." [8] Gibson's and Blackman's frustration in New Orleans was shared by Elisha Bowman and William Winans, none of whom was successful enough to get a Methodist church built in the city. That came only in the early 1820s.

Elsewhere in the deep South, however, Methodism took ready root. Early circuits were formed in the first decade of the nineteenth century—for example, Claiborne in Mississippi and Tombigbee in Alabama. Another movement was at work here, stretching westward around the south end of the Appalachians, a continuation of the southward expansion which had spread Methodism throughout what is known as the Southeastern Jurisdiction. There was the New Hope Circuit from 1778, which led to development in the Cape Fear Valley and of North Carolina in the 1790s.[9] There were Charleston, which dated from Asbury's visit in 1785, and Peedee. There were the Washington and Savannah circuits, where Hope Hull began as he devoted his life to Georgia Methodism. West to Alabama, the Tombigbee Circuit was organized in 1807. In this way another pincers movement, similar to that which brought forces from Holston and Redstone together along the Ohio River, pressed into the Gulf states and made another homeland for Methodism.

Expansion northward into New England was comparable to the rest, except for one major difference: the competition of the theologically astute New England clergy, which is better told in the context of theological development. That expansion carried across the border from New England into Nova Scotia and from New York into Lower and Upper Canada.[10] The point should be made that most of the early settlers from the United States were not English, but Dutch, Scotch, and German. Among them were the Hecks, Emburys, Switzers, and Ruckles of earlier fame in New York. Thus, when William Losee went to Canada in 1790 (formal appointment only in 1791), he found class meetings already under way. He formed a class in Hay Bay in 1791 and in the next year built the church which still survives, the first church on the first circuit in upper Canada.[11] After the break occasioned by the War of 1812, the Genesee Conference undertook to

---

[8] Holland McTyeire, *History of Methodism* (1884), 548-49. On Blackman, see Robert B. Steelman in *MH,* 5 (Apr., 1967): 8 ff; also Nola Mae McFillen in *idem,* 35-44.

[9] See C. Franklin Grill, *Methodism in the Upper Cape Fear Valley* (1966).

[10] See unpublished manuscript by Norman A. McNairn, "Mission to the North," 1970, which contains much valuable data, esp. 48, 52.

[11] See Arthur Reynolds, "The Story of Hay Bay Church, 1792-1964," pamphlet, n.d., 22 pages.

restore the work, but it was hampered by the political tensions of the times. William Strong, from the British Wesleyan Missionary Society, came on invitation to Montreal in 1814. From then on, Methodism in Canada was divided, more or less, into American and British sections. In 1817, the Genesee Conference was held for the first time in Canada. Nathan Bangs was among the American Methodists active in Canadian work.

The results of this spectacular expansion can be seen in the statistics for membership and in the multiplication of annual conferences after 1796, when the first six were defined. The general minutes record a membership of 64,894 in 1800. By 1850, including the three branches then in existence, the figure was 1,259,906.[12] That meant a growth rate of almost twentyfold (1,939 percent). During the same half century, the general population increased from some 5,308,000 to 23,192,000, four and a third times over (437 percent). In 1800, Methodists comprised about 1.2 percent, of the total population; in 1850, they had about 5.4 percent. These figures do not include the important numbers of other Methodist groups, especially the black denominations, two of which were thriving (African Methodist Episcopal and African Methodist Episcopal Zion). With statistics like these to play with, what wonder that Methodists were said to be obsessed with numbers! There was a certain intoxication with the miracle of growth. God had indeed blessed America, but his favor appeared to have fallen more bountifully upon the Methodists. At least, so it seemed to many Methodists at mid-century.

Of course, Methodism did not have the field to itself. The Baptists, with their farmer-preachers and independent spirit, were always running neck and neck, providing an exciting competition, especially in the South. The Presbyterians, in spite of theological and ecclesiastical tensions, were able to adapt effectively to the frontier without running the risk of "barbarism," a charge they leveled against Methodists and Baptists. Many circuit riders developed feelings of inferiority when confronted by a well-trained, theologically sophisticated Presbyterian minister. Of course, not all Presbyterian ministers actually came up to that standard; nor were all Methodist preachers ignoramuses. All three of these groups, each in its own way, adjusted to the conditions of the frontier and marked up many victories. New England Congregationalists like Horace Bushnell and Lyman Beecher (*Barbarism, The First Danger* (1847) and *A Plea for the West*

[12] *M.E.:* 1790, 57,631; 1810, 174,560; 1820, 256,881; 1830, 476,153; 1840, 580,098; 1850, 689,682. *M.P.:* 1830, c. 5,000; 1840, 41,600; 1850, 65,694. *M.E.S.:* 1850, 504,530. All these figures reflect a lag of one year in reporting.

(1835) might fret over the peril inherent in a growing West versus a shrinking East, but the Presbyterians, Baptists, and Methodists were busy doing something about it. In areas to which New Englanders migrated, such as the Western Reserve and Marietta, Congregationalism flourished and offered a different kind of competition to the frontier groups. All Protestants found hard going in the established Roman Catholic cultures of the French and Spanish settlements along the Mississippi.

The net effect of this westing experience on the nation and the churches is difficult to pin down. In many ways Americans remained the same. Until after the Civil War the country was agrarian, individualistic, and suspicious of power in high places. But, in other ways, the movement was a *new* thing which brought out differences. Some of these are discussed in the next chapter.

Chapter 14
Revivalism and Camp Meetings

Culturally speaking, revivalism is to be seen in the context of romanticism as it found expression in the Romantic movement of the late eighteenth and early nineteenth centuries. An early form of it has already been noted as the Great Awakening of the 1740s. As the Methodist Episcopal Church got under way and began its spectacular westward advance, another wave of revivalism spread over American Protestantism. Only two years after the formation of the church, in 1787, Methodists in Virginia were caught up in an exciting experience. Romanticism found expression in the rather sophisticated intellectual movements associated with people like Thoreau, Irving, and Longfellow, and especially in New England Transcendentalism. It also found expression in a more popular form of emotional religion which led to mass revivals and the camp meeting. People, generally, would know nothing of literary and philosophical romanticism; but they knew from personal experience all about conversion.

Revivalism

One should not make the mistake of assuming that what is called the Second Great Awakening, toward the end of the eighteenth century, was solely a frontier phenomenon. A reminder that at Yale, under Timothy Dwight, one-third of the student body was converted should redress the balance. This revival took place as readily on college campuses and in cities as it did in the primitive wilderness of Kentucky. The revivalistic spirit, which found classic expression in the Great Awakening, pervaded American religion and left a permanent mark. Its influence varied from denomination to denomination and from region to region. It was particularly important for the development of Baptists, Methodists, and Presbyterians. It helped define southern culture as a special way of life.[1] None was more deeply affected than Methodism. After the first truly ecumenical phase, Baptists and Presbyterians, concerned about closed communion and theological purity, began to have second thoughts about what some

[1] See the stimulating monograph by John B. Bales, *The Great Revival, 1787–1805, The Origins of the Southern Evangelical Mind* (1972), esp. 94-95, 100. Criticism of the "new measures" is typified by John W. Nevin, *The Anxious Bench* (1844).

regarded as the excesses of revivalism. Methodists rode out the storm, mastered the wild forces, and eventually settled down like the rest.

It is idle to speculate about the causes of such historical manifestations as revivals. Reasons and explanations can vary from direct intervention of the Holy Spirit to earthquakes. Indeed, the great midwest earthquake of 1811 did have a measurable effect on response to religious appeals. Both James B. Finley and Peter Cartwright testify to the reverberations in western Methodism. A great increase in membership was recorded in the Western Conference in 1812.[2] All one can justifiably say is that revivals tend to come in waves, following longer or shorter periods of disinterest.

In the wake of the Revolution such a revival broke out in Virginia, especially in 1787. An earlier revival in the same parts in 1776 had been reported by Devereux Jarratt.[3] This was a strong movement, but limited in extent. Around the turn of the century something arose which covered almost all regions and almost all churches—the Second Great Awakening. Methodists shared fully in its manifestations and took up its spirit permanently as part of the Methodist way. Not only in Virginia but throughout the church revivals broke out and mass conversions were reported.[4] These revivals took place both in and out of churches.

As the nineteenth century wore on, the forms of revivalism changed to fit the times. The most significant figure in the entire period was Charles G. Finney, a Presbyterian-Congregationalist deeply influenced by Wesleyan perfectionism. He began his work in New England and the East, and in 1835 became professor of theology in Oberlin, Ohio, where a new seminary was rising. He personifies the individualistic approach to religion, which emphasizes the importance of personal religious experience as a basis, not only for religious life of the individual, but also for the ultimate transformation of society. Society will change by changing people. This outlook was congenial to a society which accepted the *laissez-faire* philosophy of social development and government. He did not ignore the social ramifications of Christianity; rather he recognized them as inherent in the conversion of individuals. He represents the end result of the

[2] See Walter B. Posey, "The Earthquake of 1811 and Its Influence on Evangelistic Methods in the Churches of the Old South," *Tennessee Historical Magazine*, 1 (Jan., 1931).

[3] Sweet, *Virginia Methodism*, 121; Leroy M. Lee, *The Life and Times of The Rev. Jesse Lee* (1856), 204.

[4] See, for example, the Baltimore Conference area, (in G. P. Baker, ed. *Those Incredible Methodists* (1972), 89) where two hundred conversions were reported even at the meeting of the General Conference in 1800!

changing New England theology, from the Calvinism of Edwards through the various stages of the "new theology" to the theology of revivalism.[5]

At all stages in the revival, Methodism was involved, along with many other denominations. Mention of Phoebe Palmer, a Methodist lay woman who was active in the New York revivals beginning in 1857, is illustrative. She is best considered in the context of the holiness movement. Whether these revivals took place in the urban East or the rural West, in churches or in wilderness groves, Methodism was caught up and marked. However, the rise of the camp meeting was crucial.

Camp Meetings

The romanticism inherent in the camp meeting is illustrated by a comment of A. P. Mead as he recalled his camp meeting days in *Manna in the Wilderness:* "The heart that has offered incense at the cross, is best prepared to kneel at nature's shrine." [6] Throughout his memoirs two themes are intertwined: strongly emotional personal religious experience and a woodsy setting. Both are essential. Other religious communities have emphasized an emotional or enthusiastic response, and others, usually through poverty or persecution, have held meetings outdoors in a forest setting. The American camp meeting is almost unique in giving positive emphasis to both.

The institution of the camp meeting went through several distinct stages. The first stage, lasting only a few years, took place in an ecumenical relationship which included Presbyterians, Baptists, and Methodists. It also exhibited some of the cruder expressions of excessive emotionalism, such as the "jerks" and other physical manifestations. These, it must be emphasized, were largely limited to the early years and to Kentucky and Tennessee. Already by 1805, only four years after the traditional beginning of the movement, the physical displays declined. The closer to the actual frontier, the stronger the emotional expression. The explanation of this phenomenon lies

[5] In the huge literature on revivalism the following books are recommended: Charles C. Cole, *Social Ideas of the Northern Evangelists, 1826–1860* (1954); Whitney R. Cross, *The Burned-Over District: Social and Intellectual History of Enthusiastic Religion in Western New York* (1950); Sydney G. Dimond, *The Psychology of the Methodist Revival* (1926); Charles A. Johnson, *The Frontier Camp Meeting* (1955); Timothy Smith, *Revivalism and Social Reform* (1957); W. W. Sweet, *Revivalism in America* (1944); Bernard A. Weisberger, *They Gathered at the River* (1958).

[6] A. P. Mead, *Manna in the Wilderness; or, The Grove and its Altar, Offerings and Thrilling Incidents. Containing a History of the Origin and Rise of Camp Meetings, and a Defense of this Remarkable Means of Grace; also, An Account of the Wyoming Camp Meeting* (1860), 415.

mainly in the loneliness and isolation characteristic of frontier life. Camp meetings were the few occasions when people were gathered together in large numbers. The result was sometimes explosive.

After an intermission occasioned by the War of 1812, the revivals returned, but they tended to become somewhat more decorous. In some regions, camp meetings never displayed the extreme behavior which turned some people away. In the Old Southwest, the camp meetings long retained some of the early features. They also reflected the development of southern culture, as the habit developed of holding two meetings simultaneously side by side, one white and one black.[7] Sometimes, it was said, the Blacks would go on with their meeting into the small hours, long after the white seekers of salvation had gone to bed. This was the environment for the creation of a major form of church music, the Negro spiritual. Around the flickering campfires were heard the rich harmonies of "Roll, Jordan, Roll"; "O Sinner, Run to Jesus"; and "Hark, from the Tomb the Doleful Sound."

If the excesses of the participants subsided, the obstreperousness of the hangers-on persisted. Most large camp meetings had their outer fringes, in which worldlings gathered for reasons of curiosity, business, or plain orneriness. Accounts are full of descriptions of troubles with "rowdies" and the measures taken against them. This gave currency to the saying, "The good people go to camp meetings Friday, backsliders Saturday, rowdies Saturday night, and gentleman and lady sinners Sunday." Francis Asbury was usually able to keep control of a situation by his mere presence. One time, Jacob Young reports, Asbury came to the stand near midnight and within a quarter hour had brought a chaotic crowd to complete silence. He took advantage of the opportunity to remind the trouble-makers that, though the Methodists were all seeking salvation, they were not yet all sanctified and might be provoked to retaliate.[8] They had a remarkably quiet night.

Alfred Brunson was quite capable of taking care of his own quelling. Claiming to be a patient man, he said, "I could bear to be ridden over crosswise; but when it came lengthwise, and rough shod at that, I could not help squirming a little. I could bear a large amount of personal abuse, but when the Church and the cause of God were imposed upon, I could but feel the lion in me rise." He had a way of singling out a few rowdies to make them conspicuous and then ex-

[7] Johnson, *The Frontier Camp Meeting,* 114-15.
[8] Young, *Autobiography of a Pioneer* (1857), 295-96. Compare the similar account in J. B. Finley, *Autobiography* (1853), 252-53.

coriating them for their violation of the Constitution and laws of the land and their defiance of God. It was quite enough to make them skulk off. Maxwell Gaddis told of a unique scheme for overawing the trouble-makers. Gathering together the chief singers, elders, and young men, a battalion was formed with a trumpeteer leading, which marched around the fringes of the camp crying, "The sword of the Lord and' of Gideon." In closer concentric circles the rowdies were driven toward the center of the camp, where many of them broke down in terror.[9]

These were some of the negative and unproductive aspects. Let those who shared in these events describe the indelible experiences they carried with them the rest of their lives. Shadrach Bostwick wrote, in a letter to Laban Clark in 1820:

> The Lord was eminantly present at our Camp Meeting, Braceville, May 28th, 29, 30. On the Sab[bath] and through the night the mighty power of God came down, and it was supposed that about thirty precious souls were converted. Many more were deeply mourning which had not obtained peace. Satan and his host seem'd to try their utmosts to keep the ground and take the lead, but failed. The Hotest Cannonading was at the time of the sacrement, which was perform'd by Candle light Sunday Evening. The Cries of the wounded were heard, and their mourns pierced the Ear from every direction of the encampment. One mourning, trembling Candidate, ventured to the Table of the Lord on an Invitation given to such, of whom there were a number as Spectators. Peace poured upon his soul whilst communing, he arose shouting Glory, and called aloud, where is such and such and calling their names saying I have found the Lord, I've found the Lord![10]

William Milburn remembered that camp meeting time came "between the wheat harvest and the time for gathering corn."

> A grove of sugar maple or beech, with abundant springs and pasturage near at hand, is selected, and here the tents of canvas, logs, or weatherboards, are erected in the form of a parallelogram, inclosing from one to four acres. Within this area, upon which all the tents open, are arranged the seats, the altar, and the pulpit, or stand as it is called. Spaces for streets are left open at the four corners of the square. In the rear of each tent, a large, permanent table is erected; for the meeting is sacred to the rites of hospitality as well as of devotion. The tenters move into their temporary abodes on Thursday or Friday, and the religious exercises commence at once. A horn is blown about daylight as the signal for getting up; after a while, it sounds for family prayers, and soon you may hear strains of song from every tent, celebrating the praise of Him who hath given the slumber and safety of the night. The blast summons the

[9] Brunson, *A Western Pioneer*, I, 283; Gaddis, *Foot-prints of an Itinerant*, 160.
[10] Printed in F. A. Norwood, "Some Newly Discovered Unpublished Letters, 1808–1825," *MH*, 3 (July, 1965): 12-13.

people to the stand at eight and eleven A.M., at three P.M., and again at early candle-lighting. The meeting continues from four to six days. It is a grand sight to behold several hundreds—sometimes swelled to thousands—of people gathered beneath the shadow of the green wood, worshipping in the oldest and noblest of cathedrals; its aisles flanked by straight or twisted shafts springing from a verdant floor to a light, waving tracery unapproachable by man's poor art. The scene is one to furnish inspiration to the speaker, and to open for him the surest and swiftest access to the hearers' hearts. But it is at night that the ground wears its most picturesque appearance. From fire stands, placed at short distances over the encampment, heaps of blazing pine knots shed a brilliant light upon the assembly, and strive to illumine the dim, whispering vaults overhead, through which the stars, those candles of the Lord, may be seen blazing in their far distant sockets. Never have I been so moved by music, as when the great congregation have stood up on such a spot, and poured forth a hymn with one heart and voice.[11]

Or hear the recollection of Maxwell Gaddis of a camp meeting during his first year of itineracy:

On the last night of the meeting I was appointed to preach at seven o'clock; but at the time of sounding the trumpet for preaching the prayer meeting was still in progress, which had begun immediately after the close of the afternoon sermon. The lamps were all lighted and the wood-fires burning brightly. The altar was filled with weeping penitents; and when the time arrived for preaching, the battle-cry was so loud the sound of the trumpet was not heard by those engaged in the prayer meeting. It was finally agreed not to interrupt the altar exercises, but to let God work in his own way. The meeting progressed with power and great glory. Sinners by scores "fled for refuge to lay hold on the hope set before them." The exercises, without the slightest degree of abatement, continued till eleven o'clock . . . . As it was to be my farewell sermon, I selected for my text the following appropriate words: "Casting all your care upon him, for he careth for you." The scene before me was grand and imposing. The whole congregation were standing on their feet, and many already bathed in tears. At first my voice faltered, but I then heard the well-known voice of the venerable Collins behind me in the pulpit, saying, "Be not afraid of their faces, for the Lord hath given you the city." It gave me great encouragement . . . . The battle waxed hot the remainder of the night. More than fifty souls found peace in believing before the sun arose on our tents in the wilderness.[12]

After several days of what for many was an emotional jag, came the solemn, joyful, tearful day of parting. Sometimes an extensive ritual accompanied this leave-taking. The bell or the trumpet roused the exhausted campers, and a great bustle followed as packing to leave

[11] Milburn, *Ten Years of Preacher-Life*, 62-63.
[12] Gaddis, *Foot-Prints of an Itinerant*, 159, 161.

mingled with breakfast and morning devotions. Separate little groups prayed or sang hymns. The leader, who was sometimes the presiding elder, gave a final address. Then a great procession began around the inner circle, as everyone shared greeting and farewell with everyone else. Again A. P. Mead:

> The procession has passed, and now the ministers shake hands. The one at the extreme left turns to the right and, facing his brethren, begins the farewell. As he passes on, each in his turn imitates his example, until all have shaken hands. The scene is too touching for description. Our tears flow freely. O, beloved brethren, we shall be done by and by. We can sympathize with each other in our toils and trials. We are engaged in one work. Let us not count our lives dear unto ourselves, so that we may win Christ, and be found of him in peace. We have spent a week here in the grove, laboring for souls, and now we part.
>
> > When we asunder part,
> > It gives us inward pain;
> > We'll still be joined in heart,
> > And hope to meet again.[13]

This unashamed display of emotion may embarrass a twentieth-century gathering raised on less heady, more rational religious fare. But it may better be understood by a generation of youth accustomed to call one another "brothers" and "sisters." Fashions of romanticism are subject to change, as all else.

Around mid-century signs of decline set in. The camp meeting had settled into a rigid format and had become stereotyped. Books and pamphlets were published which endeavored to keep alive the spirit of the camp meeting and to give directions for its conduct. Most of these came from the pens of rearguard conservatives who sought to preserve the institution which had meant so much to them. The same thing was happening to the class meeting, and similar books were being written about it. The process was already under way which, within a quarter century, would transform the camp meeting into a chautauqua center, the chief purpose of which was not conversion, but either edification or education or both. The original Chautauqua Assembly was organized in New York State in 1874 by Bishop John H. Vincent and Lewis Miller, a manufacturer, both of whom were active in the Sunday school movement.

In spite of a decline in some areas, camp meetings continued in use, and some new ones were organized. Illinois had at least six centers, most of them begun after the Civil War. Ethnic branches had their own institutions. The first German *Lagerversammlung* was organized

---

[13] Mead, *Manna in the Wilderness*, 402-15.

in 1839 near Cincinnati.[14] While Lincoln was campaigning for president in 1860, the Swedish Methodists started the Des Plaines Camp Ground west of Chicago.

What came of all the furor and shouting? Most of the contemporary observers were very positive in their evaluations. Jesse Lee, who wrote before the camp meeting had progressed very far, was of the opinion that "It has been frequently observed, that there was never any remarkable revival of religion, but some degree of enthusiasm was mingled with it." [15] Nathan Bangs was more restrained, admitting that some problems attended camp meetings. But he, with the others, decided that what happened at camp meetings was a marvellous work of God.

Modern historians have differed in their judgments, and it is difficult to avoid the conclusion that their differences reflect more their own stance than any objective interpretation of the sources. One of the most balanced judgments is that of Charles Johnson, who discerns the working of the democratic spirit. A popular camp meeting song ran:

> Come hungry, come thirsty, come ragged, come bare,
> Come filthy, come lousy, come just as you are.

He sees in this "Methodist equalitarian theology" a powerful force which "helped lay the foundations for the reform crusade that aimed at the perfection of man and the moral state." [16] Much the same point is made by Timothy Smith, writing more broadly about revivalism in and after the mid-nineteenth century. The effect on individuals of the camp meeting, based so largely on emotional appeal, may have been impermanent. Many who were saved had to be saved all over again next year. The whole movement eventually fell into various stereotypes. Nevertheless, the camp meeting left its own permanent mark on Methodism, especially in the South. If some lost the marks of grace too easily, others retained deep convictions for the rest of their lives. Certainly, a church enlivened by camp meetings was not likely to suffer early senility.

---

[14] C. Ulrich, "Die erste deutsche Lagerversammlung in Amerika," *Der Christliche Apologete*, 51 (1889): 467; John O. Foster, "The First Des Plaines Camp Meeting, Des Plaines, Illinois, August, 1860," Illinois State Historical Society, *Journal*, 24 (Jan., 1932): 3-19.

[15] Lee, *Short History*, 50; Bangs, *History*, II, 113; Smith, *Revivalism and Social Reform*, passim.

[16] Johnson, *Frontier Camp Meeting*, 211, 176.

Chapter 15
The Beginnings of Black Methodism

Black people have been part of the Methodist story almost from the beginning. Although that part of the story has been told to some degree, it has usually been isolated from the accounts related to the Methodist Episcopal tradition, and it has not received the attention its importance deserves. As a result of the long neglect of the theme, many valuable sources have disappeared, or have never been collected in proper archives or published. The difficulties in the way of research in black Methodism, and in black church history generally, are monumental.[1]

The Negro in American Christianity

Out of about 5,300,000 Americans, over one million were black, about one-fifth of the population in 1800. Approximately one out of ten was free; the rest were slaves.[2] Although the slave population more than doubled by 1830, the proportion of free Blacks increased slightly to about one in seven in the decades before the Civil War.

Disagreement exists over the degree to which elements of African religion survived the traumatic transplanting of Africans to the Western Hemisphere. The evidence is clearer for movements to South America than to North America. Certainly, black religion contains elements other than Christianity, but there are disputes over specifics, such as the relation of native river cults in Africa to the popularity of Baptist beliefs among American black people.[3] Nevertheless, religion

[1] See however the bibliographical studies by William B. Gravely, "The Afro-American Methodist Tradition: A Review of Sources in Reprint," *MH*, 9 (Apr., 1971): 21-33; and Gordon Melton, *A Bibliography of Black Methodism* (1970). Other projects are under way to gather and preserve sources for the history of black Methodism, and include the archival efforts of the United Methodist Commission on Archives and History.

[2] Leonard L. Haynes, *The Negro Community Within American Protestantism* (1953), 85. One of the best general histories is Benjamin Quarles, *The Negro in the Making of America* (1964, rev. 1969). Excellent also are two books by E. Franklin Frazier, *The Negro in the United States* (1957), and *The Negro Church in America* (1963); the various works of John Hope Franklin; and J. R. Washington, Jr., *Black Religion: The Negro and Christianity in the United States* (1964).

[3] Cf. Frazier, *The Negro in the United States*, 15-16. Frazier believes the congregational polity of Baptists has been more influential.

among Negroes has some special characteristics which are rooted in the past. Furthermore, the black churches have enjoyed an almost unique relation to the black community, in so far as for long periods they have been the dominant institutional forms owned and controlled by black people. Five characteristics have been noted: the black churches (1) have been black-controlled; (2) have been involved in the everyday life of the people; (3) have given members a sense of worthiness, identity, "somebodiness"; (4) have emphasized evangelism with direct witness to saving love in Jesus Christ; and (5) have adjusted to changing conditions of society over the long run.[4]

Just as there are special qualities in Negro Christianity, so some central themes, such as the thrust of the westward movement, do not apply as forcefully. That which looms large in the development of white denominations may be of little significance for black church history. Nevertheless, for better or worse, black Christians and black churches have had common experience with white Christians and white churches in the American scene. This is well illustrated by the development of the two main denominational families which have involved large number of Negroes: the Baptists and the Methodists.

More black Christians have found a church home among the Baptists than in any other denomination. Before the end of the eighteenth century, Negroes were gathering on the Baptist model into local congregations, which allowed them to escape control and supervision by white institutions. This was easier to accomplish in the North than in the South. The first decade of the nineteenth century saw the organization of African congregations in New York, Boston, and Philadelphia. In the South the more common pattern was the inclusion of Blacks in Baptist congregations with mixed membership. Occasionally, Blacks would outnumber Caucasians by a large percentage; but control always rested with the white leaders, even in those rare instances in which Blacks were separated in congregations of their own. Black Baptist organization dates back to the 1830s with the Providence Baptist Association and the Wood River Association in the Midwest.

Next to the Baptists came the Methodists, whose missionary zeal knew no race barriers. If they could not offer the same degree of local autonomy as the Baptists, they could and did offer a style of religious expression which appealed to Blacks and Whites alike in early America. It was lively, emotional, fervid, and powerfully encouraging

[4] Frank L. Horton, "Reclaiming the Richness of Our Black Heritage," MS address to Black Methodists for Church Renewal, 1971, loaned through courtesy of Julius E. Del Pino.

to people caught in difficult circumstances. Its revivalistic spirit offered a means of escape from sometimes intolerable economic and social conditions. Along with the other forms of Protestant Christianity, it offered a unique chance for sociability as well as Christian witness. The existence of a large body of Americans untouched by the gospel (only 12 percent of the Negroes were church members as late as the Civil War) was an irresistible challenge to Methodists bent on spreading scriptural holiness over the land. As a result, the Methodist family of churches could boast of a larger black membership than any except the Baptists. For a while the Methodists outnumbered the Baptists. On the eve of the Civil War, there were about 215,000 Methodists and 175,000 Baptists. Later, the Baptists surged ahead.

Early Black Methodism

Symbolic of the early involvement of Negroes is the presence of a black girl in the little class Philip Embury formed in New York in 1766. From then on black people have played an important part in Methodist history. They were active not only in New York but also in the log chapel on Sam's Creek and in Lovely Lane and at St. George's. Both Boardman and Pilmore make reference to Blacks in the societies they formed.[5]

In the North, many of the meetings were integrated in the early days. "We met together to break bread" in a love feast, says Pilmore, in which the black people gave testimonies along with whites. He also notes receiving a pathetic letter from a slave who could not get permission to attend watch night or class meeting. In the first period in John Street Church "there were no Negro pews, no back seats, nor gallery especially provided for the dark-skinned members. They were welcome in common with other members to all the privileges of God's house of worship." [6] But in the South it was already different. During his visit to Norfolk, Pilmore discovered that, when the crowd became too large for the house, leaders appointed men to stand at the door to keep black people out until the white people got in. Whether provi-

[5] Bangs (*History,* I, 63) quotes from a letter Boardman wrote to Wesley on 24 April 1770, in which he says of New York City, "The number of the blacks that attend the preaching affects me much." Pilmore's *Journal* is full of references; for example, 58, 96, 107, 137, 149-150. Also see letter of Pilmore, dated probably in 1770, in *MH,* 10 (Apr., 1972): 56-58. The only general history is J. Beverly F. Shaw, *The Negro in the History of Methodism* (1954). There exist a number of special monographs and conference histories. See Melton, *Bibliography,* 28-34.

[6] J. W. Hood, *One Hundred Years of the African Methodist Episcopal Zion Church* (1895), 203.

dentially or not, it turned out that the pulpit fell down and Pilmore had to preach outside to the whole crowd anyway! He himself refers to formation of a class for some twenty black women in New York.

Francis Asbury was always deeply interested in bringing the gospel to the black population. He was affected by their "sable countenances" and good singing in Methodist meetings. He was repelled at the sight of cruelty and was well aware of the issue of segregation, although he didn't know any way to affect public policy on these matters. Apparently some gatherings were not segregated, but it is difficult to determine which: "We had a melting sacrament with white and coloured people." [7] In addition to the frequent references and expressions of concern in his journal, we have an interesting letter, only recently published, in which Lewis Myers recalled the bishop's abiding interest:

> The poor blacks were objects of his peculiar attentions—he appear'd to feel the weight of our Lords words in all their force when applied to them—namely—"Unto the poor, the Gospel is preached." He frequently advised us, by no means to neglect them in our c[ircui]ts, stations, & districts. When in Charleston in his annual visits, he never failed to attend to the state of the classes among the coloured people: & gave such counsel & left such directions as were calculated to further the work of God among them—all which numbers have requited, by retiring from the bosom of the Church & setting up for themselves!! But many remain with us, & are faithful, zealous, useful & happy in God. [8]

Richard Whatcoat also reported many activities which involved Negro members, although his evidence points toward increasing segregation. [9] He held love feasts for Blacks early in the morning and then later for Whites, even though in one case "the house might have held them all." On one day he met the white class, on the next the black. But the meetings were not always segregated.

No one will be surprised to discover an ineradicable element of paternalism in all this attention to the black members. It becomes obnoxiously apparent in Question 25 of the minutes for 1780: "Ought not the assistant to meet the coloured people himself, and appoint as helpers in his absence proper white persons, and not suffer them to stay late and meet by themselves? *Ans.* Yes." Southern influence, ever sensitive to the perils of permissiveness to Blacks, is clear. Pilmore, Asbury, Coke—all the early leaders—came up against the hard facts of a congealing social system and were forced to adjust. This social system

---

[7] *Journal*, II, 44 (1 Mar. 1795). Also references in index to the *Journal and Letters*.

[8] Robert Bull, "Lewis Myers' Reminiscences of Francis Asbury," *MH*, 7 (Oct., 1968): 7.

[9] MS Journal, 1794: entries for 20 July, 3 Aug., 10 Aug., 21 Sept., 8-9 Nov.; and 14 Mar. 1796.

would not be limited to southern areas of the country. It was in defiance of this oppressive system that the Methodist Episcopal Church made provision for at least limited participation by Negroes in the affairs of the church. The 1800 General Conference permitted ordination of black preachers as deacons and put the regulation into effect, but did not dare print the rule in the *Discipline.* Ordination of elders was authorized in 1812. When the American Colonization Society was formed in 1817 to facilitate the migration of free black people to Africa (Liberia), the Methodist General Conference gave only qualified approval, being aware of the ulterior motive to get rid of free Blacks. At this date the church was by no means convinced that the policies of the Colonization Society were defensible.

By all odds the most famous black preacher in the early days was Harry Hosier, "Black Harry," of whom more would be written if more were known. He was a favorite of both Asbury and Coke and had two chief claims to fame: as preacher in his own right and as traveling companion to both bishops. He must have been very effective, if Oxford-educated Dr. Coke could make this estimate of the vigorous but uneducated preacher:

> Monday 29, I preached at one *John Purnell's.* I have now had the pleasure of hearing *Harry* preach several times. I sometimes give notice immediately after preaching, that in a little time *Harry* will preach to the blacks; but the whites always stay to hear him. Sometimes I publish him to preach at candle-light, as the Negroes can better attend at that time. I really believe he is one of the best Preachers in the world, there is such an amazing power attends his preaching, though he cannot read; and he is one of the humblest creatures I ever saw.[10]

It is said that Richard Allen, founder of the African Methodist Episcopal Church, tried to teach him to read and write, but Harry gave it up when he discovered that it constricted his freedom of speech. One time in Virginia, Asbury reports, "Harry, a black man, spoke on the barren fig-tree. This circumstance was new, and the white people looked on with attention." He spent many years in the service of Methodism, and died in 1806.[11]

Hosier's successors continued in the Methodist Episcopal Church, which has always had a large percentage of Negro members and ministers. Among the three congregations that resulted from the segregation at St. George's Church in Philadelphia was African Zoar, the

[10] *Journal* (1793), 18.
[11] Not as usually recorded in 1810. Cf. note by Gordon Melton in *MH,* 8 (Oct., 1969): 88-89, citing evidence from William Colbert's *MS* Journal.

oldest black congregation in United Methodism. It was begun in 1794 in downtown Philadelphia by the dissidents who left St. George's, but did not associate with either Allen's movement or the Episcopal movement of Absalom Jones. This church observed its one hundred seventy-fifth anniversary in 1969. Many were drawn off into the separate black denominations discussed below. The conclusion of the Civil War and the establishment of emancipation brought the separation of almost all Negroes from the Methodist Episcopal Church, South; but most have remained loyally within the Methodist family. All the founders of the black Methodist denominations got their start in the Methodist Episcopal Church. Unfortunately, they also encountered facets of discrimination there that convinced them they could better serve the gospel in a separate church.

The Early African Methodist Episcopal Church

The stories of the formation of the several black Methodist denominations demonstrate a common pattern. This pattern is composed of various stages on the way from integrated participation in the life of the Methodist Episcopal Church to independent denomination: (1) integration, (2) segregation, (3) separate meeting time, (4) separate meeting place, (5) autonomous local organization, (6) independent local church, (7) regional denomination. The more successful eventually became denominations of national extent and influence. Each step meant further separation from the Methodist Episcopal Church and greater self-consciousness as an independent institution. These steps are well illustrated by the rise of the two most important churches of black Methodism, the African Methodist Episcopal (A.M.E.) Church and the African Methodist Episcopal Zion (A.M.E.Z.) Church. The two grew up together in close relations; but, like brothers in a family, they didn't always get along well. The A.M.E. Church, which has a slight edge chronologically, is taken first.

One of the great black men of America is Richard Allen, a slave ✳ who bought his own freedom and rose to a position of power as the first bishop of the A.M.E. Church.[12] He worked as a woodcutter,

[12] One of the prime sources for black Methodism is his autobiography, written between 1816 and 1831 and published in 1880, recently reprinted as *The Life Experience and Gospel Labors of the Rt. Rev. Richard Allen* (1966). See also Carol V. R. George, *Segregated Sabbaths* (1973). Among the more useful general treatments are George A. Singleton, *The Romance of African Methodism* (1952); John T. Jenifer, *Centennial Retrospect History of the African Methodist Episcopal Church* (1916); Daniel A. Payne, *A History of the African Methodist Episcopal Church* (1891). There is also a valuable *Encyclopedia of the A.M.E. Church* (1947).

bricklayer, and salt-wagon-driver before he established himself as a business man. He was converted early, soon began preaching, and is said to have attended the Christmas Conference. He was active in the St. George's society in Philadelphia before the troubles began, was licensed to preach in 1784, and was ordained deacon by Asbury in 1799. He preached frequently at St. George's and organized prayer meetings among the black members.

The year 1787 was crucial, because it marked Allen's leadership in helping to organize the Free African Society, the first Negro institution intended to improve the lot of black people, and because it marked the "walkout" from St. George's church. As the culmination of a series of discriminations, including segregation in the gallery, two trustees of the church tried to pull two black worshipers up from their prayers. Allen led them out, and others followed. They began to worship separately, and in 1794 Asbury himself dedicated a building for their use. This was the beginning of "Mother Bethel" Church. More or less friendly relations continued with the leaders and the M. E. churches in Philadelphia.

However, a problem soon developed with regard to control of church property. In the Wesleyan tradition, ever since Wesley's "Model Deed," there had been good reason for vesting control in the church at large rather than in the local congregation. This standard became the law of the church in the *Discipline*. The black members, who were struggling against great odds to obtain places in which they could worship by themselves, would naturally be suspicious of regulations which would vest control in the annual conference. They wanted, plainly and simply, church buildings owned and controlled by themselves and no one else, but this was "congregationalism." Methodist leaders were caught between the two principles, and presiding elders tended to follow the rule of the church. Considerable tension and misunderstanding arose from these disagreements. The black churches gained their own control, but the difficulty was one further cause of eventual schism. They could have their own churches, it seemed, only by organizing their own denominations. In 1796, nine men joined in signing the Articles of Association of Bethel A.M.E. Church.

This was one of two main local centers which, with several other smaller groups, came together to form the A.M.E. denomination in 1816. In Baltimore, Daniel Coker ably carried through a process remarkably similar to Philadelphia. Born in Maryland, he ran away from slavery to New York, where he became a Methodist and was ordained deacon by Asbury. Back in Baltimore, having bought his freedom, he taught school and was active in Methodist churches there. When segregationist policies appeared in both Lovely Lane and Strawberry Alley chapels, Coker helped in the process of separation by stages. Shortly before 1816, they had organized as an independent church, just as in Philadelphia. Almost identical factors, including the property question, affected developments in Baltimore.

At last, on April 7, 1816, representatives to a constitutional assembly assembled in Philadelphia, with six delegates from Baltimore, five from Philadelphia, three from Attleborough, Pennsylvania, one from Wilmington, and one from Salem, New Jersey. The Salem delegate was from Mt. Pisgah Church, which from 1813 was organized into the Union Church of Africans. From Wilmington came Peter Spencer, another able black man who obtained his freedom when his master died. He was active in the organization of the Ezion Church there, which went through the same process of separation. He attended the organizing conference of 1816, but withdrew and took part in the organization of the African Union Church. The convention proceeded to organize the new denomination, which was and remained, in effect, a thoroughly Methodist church with articles of religion, general rules, discipline, and polity almost identical with the M.E. Church, except that the office of presiding elder was abolished. Richard Allen was elected bishop, after complications from the candidacy of Coker who returned to Baltimore and served as minister. Later he went on missionary service to Liberia. A fundamental rule was adopted prohibiting church membership by slave owners.

Two important aspects of the rise of the A.M.E. Church go beyond the strictly ecclesiastical. From the beginning, this denomination took a strong stance against segregation in church membership and as a consequence has always counted some white persons among its members. Furthermore, the work of Allen can be seen as an early expression of Black Power or Nationalism, since he engaged actively in projects for the economic and political betterment of black people, which included the boycott of slavemade goods.[13] A sort of Methodist antecedent of the National Association for the Advancement of Colored People may be seen in the Convention of the Colored Men of the United States, 1830, over which Bishop Allen presided, held in Bethel A.M.E. Church in Philadelphia. With its church-sponsored secular overtones, it foreshadowed the NAACP nearly a hundred years later. Among early famous A.M.E. personages were Bishop Morris Brown;

[13] See Alain Rogers, "The African Methodist Episcopal Church, a Study in Black Nationalism," *The Black Church* 1 (1972):17-43.

William Paul Quinn, circuit rider in the Midwest; and Denmark Vesey of Charleston, South Carolina, a revolutionary. The church had a brief early development in Charleston, but was caught in the reaction to Vesey's revolt and suppressed until after the Civil War. Quinn was typical of the leaders in the westward movement of black Methodism and was the first to serve circuits beyond the Alleghenies. Quinn Chapel in Chicago, begun in 1844, is named after him. Moses Freeman founded Allen Temple in Cincinnati in 1824. Certainly A.M.E. Methodism, although it was not particularly a frontier church, was on its way west. The membership in 1826 was almost seven thousand; by 1848, it had reached seventeen thousand. In that year the church paper, *The Christian Recorder,* was founded, although under another name. It claims to be the oldest journal published by black people anywhere in the world.

The Early African Methodist Episcopal Zion Church

In general terms the process of formation of the A.M.E.Z. Church ran parallel to that of the A.M.E. Church. The stages developed in proper sequence from segregation through organization of a separate denomination. There were complications, however. A web of conflicting interests interfered with the usual pattern of evolution. In addition to the basic black-white conflict, the New York episode also exhibited a rivalry between two autonomous black congregations (Zion and Asbury). There was a struggle for leadership between the Allenites and the Zionites—that is, between Philadelphia and New York; there were pressures from a white schism in New York Methodism (Stillwellites); and finally, issues of Methodist polity on the relation of annual conference to general conference brought differences between the Philadelphia and New York conferences of the M.E. Church. All this made much more difficult the development of the sort of autonomous church desired by the black Methodists of New York. Little wonder if confusion sometimes existed!

In the 1780s, as a result of crowded conditions in the John Street Church, black members sought to have their own meetings at a separate time. By 1796 they sought to have a separate meeting place. Among their representatives was Peter Williams, already noted as the renowned sexton of John Street Church and confidant of preachers and bishops. Williams was in good relations with the church leaders, and had, by his remarkable ability, paid back to the church the purchase of his freedom. He ran a flourishing tobacco shop. During the process of formation of the A.M.E.Z. Church, he took an active part in helping his black friends while yet remaining active in the life of John Street Church. When the Zion congregation built its first church building, the African or Zion Chapel, in 1800, Williams was among the trustees and laid the cornerstone.[14]

In 1801, the "African Methodist Episcopal Church in the City of New York" (Zion Chapel) was incorporated with the property held by a black board of trustees while the ministerial direction remained with the New York Conference. For a time white ministers from the John Street Church preached and administered the sacraments. Three black preachers, Thomas Miller, June Scott, and Abraham Thompson, were licensed to preach.

Early in the nineteenth century, the situation was complicated by (1) a schism in the Zion congregation which led to organization of Asbury Church, which was in and out of the M.E. Church, the A.M.E.Z. Church, and finally settled in the A.M.E. Church; (2) the Stillwell secession from the M.E. Church; and (3) the property and ministry problems. These complications led to much controversy and confusion. The Zion people did not want to join with the A.M.E. Church, which was already spreading into New York. They did not want to remain fully in the M.E. Church, but they did not want to break with it completely. William Stillwell, who led a congregationalist-oriented schism from New York Methodism in 1820, drew the Zion Chapel into his movement for a time, because he was able to play on the natural black suspicion of disciplinary provisions for vesting control of property in the annual conference. For long, a problem continued over ordination of Negro preachers. Approaches to Allen, to Bishop McKendree, and to Episcopal Bishop Hobart, failed. At last, the congregation elected Abraham Thompson and James Varick as elders, following a principle of full democracy for all members, both male and female.

Until the Asbury group broke away, there were two local churches in New York. These joined with groups in New Haven, Philadelphia (Wesley), and Long Island, to ask the Philadelphia and New York conferences of the M.E. Church to establish them as a separate black annual conference. This was agreed to by the Philadelphia Conference, but was rejected by New York. Hence, they joined together in 1821 as the African Methodist Episcopal Zion Church in America and

---

[14] The basic history of the A.M.E.Z. Church is David H. Bradley, Sr., *A History of the A.M.E.Zion Church*, Part I, 1796–1872 (1956). There is a sequel for the modern period. An early history, and prime source, is Christopher Rush, *A Short Account of the Rise and Progress of the African M.E. Church in America* (1843), which uses an early name for A.M.E.Z. Much valuable material, especially on John Street origins and Peter Williams, is in J. B. Wakeley, *Lost Chapters Recovered from the Early History of American Methodism* (1858).

held a conference under the chairmanship of William Phoebus, M.E.
elder, with Joshua Soule as secretary. Freeborn Garrettson also attended. The next year the process was completed in another conference in which several elders were formally ordained, including Abraham Thompson, James Varick, and Christopher Rush. Varick was
elected first general superintendent (bishop). When the M.E. General
Conference of 1824 failed to take any helpful action, the break was
complete. The A.M.E.Z. Church was on its own, burdened with many
problems, very few of which were of its own making. The denomination grew quite slowly down to the Civil War. By 1831, there were
1,689 members and two conferences, New York and Philadelphia. By
1860, there were 4,600 members. Varick, a somewhat mysterious and
little-known figure, served briefly as the first bishop, and was followed
by a much more important figure, Christopher Rush, elected in 1828.

A third black denomination, the African Union Church (originally
the Union Church of Africans), traces its history to the same time as
the two African churches. However, its center was Wilmington, Delaware, and its leading figure was Peter Spencer, the same who had
attended the A.M.E. organizing conference of 1816, but had withdrawn. The background of Ezion Church, erected in 1805, was similar to the other churches. The same process of segregation led by
stages to separate meetings and separate houses. By 1812, a conflict
arose over the power of appointment of preachers for Ezion. Within a
year the black schism was organized into the African Union Church in
Wilmington, Delaware with William Anderson and Peter Spencer as
preachers. As churches were added, the denomination grew in the
East. It was Methodist in polity with the major difference that ministers were chosen by congregations, and bishops were called presidents. After the Civil War, a merger took place with a split from the
A.M.E. Church called the First Colored Methodist Protestant Church.
The resulting denomination rejoiced in the name, African Union
First Colored Methodist Protestant Church of the United States of
America or Elsewhere (1865). A division of this body in 1875 brought
into existence the present denomination.

The M.E. Church experienced considerable loss of black membership through the organization of independent black churches, but
many remained in the white church. By the time slavery became a
crucial issue in American history, there were many black Methodists
in both North and South. The black denominations had their
strength in the North. Almost all the members in the South were in
the M.E. Church, South. This, then, was the Methodist stage-setting
for the great debate over slavery.

Chapter 16
The Reform Movement and the Methodist Protestant Church

John Wesley left no doubt about the fountainhead of authority in his movement. His associates in the revival, preachers in charge of circuits, he called "assistants." Their associates were "helpers." Lest class leaders develop a sense of power, he reminded them they were "the lowest wheel but one" in the hierarchy.

Rankin and Asbury saw to it that the message came through to the American followers. Most of the preachers and people accepted the plan as a central feature of Wesley's movement, if not indeed of God's universe. Most, but not all. Laced through the growth of Methodism in the first three decades of the nineteenth century was a strong thread of concern for broader participation of both preachers and people in the life of the church. Every general conference from 1808 through 1828 experienced agitation for election of presiding elders, rights for local preachers, and representation of laymen. Now and then even women were heard, but not much hearkened to. At one time, Laban Clark, otherwise a stalwart supporter of the Asburian structure, defied the bishop in advocating election of presiding elders. He sought to mollify Asbury in an explanatory letter: "My reasons for wishing such a change is to prevent a greater one taking place in some future period: I mean the entire rejection of that office from among us, which is wished for by some. . . . But would it not be a means of conciliating the affections of the preachers, if they could have a choice of their rulers?" Asbury, characteristically, took offense while at the same time claiming to permit free dissent: "I will freely turn my Back, and my children shall freely speak against me or my administration. I wish difficulties may be brought. But am I not your Father? What have I said, what have I done?" [1]

The preachers wanted their choice of presiding elders. The local preachers wanted conference rights. The lay people wanted representation. The old issues raised by O'Kelly, and by Strawbridge before him, would not go away. In fact, with the heady decade that ushered in Jacksonian democracy in political councils, the church was rocked by a major crisis, which at first appeared to promise the

[1] Norwood, "Some Letters." *MH*, 3 (Jul., 1965): 9-11.

introduction of democratic reforms, but at last produced the second major schism in Methodist history.[2]

Debate: The Reform Party, 1820–24

The brew bubbled over at the General Conference of 1820, which met in Eutaw Street Church, Baltimore, where Francis Asbury rested beneath the pulpit in his penultimate grave. Present and in the flesh were Bishops McKendree, Enoch George, and Robert R. Roberts, together with eighty-nine traveling preachers. By what turned out to be an ironic coincidence, one Alexander McCaine was elected secretary. In the second week, a motion providing for the election of presiding elders by the members of annual conferences was introduced and debated. A compromise was then brought in by Ezekiel Cooper and John Emory, which restricted the election to nominees, three times the number needed, submitted by the bishops. This in turn was debated and finally passed, with the additional provision that the presiding elders should constitute an "advisory counsel" to the bishop in stationing the preachers. The vote, sixty-one to twenty-five, is significant. It means that over two-thirds of the general conference voted in favor of reform. It was a crucial vote and indicated the strength of the reform movement.

All the more startling, then, is the role next played by Joshua Soule, who was elected bishop in the midst of the debate.[3] Impressive in body and bearing, he was one of those men who instantly took command by his mere presence. He had been active in the councils of the church ever since the constitutional construction of 1808. Now, with the assistance of McKendree and Stephen Roszel, he stood in the breach of episcopal defenses, defied the majority, and finally won a postponement of the action taken. This was accomplished at the cost of his refusal to accept the office of bishop in 1820. After several hectic days, the general conference refused to implement its own decision. "It seems fair to say," concludes Albea Godbold, "that largely because of the conviction, determination and persuasiveness

[2] A thoroughgoing and thoroughly documented account, although biased in favor of the reform movement, is Edward J. Drinkhouse, *History of Methodist Reform* (2 vols., 1899). Basic source materials include the periodicals *Wesleyan Repository* (1821–23), *Mutual Rights* (1824–28), and *The Methodist Protestant* (from 1831); Alexander McCaine, *The History and Mystery of Methodist Episcopacy* (1827); Nicholas Snethen, *Snethen on Lay Representation* (1835); and Samuel K. Jennings, *An Exposition of the Late Controversy in the Methodist Episcopal Church* (1831). On the other side, the two works by John Emory, *Defense of Our Fathers* (1827) and *The Episcopal Controversy Reviewed* (1838) were very influential. Nathan Bangs stated his conservative views in his *History* (III).

[3] See Albea Godbold, "Joshua Soule—Methodist Lawgiver," in *Forever Beginning* (1967), 14-27, quote on p. 21.

of one man, Joshua Soule, the Methodist Episcopal Church continued to appoint rather than to elect presiding elders." Alexander McCaine, a witness to these proceedings from the secretarial chair, was not so deliberate in his judgment. Soule was a "despot." Nicholas Snethen, always the responsible, concerned observer, wrote: "When our countrymen find every idea which they have been in the habit of attaching to a constitution reversed, and instead of this instrument being a palladium of liberty, as they supposed, becoming a mere charter of self-created and monopolized power, must they not lose all confidence in the agents who produced the transformation."[4]

In spite of the domination of the general conference by the issue of the election of presiding elders, the assembly was able to accomplish other, more positive, works for Methodism. A system of district conferences was set up for the benefit of local preachers, who were beginning to feel slighted, being neither ministers nor laymen. The effort, well intended, offered little and soon languished. More important and far more durable was the organization of a missionary society, the first of a long series of institutional adventures which made Methodism mighty—and to some, monstrous. Stimulated by the highly original activity of black lay preacher John Stewart who worked among the Wyandot Indians of Ohio, the general conference gave its blessing to the infant organization in its purpose to spread scriptural holiness by means of a special agency. For the first time, the Methodist Episcopal Church made a distinction between itself, understood totally as a missionary movement ("to spread scriptural holiness"), and a special department whose responsibility was mission. This distinction would have significant effects on the church's self-understanding in later years.

Some immediate results of the battle over presiding elders were not foreseen. In the following year there appeared in some Methodist homes a paper which was stringently excluded from others: the *Wesleyan Repository and Religious Intelligencer.* Since the only publication of the church at this time was the rather sober-sided monthly *Methodist Magazine (MQR),* the new paper was designed to promote the cause of reform. For three years it did its job, always on the verge of starvation, until it succumbed. One effect was the closing of the pages of the *Methodist Magazine* by its editor, Nathan Bangs, to any reformist material. Because of the controversial nature of the articles, the authors' names were hidden behind pseudonyms. This practice lent a conspiratorial atmosphere to the activities of the entire decade, as both sides charged the opposition with secrecy and subterfuge.

[4] Drinkhouse, *History,* II, 16.

One of the liveliest contributions came from the pen of "A Methodist" (Ezekiel Cooper), "The Outlines of a Proposed Plan for a Lay Delegation." The core of this plan, which established equal lay delegation, became the basis for the later lay participation in the Methodist Protestant Church. "Let it now be noticed, that this proposed plan gives, both to the Laity and to the Ministry, an equal representation, and an equal voice in the choice of them, and that reciprocally by a joint ballot, without creating or promoting two distinct opposing interests or parties." [5] The proposal induced extended correspondence among various groups of reformers, some of whom thought the local preachers should feel insulted at their inclusion among the laity.

Tough old conservative Alfred Brunson would have no truck with these subversives, whose "radicalism" was "ecclesiastical treason" and "that heresy." [6] Thus the lines were drawn. The *Methodist Magazine* became spokesman for the *status quo;* the *Wesleyan Repository* and its successor, *Mutual Rights,* beat the drums of reform; the *Christian Advocate and Journal* (the New York *Christian Advocate*) from 1827 was the chief popular defender of established authority. The debate of 1820 spurred the dissent of the 1820s.

Dissent: Union Societies, 1824–28

If the impasse of 1820 has been somehow resolved in 1824, *if* the publications of the church had remained open for discussion of the issues, *if* the reformers had been more moderate; what might have happened? Could the Methodist Protestant schism have been avoided? Could the reformers' proposals have been negotiated into the structure then, rather than in part and piecemeal over later decades? It was not to be. Personal antagonisms, vested interests, and the muffling of debate opened the channel toward schism.

The direction became clear at the General Conference of 1824, which, by a desperately narrow margin, 63 to 61, declared the reform resolutions of 1820 unconstitutional and null. The election to episcopacy all over again of Joshua Soule was not equally balanced by the election of moderate Elijah Hedding. The old bishops signed an address which specifically rejected the argument for democratic reforms in the church based on political precedents in government.

---

[5] *Wesleyan Repository,* 3 (1823): 258. The *Western Recorder* (Feb.-Apr., 1850) gives a history of the *WR*, with names of pseudonymous authors. See also Lester B. Scherer, "Ezekiel Cooper," (Diss., Northwestern, 1965).
[6] *A Western Pioneer,* I, 328-29.

Obviously, although Andrew Jackson cast long shadows over Wesley's children, not all were impressed. Methodism was well into the process of being Americanized, but not without protest. Assisted by Bishop Soule, able successor to the mantle of Asbury and McKendree, the Wesleyan standard of authority stood up remarkably well against the buffetings of populism.

The voice of the people was strongly expressed, however, in the new periodical which appeared in 1824, *Mutual Rights*. Nicholas Snethen, who liked his own name best, shared space with "Nehemiah" (Alexander McCaine) and "Bartimeus" (Asa Shinn). This new venture grew out of a meeting in Baltimore during the general conference, which gave rise to the first of a series of "union societies." For the next four years both the magazine and the union societies spread and flourished. The reform movement was still within the church, but it was outside the control of the established authority. It now had an effective means of communication and an autonomous organization. Union societies joined together in a web of common interest, unifying the drive for reform which was being thwarted in the official channels.[7] All three major aspects received attention: sharing of authority with traveling preachers, rights for local preachers, lay representation. Everybody got into the act, not always marching in the same direction.

Halfway through the quadrennium, Asa Shinn, acute observer that he was, concluded reluctantly that the net result would be division.[8] Step by step the apparently inevitable ensued. In November, 1826, a first convention brought the local union societies together. In April, 1827, the Baltimore Annual Conference censured one of its members, Dennis B. Dorsey. In May, Alexander McCaine dropped his bombshell, *History and Mystery of Methodist Episcopacy*. In the fall, Samuel K. Jennings and other local preachers were suspended. In November, the first official General Convention of Reformers met in Baltimore, which prepared a memorial to the coming general conference. On the last day of the year, a group of women placed themselves squarely in support of the reforming men. In January, 1828, the local preachers noted above were expelled. In April, the Baltimore Annual Conference not only deprived Dennis Dorsey and another minister, William C. Poole, of their conference membership, but also expelled them from the church. Hence, by the time the general conference assembled in May, the rush of events had almost predetermined the subsequent course. By this time the issues had been thoroughly

---

[7] Drinkhouse, *History,* II, 71-95.
[8] *Ibid.,* 95.

opened and probed in a remarkable series of publications which altogether constitute a library of Methodist political debate, the end of which is not yet.

Among the leaders was formidable Alexander McCaine, the "Agamemnon" of the reformers as Drinkhouse characterized him. Tall and strongly built with an impressive rough-hewn head, he demonstrated in his physique the combativeness which dominated his activities in the 1820s. His *History and Mystery of Methodist Episcopacy* (1827) marks the beginning of an important interchange of views on the essence of the Methodist structure of authority. McCaine maintained that the office of bishop, properly understood, is a third order of ministry; that Wesley did not intend to establish such an office or order in "ordaining" Coke; and that, therefore, "the present form of government was surreptitiously introduced, and was imposed upon the societies under the sanction of Mr. Wesley's name." To this tract John Emory replied with *Defense of "Our Fathers" and of the Original Organization of the Methodist Episcopal Church Against the Rev. Alexander M'Caine and Others*. He refuted, point by point, the arguments of McCaine and sought to show that the evidence was either inconclusive, inaccurate, or susceptible of other interpretations. In his view, the term bishop applies to different forms of the office, including that meant by Wesley when he made Coke superintendent. He entitled Chapter 18 " 'History and Mystery' of Mr. M'Caine's Inconsistency." By the time McCaine took his turn with *Defense of the Truth,* the inexorable course of events had determined the issue in its own way.

Among the voluminous writings of the reformers, one of the most cogent is the collection of essays by Nicholas Snethen published in 1835, most of which had appeared in *Wesleyan Repository* and *Mutual Rights*. His introductory theme, which threads in and out of a decade's production, is the corruptibility of power. "Power combined with interest and inclination cannot be controlled by logic. But even power shrinks from the test of logic." For this reason he urges lay representation in the councils of the church. Only by such checks can episcopal power be controlled. These checks must be applied before power has become irresistibly centralized. "A carriage, which has no break [brake] upon its wheels, when descending a hill cannot be stopped to provide one." [9] Snethen had no objection to the original concentration of power in the hands of "Father" Wesley, but only to the continuation of that concentration after him. Moreover, he had no objection to bishops, but only to bishops without constitutional limits. Snethen had learned well the lesson on checks and balances applied

[9] Snethen, *On Lay Representation,* vi, x.

by the founders of the American nation, a lesson based ultimately on the doctrine of original sin.

In reviewing the General Conference of 1820 he expressed regret that the hard-won "reconciliation" was then suspended and the good will "all thrown to the winds. . . . Those who think they do God service by propagating their own suspicions against their brethren, may remain blind to the consequences, but to us who take no part in this election campaign of four years long [the rounds of annual conferences], and have no immediate interests in the issue, it is plain that they are making a schism among travelling preachers, and are using the very means to render it incurable." By 1827 the course had transpired as he feared. The reformers would be going like "lambs among wolves," since the majority had "all the claws and all the teeth. . . . *We are not to be reasoned with, but punished.*" Hence,

> I deem it proper, brethren, that in this portentous change, in this state of your affairs, that you should hear my voice, should see my name. It will, I know it will, it must be asked, now the time is come to try men's souls, where is Philo Pisticus? Where is Adynasius? Where is Senex? Where is the man who was among the foremost to challenge us to the cause of representation? Where is Snethen? I trust that while he is among the living, but one answer will be given to this question—he is at his post, he is in the front of the contest, he is shouting *on,* brethren on! and if he fall, it will be with a wound in his breast, and with his head direct towards the opponent.

In the spirit of Wilfred Grenfell inviting young persons to accept the challenge of hard work for little reward, Snethen then issued a candid warning to young ministers who might be looking for advancement. He and the reformers would attempt to prevent a normal succession of ambitious youth to the seats of power. "You will have to meet the church and the local ministry, by their representatives in the General Conference, as your equals, and they to meet you as their equals." [10]

Division: Methodist Protestant Church, 1828–30

And so it turned out. At the General Conference of 1828, a formal memorial was submitted by those who were already expelled, calling for the long-sought reforms and the end of persecution. Nathan Bangs, expressing the conservative viewpoint, thought so much of the committee's reply, written by Emory, that he quoted it entire.[11] The

[10] *Ibid.,* 68, 343-45, 366.
[11] Bangs, *History,* III, 413-29.

memorial was rejected, and its authors charged with contumacy. Along with the memorial, fell the appeal of Dorsey and Poole —although with a narrow majority of twenty votes. Asa Shinn once again mounted a superb defense, all the more impressive in defeat. It recalled the stirring appeal he had made in behalf of the men at the Baltimore Annual Conference:

> Will your daring efforts to abridge the freedom of thought and discussion, pass unnoticed in this land of justice and independence, which reflects the light of civil and religious liberty over both hemispheres? Will the free born sons of America, whose fathers had such struggles to cast off the yoke of European despotism, be silent and respectful spectators of your ecclesiastical march after absolute dominion? Will not Methodists every where open their eyes, and see that the efforts of reformers have not been made without a cause? [12]

Filled with the spirit of political democracy, the appeal recalls the republican principles of James O'Kelly. The only action of the conference that suggests the possibility of reconciliation was passage of a resolution submitted by Emory which offered restoration of membership and rights to those who resigned from union societies and gave up the reformist publications. The language was not calculated to bring in many penitents.

Almost immediately, the union societies were stirred to action with protests and plans for a general convention. The convention took place in Baltimore in November, 1828. The "Associated Methodist Churches," as they were now being called, were moving toward the formation of a separate denomination. Soon twelve annual conferences were organized under the tentative plans, together with many scattered congregations. The first was the North Carolina Annual Conference, formed in Whitaker's Chapel (Halifax County near Enfield) in December, 1828. This little church, charming in its country location now as then, is a historical shrine of United Methodism.

The Methodist Protestant Church was formally organized at the constituent general convention held in Baltimore in November, 1830. The final form of the constitution contained several compromises unpleasing to the purists. Although local churches gained a degree of autonomy, the connectional system was preserved, however, without bishops. Laymen gained equal representation in annual and general conference, but local preachers were denied membership in the annual conference. Although women had been given the vote in the "Associated Methodist Churches," they did not have it now.

---

[12] Jennings, *An Exposition of the Late Controversy*, 205.

Moreover, slavery was not rejected. McCaine, who was so fiery on the rights of people in church life, was strong in defense of slavery. Although bishops were dispensed with, a president of an annual conference made appointments, "subject to revision by a Committee of Appeals." Shades of James O'Kelly! A book committee, a new periodical *(The Methodist Protestant),* a discipline, a hymnbook, and other trappings of Methodism were provided for. The curious amalgam of disparate forces which went into the making of the Methodist Protestant Church is reflected in the eleven "Elementary Principles" which formed a preamble to the new constitution:

1. A Christian Church is a society of believers in Jesus Christ, and is of divine institution.
2. Christ is the only Head of the Church; and the word of God the only rule of faith and conduct.
3. No person who loves the Lord Jesus Christ, and obeys the gospel of God our Saviour, ought to be deprived of church membership.
4. Every man has an inalienable right to private judgment, in matters of religion; and an equal right to express his opinion, in any way which will not violate the laws of God, or the rights of his fellow-men.
5. Church trials should be conducted on gospel principles only; and no minister or member should be excommunicated except for immorality; the propagation of unchristian doctrines; or for the neglect of duties enjoined by the word of God.
6. The pastoral or ministerial office and duties are of divine appointment; and all elders in the church of God are equal; but ministers are forbidden to be lords over God's heritage, or to have dominion over the faith of the saints.
7. The Church has a right to form and enforce such rules and regulations only, as are in accordance with the holy scriptures, and may be necessary, or have a tendency to carry into effect the great system of practical Christianity.
8. Whatever power may be necessary to the formation of rules and regulations, is inherent in the ministers and members of the Church; but so much of that power may be delegated, from time to time, upon a plan of representation, as they may judge necessary and proper.
9. It is the duty of all ministers and members of the Church to maintain godliness, and to oppose all moral evil.
10. It is obligatory on ministers of the gospel to be faithful in the discharge of their pastoral and ministerial duties; and it is also obligatory on the members, to esteem ministers highly for their works' sake, and to render them a righteous compensation for their labours.
11. The Church ought to secure to all her official bodies the necessary authority for the purposes of good government; but she has no right to create any distinct or independent sovereignties.[13]

[13] Drinkhouse, *History,* II, 258, where the constitution is given in full.

Here, then, is a classic recipe for the making of a schism. Begin with a long frustrating controversy over certain principles. Mix in strong personalities, parliamentary maneuvers, gag rules, reprisals against opponents, individual test cases; increase the pressure and heat. Box in the forces of change till there is no way out. Then expel the dissidents. There will be losses along the way. Ezekiel Cooper, who for long sympathized with the reform proposals, retired when schism threatened. Many who began liberal turned conservative, sometimes for admirable motives. Among them were McKendree himself, Elijah Hedding, John Emory, Beverly Waugh (all three eventually bishops), Nathan Bangs, and Thomas E. Bond. Some, undoubtedly, were ambitious men. All loved the church too much to cling to reform if that meant schism. Among the radical reformers, a similar mixture of motives is observable. Some regarded themselves too highly; others were unable to compromise; some were willing to sacrifice personal fortune in commitment to great principle. The result was tragedy, for individuals and for Christian community.

At its organization, the membership of the Methodist Protestant Church was 5,000. By 1880, it had grown to 118,000, and by 1939, the year of reunification, 197,000. It served a great symbolic purpose in witness to the democratic or populist element in American Methodism.

Chapter 17
Slavery

Thomas Jefferson once said, "I tremble for my country, when I reflect that God is just; that his justice cannot sleep forever." Henry Clay perceived in the Methodist schism of 1844 a troubling adumbration of an irrepressible national destiny. Abraham Lincoln brooded over the mysteries of God's providence while Americans engaged in fratricidal struggle. In this manner the entire nation was enmeshed in the problem of slavery, a basic moral issue that inevitably sharpened theological differences. However important the economic factors were for the nation and the constitutional issues were for Methodism, in the end the problem of slavery was a moral and theological problem. Hence, people of all philosophies and religions had to face it in terms of faith. Methodists were different only in that their church was so successfully permeating the whole country that the problem could be neither evaded nor resolved.

The Early Stance

Many studies, some of them recent, have been made of the involvement of the American churches in slavery. Among them are excellent monographs on Methodism.[1] All that can be attempted in a brief survey is summarization of major developments and an interpretation of their meaning.

The problem of slavery marked American history almost from the beginning. The Revolution raised troubling questions about keeping slaves while fighting for liberty. Although some denominations were able to avoid the issue because of their regional character, Baptists and Presbyterians, along with Methodists, were caught squarely in the middle. All three in one way or another were split before the Civil War divided the nation.

[1] In addition to treatments in general works, see especially Richard M. Cameron, *Methodism and Society in Historical Perspective* (1961), Chap. 4; Donald G. Mathews, *Slavery and Methodism* (1965); Lewis McCarroll Purifoy, Jr., "The Methodist Episcopal Church, South and Slavery, 1844–1865" (Diss., Univ. of North Carolina, 1966); Marie S. White,"Antislavery Leadership in Illinois Methodism, 1844–1861" (Thesis, Northwestern University, 1970); several excellent articles in *MH* and elsewhere referred to below. Lester Scherer has an unpublished manuscript of a first-rate study of slavery in the larger religious context.

In the early days of small and simple beginnings, Methodists were able to take a strong stand against the evil institution. Rankin vehemently and Whatcoat gently decried it.[2] Garrettson and Gatch both hated it. The latter explained his migration to Ohio as a protest: "I felt unwilling to lay my Bones there [Virginia], and leave my Children whom I tenderly loved in a land of slavery not knowing what the Evils there of would amount to in there time." [3] Benjamin Lakin cried out in 1814, "Oh the curse of Negro slavery!" Of all the early leaders, George Whitefield was the only one who was not completely against slavery. Asbury recorded many entries indicating his opposition to the institution and his sympathy with the slaves. Both before and after 1784, he took an open stand against it.[4] But at the same time, he is the best example of the ultimate compromise. Although he led a second drive against slavery among Methodist members in the 1790s, he "had to settle," in the words of David H. Bradley, "for freedom of the soul as against freedom of the body." [5] His reluctant adjustment typifies the accommodation made by Methodists as the decades wore on. Bishop McKendree further adjusted the stance of the church when he significantly altered (in addressing the General Conference of 1816) the revered purpose "to reform the Continent, *and* to spread scriptural holiness over these lands," so it would read, "to reform the continent *by* spreading scriptural holiness over these lands." Thus, the theme of reform was submerged under the evangelistic message to individuals.

Of all the founders, Thomas Coke stands supreme for forthright and uncompromising opposition to slavery. Even he had to trim his sails to the wind, but not before he had raised a storm. In Virginia he was virtually mobbed until he learned to become more adroit in his attack. "Here I bore a public testimony against slavery, and have found out a method of delivering it without much offense, or at least without causing a tumult: and that is, by first addressing the negroes in a very pathetic manner on the duty of servants to masters; and then the whites will receive quietly what I have to say to them." [6] Neverthe-

[2] See Rankin, "Journal," 20 June, 20 Sept., and 1 Jan., 1775–76; Whatcoat, "Journal," 29 Apr. 1795, 25 Aug. 1798. Both of these are unpublished manuscripts in the library of Garrett Theological Seminary.

[3] Gatch to Dromgoole, 1802, in Sweet, *Religion on the American Frontier*, IV, 152. Cf. 157, 159, 171, 175, 248.

[4] See William B. Gravely, "Methodist Preachers, Slavery and Caste: Types of Social Concern in Antebellum America," *Duke Divinity School Review*, 34 (1969): 209-29.

[5] From an address at the International Methodist Historical Society, Denver, 1971.

[6] See John Vickers, *Thomas Coke, Apostle of Methodism* (1969). Manuscripts by Warren Thomas Smith, "Thomas Coke's War on Slavery," and "Thomas Coke, the Early Years," made available by courtesy of the author.

less, Coke persisted so strongly in his witness that at least once more his life was threatened, and he had to parry law suits. He joined with Asbury in addressing a petition to George Washington in behalf of the Methodists for emancipation of slaves in Virginia. With obvious pleasure he recorded in his journal that the general was sympathetic with their views.

Inevitably, the original high stand of the church, established formally in the first *Discipline,* had to be modified if the church were to survive in those areas of its earliest strength. That rule was suspended within six months. Although the *Discipline* continued to take a strong stand against the moral evil of slavery, its teeth were progressively drawn. It became possible to ignore the rule, or to reinterpret it in innocuous fashion. Now and then, the race issue, in which the slave issue was inextricably bound, led the leaders to connive in disreputable devices, such as the suppression of publicity about the ordination of black deacons and the printing of a thousand special copies of the *Discipline* of 1808 for use in South Carolina, in which the rule on slavery was omitted. By 1816, a sense of hopelessness had developed, since there seemed no way out of the contradiction between profession and performance. A committee reported to the general conference of that year:

> The committee to whom was referred the business of slavery beg leave to report, that they have taken the subject into serious consideration, and, after mature deliberation, they are of opinion that, under the present existing circumstances in relation to slavery, little can be done to abolish a practice so contrary to the principles of moral justice. They are sorry to say that the evil appears to be past remedy; and they are led to deplore the destructive consequences which have already accrued, and are likely to result therefrom.[7]

The story of slavery in the United States invites an economic interpretation, and historians have not been slow in accepting the invitation. This is not the place to engage in a survey of the literature. The point is that in slavery we have a clear case of the unavoidable mingling of church history and economic history. Try as they would to stay out of secular affairs, churchmen were caught up in events. Slavery, slave revolts, and the underground railroad pressed in upon the church as powerfully as upon business and finance. Churchmen might claim to stay out of politics—but they could not.

There were some hard facts. The price for a first-class slave in 1790 was three hundred dollars, in 1830, twelve hundred dollars, in 1860,

---

[7] *JGC,* 1816, 169-70.

two thousand dollars. If Dr. Coke had trouble being an antislavery witness in Virginia, he should have known that Virginia held twice as many slaves as in any other state, almost three hundred thousand. The fears aroused by even a few slave revolts raised specters to haunt southern property owners for decades. Many Methodists, along with Quakers and others, were deeply involved in the illegal operations of the Underground Railway, by means of which slaves escaping from the South were hidden away and transported to freedom in Canada. Many are the tales of that risky business. Jermain Loguen, a slave in Tennessee who escaped and later became a bishop of the African Methodist Episcopal Zion Church, wrote to Frederick Douglass to report his experience twenty years later:

> Twenty-one years ago—the very winter I left my chains in Tennessee—I stood on this spot, penniless, ragged, lonely, homeless, helpless, hungry and forlorn—a pitiable wanderer, without a friend, or shelter, or place to lay my head. I had broken from the sunny South, and fought a passage through storms and tempests, which made the forests crash and the mountains moan, difficulties new, awful, and unexpected, but not so dreaded as my white enemies who were comfortably sheltered among them. There I stood, a boy twenty-one years of age (as near as I know my age) the tempests howling over my head, and my toes touching the snow beneath my worn-out shoes—with the assurance that I was at the end of my journey—knowing nobody, and nobody knowing me or noticing me, only as attracted by the then supposed mark of Cain on my sorrow-stricken face. . . . No Underground Railroad took me to Hamilton. White men had not then learned to care for the far-off slave, and there were no thriving colored farmers, mechanics and laborers to welcome me. . . . My dear Douglass, you will not think it strange I speak of my case in contrast with the now state of things in Canada. Hamilton was a cold wilderness for the fugitive when I came there. It is now an Underground Railroad Depot, where he is embraced with warm sympathy. . . . Fortunately for me, I gained the favor of the best white people. . . . All the country around is familiar to me, and you will not wonder I love to come here. I love it because it was my first resting place from slavery, and I love it more because it has been, and will continue to be, a city of refuge for my poor countrymen. [8]

A white Methodist minister's acquaintance with the Underground Railroad is colorfully reported in Brunson's autobiography. The most famous "engineer" was Harriet Tubman, a Zion Methodist, who made nineteen trips into the South and helped some three hundred persons escape.

The black Methodist churches were involved in some of the various

---

[8] David H. Bradley, Sr., *A History of the A.M.E. Zion Church* (1972), Part I, 1796–1872, 118-19. See Brunson, *A Western Pioneer,* I, 269-72.

slave revolts. Biblical parallels sprang to mind as Negroes worshiped together and sang "Go down Moses . . . Let my people go."

> And before I'd be a slave I'll be buried in my grave,
> And go home to my God and be free."

Denmark Vesey, who scared the wits out of the people of South Carolina, was a Methodist class leader. He received help from the A.M.E. congregation in Charleston, even secretly from Bishop Morris Brown. After he was hanged in 1822, the A.M.E. work was prohibited in that state.[9] On the other hand Nat Turner was a Baptist local preacher, who became convinced he was a black prophet assigned to lead his people to freedom. An eclipse of the sun in February, 1831 was thought to be the sign to slaughter the white people of Virginia without regard for age or sex.

However the ecclesiastical facet of the problem is delineated, the underlying economic (and therefore political) factors provide the frame of reference. Long before the Civil War, churchmen were divided along economic and racial lines which bore a close relation to their religious perspectives. An analysis of southern clerical representation in the General Conference of 1844, shows a high proportion of slave-holding ministers among the southern delegates. The average southern delegates were "southerners first, farmers with families to support second, and theologically-untrained ministers third."[10] Of fifty-one delegates, four had a college education. The more well-to-do had dozens of slaves who worked plantations of up to three thousand acres. Altogether, these preachers owned slaves estimated at a value of over two hundred thousand dollars.

Hardening of the Positions

Other works have attempted to study the development of arguments by churchmen for and against slavery. All we can do here is suggest some examples to demonstrate the hardening of the positions between increasingly radical extremes. Under the growing agitation of abolitionists, the northern churches, including the various Methodist bodies, developed a strong abolitionist wing, both in the East and Midwest. In New England, younger preachers like Gilbert Haven argued, in and out of the pulpit, that slavery was not only a moral evil but a pestiferous sin that must be uprooted. Whenever

---

[9] See Haynes, *The Negro Community Within American Protestantism*, 148; E. Franklin Frazier, *The Negro in the United States* (1957), 87, 89; Lester Scherer, manuscript, read through courtesy of the author.

[10] Joseph Mitchell, "Traveling Preacher and Settled Farmer," *MH*, 5 (July, 1967): 3.

such abolitionists were able to get their message across, the result was violent reaction from the South. Brunson, reporting on the General Conference of 1832, wrote, "Such was the sensitiveness of the public mind upon this subject, and especially those in the slave regions, that the slightest allusion to the race held in bondage, whether it be in Church or State, was like the spark thrown upon powder—an explosion was sure to follow." [11] Brunson, it may safely be said, made more than allusion to the issue of slavery, which he strongly opposed.

When moderate forces in church councils appeared to drag their feet, black Methodists lit a few fires. They never ceased to raise the moral issues and to demand action by their churches. Black members of the New England Conference, for example, sent a petition of protest against the do-nothing policies of the General Conference of 1840, especially against the rejection of Negro testimony in church trials.[12] Since most black preachers in the M.E. Church were exhorters or local preachers, they have not left much evidence of their activity.

In the Negro denominations the record is clearer. Both Richard Allen and Daniel Coker took strong antislavery positions. Daniel A. Payne, long before he rose to episcopal eminence in the A.M.E. Church, addressed a Lutheran synod after his graduation from Gettysburg Seminary on the theme that American slavery brutalizes man, destroys his moral agency, and subverts the moral government of God. Most impressive was the denunciation of slavery written by Hosea Easton, a minister of the A.M.E. Zion Church, *A Treatise on the Intellectual Character and the Civil and Political Condition of the Colored People of the U. States; and the Prejudice Exercised Towards Them* (1837). He showed how slavery was degrading the black man into an inferior being, for "the slave system is an unnatural cause and has produced its unnatural effects." Much white prejudice and discrimination could be attributed to slavery. There is something enduring about his appeal:

> They ask priests and people to withhold no longer their [black people] inalienable rights to seek happiness in the sanctuary of God at the same time and place that other Americans seek happiness. They ask statesmen to open the way whereby they, in common with other Americans, may aspire to honor and worth as statesmen—to place their names with other Americans—subject to a draft as jurymen and other functionary appointments, according to their ability. They ask their white American

---

[11] Brunson, *A Western Pioneer*, I, 391.

[12] Haynes, *The Negro Community*, 199, 201; Gravely, "Methodist Preachers, Slavery and Caste," 209-29.

brethren to think of them and treat them as American citizens, and neighbors, and as members of the same American family. They urge their claims in full assurance of their being founded in immutable justice. They ask them from a sense of patriotism . . . from the conviction that God, the judge of all men, will avenge them of their wrongs, unless their claims are speedily granted.[13]

Several well-known black figures, including Harriet Tubman, Frederick Douglass, and Sojourner Truth, were either members of or associated with the Zion Methodists.[14]

In the South, powerful reaction exploded against even the gentlest hint of criticism of the South's institution—and abolitionist critics were anything but gentle! A large literature appeared, produced in large part by southern Methodists, designed to provide justification for slavery on moral and religious grounds. Illustrative is the essay by Holland McTyeire, which was published as first prize by the Baptist Convention of Alabama and later was expanded into a book published in 1859 by the Southern Methodist Publishing House under the title, *Duties of Christian Masters.* It made much of the principle of mutual kindness and respect which characterized the system at its best.

In dealing with the importance of justice toward one's slaves and consideration for their rights as persons, McTyeire used reasonable arguments which, if carried on to the logical conclusion, would have made him an abolitionist. At that point, however, he fell back on biblical texts to demonstrate the reality of slavery in an imperfect world. The most explosive problem was teaching slaves to read. This skill would seem to be advised in order that slaves might be instructed in the Christian faith and be able to read the Bible. However, it might also make them dissatisfied and dangerous potential rebels against society. Therefore, this very able man, who became one of the most influential and progressive bishops of the southern church, concluded that slaves were better left illiterate, taught only by the spoken word, like thousands of poor peasants in "enlightened" Europe.[15]

More systematic was the treatise by William A. Smith, *Lectures on the Philosophy and Practice of Slavery,* published in Nashville in 1856. He was candid: "Slavery, *per se,* is right. . . . The great abstract principle of slavery is right, because it is a fundamental principle of the social state; and . . . domestic slavery, as an *institution,* is fully justified by the

---

[13] Easton, 49-50, quoted in Gravely, "Methodist Preachers, Slavery and Caste," 228.

[14] See discussion in Bradley, *History,* 107, 123; cf. *African Methodist Episcopal Zion Quarterly Review,* 63 (1951): 193-96.

[15] McTyeire, *History,* 156-58.

condition and circumstances (essential and relative) of the African race in this country, and therefore equally right." [16] Laying his ground on philosophic principles, Smith came to the conclusion that, since slavery was part of the natural order and hence ordained of God, it was not wrong. Ideas based on rationalism, which favor equal rights for all men, are not valid if they conflict with the divinely ordained structure, which posits inequality among men. When slavery may be shown to be in accord with the will of God, the institution is good, not bad. Finally, Smith buttressed his argument with biblical citations.

Capers was not a philosopher and contented himself with biblical arguments, supplemented by illustrations of the beneficent aspects of slavery in giving sustenance to inferior races and in offering them hope of salvation. What John C. Calhoun worked out in political terms, Smith, Capers, and many others in the South worked out in biblical and philosophical terms. Methodists were not the only ones to devise arguments in favor of slavery; so did most of the other denominations with heavy investment in the South. A substantial review in the *Methodist Quarterly Review* (southern) of two proslavery books, Albert T. Bledsoe, *An Essay on Liberty and Slavery* (1856), and Thornton Stringfellow, *Scriptural and Statistical Views in Favor of Slavery* (1956), gave high praise to both. [17] "If the Bible sanctions slavery, we will commend it," was the central thesis. No one had real trouble with the Old Testament; but the New Testament required more adroit maneuvering. The principle of the Golden Rule, frequently cited in the North, was dealt with directly. That great principle includes the law, but does not exclude God's order; therefore, it cannot be used against slavery. "The principle of slavery does not conflict with the proper lines of the law of Human love."

In between the radicals on both sides were the moderates—persons who refused to take an extreme position for various reasons. Some hoped the problem could be resolved peacefully. Some were congenital postponers. Some favored partial emancipation, others partial slavery. Some simply loved the church too much to see her rent. For these and other reasons, many Methodists grasped at the promise of the American Colonization Society, founded in 1816, which proposed to solve the problem by removing the Negroes to Africa. It was

---

[16] Quoted in Harmon L. Smith, "William Capers and William A. Smith," *MH*, 3 (Oct., 1964): 25. Those interested in the use of the Bible to justify slavery may consult the following: Gen. 9:25-27, 16:9, 17:12, 30:43; Ex. 14:14, 21:2-8; Lev. 25:39-46; Deut. 15:12; Philem.; Luke 7:2-10; I Cor. 7:20-23; Titus 2:9-10; I Pet. 2:18; Col. 3:22-25; I Tim. 6:1-9.

[17] "The Scripture Argument for Slavery," *MQRS*, 11 (1857): 30, 40-41.

directed specifically at the embarrassing presence of free Blacks. It occupied much the same place in people's thinking as the mission to the slaves, which connived at slavery in order to gain access to the black man's soul. It provided yet another motive for compromise —missionary zeal. If Negroes were sent to Africa under Christian auspices, they could spread the faith there. At bottom, both the Colonization Society and the mission to the slaves contradicted the very purpose they were designed to promote: spreading scriptural holiness. They had a gospel, but it was a tainted gospel. Richard Allen, who would have none of this plan—although a considerable number of black Christians favored return to Africa—was active in the Convention of the Colored Men in America, meeting in 1830 in the Bethel A.M.E. Church in Philadelphia. This organization was strongly opposed to colonization schemes.

Nevertheless, many Methodists gave continued support to both enterprises and did so in the conviction that they were doing the Christian thing. Many moderates like Nathan Bangs thought such activities might avoid schism, in his judgment the worst outcome.[18] Hence, the moderates in the General Conference of 1840 were almost unanimously in favor of supporting the American Colonization Society.

Some of the adjustments, however well meant, amounted to perversion of the church's mission. In this category was the attitude that, since the issue was secular, it was none of the church's business. Moses Henkle concluded simply: "It is impossible to regulate this matter by ecclesiastical action; for it involves a civil relation, with which the Church cannot safely intermeddle." [19] Most unsavory was the controversy over the case of Silas Comfort, which caused great debate in the General Conference of 1840. It was not related specifically to slavery, but it stirred up identical opposing forces. This presiding elder of the Missouri Annual Conference had been censured by his conference for admitting testimony of a Negro in a church trial. The general conference sustained his appeal and rejected the conviction of the annual conference. Nevertheless, debate led to passage of a resolution which condemned black testimony in church trials in states which prohibited it. All the explaining by Bishop Soule, that this did not mean to prohibit such testimony in church trials everywhere nor to cast aspersions on the characters of black members, did nothing to clear away suspicions and bad feeling.

The moderates were not all connivers and opportunists. They had

[18] Bangs, *History*, IV, 242-65.
[19] Moses Henkle, *Primary Platform of Methodism* (1851), 182.

cause to resent the intemperate words and actions of extremists on both sides, which did more harm than good. They wanted desperately to save the church. Hence, a pattern rose in successive general conferences of the thirties and forties, which resulted in an uneasy coalition of moderates with Southerners through 1840. We see the consequences of this coalition in the general conferences of 1836 and 1840, which set the stage for the surprising reversal of parliamentary forces in 1844.

These great quadrennial assemblies were held under an immense threatening shadow. One of the delegates on May 23, 1836 wrote to Laban Clark that the southern delegates were trying to impose the principle of slavery on the whole church. "Tomorrow will determine the business and will perhaps decide the momentous question whether the Methodists shall any longer be a united people." [20] Delegates from New England were ready for a confrontation, but were frustrated by the tactics of the moderate majority who were concerned about keeping the South from bolting. Abolitionists were a rather small minority. Among them was Orange Scott, one of the delegates from the New England Conference. The tone of the meeting was set early by the bishops in the Episcopal Address, which was a classic example of head-hiding: "From every view of the subject which we have been able to take, and from the most calm and dispassionate survey of the whole ground, we have come to the solemn conviction that the only safe, scriptural, and prudent way for us, both as ministers and people, to take, is wholly to refrain from the agitating subject." [21]

The episcopal address four years later was not very encouraging to those who wanted to rid the church of slavery. It took up where the Conference of 1836 left off, and went on specifically to criticize the New England Conference for continuing agitation. This general conference also saw the sad debate over Silas Comfort's appeal regarding testimony by Negroes. In issue after issue, the sessions of 1840 demonstrated the power of the South, aided by those who wished to prevent schism at all costs, to impose its will on the church. In addition to the censure of the New England Conference and the debacle over Comfort's appeal, the case of Daniel Dorchester also went against the abolitionists. As presiding elder, he had obstructed an antislavery resolution in a quarterly conference and had been convicted by the New England Conference of exceeding his powers. This decision the general conference reversed. Once again, the strong approval of the American Colonization Society went against antislav-

---

[20] David Ostrander to Clark, Laban Clark MSS, Garrett Theological Seminary.
[21] In Lucius Matlack, *The History of American Slavery and Methodism* (1849), 43.

ery interests. Finally, the general conference went on record as defending the right of all ministers to hold slaves in states in which manumission was not possible. The wall against abolitionism was raised and closed. It looked as if the church might weather the storm over the great national issue without schism, but the defenders of the wall forgot to lock the back gate.

The Wesleyan Methodist Church: Out the Back Way

While everybody was watching with bated breath, hoping the unreconciled Southerners would not bolt and sunder the church, another movement marched out in the other direction, the followers of Orange Scott and La Roy Sunderland who formed the Wesleyan Methodist Connection. Both these men had been active during the 1830s in the cause of abolition. Scott, presiding elder for six years and delegate to three general conferences, was one of the most able leaders in the church. He came to public attention at the General Conference of 1836, when he made an effective defense of two abolitionist delegates who were up for censure.[22] His bearing made a favorable impression on those observers. He repeated his performance in 1840, and then, broken in health, retired in 1841 for a time. La Roy Sunderland had been active for many years in antislavery work. He helped form the American Antislavery Society, and was the first editor of *Zion's Watchman,* which began publication early in 1836. He was in and out of church trials, in most of which he was acquitted. On the occasion of one of these trials, he confronted Bishop Joshua Soule in an unprecedented manner. When the bishop, who was presiding, tried to stop him from reading a letter in his own defense, he replied, "I will read the Davis letter in spite of all the bishops in the land." When Soule charged him, "In all my experience and in all my intercourse with my fellowmen, I have this to say, that La Roy Sunderland is the first man that ever dared to speak to me in that manner," the defendant came right back: "I thank God, sir, that you have lived long enough to find one man who will tell you to your face what many others say of you behind your back." [23]

These were the leaders of the movement which came in 1842, as a

[22] The best volume on this body is Ira Ford McLeister, *History of the Wesleyan Methodist Church of America* (1959). Valuable as a source is Lucius C. Matlack, *The History of American Slavery and Methodism, from 1780 to 1849; and History of the Wesleyan Methodist Connection of America* (1849). The events of 1836 are reported pp. 18-26 and 118-27 respectively.

[23] Edward D. Jervey, "La Roy Sunderland: Zion's Watchman," *MH,* 6 (Apr., 1968): 29.

small band of preachers and followers withdrew from the Methodist Episcopal Church. They began a new paper called *The True Wesleyan* and called for a convention to meet early the next year. They announced their intention in the first issue of the paper in an extended statement entitled "Withdrawal from the M.E. Church": "We wish it may be distinctly understood, that we do not withdraw from anything essential to pure Wesleyan Methodism. We only dissolve our connection with Episcopacy and Slavery. These we believe to be anti-Scriptural, and well calculated to sustain each other." [24] This statement says much, both explicitly and implicitly, about the original motives for the formation of the new group. Here was, in the first place, another antiepiscopal reform movement similar to those of the Methodist Protestant reformers of the 1820s. Secondly, the break was over the specific issue of slavery. Above all, the Wesleyan Methodists were an antislavery movement. Just below the surface, not yet clearly expressed, was the element which later became dominant: emphasis on pure Wesleyanism, especially sanctification.

At the Andover and Utica conventions of 1843 were forged the elements of the Wesleyan Methodist Connection (not designated a church until 1947), with an initial membership of six thousand. Scott led the movement until his death in 1847. Sunderland was another important figure. Lucius C. Matlack, an excellent writer and editor, joined for a while. He was among several who returned to Episcopal Methodism after the Civil War. The first general conference was held in Cleveland, 1844, at which a membership of fifteen thousand six hundred was reported, organized into six annual conferences.

Thus, the schism which was so much feared took place anyway, but in the form of a small separation in the opposite direction. Shock waves shook the church during the crucial quadrennium of 1840–44. When the next general conference met, dark clouds of foreboding had gathered, and the storm, held off by desperate and sometimes questionable measures for so long, broke. The most succinct comment is that which James Gilruth confided to his journal when, in 1835, he witnessed his Ohio Annual Conference approve a committee report which opposed abolition and favored colonization: "O God!"

[24] The full text is in Matlack, *History of American Slavery*, 308-17; 315.

Chapter 18
Division and Dissension

From one point of view the outcome of the General Conference of 1844 was unexpected. A showdown had been avoided for sixty years. From another point it was inevitable—when pressures rise beyond tolerable limits without any safety release, explosion results. Only one aspect could not have been anticipated with certainty—the break was accomplished with forbearance and without violence, although the aftermath brought its sorry train of recrimination and malevolence. The Methodist Episcopal Church embarked on a course determined by factors beyond its control, which in a few years would open the floodgates of war, threaten the bulwarks of the Union itself, and finally alter permanently a way of life known as the antebellum South. One immediate cause which brought on the crisis of 1844 was the departure of Orange Scott and part of the abolitionist force in 1842.

The General Conference of 1844

Any account of the General Conference of 1844 is complicated by the fact that two issues, not simply one, became interwined in the extended debate. From May 1 to June 1, the weary delegates struggled to determine the best way out of an impossible situation. Greene Street Church in New York city became the scene of powerful debates, sometimes fiery, sometimes poignant, always crucial for the future of the church. Without any doubt whatsoever, the fundamental issue which led to separation was slavery. Equally without doubt is the fact that most of the language of the debate centered on another fundamental issue, the authority of the general conference versus the integrity of the episcopal office. The conflict cannot possibly be understood without reference to both issues.

The church had five bishops: Joshua Soule, senior in point of service, already famous as the cause of a constitutional crisis in 1820, and a New Englander who would cast his lot with the southern branch; Elijah Hedding, elected in 1824, another Northerner known for strict discipline; James O. Andrew, a Georgian who became bishop in 1832 and whose slaves became the focal point for both basic issues; Thomas A. Morris, elected in 1836 from a ministry in Ohio;

197

and Beverly Waugh, a Virginian, also elected in 1836, who would remain in the M. E. Church.

Since by tradition bishops did not participate in direct debate, they were not the prime floor leaders nor the most significant voices.[1] Northern delegates like John A. Collins and Stephen Olin and Southerners like William A. Smith and William Capers participated in extended and complex debates interwoven with parliamentary maneuvers. The first test of strength came with the case of Francis Harding's appeal from the decision of his Baltimore Annual Conference to suspend him for failure to free some slaves he had acquired by marriage. The vote, 117 to 56 to reject the appeal, said much about the new stance of this general conference. It was clear that the moderates were voting with the antislavery forces, not with the southern delegates. The vote was especially significant in that the issue here was slavery without the constitutional complications which attended the case of Bishop Andrew.

The case of Harding was a sort of dress rehearsal for the more crucial case of Bishop James O. Andrew. He also was, unwillingly, a slave owner. He had a young mulatto girl, Kitty, and a young boy bequeathed to him from his first wife's estate. The girl did not want to leave, and the boy was too young. Georgia law prohibited emancipation. In addition, his second wife owned several slaves, in whom the bishop had no ownership or control. Thus he could and did claim that he had never bought or sold a slave and that his only involvement was unwillingly as trustee. Almost everyone understood these facts and considered the case on the broader ground of propriety, not morality or church law. At first he was requested by resolution to resign his office, but this led to strong debate which resulted in a compromise resolution to the effect that he should "desist from the exercise of this office so long as this impediment remains." The final vote was 110 to 68 in favor of the compromise resolution.

It was really no compromise, for by this time the sense of the conference was such that this vote meant almost certain division.

---

[1] Still the most complete analysis of the process of division is John N. Norwood, *The Schism in the Methodist Episcopal Church, 1844: A Study of Slavery and Ecclesiastical Politics* (1923). The principal literature on slavery has been listed in the preceding chapter. No less than three doctoral dissertations offer interpretations of the episcopal office: Jesse Hamby Barton, "The Definition of the Episcopal Office in American Methodism" (Diss., Drew, 1960), Norman W. Spellman, "The General Superintendency in American Methodism, 1784–1870" (Diss., Yale, 1962), and Gerald F. Moede, *The Office of Bishop in Methodism, Its History and Development* (Diss., Yale, 1964). The reader may wish to compare two constitutional histories: James M. Buckley, *Constitutional and Parliamentary History of the Methodist Episcopal Church* (1912), and John J. Tigert, *A Constitutional History of American Episcopal Methodism* (1916).

While a Committee of Nine worked on a plan of separation, there appeared the first in a series of documentary papers, "Protest of the Minority of the General Conference Against the Action of that Body in the Case of Bishop Andrew." Soon there appeared a "Reply" to the "Protest." On June 8 the Committee of Nine reported with a "Plan of Separation." [2] It was intended to provide a procedure in case the annual conferences in the slaveholding states decided that separation was necessary. Provision was made for the establishment of a boundary, which would allow individual societies, stations, and conferences along the border to determine by majority vote to which part of the church they wished to adhere. Ministers were given free choice of allegiance. A beginning was made in providing equitable division of publishing house property and in assigning church property south of the border to the proposed M. E. Church, South.

When this long general conference finally adjourned on June 11, the church was not yet separate, but provision had been made for lawful separation if the South should so decide. There was little doubt of that decision. The process of implementing the separation plan was filled with frustration, misunderstanding, and ill feeling. The wounds, instead of healing, were left to fester. They produced deep scars which took a hundred years to heal and have not yet disappeared. All too accurately, the experience of the church foreshadowed what was about to happen to the nation.

The Meaning of the Separation

The national perspective in which the division of Methodism should be seen is well illustrated by a letter from John C. Calhoun, famous antebellum statesman of South Carolina, to William Capers, dated June 4, 1844, and sent by Capers to the *Richmond Christian Advocate:*

Dear Sir:
    I have felt a deep interest in the proceedings of your conference in reference to the case of Bishop Andrew. Their bearing, both as it relates to Church and State, demands the gravest attention on the part of the whole Union and the South especially.
    I would be glad if you and Judge Longstreet, and other prominent men of the conference, would take Washington in your route on your return home, and spend a day or two with us, in order to afford an opportunity of exchanging ideas on the subject of such vital importance.[3]

---

[2] *JGC,* 1844, 135-37. The major portions are in *HAM* II, 62-63.
[3] Quoted in Sweet, *Virginia Methodism,* 228.

For over a hundred years, Methodists have looked back and in upon themselves in an effort to discover how it could have happened that way, and why. The further they looked, the deeper they probed into the centers of motivation, into the heart of their calling as Methodist Christians. We are dealing here with a theological problem, not simply a question of historical causation. Methodists were not, in the main, systematic theologians. Nevertheless, they were informed by a strong theological tradition derived from the Wesleyan Revival, which was by no means dead in the first half of the nineteenth century. They, as much as any other group of Protestants, were affected by the primitive conditions of the frontier. From Wesley on, an ineluctable strain of expediency permeated their thinking. Consequently, they repeatedly tended to discover programs that would work in the face of a clearly demonstrated need, and only later tried to define and justify them theologically in terms of the doctrine of the church and the church's mission in the world. By trial and error, making prophetic witness while spreading scriptural holiness over the land, Methodists stumbled into schism over the issue of slavery as earlier they had stumbled into churchhood.

Methodist attitudes toward slavery may be charted in a general curve. It looks concave; beginning rather high on the scale of Christian awareness of moral evil, falling to the nadir in relentless compromise with the forces of the Cotton Kingdom, finally, rising once again, inspired by the dual influences of revivalism and abolitionism. We have seen how the Christmas Conference required all members, with certain exceptions, to free their slaves within a year. Although the original disciplinary prohibition had to be suspended, the high principle and expectation of the founders were clear enough. This direct attack on slavery was still lively in 1808, when the open-ended Western Annual Conference, meeting at Liberty Hill, Tennessee, passed a strongly worded resolution to the effect that any member who bought or sold a slave except "in a case of mercy or humanity" should be summarily expelled by the quarterly conference.[4]

But even those original high principles must be qualified by the involvement of the founders themselves. Neither Wesley nor Asbury stand out as champions of absolute freedom for slaves. Asbury was well aware of the temptation to use excuses for not doing anything about the evils of slavery. But, as John Wesley Bond judiciously recalled, "Under such circumstances he did not see what we as a ministry could do better than to try to get both masters and servants

[4] Western Annual Conference, *Journal,* 1808; in William W. Sweet, *The Rise of Methodism in the West* (1920), 148.

to get all the religion they could, and get ready to leave a troublesome world." [5]

There was a deep-rooted conflict between the individual and social aspects of sin as experienced in the local Methodist societies and classes. One of the unanswered questions of history is the experience of slavery in the most personal of all Methodist associations, the class meeting. What about the great impersonal sins of society, in which everyone was involved willy-nilly, sometimes without even being aware of sin? What about Methodist witness on slavery in the societies and classes? What social relations lay behind the repeated references of William Colbert in his unpublished journal of working with the "black classes"? [6] What led Richard Whatcoat to arrange a "lovefeast for the Blacks at 6 o'clock and for the whites at 9"? [7] Much work needs to be done at the point of local involvement before substantial generalization can be made.

However it was at the local level, tension reigned at the top. Leaders in the North were torn between an uneasy conscience which recognized the sinful proportions of the institution of slavery and an abiding sense of responsibility to the church which had nurtured them. On the other hand, leaders in the South, finding their feet stuck more and more in the muddy environment of the Cotton Kingdom, felt pressed to justify what they at first recognized as an evil by claiming that it was not also a sin. They too were seeking to distinguish between personal sins which stood under unremitting attack in society and class and the social evils of the day which were somehow different. The outspoken William Smith of Virginia found himself deeply enmeshed as he tried to stand against the "great evil of slavery" while maintaining that *slavery was not necessarily sinful.* [8]

Here was a clear theological issue which did not receive very clear theological treatment. Could slavery, a man-made institution, be an evil without involving men in sin? The element of sin would make a great difference in so far as it would lead, hopefully, to repentance and amendment. Step by step, southern defenders backed away from this excruciating conjunction of evil and sin toward a disjunction between the evil institution which was the business of the state, and the sinful involvement which was the personal business of members in

[5] Robert Bull, "John Wesley Bond's Reminiscences of Francis Asbury," *MH*, 4 (Oct., 1965): 22.

[6] "Journal," I, 20, *et passim*, in typescript copy in Garrett Theological Seminary library.

[7] Whatcoat, "Journal," II, under 20 Jan. 1794. See also under 3 Aug. and 10 Aug. 1794.

[8] *Report of Debates in the General Conference of the Methodist Episcopal Church* (1844), 26, 44.

societies and classes. In this way, men could participate as citizens in the institution of slavery without being involved personally in sin. Many northern leaders, until after 1840, would have had no real disagreement with the judgment of the Committee on Organization of the nascent Methodist Episcopal Church, South, that the new church should have no part in discussion and agitation on the subject.

One ought not deride the motivation of church leaders under these circumstances, as certain contemporary authors, writing from the stance of the civil rights movement, have done. This is to ignore completely the original and continuing dilemma—how to speak to the slaves' social needs while still communicating the gospel of redemption in Jesus Christ. Whatever else southern ministers knew, they knew clearly that they could not hope to be pastors to slaves if they so much as hinted at antislavery views. Only with this in mind could gentle Bishop James Andrew speak of "slaveholders for conscience' sake." These men may have been misguided. Their views on slavery may have doomed their hopes of evangelism, but they were not perpetrating a fraud. The historian must always beware of reading back into history his own presuppositions.

Understanding the presuppositions and conditions of their ministry, we can then understand their justifications and rationalizations. The non-antislavery position became a proslavery position, which included a biblically based defense of the institution. This became especially important in the period between the schism and the Civil War. There was a good deal of self-delusion and quiet desperation in the citing of texts designed to show the permanent degradation of the sons of Ham under the curse of servitude. However misguided they were, these efforts must be taken as a serious attempt at responsible biblical exegesis and must be regarded more carefully than they have been hitherto in studies of attitudes toward slavery. On the other hand, equally serious attention must be paid to the relative failure of abolitionists and others to make full use of biblical resources in their attacks on slavery. Many abolitionists were quite secular in outlook.

Some ministers were completely devoted to their pastoral calling, which they understood to include Negroes. William Capers is, perhaps, the most tragic figure in a doomed society, as he sought to bring the consolations and rewards of the Christian faith to the Negroes at great cost to his energy and status in southern society. For many long years, against the strong opposition of slaveholders, he worked diligently to carry the gospel to the Negroes. At the same time, during the general conference and afterwards, he was one of the most vigorous proponents of the southern view and a key figure in the formation and development of the new southern church.

The real issue, once again, was a theological one. Which is more important: the forthright proclamation of the gospel to people or a prophetic judgment on society? If social attitudes based on Christian conviction conflict with the Christian's calling to give witness to Jesus Christ, what then? But these considerations were beyond the capacity of most Methodists—most Americans—in the middle of the nineteenth century. A nondenominational layman, himself deeply involved in the struggle that ensued, perceived the profound theological significance of the war and the disputes over slavery. Abraham Lincoln brooded, occasionally in public, on the mysterious judgments of a God who refused to recognize righteousness on either side.

Only a few learned that other hard lesson, the dangers of extremism as well as the dangers of compromise. Whereas many well-meaning persons were pushed, step by step, into intolerable compromises with unjust society, many others through emotion or bent minds rushed without thought of consequences into attacks on all who disagreed with them. Resorting to sordid name-calling, they reduced the complex issues to simple and artificial choices between good and evil, Christian and pagan, true and false, as if life offered no complications that rendered such simplicities impossible. How were they to deal with a situation like that in western Virginia, where the poor whites joined the southern church in large numbers, while the landed slaveholders joined the northern church? Or with Bishop Andrew, who could not be made into a villain? Or with Orange Scott, who loved the church? Or with William Capers of South Carolina, who loved the Negroes? Or with slaveholding Unionists and antislavery Confederates? The deepest wounds were inflicted by the tongues, and, rarely, the fists of emotion-ruled extremists. One of the few rational acts in the unhappy drama was achieved by the separation plan, because the northern extremists for once kept their mouths shut and the southern extremists had to settle for separation.

And yet, what would the church have done without those determined men who were able to stand by their convictions no matter what the cost? Without Orange Scott and Joshua Soule, to mention only two of the many "trouble-makers" who kept things stirred up, the church might have succumbed utterly to the secular culture which threatened to swallow it up. They at least saved the church from gradual self-strangulation through compromise.

Something more needs to be said regarding the relation of the antislavery impulse to theories of racial equality. We must beware of reading back into the nineteenth century racial attitudes characteristic of our own time. Abolitionists were not necessarily committed to the principle of the equality of all races. Many persons who hated slavery nevertheless assumed that the Negro was of inferior stock. On the other hand white southern slaveholders were not necessarily committed to segregation of the races, much less to that later development, Jim Crowism. The wide-spread fear of slave rebellion reveals a belief, probably subconscious, that the black man, if provided with tools of education and weapons of power, might prove to be entirely too capable.

Another sticky, murky problem is the legal regulation of manumission. At the very outset, the strict rules on slavery had been qualified by reference to laws which prohibited manumission. The regulation enacted by the General Conference of 1816 specifically provided, not only that the states must legally permit freeing of slaves, but also that the states must "permit the liberated slave to enjoy freedom." [9] Otherwise, the Methodist regulations could not apply. The tendency among southern legislators was to permit emancipation if the slave was removed from the state in which he resided. Freedmen could remain in Delaware, Kentucky, and Missouri if the former owners guaranteed their support. Mississippi, North Carolina, and Texas provided the same privilege if application were made to the state legislature on grounds of good work. Georgia and South Carolina placed the right of manumission directly in the legislature, but had no specific regulation against remaining in the state. In Georgia, in 1818 and 1829, additional penalties were imposed upon those who freed slaves by will or deed of trust, thus giving evidence that considerable illegal emancipation was taking place. A cursory inspection of state laws would seem to indicate that emancipation of slaves was entirely possible in almost every case, if the owner were seriously desirous of doing so. To what extent, we may ask, were the supposed laws against manumission used by Methodists as an excuse for doing nothing? This matter would bear further study.

There remains the old constitutional issue. Let us be clear. Slavery, from start to finish, was the issue over which the church broke in 1844. Neither secular "revisionists" who would set the whole struggle in terms of economics rather than morality, nor ecclesiastical "constitutionalists" who would debate the relationship between bishops and the general conference, can evade the inexorable problem of slavery as a moral and, therefore, theological issue.[10] This does not

---

[9] *JGC*, 1816, 169-70.
[10] Cf. Melvin Drimmer, ed., *Black History: A Reappraisal* (1968), 99-101, 180, 222.

mean, however, that the problem of Bishop Andrew did not involve real constitutional problems. Anyone who has studied the ecclesiastical development of the Methodist Church from a small exclusive gathering of societies into a major denominational church will recognize the relevance of the constitutional issue in the case. From the day in 1792, when James O'Kelly introduced into the general conference his resolution providing for an appeal by the minister from the bishop's appointment, to that day in 1966, when another special general conference rejected the plea of the Evangelical United Brethren for a term episcopacy in the projected United Methodist Church; the problem of episcopal authority in relation to the power of the general conference has been with us. It would be impossible to explain the role of Joshua Soule solely on the basis of his attitude toward slavery. His convictions on constitutional law, which threw the General Conference of 1820 into utter confusion, guided in large part his ultimate determination to cast his lot with the southern church. Yes, Bishop Andrew unhappily possessed slaves, and that was the nub of the trouble; but delegates to the general conference were quite within their rights in disputing the authority of that body over the tenure and performance of a Methodist bishop. Suffice it to say that the ugly reality of slavery, as the basic issue in dividing the church, does not mean that the constitutional issue was either irrelevant or ersatz.

Having finally confronted the issues directly and having decided on the way of separation, only one more step was needed—to implement the settlement.

Organization of the Methodist Episcopal Church, South

The M. E. Church, South, was formed in consequence of five major steps: (1) the separation plan, (2) the call by southern delegates to the general conference for a constitutional convention in Louisville, (3) the action and election of delegates by southern annual conferences, (4) the Louisville Convention of 1845, (5) the first general conference of the new church in Petersburg, Virginia, 1846. During the early stages many efforts were made to head off division and preserve unity. As late as November, 1845, Bishop Hedding replied to a letter from Laban Clark, who had yet another plan for healing the incipient schism.[11] He said that affairs had already gone too far.

Indeed they had. In addition to the formal actions taken, there was

[11] MS Laban Clark papers, Garrett Theological Seminary.

overt evidence of resistance to any plan of separation which would allow the South to escape the onus of schism. There was southern irritation and sensitivity and increasing bitterness over the tough problems of definition of the border, mutual publishing interests, and ownership of church property.

Under these circumstances southern annual conferences elected delegates to the forthcoming convention in Louisville. The Kentucky Conference, which was the first to meet, set a sort of pattern or the rest. It appointed a committee to propose procedures for implementing the separation plan and invited such bishops as wished to attend the convention. Following Kentucky came Missouri, Holston, Tennessee, North Carolina, Memphis, Arkansas, Virginia, Mississippi, Texas, Alabama, Georgia, South Carolina, Florida and the Indian mission.

The delegates, along with a large number of visitors and a few curious observers from the North, met in Louisville, May 1, 1845.[12] Bishops Andrew and Soule were in attendance. William Capers, Lovick Pierce, Thomas N. Ralston, John Early, William A. Smith, and Thomas O. Summers were active in leadership. After voting in favor of separation, resolutions were almost unanimously approved to form a Methodist Episcopal Church, South; to set up new annual conferences with provision for adherence of border circuits and stations; to call a first general conference to meet the following May in Petersburg, Virginia; and to take care of numerous details attendant on separation.

Between the convention and the Petersburg General Conference, a literary war broke out, especially in the pages of the various *Advocates,* led by Dr. Thomas E. Bond of the New York *Advocate.* Polemical works began to appear in print. Northern annual conferences began to react to what they considered a secession. Andrew was the only bishop clearly aligned with the South. Soule was favorable, and presided at the Louisville Convention, but declined to commit himself. The difficult problem of establishing a boundary between the two churches arose, and the debate over the bearing of the Sixth Restrictive Rule on the division of Publishing House property began. All these activities and issues would continue into the next decade.

---

[12] A voluminous literature developed, some of it polemic. In addition to the *Protest of the Minority* and the *Reply of the Majority,* both resulting from the General Conference of 1844, there is the official record prepared by the M. E. Church, South, *History of the Organization of the Methodist Episcopal Church, South* (1845); Henry B. Bascom, *Methodism and Slavery: A Review of the Manifesto of the Majority in Reply to the Protest of the Minority* (1845); George Peck, *Slavery and the Episcopacy: Being an Examination of Dr. Bascom's Review* (1845); and Charles Elliott, *History of the Great Secession* (1855).

A last step in the formation of the M. E. Church, South was the action taken by the general conference in Petersburg in 1846. At this meeting Joshua Soule, with a fine sense of the dramatic, declared his adherence to the southern church. To him the constitutional issue, around which he had organized his career, was more important than the moral issue of slavery. This general conference elected two new bishops, William Capers and Robert Paine. It authorized *Advocates* in Nashville, Charleston, and Richmond and a quarterly review. Provision was made for a new hymnal and discipline.

Between Division of the Church and Division of the Nation

The story of Methodism between 1845 and 1860 is largely one of competition between the two branches. An early victim was the Plan of Separation, which was well intended but inadequate. One of the more bitter and enduring conflicts ensued over the border. The original idea had been that a line should be established between non-slaveholding and slaveholding annual conferences, with modifications based on local situations. "Societies, stations, and conferences" on the border could decide by majority vote which branch to join. After such vote, the minority side should not attempt to establish a competing church. A distinction was made between *border* and *interior* situations, the latter meaning points separated from the border by intervening points.

This arrangement left several unanswered questions. First, just how was a vote to be taken? Again, did the border shift as charges and conferences voted one way or another? How long could efforts continue to gain adherence? Could individual points within a circuit make independent decisions? Occasionally confusion, misrepresentation, and downright chicanery influenced the outcome. On Virginia's eastern shore it was argued that charges were interior because of thirty miles of intervening water. Voting procedures might exclude large numbers of members. The situation in Maysville, Kentucky was particularly touchy, because the minister and the presiding elder were for the South, whereas the leading layman, Dr. Tomlinson, President of Augusta College, was for the North. Preliminary petitions, which were regarded by some as the actual vote, included 139 for the North; but the congregational meeting at which the vote was taken went 109 to 97 for the South. After lengthy legal battles, the state supreme court reversed a lower court and gave the entire property to the South.

In general, the southern church was more aggressive than the northern. The Virginia Conference (South) encroached successfully on both the Baltimore and Philadelphia Conferences (North). The practice of ignoring the distinction between border and interior points was very common. For example, although Parkersburg, West Virginia, was in the Kanawha District of the Ohio Conference and was 75 miles from the border, the members drove off the appointed minister and received one from the Kentucky Conference. The membership was closely divided on preference. Two southern churches were established in Cincinnati, although both were located with northern churches between them and the border. Fiercely fought over were the middle portion of western Virginia and the part of the Baltimore Conference north of the Rappahannock River.[13] There was some encroachment by the northern church, not very successful, in the slaveholding states of Kentucky, Missouri, and Arkansas.

The final failure of the separation plan was made clear when it was rejected by the northern General Conference of 1848. The struggle over the property of the Publishing House dragged on until a decision by the United States Supreme Court in 1854 supported the South. After this, the struggle over church property generally waned. The decline of the conflict allowed members to enjoy the luxury of debate over other issues, such as lay representation in annual and general conferences. It turned out that the day of the layman, except in the Methodist Protestant Church, was not yet. Both northern and southern General Conferences of 1852 and 1854 strongly rejected the proposal.

As the conflict over the separation plan declined, that over slavery warmed up. Curiously, neither branch made any formal change in the rule on slavery until the time of the Civil War, but attitudes and interpretations changed considerably. The northern church was plagued by the fact that it had a major interest in slaveholding areas where the Methodists had adhered to the northern branch. This was particularly true of Kentucky, where a northern Kentucky Conference was established in 1853. The southern church also hesitated to make a formal change in the rule because of concern over border conferences. This did not prevent the General Conference of 1854 from giving it a narrow interpretation, limiting its application solely to the slave trade. Throughout the period, although the M. E. Church, South assumed a serious responsibility for a mission to the Negroes, the church refrained from any interference in the institution.

[13] See especially data in Lewis M. Purifoy, Jr., "The Methodist Episcopal Church, South, and Slavery, 1844–1865" (Diss., 1966), 87-118; and Gordon Pratt Baker, ed., *Those Incredible Methodists*, Chaps. 8 and 9.

In the North, the issue of slavery took center stage for a time at the General Conference of 1856, in which a vigorous attempt was made to change the rule, but again without success. Arguments based on constitutional law and expediency overcame moral scruples. By this time there were six annual conferences partly or wholly within slave territory, with white membership of 143,000 and black membership of 28,000. Once again, the conservatives were allied with the constitutionalists to defeat the abolitionist forces. Nevertheless, it was clear that a strong majority of the northern delegates were opposed to slavery in any form. For the next quadrennium, discussion of the issue was open and vigorous.

Finally, in 1858, the M. E. Church, South got around to removing the rule on slavery from the *Discipline,* an action which had been urged ever since separation in 1844. On the other hand, the northern church conservatively retained the rule, even under threat of yet another antislavery schism. Only the outbreak of the Civil War submerged these internal struggles in a larger drama. It thus remained for that unchurched layman, Abraham Lincoln, to make the decisive move.

Chapter 19
Books and Teachers

"Beware you be not swallowed up in books: an ounce of love is worth a pound of knowledge," John Wesley wrote in 1768. Then, eight years later: "Our little books you should spread wherever you go. Reading Christians will be knowing Christians." [1] Thus has it been with his followers to this day—an elemental suspicion of book learning at war with a fundamental drive toward Christian education. At least some facets of this opposition reflect that underlying tension which constitutes one of the major themes of Methodist history: authority versus democracy. Sometimes it has seemed that the disciplined understanding of the faith (reading and learning) has stood in conflict with the free expression of the Spirit. This chapter shows some of the ways in which tension, although never eliminated, has been resolved.

The Methodist Publishing House

Traditionally, The Methodist Publishing House has been dated from 1789, when John Dickins was appointed book steward. The story really begins much earlier, specifically with the appearance in 1737 in Charleston, South Carolina, of a little hymnbook entitled *A Collection of Psalms and Hymns,* "America's first Methodist-related imprint," as well as the first collection of hymns for use in the Church of England.[2]

Among the more ambitious unauthorized early enterprises was the publishing venture of Robert Williams (1769–73), who undertook all on his own to reprint and distribute some Wesley tracts until he was forbidden by action of the first conference. At the same time that Thomas Rankin acted to stop Williams, he set about distributing large numbers of Wesley's tracts he had imported from England. From this

[1] To Joseph Benson, 7 Nov. 1768 and Richard Boardman, 12 Jan. 1776, *Letters,* V, 110, and VI, 201.

[2] Leland D. Case, "Origins of Methodist Publishing in America," Bibliographical Society of America, *Papers,* 59 (1965): 12-27; also his contribution to Joseph Pilkington, *The Methodist Publishing House,* I (1968). This history, which carries the story to 1870, together with the equally substantial work on the publishing history of the Evangelical United Brethren by John H. Ness, Jr., *One Hundred Fifty Years* (1966), are by far the best sources.

time on, there was some kind of elementary system for book distribution, but not yet any formal organization for publication. During the time of the Revolution, as we learn from the supplementary minutes kept by William Duke and Philip Gatch, there already existed a plan for distribution of religious books centered in Philadelphia. By 1781, three Wesley hymnbooks had been independently printed in Philadelphia. After the formation of the Methodist Episcopal Church, official publications included Coke's Christmas Conference sermon on the Godhead of Christ, the early disciplines printed each year, and the general minutes (called "Minutes of the General Conference").

Then, in 1789, John Dickins, whose primary appointment was St. George's Church in Philadelphia, was also appointed book steward. This regularizing of the "book business" (one of the early terms) constituted the formal beginning of The Methodist Publishing House. It was still a small activity, however. Dickins was expected to take care of it on the side. There was no property, no printing, no publishing, and especially, no money. The first two book stewards had to keep the infant enterprise going out of their personal funds, but from then on an ever increasing list of books was made available for the edification of Methodists. Wesley's abridgment of Kempis' *Imitation of Christ* (titled *An Extract of the Christian's Pattern*) and an American edition of Wesley's home-remedy book, *Primitive Physic*, made their appearance. An abortive attempt to start an American Methodist magazine brought forth two years of the *Arminian Magazine,* which was really a reprint of Wesley's periodical of the same title. From these curious insignificant beginnings grew the massive Methodist Publishing House. The book concern, however falteringly, was on its way—more editions of the hymnbook, early portions of Asbury's Journal, and another attempt to start a *Methodist Magazine* (which also lasted two years, 1797-98). In 1798, Dickins, who had cherished the book concern as a personal labor of love, died in the great Philadelphia plague, mourned by all.

Ezekiel Cooper, the second book steward, entered on his responsibilities reluctantly because the enterprise appeared to be sinking under financial burdens. His greatest service was to rescue the business and keep it going until a day of greater opportunity dawned.[3] Owing in part to intramural troubles in St. George's congregation, the business was moved to New York in 1804. Ten years later, the list of books and tracts offered read as follows with the most expensive books listed first and the cheapest last: "Coke's Commentary on New

[3] See Lester B. Scherer, "Ezekiel Cooper, 1763–1847: An Early Methodist Leader" (Diss., Northwestern, 1965).

Testament"; "Wesley's Notes on New Testament"; "Wesley's Sermons," 9 vols.; "Wood's Dictionary," 2 vols.; "Fletcher's Checks," 6 vols.; "Benson's Life of Fletcher"; "Portraiture of Methodism"; "Experience of several eminent Methodist preachers," 2 vols.; "The Saint's Everlasting Rest"; "Methodist Hymns," 2 vols., bound together; "Law's Serious Call to a Holy Life"; "Experience and Letters of Hester A. Rogers," "Fletcher's Appeal"; "Abbott's Life"; "Alleine's Alarm and Baxter's Call"; "Family Adviser and Primitive Physic"; "Methodist Discipline"; "Extract from John Nelson's Journal"; "Watters' Life"; "Confessions of James Lackington"; "Truth Vindicated"; "Thomas à Kempis"; "Mrs. Rowe's Devout Exercises," abridged; "A Scriptural Catechism."

Coke's *Commentary* was by far the most expensive, being imported from Europe. Only three works of American origin are on the list: the autobiographies of Benjamin Abbott and William Watters and the *Scriptural Catechism.* So much for American independence—at least intellectually!

In 1816, Joshua Soule, already famous but still at the outset of a remarkable career, became another of the reluctant book stewards, and once again the financially faltering institution was rescued, but this time without the desperate recourse to personal funds. In 1817 the first Bible was published, and more and more materials designed for children came out. At last, in 1818, after two abortive earlier attempts, the *Methodist Magazine* began its unparalleled record. Published every year except 1829, under varying titles, until 1932, it was then succeeded by its depression-born child, *Religion in Life.* Under the generic title of *Methodist Quarterly Review* it has had a longer life than any other religious publication.[4]

If 1818 marks the turning point in publication of a religious magazine, 1820 is the turning point for the entire business. In that year Nathan Bangs entered on his responsibilities and presided over the expansion of the Methodist Book Concern as it entered on its amazing history of growth and service. The day of great things had at last arrived. Let us review the development of magazine projects.

The *Methodist Magazine (MQR)* began life as a forty-page monthly in

---

[4] For convenience we use the abbreviation *MQR* for the *Methodist Magazine* (1818–28), monthly; *Methodist Magazine and Quarterly Review* (1830–40), quarterly; *Methodist Quarterly Review* (1841–48), quarterly; and *Methodist Review* (1885–1931), bimonthly. The *Methodist Quarterly Review* of the M. E. Church, South (1847–1930), abbreviated as *MQRS*, went under the titles *Quarterly Review of the Methodist Episcopal Church, South* (1847–61, 1879–86, 1889–94); *Southern Methodist Review* (1887–88); *The Methodist Review* (1895–1903, 1906–08); *The Methodist Quarterly Review* (1903–06, 1908–30).

which the influence of Nathan Bangs was determinative until 1836. Areas of interest were arranged in the contents to include such heads as Divinity, Biography, Scripture Illustrated, the Attributes of God Displayed, the Grace of God Manifested, Miscellaneous, Religious and Missionary Intelligence, Obituary, and Poetry. Since Bangs had to do much of the writing as well as most of the editing, many pieces were reprints from British Methodist publications or other religious papers in the United States. By 1841, the publication had become not only a quarterly of impressive size, but also more truly a *review* in which major attention was paid to book reviews of current religious publications. Circulation difficulties led the General Conference of 1848 to recommend, "Resolved, that while we highly prize the Quarterly Review in its present character, it is our firm conviction that, were it made more practical, it would be more popular and useful." Although John McClintock (the first editor who was a college graduate) was all in favor of usefulness and popularity, he did not believe that making the magazine "more practical" was the way. His brilliant scholarly bent preserved the high intellectual quality which distinguished the *MQR* in its finest years. While the *Advocates* served the needs of the popular religious press for all the people, the *Review* continued to emphasize the more serious intellectual concerns. Its greatest days would come after the Civil War.

One might assume that the next large periodical venture was the *Christian Advocate;* but that is not true. In 1823 appeared the first of many impressive efforts to serve the needs of the church's youth, the *Youth's Instructor and Guardian,* which, along with the *Child's Magazine* of 1827 and its successors, took account of children, the future of all institutions. After 1841 came the *Sunday School Advocate,* published in newspaper form for some 200,000 subscribers. Another project was the "Sunday School and Youth's Library," a series of cheap books on all sorts of subjects, which by 1842 had run to some two hundred titles, and the even cheaper "Juvenile Books," of stitched paper.

The history of the *Christian Advocate* is yet to be written. The riches to be found in those almost endless pages, illustrative of the religious, social, and cultural life of the common people, has been sampled only slightly in historical monographs and articles.[5] On September 9, 1826

---

[5] The complex skein of regional *Advocates* is becoming more readily available through the microfilm project sponsored by the Methodist Librarian's Fellowship and the Commission on Archives and History. Only the archives of the United Methodist Commission on Archives and History, the library of The United Methodist Publishing House, and several seminary libraries possess more than a scattering of the originals. For an analysis and locator, see the work edited by John D. and Lyda K. Batsel, *Union List of United Methodist Serials, 1773–1973* (1974). The *Advocates* also went through a complicated change of titles.

appeared the first number of the first volume of a people's magazine which in one form or another has continued in publication to the present and which quickly became the largest circulating periodical in the country with a subscription in 1828 of some 25,000. It was, of course, officially supported by the church. It was preceded in fact by two other kinds of unofficial papers: (1) regional enterprises like *Zion's Herald* in New England (1828) and the *Wesleyan Journal* in Charleston, South Carolina (1825); and (2) the publications of the reformers of the 1820s, the *Wesleyan Repository* and *Mutual Rights*. The reformist magazines were started because their supporters found the pages of the *MQR* closed to them. Hence, a principal cause for the foundation of the *Christian Advocate* was to counteract the influence of the magazines being distributed by the reformers. Apart from that pressure, however, Bangs had hit upon a red-hot journalistic opportunity, fulfilling an immense need which had only to be tried to be recognized. Not only did the *Advocate* grow by leaps and bounds, but it spawned numerous regional offspring which provided plenty of competition. Among the earlier regional forms, which combined general features used by all editions with particular regional news and local articles, were the *Western Christian Advocate*, which, beginning in 1834, became the second most influential edition, closely rivaling in circulation and geographical spread the national New York *Advocate;* the *South-Western Christian Advocate* (Nashville, 1832); the *Pittsburgh Christian Advocate* (1833); the *Southern Christian Advocate* (Charleston, 1837); the *Richmond Christian Advocate* (1839); the *Northern Christian Advocate* (Syracuse, 1841). In the early fifties came the St. Louis, Northwestern (Chicago), and California *Advocates*. And that was not the end. These editions varied in the closeness of their relation to the editorial authority of The Methodist Publishing House. After 1845, of course, the southern editions came under the control of the M. E. Church, South. The *Central Christian Advocate* was a northern voice in St. Louis. Many of the editors won national recognition, such as Thomas E. Bond, Abel Stevens, Matthew Simpson, Charles Elliott, T. M. Eddy, and John B. McFerrin.

A venturesome experiment in a women's magazine began in 1841, the *Ladies' Repository and Gatherings of the West*. It was designed to counteract from a modest Christian stance the newly popular fashion-conscious *Godey's Lady's Book*. Published in Cincinnati and edited by Leonidas L. Hamline, who also had to do most of the writing, it was by far the most sumptuous Methodist publication of its day. It expressed the democratic spirit of the West, which encouraged women to play a more active role. It took a more daring position on some aspects of modern culture, such as the novel, but it certainly was no rallying point for women's liberation. The editorial policy sought to describe the religious duties of women to God and other human beings, assist in doing these duties, illustrate virtue through biographies of fine women, discuss biblical texts, and encourage domestic economy. There was a section for children and even occasional material for other readers (men). It exuded victorianism and romanticism. It was eagerly snapped up, especially by culture-starved women of the great Midwest.

The publication of various magazines was only a part of the increasing activity. The book list grew year by year. It included one major enterprise still in print: Adam Clarke, *The Holy Bible* (usually called *Commentary*), 1824, in six volumes. In 1856, it was reported to the M. E. General Conference that 15,588,926 tracts had been distributed during the quadrennium. As the Sunday school movement grew, the publishing house undertook to provide all kinds of study supplies. No wonder that the problem of space and equipment burgeoned! New quarters on Mulberry Street in New York were acquired along with presses and other necessary equipment, only to be totally destroyed by fire in 1836. Nathan Bangs, who was an eyewitness to the disaster, groaned to see the irreplaceable records and documents, including Asbury's journal, go up in flames. The vigorous organization, however, survived the fire, legal complications over the division of 1844, copyright infringements, and even financial scandals.

The southern book concern had much the same history, except for additional difficulties attendant on the church property case which was dragged all the way to the United States Supreme Court and the dire catastrophe of the Civil War. Nashville became a publishing center for southern Methodism, and the Nashville *Christian Advocate* was the most influential voice. The *Southern Methodist Quarterly Review* tried to emulate, if not surpass, the best in the northern intellectual quarterly. In general, its stance was somewhat more conservative on cultural as well as social matters, reflecting the views of its early editors, H. B. Bascom, D. S. Doggett, and Thomas O. Summers.

The much smaller Methodist Protestant Church had its own publishing program, and gamely kept in circulation two church papers, *Mutual Rights and Methodist Protestant* (later *Methodist Protestant*) and *Methodist Correspondent* (for the West, eventually *Methodist Recorder*).

Finally, the German Methodists became numerous enough in the 1830s and 1840s, especially in the Ohio valley, to need a religious paper of their own: *Der Christliche Apologete*, which began in 1839 and was edited for fifty-seven years by one man, William Nast. Nast was a well-educated convert to Methodism serving as missionary to the Germans around Cincinnati when he was chosen editor. This German-language Methodist magazine continued in publication until 1941.

United Brethren and Evangelical Association

In spite of the relatively small size of these churches, both former branches of the Evangelical United Brethren maintained an impressive publishing program. Both began issuing printed material early in the nineteenth century, and both made a major change of location and program in the early 1850s. We begin with the Evangelical Association, which had a slight edge in point of time.[6]

The *Evangelische Gemeinschaft*, the widely used name of this German-rooted organization, began publishing almost as soon as the church was gathered, although a church-operated press was not set up until 1815. Apparently the first item was a German *Discipline*, prepared by George Miller in 1809 on the basis of the Methodist *Discipline* of 1808. It was printed in Reading, Pennsylvania, and bore the title *Glaubenslehre und allgemeine Regeln christlicher Kirchen-Zucht und Ordnung der sogenannten Albrechts-Leute.* That same year John Dreisbach brought out a catechism, always a popular form of instruction, *Die kleine Biblische Katechismus;* and next year the first hymnal appeared, John Walter's *Geistreicher Lieder.*

The first significant step was the establishment of a publishing house and printing press in New Berlin, Pennsylvania in 1815–16. This was largely the work of young John Dreisbach, then only twenty-five years old. A small printing shed and a hand-operated wooden press—this was the first form of the Evangelical Publishing House, of which Solomon Miller was elected first book agent by the General Conference of 1816. Dreisbach was the second book agent. A revised edition of the *Glaubenslehre und Kirchen-Zucht-Ordnung* was published the next year. Not until 1836 did the general conference authorize an English edition of the *Discipline,* as well as an English hymnbook. That year also saw the appearance of the first issue of the long-lasting *Der Christliche Botschafter,* which remained in publication until 1946 as the oldest German-language religious periodical in America. Not until 1848 did the *Evangelical Messenger* begin as an English language paper.

In the 1830s the plant was large enough to move into new quarters, a substantial brick building. Slowly the work expanded, but it was limited by the small membership and by a peculiar policy of appoint-

---

[6] An excellent recent study is that of John H. Ness, Jr., *One Hundred Fifty Years, A History of Publishing in the Evangelical United Brethren Church* (1966).

ing as book agent men who appeared to be too sick to travel. By 1850, the year of the jubilee celebration of fifty years since the first organization of classes by Jacob Albright, the business had grown to the point where the general conference decided to move to a central location. Cleveland was chosen, and in 1854 the move was made.

The United Brethren began publishing early in similar fashion with hymnbooks and disciplines. But nothing really significant came until the General Conference of 1815 authorized an official *Discipline,* which was printed in Hagerstown, Maryland in 1816. A German hymnbook was also provided. In 1826 came the first English hymnbook, several years earlier than the Evangelical hymnbook. A first effort at a religious magazine was *Zion's Advocate,* printed in 1829 in Indiana. After this came the *Union Messenger.* The most significant enterprise was the beginning of an official denominational magazine called the *Religious Telescope* in 1834, one of the first fruits of the organization of a new publishing house in Circleville, Ohio. This paper had a long history in service to the United Brethren. William R. Rhinehart, the first editor, was a reformer at heart and did much to bring progressive views to the church, but his views did not become widely popular, and circulation remained a problem, especially since this semi-monthly was the largest single activity of the publishing house. As in Methodism, a bitter debate raged over the propriety of carrying the issue of slavery into the pages of the paper. Although a gag rule was never fully imposed, limitations were such that free discussion was impossible.

As with the Evangelical Association, materials were brought out in both German and English. *Die Geschaeftige Marthe* ("Busy Martha") and *Der Deutsche Telescop* were papers for the German readers. In 1845 the *Religious Telescope* became a weekly, and finally had over three thousand subscribers, which rose to over five thousand by 1851. Continual growth in spite of financial handicaps made a change of location desirable. As a result, in 1853 (one year before the Evangelical move to Cleveland), the publishing house was moved to Dayton, where it entered a new era of growth.

Education

Methodists were rather obviously behind many other denominations in their approach to the higher branches of education. Several strong universities already had a long history before the M. E. Church was even founded. On the other hand, none could claim prompter attention to the needs of elementary education, religious and general. Although Robert Raikes is properly recognized as the founder in

1780 of an organized Sunday school movement in England, Methodist preacher Hannah Ball had a lively school for children going at High Wycombe ten years before. Sunday schools quickly developed in both England and America. Thomas Ware, for example, told of the organization of a Sunday school for poor children in 1790.[7] Undoubtedly, there were other schools started in the 1780s. Out of sheer necessity these schools, although intended to advance religious education, included reading, writing, and arithmetic. The strong growth of these schools created the demand for the broad selection of literature for children provided by the publishing house. Thus, the original educational stimulus from Wesley, who laid responsibility for training of children on his preachers, merged with the new Sunday school movement. Gradually, the elements of general education gave way to specifically religious education, as other agencies undertook the broader task.

Methodist higher education got off to a premature start with Cokesbury College, the fond project of Thomas Coke, Francis Asbury, and the Christmas Conference. It opened in 1787 in a new building and had a brief struggling existence before it burned to the ground in 1795. The idea was to provide the rudiments of classical education with a Christian emphasis to preachers' sons, poor orphans, and paying students. Only briefly did it attempt to provide college work, and actually it was an elementary and secondary school.

Ebenezer Academy in Virginia was one of several schools founded by Methodists in the last two decades of the eighteenth century. There was a Kentucky Bethel and a South Carolina Bethel and others, all of which came to untimely ends. Before the General Conference of 1820 urged annual conferences to undertake responsibility for establishing institutions of higher education, the only attempts were the foundation of Asbury College in Baltimore, Wesleyan Academy in Wilbraham, Massachusetts, and Wesleyan Seminary in New York. The Wilbraham institution was destined to have a long and varied history.

After the church officially gave encouragement to the development of colleges under the auspices of annual conferences, a number of projects surfaced. The Ohio and Kentucky Conferences cooperated in establishing Augusta College in Kentucky on the Ohio River. Although it was a casualty of the division of the church in 1844 and ceased all operation in 1849, it counted among its alumni Bishop Randolph S. Foster and Professors John Miley and W. G. Williams. Depending on the criteria for measuring the foundation of a college,

[7] Ware, *Sketches* (1842), 183.

the first permanent *Methodist* institution would be either McKendree College in Illinois (founded as a small academy in 1828) or Randolph-Macon College in Virginia (chartered 1830, opened 1832), whose first president was Stephen Olin. Wesleyan University, founded through the agency of Laban Clark and presided over in its early years by Wilbur Fisk, was chartered and opened in the interval between the two steps which gave rise to Randolph-Macon. Fisk brought many original ideas to Wesleyan, especially an emphasis on modern languages and science.[8] Dickinson College in Pennsylvania, although it possesses a charter carrying the date 1783, became a Methodist institution only in 1833. Something of the same may be said of Allegheny College, chartered in 1817 and made Methodist in 1833. In the Southeast appeared Emory College at Oxford, Georgia in 1836, an institution unique in that it was the occasion for the rise of a town and not vice versa. The town and college have been preserved so well that they have been designated collectively a United Methodist historical shrine. About the same time Emory and Henry College began in western Virginia. Indiana Asbury University was established in Greencastle, Indiana, chartered in 1837, and opened in 1838. Matthew Simpson was the first president. Ohio Wesleyan University began in Delaware, Ohio in 1844.

The oldest college for women in the world is Wesleyan College, Macon, Georgia, started in 1836, became Methodist in 1839. Greensboro College in North Carolina began classes in 1846. Both of these institutions are still in operation. A third women's college, Cincinnati College for Young Women, made a good beginning but later declined and closed.

While the larger M. E. Church was busy founding colleges, the much smaller but growing Church of United Brethren and Evangelical Association were beginning to provide for themselves. Both carried on Sunday school programs supported by their publishing houses. At the General Conference of 1845, the United Brethren took an important step in giving official support to the establishment of a church-related college. The result was Otterbein University in Westerville, Ohio, which opened in 1847. Evangelicals started Albright Seminary in New Berlin, Pennsylvania in 1853. Unlike Otterbein, it closed after a brief struggle. Not until after the Civil War did other educational enterprises get under way.

The only black Methodist college which was founded before the Civil War and survived was Wilberforce University, whose beginnings

[8] See Wilbur Fisk, "The Science of Education," *MQR*, 13 (1831): 419-41, his inaugural address.

go back to 1844, but actually was opened in 1856 as a joint venture of the African Methodist Episcopal and M. E. churches. After a brief closing during the Civil War, it reopened as an A.M.E. institution under the presidency of Daniel Payne. The only effort made by the A.M.E. Zion Church during this period was Rush Academy (1848), which never really got going.

Methodists, who got a very late start, caught up rapidly in the establishment of colleges. Under the wing of the M.E. Church had come thirteen institutions between 1822 and 1844, which placed Methodists second only to Presbyterians. Eleven of those thirteen survived as permanent institutions. It should be noted in conclusion that all these institutions aspired to the ideal of liberal arts education based on the classics. Furthermore, although they definitely professed a Christian purpose, they carefully avoided any pretension to theological study as such. This was a reflection of the widespread suspicion of formal theological training for the Methodist ministry.

"The Happy Art of Winning Souls"

The title above was used by Thomas Ware in a discussion of early theological education.[9] Part of that "art," he readily admitted, was sufficient learning to get the true message across. That was the attitude of most of the early leaders, very few of whom had much formal training and almost none college degrees. Theological education in its first form was completely personal; one man learned from another more experienced. Young Thomas Smith, for example, met and was examined by none other than Asbury himself, who accepted him and concluded, " 'Thomas, be faithful to God, be faithful to his church, be faithful to yourself.' When he dismest me I thought a thousand blessons on his soul, for his good advice."[10] Shadrach Bostwick, a well-educated preacher who located in Ohio, was an elder brother to men like Alfred Brunson who wrote he was "a father to me, . . . a professor and teacher in our 'Brush College.' "[11] William Milburn called it "Swamp University." The presiding elders were key figures in this early form of theological education. They took the younger men under their wing and showed them how. According to Brunson, ministers should exhibit four leading characteristics: conversion, fruits, calling of God, seals from the church. Their qualifications were of three types: natural, gracious (aid through the Holy Spirit), and acquired. Only the latter required training, and that

[9] Ware, *Sketches,* 107.
[10] Thomas Smith MS, Drew Theological Seminary, 8 May 1799.
[11] Brunson, *Western Pioneer,* I, 235; Milburn, *Ten Years of Preacher-Life,* 82.

better in the field than in school.[12] He favored the "Conference course of study," but not college education. Unlike some of his predecessors, including Pilmore and Asbury, he did not think Greek and Hebrew were important, because the English Bible was best anyway.

A major turning point was the beginning of the course of study in 1816, the first form of which was the responsibility of annual conferences. The Committee on Ways and Means of the General Conference of 1816 brought in a recommendation that annual conferences should set up "a course of reading and study proper to be pursued by candidates for the ministry," to be directed by presiding elders. During the early years this course, if instituted at all, was very limited and the examinations superficial. Gradually the idea caught on and was developed more seriously in some annual conferences than in others. The Baltimore Conference, for example, had a well developed plan by 1817.[13] Numerous other conferences had developed courses during the 1820s. Most of the books recommended, in addition to the standard works of Wesley, included Fletcher's *Checks* or other works, Baxter's *Saints' Everlasting Rest,* Law's *Serious Call,* and others which Wesley himself had emphasized. Also likely assignments were Rollins' *Ancient History,* Josephus *Antiquities,* and various works on English and geography.

In 1848 the general conference of the M. E. Church (1878 in M. E. Church, South) standardized this course of study with a list for use throughout the church.[14] It did not change until the period after the Civil War. This plan for a course of study had two major effects on the intellectual climate of American Methodism. In the first place, it provided a design for theological education which would equip ministers with a more substantial understanding of the meaning of Christianity and its history, together with the tools for practice of ministry. In the second place, it established a bulwark against any pretension to theological schools. These, it could be argued, simply were not needed. There persisted until well after the Civil War a deep suspicion of theological schools as such. Although two such schools did make appearance in the period under consideration (Boston and Garrett), they were for long on the defensive. Bishop Enoch George urged, as a prime reason for supporting the course of study, that it would protect young men from "metaphysics," which he suggested

[12] Alfred Brunson, *The Gospel Ministry, Its Characteristics and Qualifications* (1856), 6 ff, 27-29.
[13] *Those Incredible Methodists* (1972), 132-33. Cf. Kenneth E. Rowe, "New Light on Early Methodist Theological Education," *MH* 10 (Oct., 1971): 58-62. Also the Journal of the Illinois Conference in Sweet, *Religion on the American Frontier,* IV, 303-04.
[14] See lists in *HAM,* II, 654-55.

they would encounter in schools.[15] In a strong argument in favor of Methodist support for higher education, Nathan Bangs was careful to add: "I am no advocate for theological seminaries, considered distinct and apart from our colleges, though I am far from believing that they either have been or are the nurseries of heresies. Nor can I see any reason why sound theology may not be taught, guarded, and defended as thoroughly in a theological school, as it can be in the closet or in the pulpit."[16] He thought the best way to guard against heresy was to provide sound theological education.

That was about as far as one could go. The editor of the *Christian Advocate* was attacked for being "anti-Methodistical, not to say anti-Christian," for giving support to theological seminaries. When La Roy Sunderland wrote an article in the *MQR* in favor of theological education, he had to make clear he did not mean theological seminaries.

A similar distaste for formal theological training permeated the United Brethren and Evangelical Association. The *Christliche Botschafter* warned against *tiefsinnige philosophische Spekulationen* ("profound theological speculation").[17] The Evangelicals tended to more open opposition than the United Brethren. Bishop John Seybert wrote of "university educated and pharisaic hypocrites," but Albright was not against education, and Seybert himself was a wide reader. Among the United Brethren the influence of university-educated Otterbein was strong. Hence, the *Religious Telescope* took a more favorable attitude toward formal theological training, and in 1839 the magazine began a compaign for more adequate ministerial training. In 1841, the United Brethren General Conference appointed a committee to prepare a course of study, which was very similar to the Methodist list. It was in effect by 1845. In 1843, the Evangelical Association had also come to develop a course of study. Both contained writings of Wesley, Fletcher, and Watson. In the mid-1850s, John Dreisbach explained in behalf of the Evangelical Association that opposition was not directed to theological education as such, but only to the preparation of persons who "are not in a regenerated state by grace, and consequently not called of God to this sacred office." Theological schools as such had to wait till the post-Civil War period.

[15] Letter to Laban Clark, 25 May 1825, *MH*, 3 (Jul., 1965): 18-21.

[16] Nathan Bangs, *The Present State, Prospects, and Responsibilities of the Methodist Episcopal Church* (1850), 303-304.

[17] Much valuable data is in a thesis by William H. Naumann, "Theology in the Evangelical United Brethren Church" (Diss., Yale, 1966), which provides references to *Chr. Botschafter*, II (1837), 49-51; Seybert, *Journal*, I, 5; *Religious Telescope*, 7 Aug. 1839, p. 63; 18 Aug. 1841, p. 10; *Evangelical Messenger*, 26 Dec. 1855, p. 204.

Chapter 20
Early Theological Expression

If one is interested in hitting the high points of theological development in America, he will not begin with the Methodists. He will first
take account of colonial Puritan thought in New England; study the
rationalistic reaction associated with the Enlightenment, Unitarianism
and Transcendentalism; and then move on to the Presbyterian controversies of the early nineteenth century swirling around the old and
new schools. This is not to say that Methodism had no theological
development, but rather that it took place in the context of theological
issues which went considerably beyond the denomination and religious centers elsewhere. Inevitably, Methodism was affected by the
powerful intellectual forces which were molding the outlook of
American Protestantism. Most of these forces, as Winthrop Hudson
reminds us, were European in origin, but they were all subject to
uniquely American influences, for better or for worse.[1] No less an
authority than Horace Bushnell regarded the Methodists as pioneers
in the Americanizing process; responding ably to the challenge, but
also caught in the perils of an unstable, changing society.

> Thus, the Methodists, for example, have a ministry adapted, as regards
> their mode of action, to the new west—a kind of light artillery that God
> has organized, to pursue and overtake the fugitives that flee into the
> wilderness from his presence. They are prompt and effective in action,
> ready for all service, and omnipresent, as it were, in the field. Our
> Methodist brethren have put on their armor too against the enemies of
> learning among themselves. They are building colleges, and one among
> the number, which they mean to make the most complete and best
> endowed university in the west. If sometimes their demonstrations are
> rude, and their spirit of rivalry violent, still it is good to have such rivals,
> for their labor is still ours, and when they have reached the state of
> intelligence they are after, they are sure to become effectually, if not
> formally, one with us. Therefore let there be, if possible, no controversy
> with them; but let us rather encourage ourselves in a work so vast, by the
> fact that we have so vast an army of helpers in the field with us.[2]

This somewhat patronizing view of the role of the Methodists describes accurately the problems faced by the young denomination in

[1] In Gerald C. Brauer, ed., *Reinterpretation in American Church History* (1968), 154-55.
[2] Horace Bushnell, *Barbarism the First Danger* (1847), 31. This essay grew out of an
address to the American Home Missionary Society.

adhering to its original calling to spread scriptural holiness throughout the land, while yet retaining and refining the theological heritage
so powerfully and effectively provided by John Wesley.

Intellectual Interest

First of all, the student must divest himself of the stereotype of
Methodist preachers as homespun ignoramuses. This prejudice derives from the classical tradition in the univerity which defines education in terms of the literary and philosophical heritage of ancient
Greece and Rome. In this tradition the preachers had little part, for
with few exceptions, they were not formally educated. Yet, consider
Joseph Pilmore, an early pioneer, diligently studying Hebrew during
his first year in America, his reason being "a desire to be more
extensively useful in the world and more effectually promote the
glory of God." [3] Much the same can be said, with ample evidence
from his journal, of self-educated Francis Asbury. One is astounded
to discover the extent of purposeful reading done by many of the
early leaders. If their literary style did not always demonstrate mastery of Dr. Johnson's English, it was eminently suited to communication with the people. If scholarship would make them "more extensively useful," they were all for it.

Thus, one is not surprised to discover that the theological enterprise of early Methodism was considered an adjunct to the main
business, preaching the gospel. It was "salvation theology." [4] This is
especially true of Francis Asbury, who has survived many biographi-
cal studies without a hint of theological competence. Some writers
have gone out of their way to indicate that he had no theological
understanding at all. This view is simply not true and is no longer
tenable.[5] Although his theology was certainly not in any sense systematic, his preaching was informed by a well-grounded theological
framework derived largely from Puritan sources and amplified by the
powerful influence of Wesley. His theological reading was omnivorous. An analysis of the innumerable data in his journal gives ample
evidence of impressive theological competence. He knew, in other
words, what he was talking about when he proclaimed Christ.

Mention of Wesley reminds us of his continuing, persistent influ-

[3] Pilmore, *Journal*, 27; cf. 44, 75, 102, 116, 163. He was also going through his Greek
New Testament.

[4] See the effective discussion by Charles A. Rogers, "The Theological Heritage of the
Early Methodist Preachers," *The Duke Divinity School Review*, 34 (1969): 196-208.

[5] See the dissertation by Edward M. Lang, "The Theology of Francis Asbury," (Diss.,
Northwestern University, 1972).

ence on the form of the Methodist message. It was pervasive enough not to require documentation. If anything besides the Bible was to be found in the famous saddle-bags, Wesley's works were. Time and again the preachers in conference agreed, as Jesse Lee put it referring to the Conference of 1781, to "preach the old Methodist doctrine, and inforce the discipline which was contained in the *Notes, Sermons* and *Minutes* published by Mr. Wesley." [6] Various Wesley tracts, either in pamphlet form or bound up in sizable volumes, were repeatedly kept in print.[7] The episcopal address to the General Conference of 1840 was saying nothing new as it called attention to the centennial of the beginning of the Wesleyan movement, reemphasizing the Methodist theological roots in the Wesleyan message. Perhaps with another issue in mind on which it took the same stand, the college of bishops warned against changes from those roots except "with the utmost caution."

Early Expressions

We begin with an inherited and not very well-digested statement of theological belief, the "Articles of Religion," which Wesley had prepared for his American followers in 1784. This abridgment of the Anglican Thirty-nine Articles serves as a symbol of the European origin of most American theology. Their chief significance has been to function as a bulwark against "popish pretensions" and "atheistic rationalizations." They have been very little read, but have provided a vague sort of comfort by their very presence. Hence, according to the restrictive rules, they are not to be tampered with. They do not set forth the doctrines distinctive of Wesleyan theology.

One of the earliest attempts to systematize Methodist theology was made by Asa Shinn, who brought out in 1813 *An Essay on the Plan of Salvation: In Which the Several Sources of evidence are Examined, and Applied to the Interesting Doctrine of Redemption, in its Relation to the Government and Moral Attributes of Deity.* The title gives an ample statement of purpose. All religious knowledge should be based on rational evidence, whether it be intuitive self-evident truth, reason and logic, or revelation undergirded by personal conviction. Shinn sought to show that Wesleyan theology as contained in the official documents of Methodism is in accord with that evidence.

[6] Lee, *Short History,* 70.

[7] In addition to those listed in appendices to the *Disciplines* see, for example, *A Collection of Interesting Tracts,* published by order of the general conference by Bangs and Emory, 1825. It contains those listed in the *Discipline* until 1812 with others and was revised for use as late as 1861.

Shinn's book had nowhere near the influence among Methodists as did the perennial favorite, Richard Watson's *Theological Institutes,* which came out in an American edition in 1829. This English attempt to systematize Wesley's theology continued past the mid-nineteenth century as the standard authority. That the preachers were seriously interested in theological topics is demonstrated by the impressive series of weekly discussions held by the New York Preachers' Meeting during 1817 through 1819. In one summary statement they agreed

That faith, which is the condition of justification, is simply believing the record that God has given of his Son . . . and therefore, according to the nature and fitness of things, *must* be the *act* of the creature. But as man is by nature so depraved, that he cannot do good works pleasing to God, but by Christ preventing [coming before, enabling] him, that he may have a good will, and working with him when he has that good will, the creature has no power to exercize that faith until he is excited and enabled thereto by the Spirit of God. Hence that faith which is the act of the creature is of the operation of God.[8]

They were further edified by a long report on the "unconditional benefits of redemption" leading to sanctification.

In all this, very little interest was expressed in maintaining the formal walls of orthodoxy. Methodism has been remarkably free from doctrinal trials. Now and then minor overtones may be heard. The Committee on Safety of the General Conference of 1816 professed to have discovered some "dangerous tendency" toward the "ancient doctrines of Arianism, Socinianism and Pelagianism," together with departure from the principles of the Reformation and Wesley. But nothing apparently happened as a result of the exposé. Interest in theological topics continued, as is illustrated by the invitation sent in 1832 to the elder scholar of English Methodism, Adam Clarke, to come for a series of lectures in America.[9]

Controversy

The bulk of Methodist theological writing in the early period grew out of the various controversies with Deists, Unitarians, Calvinists, and other denominational opponents. Nathan Bangs was much concerned about "enlightened" philosophers who were explaining away the Christian faith based on revelation. He wrote a long letter to Laban Clark to emphasize that the limitations of reason are such that

[8] Manuscript records kept for the New York Conference by the New York Public Library; see especially entries for 16 Apr. and 18 Oct.

[9] See letter of 6 Feb. 1832 in *MH,* 3 (July, 1965): 22-24. The Bangs letter below is on pp. 4-8.

revelation becomes necessary for religious knowledge. He also expended much effort to prove that Methodist polity was in accord with Scripture and ancient tradition.[10] Furthermore, he was not slow to enter the great Calvinist controversy with *The Errors of Hopkinsianism* (1815) and *An Examination of the Doctrine of Predestination* (1817).

The debate with New England Calvinists and Revisionists lasted a long time. In the 1780s and 1790s, Thomas Ware essayed to show New England Christians "the better way," by which he meant free grace. Fundamental relations between church and state were involved, as is shown by Henry Boehm's report of the situation in Vermont, where Methodists defied the practice of taxing everyone for the support of the Congregational churches.[11] From the standpoint of the established clergy, Methodist circuit riders were thrice condemned interlopers: they were from the South—strike one, they were uneducated—strike two, and their work was unauthorized —strike three! [12]

Of all the pioneers in New England, beyond Jesse Lee, Nathan Bangs, and Laban Clark, Wilbur Fisk stood as the most competent Methodist defender against Calvinism. He was one of the few preachers with a college degree (Brown University B.A.), was a member and presiding elder in the New England Annual Conference, and in 1830 was elected first president of the newly-founded Wesleyan University in Middletown, Connecticut. That same year he delivered his "Discourse on Predestination and Election," which proved to be the opening shot in a long theological exchange, chiefly with the colleagues of Nathaniel Taylor at Yale University on the theological issues between Methodists and Congregationalists. Fisk's central point was that the Calvinist view destroyed any possibility of man's response as a free agent. He was well aware that old-line Calvinism had already gone through modifications in Samuel Hopkins, and was undergoing more change with Taylor. In fact, by this time Taylorite views on predestination were not far from the Methodists. He tried to show that Taylor, in departing from Old Edwardianism, had landed in Pelagianism and "natural ability." If the revisionists were to ignore the Wesleyan resolution of the problem, then they had only a choice "either of going back to the old Calvinistic ground of remediless impotency, or of advancing on to the Pelagian

[10] See his *An Original Church of Christ* (1837). His *Vindication of Methodist Episcopacy* and *Defense of the Fathers* were directed largely against the Methodist Protestant reformers.
[11] Ware, *Sketches* 126, 144, 205-6, 212; of his early experience, pp. 13, 48. Boehm, *Reminiscences*, 248-49.
[12] See Douglas Chandler, "Enthusiasm vs. Education? Early Methodist Preachers in New England," *The Duke Divinity School Review*, 34 (1969): 188-95.

ground of the New Divinity." Predestination, he argued, does not necessarily follow from the depravity of man. "Although all moral depravity, derived or contracted, is damning in its nature, still, by virtue of the atonement, the destructive effects of derived depravity are counteracted; and guilt is not imputed, until, by a voluntary rejection of the gospel remedy, man makes the depravity of his nature the object of his own choice." [13] The Wesleyan stance, he concluded, makes it possible to retain the biblical doctrines of the depravity of man and the salvation by grace alone, while not denying human ability and responsibility. Whether he left a mark on the New England divines is debatable, but he certainly was not ignored. In 1837 his part of the exchange appeared in book form as *The Calvinistic Controversy*.

Polemics involving Calvinism rose as well from contacts with Presbyterians and Baptists in the middle and southern states. Benjamin Lakin reported at length on an exchange he had with Baptists, in which he attributed to them the classic doctrines of the Synod of Dort (1619), and proceeded to set against them the position of Wesleyan Arminianism.[14] The most notorious fight with the Baptists, however, centered around the attack mounted by J. R. Graves, editor of *The Tennessee Baptist* of Nashville in the 1850s. His greatest blast appeared as *The Great Iron Wheel; or, Republicanism Backwards and Christianity Reversed* (1855). It was designed to be a defense against "the most belligerent and offensive of all Protestant sects," which has turned the whole west into "one great battle-field" strewn with the literature of the Methodist Book Concern. As an original Old Landmarker he declared that Methodism was 1,747 years too young to claim any apostolicity of origin.[15] What Methodists regarded as providential he called accidental. Specifically, the "wheel" was the itinerant system, which is Jesuitism. Perhaps the vehemence of Graves's attack is partly explained by the fact that he had chiefly in mind the views of Joshua Soule, then senior bishop of the M. E. Church, South. As was customary in those days of open sectarian conflict, Graves's broadside was answered by Methodist "parson" William G. Brownlow in *The Great Iron Wheel Examined; or, Its False Spokes Extracted, and an Exhibition of Elder Graves, its Builder* (1856).

Similar exchanges, if not so boisterous, took place with the Disciples especially the Campbellites, and other denominations. Asbury was of the opinion that, while "the Presbyterians are a little contentious, the

[13] See Leland Scott, "Wilbur Fisk and the Calvinistic Controversy," in *Forever Beginning* (1967), 99-118, esp. 107, 112. Also his chapter in *HAM*.

[14] Lakin's journal in Sweet, *Religion on the American Frontier*, IV, 257-58.

[15] J. R. Graves, *Great Iron Wheel* (1855), vi, vii, 19, 140, 157, 164.

Baptists are violent." But John Smith, early circuit rider in western Virginia, was not convinced of the accuracy of the distinction. Describing a confrontation with a Presbyterian minister in church, he recorded: "At which time he fell to Abusing and blackgarding of me And Said if his office did not prohibit and forbid him to be A Striker that he would Lace me well[.] I told him I believ'd that was not all that hinder'd him. and it was as much as he could do to keep his hands off of me[.] I saw it was to no purpose to Argue with A mad man And so let him run on."

In the end, Smith concluded, he himself "kept the field." [16]

Worship

The sermon, which from the beginning was the central feature of corporate worship, had to be placed in some kind of setting. John Wesley had provided the "Sunday Service," revised from the Anglican *Book of Common Prayer,* for regular daily and weekly use. Although a few brief efforts were made to use the Sunday Service with all its liturgical forms, it very quickly disappeared on this side of the Atlantic.[17] This fact has more than liturgical significance. It is symbolic of the loss of the central concept of the church at the very moment the American societies were becoming a church. The net result was to leave the church without any stated form of worship. Although forms were later provided, the damage was done. Many Methodist ministers have felt perfectly free to follow any plan they pleased, with or without the consent of their congregations. For this reason the development of accepted practices becomes very important.

At a very early date, long before the organization of the church, a clear distinction was made between the public and the private meetings of the societies. Pilmore testifies to this distinction.[18] He also insisted on at least minimal observance of the Christian year, and warned against "wildness, shouting, and confusion in the worship of God." The sermon quickly became the center of most services, the other parts becoming adjuncts of the proclaimed message. This helps to explain the early importance of exhorting, which was a relatively brief homily or application of the message of the sermon to the immediate lives of the people. It differed from the sermon in that it took no text. Whatever else happened in the ordinary service, at the

[16] Asbury, *Journal,* I, 38; Smith, "Journal," 27.
[17] Lee, *Short History* (1810), 107.
[18] Pilmore, *Journal,* 110, 82-83, 138. Gaddis, *Foot-Prints,* 127,129.

end the "doors of the church were opened," which meant an invitation to the acceptance of Christ and membership in the church. Whether at camp meeting or Sunday service in the city church, this was the main design for worship.

Programs of worship stated in advance were rare. In 1826, however, the New York Preachers' Meeting published guidelines: (1) for morning worship reading from the Old Testament, (2) singing and prayer, (3) reading from the New Testament, (4) "sing a few verses," (5) preaching, (6) singing, (7) prayer and benediction.[19] This form may be taken as typical of the more settled societies in the East. Further instruction required the use of the Lord's Prayer in the morning service, but permitted omission of scripture lessons on sacramental occasions. Afternoon and evening services were to be the same, except that the lessons and the Lord's Prayer might be omitted. Noteworthy is the omission of any formal provision for exhortation in the services.

The New York ministers' order of worship was obviously based on guidelines in the *Discipline* of 1808. Wilbur Fisk, writing in the *Methodist Magazine (MQR)* of 1824, warned against two extremes, both of which he thought threatened Methodist worship: excessive emotional expression, "animal feelings," and liturgical rigidity as practiced in some other churches. "It is to be feared, the religious exercises of many are too sensual, in consequence of suffering their animal feelings to have an undue influence. In such cases, instead of being *spiritual* worship, it becomes *sensual* excitement." [20]

Celebration of the Lord's Supper, although long desired and finally provided for by the Christmas Conference, was infrequent, usually quarterly. The reason for this disuse of the communion may have been simply the scarcity of elders, who were stretched to the limits of their energy in getting around immense circuits.[21] Whatcoat's journal in the 1790s is full of references to administration of the sacrament to groups of all sizes, up to one hundred fifty people at once, usually in connection with a preaching service. Although the portions of liturgy which pertained to the Lord's Supper fared better than the morning service, and the *Discipline* of 1824 required use of the ritual; there is considerable evidence that some ministers followed their own whims. No legal directions were yet given for the elements, and the use of

[19] Manuscript records of New York Preachers' Meeting, New York Public Library, under 3 July 1826.

[20] Wilbur Fisk, "A Sermon on the Spirituality and Truth of Divine Worship," *MQR*, 7 (1824): 81-90, 121-30, esp. 85; cf. 125.

[21] John Thomas Tredway, "Eucharistic Theology in American Protestantism, 1820–1860," (Diss., Northwestern, 1964), 237.

ordinary wine was quite common. But differences of opinion, based on the rising cause of temperance, were beginning to appear before mid-century.[22]

Very little interest was expressed in forms for baptism, except for controversy with the Baptists. Practices varied widely and included immersion, pouring, and sprinkling, in and out of the river. The only point Methodists were inclined to insist upon was the validity of infant baptism.

All kinds of special services developed, some of them derived from Wesleyan precedents, others *de novo.* Almost universal was the rich experience of worship at quarterly and annual conferences. These, at least, would serve as some direction for the guidance of itinerant preachers and help avoid more exotic variations. Observance of congregational fasts and thanksgivings was common. Watch nights were long practiced in accordance with Wesley's precedent. Above all was the love feast, which repeatedly threatened to supplant the Lord's Supper as a sacramental occasion. Pilmore speaks of quarterly love feasts, which sometimes preceded or followed the Lord's Supper. They were common at conference meetings, and they were a central part of camp meetings. They could develop spontaneously in revival. The most succinct description of what they were all about is given by Thomas Ware: "To take a little bread and water, not as a sacrament, but in token of our Christian love, in imitation of a primitive usage, and then humbly and briefly to declare the great things the Lord had done for them in having had mercy on them."[23] Brunson states that three strong men were posted at the door to keep "rowdies" out.[24] This, of course, reflects the special conditions which prevailed on the frontier. Another common feature is that, when bread and water were not readily available, a perfectly good love feast could be held without any equipment whatever. Prayer meetings were also very common and increasing in usage.

One more aspect of worship demands attention: hymnody. If any one aspect stands out, both in the awareness of the participants and outside observers, it was the *singing.* Methodists really deserved their reputation of being a singing people. Between 1805 and 1843 at least seventeen hymnbooks were printed for Methodist use.[25] Among the

[22] Cf. Tredway, 240; Moses Stuart, "The Duty of the Churches in Regard to the Use of Fermented Wine in Celebrating the Lord's Supper," *MQR,* 17 (1835): 411-438; Gaddis, *Foot-Prints,* 339; Leland Scott in *HAM,* I, 315.

[23] Ware, *Sketches,* 63.

[24] Brunson, *Western Pioneer,* I, 87.

[25] Johnson, *Frontier Camp Meeting,* 197, 362-64. Cf. Leonard Ellenwood in *Religion in American Life,* II, 320-21.

most popular were Stith Mead, *Hymns and Spiritual Songs* (1805); Thomas S. Hinde, *The Pilgrim Songster* (1810); Orange Scott, *The New and Improved Camp Meeting Hymn Book* (1929); and *The Methodist Pocket Hymn Book* (1830). That unacceptable and unauthorized hymnbooks were also current is indicated by a prefatory warning: "We most earnestly entreat you, if you have any respect for the authority of the Conferences, or of us, . . . to purchase no hymnbooks, but that are signed with the names of your bishops."

Some of the hymns are still familiar: "Come Thou Fount of Every Blessing," and "On Jordan's Stormy Banks I Stand." Many of them reflect a strong military symbolism after the fashion of St. Paul. Forty of the hymns in Hinde's book were by John A. Granade and Caleb Jarvis Taylor, both of them Methodist circuit riders admitted to the Western Conference in 1801 and 1810 and both famous for their hymnody.[26] Many of these hymns were so familiar that almost any congregation could sing them from memory. Others had to be "lined out" by the preacher or song leader. That meant singing a line which would then be repeated by the people. Another favorite device to bring the people into singing easily was the chorus, where lines might be repeated for easy memorization. No wonder that these singers came to be called, in mixed envy and derision, "shouting Methodists"!

> They are despised by Satan's train,
> Because they shout and preach so plain;
> I'm bound to march in endless bliss,
> And die a shouting Methodist.
>
> The devil, Calvin and Voltaire
> May hate the Methodist in vain;
> Their doctrine shall be downward hurl'd:
> The Methodist will take the world.

This song appeared in various versions, all shamelessly boastful, from 1805 on.

Theology in Action

In the final view, it could be said that Methodism gave expression to its theology by marking out the royal road of salvation through the wilderness of this life. Only a minor part of the drive to spread scriptural holiness was directed toward theological polemics; the main business was to show people the way to heaven. Although the day had

[26] See B. St. James Fry, "The Early Camp Meeting Song Writers," *MQR*, 41 (1859): 401-13.

not yet come when Methodists and other Christians would make explicit the social relevance of the gospel, and although the church suffered under the horrendous moral burden of the issue of slavery, its message did carry into many facets of common life.[27] This theme becomes subject to a more systematic study in a later period, but a few observations may properly be made.

An indication of the progress of Methodism from sect to church is the appearance in the early nineteenth century of service organizations such as the Tract Society (1817). It developed a reading program for the poor which was begun on a small scale by "a few pious and benevolent females."[28] The Missionary Society (1819), formed under the leadership of Laban Clark, Nathan Bangs, and Freeborn Garrettson, supported such work as that already under way in Ohio by John Stewart with the Indians. Methodism was on the way to becoming a well-organized service institution. Tracts and missions began to spread over the land, with or without scriptural holiness.

Ever since Wesley in the general rules gave examples of "avoiding evil in every kind," Methodists had been rather good at listing individual sins to be avoided. A theme frequently repeated all through the nineteenth century was that stated, for example, by Moses Henkle in his *Primary Platform of Methodism* in 1851, urging strict observance of the general rules and particularly the sabbath. This conservative exponent of discipline listed among those activities to be avoided on Sunday, not only the common amusements and frivolous activities, but also going visiting, feasting, taking medicine, neglecting children and servants, sleeping (more than on other days), and writing letters.[29] The message is clear: Sunday is for church going, Bible study, and religious conversation.

A more socially significant issue was the abuse of alcohol. Several decades before the temperance movement began, Methodists had accepted Wesley's Rules, including the one against "drunkenness, buying or selling spiritous liquors; or drinking them (unless in cases of extreme necessity)." In the early period this rule was understood to apply to distilled liquor such as gin, which had devastated England with its cheap availability in the eighteenth century; rum made from molasses and imported from the West Indies; and whisky, which was the evil spirit of the frontier.

Already in the 1790s, regulations attempted to control buying and

[27] See for full discussion Richard Cameron, *Methodism and Society in Historical Perspective* (1961).

[28] Bangs, *History*, III, 55.

[29] Henkle, *Primary Platform*, 147. Cf. C. B. Parsons, "A Cursory View of the Evil Tendencies of Fashionable Amusements," *MQRS*, 7 (1853): 197-210.

selling. This effort did not meet with much success. Proponents of temperance had great difficulty in getting any kind of regulation of activity. Not until the General Conference of 1836 was a clear prohibition enacted against the making or selling of spirituous liquors by ministers. A few leaders like Wilbur Fisk, Timothy Merritt, James Axley, James B. Finley, and Peter Cartwright spoke forthrightly against the evils they had seen wrought in the lives of men by alcohol. A few were for teetotalism, which meant rejection of all alcoholic beverages. Most favored abstinence, which generally referred to strong drink. The New England Conference had a temperance society in 1833 and the Tennessee Conference another in 1834. Before mid-century, the church had succeeded in taking a much stronger stand on this evil, which was easily identified with individual sin, than it had achieved on the far deeper social evil of slavery, which appeared to so many to be a political issue beyond the competence of the church.

At mid-century Nathan Bangs allowed himself to take a long view of the progress of Methodism up to that time. Laying aside the troublesome problems which afflicted the church he loved, he surveyed the positive advances under the headings of numerical growth, temporal increase, education, missions, strength of doctrine and "old Methodism," tracts, Sunday schools, and temperance. He found good things to say under all categories. Most important, he found the preservation of the "vital principles" which distinguished Methodism and must never be allowed to disappear.

If, for instance, we were to relinquish the doctrine of the atonement, as generally understood by orthodox Christians, or that of justification by grace through faith, sanctification, the possibility of falling from grace, the witness and fruits of the Spirit; or were we to break up the itinerancy, or lay aside class meetings, or cease to hold love-feasts, we should no longer be Methodists, because these doctrines form our vital principles, and these usages form those peculiarities by which we are distinguished from all other denominations, and in the use of which our success, by the blessing of God, has mainly resulted.[30] He approved of the adaptation of the itinerant plan to the new challenge of the city station. But in general, he cherished the preservation of the essential old ways which had blessed the Wesleyan movement from the beginning.

His optimistic view could be supported by much evidence of growth and strength. Methodism *was* a winner! He could arrive at such favorable conclusions, however, only by ignoring other evidence of

[30] Bangs, *The Present State,* 63.

trouble. Chief, of course, was the failure to solve the problem of slavery in the church without schism. Perhaps the final willingness to divide the church, rather than further to compromise with slavery, was a victory of sorts, but it was a rueful one. Beyond this, signs were visible of trouble with some of the old essentials which Bangs cherished. Moses Henkle, another conservative, said, "We have, evidently, reached a point—a crisis—where, if the peculiarities of Methodism, in which our fathers gloried, are to be maintained, and transmitted, pure, to posterity, they must be fully and fairly explained, and defended, to the satisfaction of reasonable men and Christians." [31]

If it was indeed a crisis, as he averred, it was one of those subtle crises which sneak up without fanfare before its nature is recognized. A spate of tracts and guidebooks on the nurture and preservation of the class meeting began to appear in the 1850s, all extolling the virtues of the great experiment in religious work with small groups.[32]

Perhaps these concerned authors protested too much. If the traditional institutions of Methodism were so wonderful, why did they require so much elucidation? The truth is, at the same time the church was demonstrating so convincingly its success in Christian witness in the United States, it was paying the price of victory in becoming a great institution, burdened with numbers and organizations, increasingly displaying tares along with the wheat. Before this evidence, which Bangs chose to ignore, pressed too hard on the church; it was thrown, along with the rest of the country, into the horrors of fratricidal war. After it was all over in 1865, nothing was quite the same as it had been. Methodism was living in a different land.

The Price of Victory

During the first half of the nineteenth century, Methodism continued the process of interaction with its environment. In the East, where the church first grew and remained strong through the entire period, the principal form of society was agrarian, but subject to increasing pressures of urbanization. The early little towns, in which the first societies had begun, were by 1860 large cities. On the other hand, in the west the agrarian society remained dominant; in fact, in

[31] Henkle, *Primary Platform*, 11.

[32] Among them Charles C. Keys, *The Class-Leader's Manual* (1851); John Miley, *Treatise on Class Meetings* (1866). See also the broader themes in Osmon C. Baker, *A Guide-Book in the Administration of the Discipline of the Methodist Episcopal Church* (1855).

some areas had scarcely overcome the frontier wilderness. The journals and diaries and letters of western preachers are full of language
and metaphor rooted in the land. When preachers located as a result
of marriage or financial pressure, they almost invariably became
farmers.

Under frontier conditions the connectional system kept the
preachers in line, more or less, but it could not obliterate the strong
individualism and tradition of self-reliance which produced many
colorful characters. The odd-ball was endemic to the westward
movement, including Methodism. Some of these individuals were
altogether admirable. Take Shadrach Bostwick, for example, who
rose to the position of presiding elder in New England and in 1803
moved to the Western Reserve, married, and located. He studied
medicine on his own and began its practice, but remained an active
local preacher who had great influence on the young circuit riders
who visited him in Deerfield. On the other hand one finds James
Axley, the rough and ready frontiersman, who amused Governor
(and Methodist local preacher) Edward Tiffin with his table manners
as he ate "chicken in the rough" in the gubernatorial home. Mrs.
Trollope, who had a low opinion of the *Domestic Manners of the Americans* (the title of her book, published in 1832), must have had him in
mind. Yet, his acquaintance with frontier ways made possible his
effective campaign against hard drink.

In and out of the scene came eccentric figures like Lorenzo Dow
who, after hesitation by the annual conference, was admitted on trial
in Massachusetts in 1798 and immediately began an industrious,
spottily successful, frenetic ministry. He was never admitted in full
connection. He disappeared from his appointment as a result of a
"divine impression" that he must go to Ireland to proclaim the gospel.
Back in the United States, he traveled extensively in the South and
Southwest. Everywhere he went his eccentric appearance and manners made a startling impression. Of course, colorful personalities
were not limited to any one area or time. Methodism has had its full
share of mavericks.

The question has already been raised about the effects of the
American experience on the quality of Methodism. Of the quantity
there is no doubt. It amounts to one of the great success stories in the
history of Christianity. The question remains, what price was exacted
for this success?

One need not exaggerate in reconstructing the kind of life led by
the typical preacher riding a circuit on the western frontier between
1784 and 1850. The means of transportation were primitive: horse,

wilderness trail, long hours in the saddle, no directions, no bridges, no protection from the weather or the Indians. At the end of a long day, either some isolated log cabin or a bed of boughs in the woods. In the cabin for company, along with the pioneer and his wife (or only his wife), several urchins of the forest, infestations of roaches and fleas, cold bare floors and smoking chimney. Food catch-as-catch-can. Malaria. Typhoid. The "misery." Mosquitoes, deer flies, ticks, jiggers.

This sort of primitivism results not in a romantic idyll but in human degradation. In a world devoted to survival, the moral sense is dulled. We are not suggesting that the circuit rider played fast with the pioneer's wife. Rather, the whole of life is permeated with moral callousness. The sense of discrimination is destroyed. Life is reduced to its animal necessities. Morality inevitably suffers, because it is based on weighed and measured decisions. Weighing and measuring are luxuries not available on the frontier. Frequently, the easiest way out was a strong shot of whisky. If Methodists later ran strong against demon rum, they could be said to have lived hand-in-glove with their subject. They knew what they were talking about. Along with moral degradation went intellectual debacle. What was there to talk about? And with whom? The life of a hermit was agreeable to Henry David Thoreau in his carefully defended intellectual fortress in the woods of Walden. Five hundred miles west, Walden would have been in Ohio's Western Reserve.

Brush college was a poor center of intellectual ferment without an original fund of knowledge and thought brought in from the civilized world. Books, except notably those in the circuit rider's saddlebags, were almost nonexistent. Persons of education were also nonexistent, unless they were among those few unlucky ones who had very, very good reasons for being as far away from civilization as possible. The exceptions, like Edward Tiffin and Shadrach Bostwick in Ohio, come readily to mind and are quickly exhausted. Gradually, of course, there were log cabin schools and eventually, small colleges. The latter, however, usually devoted many struggling years to sheer survival before they were able to make much of an intellectual contribution. By this time the circuit riders had long since departed westward, along with the second and third generation Boones, Kentons, and Zanes, preparing the way for the Jedediah Smiths and Jim Bridgers.

An inevitable consequence of this intellectual famine was the disintegration of theological perspective. The finely knit interpretation of Wesley's synthesis of Anglican, Catholic, Reformation, Puritan, and Enlightenment strands suffered in the homespun environment. The distinctive meaning of the steps from conversion to perfect love was blurred as the complex facets of theology were drowned in cries of "Rescue the perishing!" Drowning men will not be finicky about the ordering of the sticks they will seize. An overnight stop in a wilderness community does not provide much opportunity to develop understanding of faith commitment. Save as many souls as possible, record their names, tote them up, and then on to the next appointment. The meaning of justification by faith, sacramental occasions, sin, mediation, redemption, atonement, and salvation of persons and worlds —let alone prevenient grace, Trinity, two natures, epistemology, secular and sacred, imputed righteousness and imperfect perfection—was lost in the exciting, but undiscriminating, spirit of the camp meeting.

It all adds up to cultural barbarization. This statement can still be made in spite of two very important qualifications. First, this view easily reflects an eastern prejudice and misunderstanding of the nature of the American West. This prejudice must be strongly discounted. Second, there were positive values of the westward experience which left an admirable mark on both nation and religion. Self-reliance, candor and honesty, simple and direct faith, eager response to human society, stalwart trust in God in the face of great peril and insecurity, heroic devotion—these are some of the benefits of the conquest of forest, mountain, and plain. Out of it came something indubitably American, for better and for worse. And right in the middle, for better and for worse, was Methodism.

III. Settled Institution
1860-1914

Chapter 21
Civil War and Reconstruction

As we approach the major turning point of American history in the
nineteenth century, the Civil War, we may first pause to ask, "What
was it like to be a Methodist in 1860?" Aside from the great issues of
the day in church and state, what made ordinary Methodists "tick"?
First, we should be clear that, although episcopal Methodisms were
growing apace with the country, many members retained strongly
sectarian views derived from the old "society" concept. There was a
good deal of tugging between the forces of growth toward ecclesiastical power and of concentration on the original dynamic of spreading
scriptural holiness. Substantial church buildings were beginning to go
up in cities, but there were complaints in the *Advocates* about for-
malism in worship.[1]

The presence of choirs led one member to cry out in a letter to the
editor: "Oh, for one good hearty song sung by a whole congregation
with hearts full of love!" As more emphasis was placed on the value of
education for ministers, more insistence was placed on the necessity
of a spiritual call to the ministry. A few isolated voices were being
raised in defense of the rights of women, but it was still pretty much a
man's world in public affairs. An editorial in the *Northwestern Christian
Advocate* remarked about the injustice of unequal treatment for moral
lapses, the women always suffering ostracism. There were many such
new ideas swirling in the minds of Methodists, but their day had not
yet come.

Rather, most attention was being given to such exciting issues as
denominational competition and the new science. Frequently, the
church papers came out with what amounted to diatribes against
"Romanists" and "Campbellites" and other rival movements regarded
as disreputable. Rome, it was thought, was "essentially and unchange-
ably unprogressive and persecuting." The fate of that church in the
unification of Italy was only what it deserved. The Disciples of Christ,
for whom the derogatory term "Campbellites" was favored, were said
to be almost Romanists themselves in their emphasis on baptism.
Were they "Jesuits in disguise?" This kind of interdenominational

[1] Most of the specific data comes from a survey of *NWCA* for the year 1860.

infighting, which is distasteful to the modern Christian outlook, was daily fare for Methodists and non-Methodists alike.

Even more disturbing was the uneasy confrontation with new ideas arising out of the scientific advances of the day. At first, this meant geology. How old is the earth? Does the record of the rocks conflict with the testimony of Genesis on creation? The Darwinian bombshell was about to burst, but the center of conflict in 1860 was Charles Lyell and the story of creation. The *Advocates* carried many articles which tried to help readers think their way into these unsettling areas. For the most part the editors did their best to state a well-founded faith without rejecting out of hand the new science. Hence, such reconciling books as *Footprints of the Creator* and *Vestiges of the Creation* were generally well received.

Through it all strode the sturdy, unbending figure of Peter Cartwright, whose fame spread far beyond his midwest homeland. In the general conference and elsewhere, with "a countenance resembling a mahogany knot," he took a conservative stance against newfangled ideas. He didn't like experiments in worship. At the general conference he spoke on a resolution which would give more power to annual conferences. "He didn't like the looks of the thing," reported the *Advocate* editor, "it had an ugly phiz, and he hoped the brat would be christened elsewhere." He signed John Scripps's autograph book with the comment, "I am a good old Methodist preacher, and am fully opposed to all innovations." Some young ministers of 1860, already being trained in the new biblical institutes, found this tough old curmudgeon hard to take.

These were a few of the influences that made Methodists "tick" in 1860, as they approached with deep concern a crisis in the nation, the proportions of which they as yet were only vaguely aware.

On the Eve

We must remember that the unfortunate division of 1844 did not solve the problem of slavery for Methodists. The conflict remained bitter between northern and southern churches. A substantial minority within the Methodist Episcopal Church continued to live in slaveholding states. Even the regional *Advocates* of the North had conflicting editorial attitudes. Southern Methodists were by no means agreed on the virtues of slavery. Church people in the border states were caught squarely in the middle. Methodists were divided almost equally between the three great regions: East, Midwest, and South, each with between four and five hundred thousand members. About one hundred fifty thousand members lived in border states. This means that the M. E. Church had a preponderance of about two to one over its southern counterpart.[2]

For the most part these church people identified themselves with the dominant political forces in their respective regions. In the East they patriotically supported Lincoln and the cause of the Union. In the Midwest they were even more fervently patriotic, especially in the Cincinnati Conference. In the South they supported the Confederacy. Along the border they were exasperated, like everybody else.

The border situation was extremely complex. In Maryland the Baltimore Conference, which included many churches in Virginia, was broken up. After the withdrawal of southern sympathizers, the remaining Baltimore Conference became strongly Unionist. In western Virginia, the forces that brought about the creation of the new state of West Virginia were apparent in the texture of Methodism. There were about twenty-one thousand northern and ten thousand southern members in the area. Every possible attitude toward slavery and the nation was represented, including proslavery Unionists and antislavery Confederates in both churches.

In Kentucky the northern Methodists were a small minority of three thousand resisting the pressures of forty-one thousand supporters of the southern church. The governor and legislature at first took a neutral position and later favored the Union. Ministers of the northern church were passionately Unionist, but Union sentiment was also strong in the southern church. When the war broke out, both the Louisville and Kentucky conferences remained loyal to the Union. The bitterest conflict occurred in Missouri, where six thousand northern Methodists were pitted against forty thousand southern. There were even two competing *Advocates* on opposite sides; the *Central* was North, the *St. Louis* was South. Most ministers of the southern church in Missouri, unlike Kentucky, favored secession. Nobody was neutral. For a time it was almost impossible for ministers of the northern church to hold services outside St. Louis. Later, the situation was reversed as southern preachers were driven from their pulpits by advancing Union armies. All in all, the Civil War was a disaster for border Methodism. That, of course, is only to say the Civil War was a disaster.

Way out west in California, the reverberations of war were felt only

[2] Still the best account of the church in the Civil War is W. W. Sweet, *The Methodist Episcopal Church and the Civil War* (1912). For the South see W. Harrison Daniel, "A Brief Account of the Methodist Episcopal South in the Confederacy," *MH*, 6 (Jan., 1968): 27-41.

vaguely.[3] Since both branches of the church had been introduced about the same time, 1849 and 1850, they grew up with relatively good will. At one time a plan was proposed for a merger of the two conferences in an autonomous California unit, but that fell through. Suspicions of ecclesiastical imperialism and the irrepressible issue of slavery (California became a free state) made cooperation difficult. There existed in San Francisco a northern *California Christian Advocate* and a southern *Pacific Methodist* (stopped in 1862). During the war southern Methodism was restricted and suffered some loss of membership, but it got along remarkably well and recovered quickly after the close of hostilities.

Methodist Episcopal Church

During the war years the M. E. Church, through its bishops, periodicals, and annual conferences, gave strong support to the Union policy of President Lincoln. The first wartime general conference did not come until 1864; but when it did, the delegates lost no time in sending formal greetings and support to the president, who replied with appreciation. Numerous patriotic observances were supported by the church and its leaders. Northern Methodism, if only because of its predominant size, was no small factor in rallying support for the Union and President Lincoln. Bishop Matthew Simpson and Bishop Edward R. Ames were most influential in their political activities. Bishop E. S. Janes, on the other hand, devoted much time to the United States Christian Commission, a service organization formed in 1861.

As the nation moved toward emancipation, the M. E. Church rather belatedly took its stand. The General Conference of 1860 finally changed the rule on slavery with a "New Chapter on Slavery" which considerably strengthened the position. In 1858 the southern church removed the rule on slavery from its Disciplinary General Rules.

It has sometimes been said that Bishop Simpson inspired Lincoln to make the Emancipation Proclamation. That is an overstatement. Although Simpson for long had been antislavery, he had nothing directly to do with the proclamation.[4] Nevertheless, his friendship with Lincoln and the support the president received during the war from the bishop has symbolic significance. Methodism was coming closer to becoming a sort of unofficial national church when Bishop Simpson

---

[3] See Barbara McClung MacVicar, "Southern and Northern Methodism in Civil War California," *California Historical Society Quarterly,* 40 (1961): 327-42.

[4] See James E. Kirby in *MH,* 7 (Oct., 1968): 35, 36.

conducted the funeral of the assassinated president in Springfield, Illinois. The pathos of the occasion permitted a genuine expression of deep emotion:

> Chieftain, farewell! The nation mourns thee. . . . Mute though thy lips be, yet they still speak. Hushed is thy voice, but its echoes of liberty are ringing through the world, and the sons of bondage listen with joy. Thou didst fall not for thyself. The assassin had no hate for thee. Our hearts were aimed at; our national life was sought. We crown thee as our martyr, and Humanity enthrones thee as her triumphant son. Hero, martyr, friend, farewell.

It is just as well that this tie between the two men was not perpetuated in stone, as some actually wished, by setting Simpson alongside Lincoln in the Memorial in Washington.

The church was involved in the war in two ways: the support of the United States Christian Commission and the encouragement of chaplaincies. Bishop Janes was active in the commission, which was formed with interdenominational support in 1861 in New York to give help to soldiers. Over the war years, about 458 Methodist ministers gave their services as volunteers. Their work was similar to that of chaplains. Less favor was shown towards the government-sponsored Sanitary Commission.

There was no central organization of military chaplains. Ministers who volunteered were usually chosen directly by their regiments, which were identified with particular states. This created several problems, one being the maintenance of standards, another being status and rank. Almost five hundred Methodist ministers became regimental chaplains. The more successful chaplains brought into being what amounted to regimental churches or congregations, reminiscent of Cromwell's New Model Army during the English Civil War of the seventeenth century. Frequently, lively revivals would break out in camp, crowned with many conversions.

The church's periodicals played a significant role in formulating and giving publicity to moral judgments on the war. The most moderate was the *New York Advocate,* which succeeded in avoiding some of the emotion and vindictiveness to be found in some of the others. All the papers were strong for union and immediate emancipation. Charles Kingsley, editor of the *Western Christian Advocate,* was inclined to outbursts of wrath and denunciation, together with no small amount of self-righteousness. Until Lincoln's assassination, however, editorial comment was surprisingly restrained. Now and then, the unexpected duration of the conflict could be cited as evidence of

God's judgment on both sides. The war itself was regarded either as a righteous cause or a necessary evil. Almost no pacifist sentiment is to be found anywhere.[5] Lincoln's plan for reconstruction was generally supported, and that support continued into the Johnson era. In spite of the fact that the *Western Christian Advocate* was repelled by the president's drinking habits, there was little overt support for the vindictive extremists before Johnson's impeachment. The *Central Christian Advocate,* edited by Charles Elliott in Missouri slave territory, refused to fold up and managed to hold on until Union troops occupied St. Louis.

The most controversial activity of the M. E. Church was its expansion into southern territory, promoted especially by Bishop Edward R. Ames. This vigorous churchman obtained an order in 1863 from Secretary of War Stanton instructing Union commanders to aid the bishop: "You are hereby directed to place at the disposal of Rev. Bishop Ames all houses of worship belonging to the Methodist Episcopal Church, South, in which a loyal minister, who has been appointed by a loyal Bishop of said Church does not officiate." The Baptists and Presbyterians were similarly privileged. In the case of churches which had been abandoned by their ministers, the policy can be understood; but when this military order supported the seizure of southern churches in such a manner as to confiscate them and to imply that they would not be returned with the end of the war, it raised many questions. President Lincoln did not learn immediately about Stanton's policy. When he found out, he quickly limited the privileges which would simply have turned over southern property to northern churches.

In general, the M. E. Church came through the war in relatively good shape. The bishops in their episcopal address of 1864 congratulated the general conference that there had been little disruption and that all annual conferences had been held regularly except in Kentucky and Missouri. "The progress of the Federal arms has thrown open to the loyal Churches of the Union large and inviting fields of Christian enterprise and labor."

Methodist Episcopal Church, South

The southern church was on the losing side. That was a main part of the difference. Whereas in the North a continuity of life and culture was preserved, in the South all was changed. At the end, the

---

[5] Students in a seminar of mine a few years ago on Methodism and Civil War found practically no evidence of pacifist opinions.

Confederacy, southern culture, and the institutions of religion were all in shambles.

At the outset, leaders of the M. E. Church, South were by no means intent on secession. The southern *Advocates* were rather restrained, urging patience and moderation, but the election of Lincoln and the firing on Fort Sumter changed all that. The Alabama Annual Conference, for example, passed a resolution in December which, while it deplored the division of the country, applauded southern efforts to resist northern encroachment and domination. As a matter of course almost all the churches joined in the struggle for the Confederacy. Perhaps because the situation in the South was more desperate, there was relatively little temptation to engage in polemics and denunciation.

In some areas Union sympathy was strong enough to find expression. This was especially true of the Holston Conference, always somewhat isolated in the mountain valleys of eastern Tennessee. Most outspoken as a Unionist was William G. Brownlow, who was active in the Methodist ministry in that region. However, southern views were sufficiently hardened in 1862 so that many Methodist voices denounced the Emancipation Proclamation as political chicanery and the work of the devil. Seventeen Methodist ministers joined with others in signing *An Address to Christians Throughout the World* to protest the proclamation.

As if to compensate for the moral morass involved in slavery, the southern church developed a vigorous mission to the slaves. This had grown during the years after separation until 327 missionaries were working with the 217,000 slave members of the church. Many church leaders, even relatively conservative ones like Bishop George F. Pierce, urged reform of the institution to encourage education and preservation of the family. Many voices were raised in the interest of reform of abuses. Almost none were heard urging abolition. Whether or not this mission served as a moral palliative that made the evil of slavery endurable, it deserves attention and appreciation in its own right. The mission to the slaves represents one of the better aspects of southern Methodism during these trying times.

Chaplaincy in various forms was another active area of Christian service. Even more than in the North, efforts were made to maintain contact with the soldiers and provide ministry to them. There were far more Methodist chaplains than any other denomination, some 209 of them. Moreover, many ministers served as regular army officers or soldiers. The southern code of honor brought many of these men into combat service. One reason why the churches of New

Orleans had no ministers was that so many of them had volunteered for the army. In addition to chaplains, there were the volunteers in the interdenominational army missions, civilians who performed services similar to the chaplains. The peculiar institution of army churches flourished, sometimes as a direct result of successful revivals among the troops. Some of these came close to being gathered congregations; others took the form of Christian Associations, which were looser in structure, like the later Y.M.C.A.

Along with the rest of the South, the church suffered heavy damage. Buildings almost everywhere were either destroyed or put to secular uses. After Union occupation in 1862, the publishing house in Nashville was taken over for use of the federal printing office. All the colleges closed. Annual conferences could not meet because the ministers were scattered, the bishops could not reach them, and military disruption made any meetings perilous. The General Conference of 1862 simply did not take place. As a result of these difficulties and the toll of war, the membership declined massively by about a third.

One big question was faced by the surviving leaders at the end of the Civil War, Is it possible, is it advisable, to attempt to go on?

Reconstruction

After the war was over, it went on in the Methodist press. All of the issues raised by Reconstruction policies were the same as the issues of war, but the setting was different.[6] As far as Methodist spokesmen were concerned, Reconstruction could mean disintegration (let nature take its course in the South), destruction, magnanimous assistance, or moral judgment. Whatever else it meant, it meant expansion of the Methodist Episcopal Church into fields (somewhat trampled) ripe for harvest. Five years after the end of the war, ten northern annual conferences were in existence in southern territory, counting over 135,000 members (88,000 Negro), served by 630 ministers (370 Negro). A *Methodist Advocate* was published in Atlanta, and after 1876, the *Southwestern Christian Advocate* in New Orleans.

The M. E. General Conference of 1868 was an occasion for self-congratulation. Bishop Matthew Simpson reported the success of the

[6] The standard work on northern activity during Reconstruction is Ralph E. Morrow, *Northern Methodism and Reconstruction* (1956). Other viewpoints are in William W. Sweet, "The Methodist Church and Reconstruction," Illinois State Historical Society, *Journal*, 7 (1914): 153-54; Edward D. Jervey, "Motives and Methods of the Methodist Episcopal Church in the Period of Reconstruction," *MH*, 4 (July, 1966): 17-25. A southern view is Hunter Dickinson Farish, *The Circuit Rider Dismounts* (1938).

church in the South with impressive statistics. This general conference met just prior to the congressional vote on impeachment of President Johnson. The air was thick with political pressures. Every success of northern Methodism in the South was regarded as a success for the Republican Party. The New York *Tribune* expressed the opinion that the role of the M. E. Church had political as well as religious ramifications. M. E. annual conferences were Republican outposts. Sourly the editor of the *St. Louis Christian Advocate* commented, "Brother Greeley and Brother Stanton know very well what Brother Simpson and Brother Ames are about." No wonder that attempts were made to bring the conference into line against Johnson. Although a resolution was passed which indirectly supported conviction of the president, another resolution calling for prayers to that end failed. Simpson, however, taking the floor, did obtain license for prayer "to save our senators from error." Senator Willey of West Virginia, who opposed conviction, was a Methodist. The *Advocates*, which had tended to support Lincoln's policies and for a while Johnson's attempts to carry them out, turned against the latter as a Southerner and a drunkard. In all, Bishop Simpson was outstanding with his persuasive oratory. Occasionally, he was able to move even a hostile southern congregation to tears as he proved himself to be once again a master preacher.

One facet of northern effort in the South, although not utterly pure in motivation, was beneficial in its effects. The Freedmen's Aid and Southern Education Society was formed in August 1866 in Trinity M. E. Church in Cincinnati. The first annual report listed forty teachers and three thousand students in nine states. Within two years fifty-nine schools were organized. By the 1870s, the society was sponsoring orphan homes; day and boarding schools; and colleges, including among the earliest, Central Tennessee College, Clark University, and Claflin University. When the society faced opposition in extending its services to Chinese, Indians, and immigrants, Bishop Edward Thomson's answer was, "Let them come! The earth is the Lord's and the fullness thereof!"[7] Thus, a reconstruction project, based on equal opportunity for the freed black man, began a long and illustrious history which would in due time become a major part of home or national missions.

It was an amazing mix of good and bad that characterized church involvement in Reconstruction. There is not the slightest doubt that the leaders of the M. E. Church took unfair advantage of the military victory of Union forces to push into the South at the expense of the

[7] Freedmen's Aid Society, *Annual Report* (1869), 20.

M. E. Church, South. There is not the slightest doubt that most leaders of the southern church were seeking ways of preserving or recovering the cherished way of life which had been wiped out by the Civil War. There is also not the slightest doubt that both sides had an honest and serious concern for the spiritual welfare of the Negro. The North may have been more willing to include also his social and economic welfare, but that is not to deny the real worth of the southern mission to the black man.

What did northern victory and southern defeat mean in terms of God's providence? It could be interpreted as vindication of God's will. It could be interpreted as judgment on the personal sinfulness of southern Christians. A good many southern thinkers said as much, explaining that the judgment of God rested not on the social sin of slavery, but on personal sins of individuals. Or it could be interpreted as the work of the devil. However understood, the broader effects meant the powerful increase of those denominations most successfully woven in the warp and woof of national expansion, the Baptists and the Methodists. The old denominations of the East, Congregationalists, Episcopalians, and Presbyterians (at least after they dropped out of the westward race), lost out in rate of growth. In spite of the sad schisms which rent Baptists and Methodists, they forged ahead on both sides of the Civil War lines. Although Christian America was still overwhelmingly Protestant, it was no longer unified in a common dream of an evangelical kingdom of God. The great turning point was past. It was a different country, a new world.

Chapter 22
Recovery South and Growth North

The New York *Christian Advocate* of 1865 reported on southern Methodism:

> So far as we can ascertain, most of its conferences are virtually broken up, its circuit system is generally abandoned, its appointments without preachers to a great extent, and its local societies in utter confusion. Its Book Concern is overthrown; its Missionary Society, Sunday-School Union, and most of its other Church enterprises, without power, if not without form. All has been submerged in the general wreck of the South.[1]

We may speculate about northern response to this obviously disastrous condition. Sympathy? Judgment? Emergency relief? Opportunity for expansion? We have already seen what happened during the era of Reconstruction. What about the South itself? Was southern Methodism caught so completely in the debacle of the Confederacy that it too must go down? The story of the recovery of the M. E. Church, South, is one of the dramatic episodes of Methodist history.

Recovery of the South

If the South practically lost a generation of young men, the churches suffered similarly. Some, especially those larger denominations with interests deeply rooted in both North and South, had suffered schism as the sectional issues circulating around slavery came to a crisis. The war brought disaster piled on disaster. Statistics (for once clearly) tell the story: The M. E. Church, South, which in 1860 had about 750,000 members (including probationers), counted in 1866 less than 499,000.[2] Many ministers, both traveling and local, had been lost or had located during the conflict. Many churches were without leadership. The desperate straits were described by a Yankee who visited the Tennessee Annual Conference in May, 1864:

> I entered the Conference room. Behold! There sat Joshua Soule and *thirteen preachers!* And this was the wealthy, proud, domineering Tennessee Annual Conference! Three years ago it mustered near two hundred

[1] New York *Christian Advocate* (16 Mar., 1865): 84.
[2] Full members: 1860: 454,203 whites, 171,857 blacks, 3,295 Indians; 1866: 419,404 whites, 78,742 blacks, 701 Indians.

ministers, and every one of them was a rebel. Lo! here are thirteen, and where are the others? Nearly all the Conference are in the South—many of them in the rebel army. Well, I sat there all day and listened to the graybacks, for nearly all the ministers were dressed in grayback cloth literally.[3]

The venerable Soule was eighty-three years old and feeble of frame, but as powerful a leader as ever. For several months after cessation of hostilities, buildings throughout the South continued to be held by ministers or groups set up by Union forces. Not until the end of 1865 were most southern church properties back in the hands of their owners. Economically, of course, all activity was at either a standstill or low ebb. No wonder, then, that some voices were raised in resigned willingness to give up and merge with northern Methodism. If the original separation had been amicably accomplished, if relations between the two branches had not been exacerbated over long years, and if Bishop Ames had not pursued so enthusiastically his expansionist policies; reunion might have been possible in 1865. It was not to be, not for another seventy-four years.

Instead, the southern church began painfully to treat its wounds, sort out the pieces, and begin to get up. At the lowest ebb, in early summer, 1865, a small group of two dozen ministers and a dozen laymen met in Palmyra, Missouri with Bishop Hubbard H. Kavanaugh. They prepared a statement which was circulated with remarkable rapidity and was known as the "Palmyra Manifesto." Its main point, fortified with many reasons, was that "we consider the maintenance of our separate and distinct ecclesiastical organization as of paramount importance and our imperative duty." Most of those reasons were based on the alleged wrongs committed by the northern church. In conclusion, then, the participants at Palmyra proclaimed:

It is, therefore, due the great mass of the people who oppose the prostitution of the pulpit to political purposes, it is due to our large membership who have been converted and gathered into the fold of Christ under our ministry, and who love our Church doctrines and discipline too fondly to seek any other fold now—it is due every principle of self-respect and ecclesiastical propriety that we maintain, with firm reliance upon the help of the Great Head of the Church, our organization without embarrassment or compromise.[4]

When the six bishops were able to meet, they issued a statement in similar vein, prepared by an upcoming minister named Holland N.

---

[3] Quoted in John J. Tigert IV, *Bishop Holland Nimmons McTyeire* (1955), 131.

[4] In W. H. Lewis, *The History of Methodism in Missouri for a Decade of Years from 1860 to 1870* (1890), 175, 177-78.

McTyeire, who had edited the Nashville *Christian Advocate* before the war. Preparations were made for a general conference, which was to assemble in New Orleans on April 4, 1866. This conference was to be one of the most significant ever held in the United States.

Of the three vigorous bishops, George F. Pierce was the most influential. He and McTyeire dominated the meeting. Here was a general conference of a church which seemed only shortly before to be on the verge of collapse. Its crucial business was survival. Amazingly, it also carried through fundamental reforms which changed the character of Methodism in the South. The most controversial issue, which actually took two general conferences to carry through, was lay representation in the government of the church. A resolution submitted by McTyeire, "Resolved, that it is the sense of this General Conference that Lay Representation be introduced into the Annual and General Conferences," passed handily by 96 to 49. It was not quite the two-thirds necessary for constitutional change, but it secured inevitable victory the next time, so completely that lay delegates were elected to be seated in 1870. When the change was made, equal lay representation was provided for the general conference and four lay delegates from each district or annual conference. How far ahead this was is measured by comparison with the northern church, which in 1872 allowed two lay delegates from each annual conference to the general conference and none to annual conferences.

But this was only the beginning. Probationary periods for church membership and compulsory attendance at class meetings were abolished. The itinerant plan of ministry was also changed, with provision for a four-year time limit on appointment to one charge. Apparently, only the stalwart opposition of Bishop Pierce prevented abolition of the time limit altogether. The only constitutional change voted by the general conference which failed to get the three-quarters vote required in annual conferences had to do with a change of name. It remained the Methodist Episcopal Church, South. Finally, this adventuresome general conference elected four new bishops: Holland McTyeire, David S. Doggett, Enoch M. Marvin, and William M. Wightman. The conference adjourned as faint glimmerings of the sun, long hidden behind clouds of controversy and war, pierced the gloom and made promise of day to come.

Development of Southern Methodism

An obvious and immediate negative result of the Civil War was the precipitous decline in Negro membership in the southern church.

This process was already well under way during the war years. The African Methodist Episcopal Church and the African Methodist Episcopal Zion Church entered the South for the first time in decades and made great strides. The M. E. Church also gained membership among black Methodists. Black membership in the M. E. Church, South, dropped from about 208,000 in 1860 to 79,000 in 1866 and only 20,000 in 1869. The next year the Colored Methodist Episcopal Church was formed under the auspices of the southern church.

In spite of these losses, leaders of the M. E. Church, South sought to continue the active mission to the Negroes which had been going on ever since division in 1844. Frustrated by poverty and competition from the North, southerners had begun to relax their intense home mission enterprise. In general, the work of the Freedmen's Aid Society was welcomed; but increasingly, political considerations and growing resistance to black participation in government and education interfered with the original evangelistic zeal personified by William Capers and others. Not until Atticus Haygood published his influential work *Our Brother in Black* in 1881 did the southern church take up once more its full responsibility.

Immediately pressing was the need to reconstruct the work in publishing, education, and missions. All had been wrecked. The publishing house in Nashville had scarcely emerged from the long legal struggle over publishing assets which ensued from separation, when the war hit hard. J. B. McFerrin, book agent from 1858 to 1862, built up a prosperous program. Then, in February of 1862, the Union army took Nashville and used the facilities for military purposes. At the end it had lost many assets and was deep in debt. A fire in 1872 added disaster to disaster. Once again McFerrin rescued the enterprise and helped it toward a new prosperity.

Along with Bishops Pierce and McTyeire, J. B. McFerrin, Thomas O. Summers, and Atticus G. Haygood were outstanding leaders. By the mid-1870s, the church had survived the reverberations of war and Reconstruction and forged ahead with remarkable energy and growth. The elite membership, which had fallen to a little over 419,000 in 1866, grew back to the prewar figure by 1869. By 1875 it was well over 700,000, and financial support had recovered and surpassed the 1860 figures.[5] Within ten years of the end of war, the M. E. Church, South, had fought back and gone on to larger fields of effort. The Indian mission, for example, which had only 700 members in 1866, had grown by 1875 to 4,335. For the rest of the nineteenth century the southern church was to excel in its efforts to

[5] Cf. D. C. Kelley, "Methodist Church Membership," *MQRS*, 6 (1884): 45-49.

take the gospel and service to the Indians of Oklahoma and the Southwest.

Sunday schools were thriving under the direction of the general secretary, Atticus Haygood. Vanderbilt University was founded under promising auspices in 1875 with Bishop McTyeire as president. Revivals, feeding on renewed interest in Christian perfection, were frequent and effective. The church was beginning to take influential stands on moral issues such as temperance. At last, after years of reluctance, the M. E. Church, South, was ready to meet its great northern friend and rival. The Cape May Conference of 1876, although it did not bring instantaneous unity, marked a turning point in fraternal relations between the two branches of Methodism. It cast a long shadow down to the year of reunion, which came at last in 1939.

Growth in the North

In many ways Methodism at the end of the Civil War was living still in an age of innocence—innocent, that is, of the complexities of modern industrial technological society. Only an agrarian society epitomized by Currier and Ives lithographs could rejoice in "The Children's Centenary Song" which was composed for the centennial of 1866:

> How many precious children,
> Burdened with sin and wrong
> Coming to Christ, the Saviour,
> Have learned the Lamb's sweet song—
> The song of *free salvation,*
> Redemption from all woe,
> Since God lit up our altars
> A century ago! [6]

Romanticism, which found little place in the grimy factories and tenements even then springing up vigorously, still held sway among traditional Methodists, along with most Protestants, who still remembered their early pioneer days and village upbringing.

But life wasn't like that anymore. A few figures may point the direction. At the outbreak of the American Revolution, five cities could claim between twenty and thirty thousand inhabitants. In 1800, New York City had a population of sixty thousand. In 1860 it had increased ten times to six hundred thousand. In 1812 the total popu-

[6] Daniel Wise, *The Children's Centenary Memorial* (1866), 17.

lation was ten million. In 1860 it was over thirty million. In 1800 there were fifteen farmers to every urban dweller, in 1830 ten to one, in 1850 five to one. The nation would for long remain agrarian, but the new forces were all in the direction of urbanization. The future lay with the city, not with the country. This shift would have very important effects on the form of the Methodist Church and on the character of its ministry, and Methodism did *not* keep step. H. K. Carroll pointed out in 1880 that, whereas the church had its beginning in eastern cities, it fell behind there first. There was one Methodist member for every twenty-nine rural people, one for every forty-six urban people. The Presbyterians, in contrast, had maintained the same proportion in city and country, and the Episcopalians favored the city three to one.[7] The Methodist answer, of course, would follow C. C. McCabe, the famous church builder, and point out the tremendous growth of Methodism all over the nation. Who, after all, was there "firstest with the mostest"? All these changing social factors bore directly on the Methodist Episcopal Church.

Outwardly all was fine. An optimism which fed on new social philosophies and on the apparently never-ending opportunities of the West promised great rewards for those who worked. One of those who labored as if he had invented the Puritan work ethic was C. C. McCabe, secretary of the Church Extension Society. If bulk of church architecture is any measure of growth, Methodism was rising high and wide. "Building two a day" became a victorious taunt against unbelieving detractors like Robert G. Ingersoll. The society was organized in 1864, two years after the Homestead Act opened the West to the most democratic movement of people to the land.

The obvious growth in numbers and substance fitted in very well with the social philosophy popularized from Darwinism. Brought into the pulpit by such facile adapters as Henry Ward Beecher, the message of success buoyed up the self-esteem of those who had made it and gave hope to those still striving. The Methodist Episcopal Church was caught up in this euphoric spirit. All indicators said Go! The membership in the M. E. Church alone went from about two-thirds of a million in 1850 to almost three million in 1900.

As ever new and larger churches were built, the people who came to worship changed also. More and more the denomination was becoming an expression of the middle class. The chief reason for this is that so many members were pulling themselves up to that status. Once the People Called Methodists had appealed to the poor, although never exclusively. Now the products of success came. They

[7] N. C. Sims, ed., *The Methodist Itineracy . . . A Discussion* (1880), 35.

became accustomed to more comfortable facilities. They wanted to hear more polished sermons. They wanted to improve the quality of music. In all of these aspects they wanted to put on a better show than the Presbyterians and the Baptists. The pressures were growing for more and better publications, for church-sponsored colleges, for a more carefully educated ministry.

Changing Styles of Ministry and Membership

A price had to be paid for this well-organized success. Part of that price was the diminution of democracy. Daniel Dorchester, in explaining Methodism in 1887, admitted, "Undemocratic it is, in some respects, and none the worse for that, but rather better; for a pure democracy is a very weak government, whether in state or Church." [8] Once again the main channel of Methodist history comes to the fore: creative tension between authority and freedom. In the period under consideration, the role of the bishop as the symbol of authority came under scrutiny. At the same time, the place of the layperson was reassessed. If we begin this discussion of changing styles with the episcopacy, we end with the ordinary member.

Before the Civil War both issues, episcopacy and lay representation, came before the General Conference of 1852. The first came to focus in the resignation of Bishop Leonidas L. Hamline for reasons of health. The issue, however, was the concept of the episcopal office, the very same that had complicated the struggle over separation in 1844. If the episcopacy was indeed a third and higher order of ministry, there was something indelible about ordination to that order. Extremists would say, "Once a bishop, always a bishop." But the conference voted overwhelmingly otherwise, and released Hamline from his responsibilities. Thus, the northern church went on record once again in favor of a more limited view of the episcopal office. The view in the South leaned more in favor of episcopal prerogative. Though the Methodist Protestant Church continued its original opposition to episcopal administration, it moved in the direction of more centralized authority with the experiment of an annual council, established by the General Conference of 1875. The agency continued after the reunion of the church in 1877, and met until 1892. Since its authority was largely advisory, however, it served more as a bogeyman subject to attack by Methodist Protestants who continued to fear any form of centralized power. Their attitude is well portrayed by the seventieth anniversary issue of the *Methodist Protes-*

[8] Daniel Dorchester, *The Why of Methodism* (1887), 109.

tant, November 9, 1898, which was full of reminders of the peril once faced and rejected.

In the M. E. Church the itineracy also came under scrutiny. After the Civil War, when the M. E. Church, South, had decided to extend the time limit on appointments to four years in one charge, the northern church had just changed from two to three years. During these years, a large literature appeared arguing both sides. Someone, who chose to publish under the name Nathan Plainspeke, brought out a pamphlet entitled *Itinerancy on Paper and Itinerancy in Fact.* "The itinerancy is a human invention. As such it is from its very nature constantly in need of repair and renovation, as such is capable of unlimited improvement, as such must be adapted to new conditions as fast as they arise." [9] W. H. Pearne followed with *Sober Thoughts for Thinking Men* (c. 1880), which marshaled many arguments for extending or even abolishing the time limit. Times, he said, are different from those of Asbury. Efficiency would be improved. The people want a change. Ministers would be more studious and devoted. An extensive series of articles in *The Independent,* reprinted in pamphlet form in 1880, presented both sides, but came down on the side of change.[10] Sims thought a change from three to five years would help, yet not destroy, the itinerant principle. That was the decision arrived at by the General Conference of 1888. That was also the conclusion of Nathan Bangs, who was certainly no radical, in 1850:

> The fact is, a competent preacher stationed in one place, if as diligent as he ought and may be, will soon familiarize himself with his people; can visit the sick, the delinquents, and incite them forward in the discharge of duty; bury the dead, perform the marriage ceremony, meet the classes, attend prayer-meetings, and perform all other pastoral duties, and then have time enough for study,—for whenever I hear a minister say that he has no time for study, or for the discharge of any other indispensable duty, I take it for granted that he is either indolent, or knows not how to economize his time.[11]

As with the ministry, so with the laity. The times were changing for them too. At every point pressures were building for change—change in terms of membership, change in structure of class meetings, change in disciplinary requirements, change in forms of worship, change in camp meetings and revivals. These pressures were espe-

---

[9] Pub. after 1864, p. 11.

[10] Sims, ed., *The Methodist Itinerancy,* esp. p. 40. The development of the itineracy is discussed more thoroughly in Frederick A. Norwood, "The Americanization of the Wesleyan Itinerant," in Gerald O. McCulloh, ed., *The Ministry in the Methodist Heritage* (1960), 33-66.

[11] Bangs, *The Present State,* 75.

cially strong in the North, although they affected the South also. *The Methodist Quarterly Review* of the M. E. Church, South, carried in 1853 an article on "Obsolete Disciplinary Laws." [12] There were conservative voices; but Osmon Baker and Moses Henkle, one North and the other South, both of whom wrote to defend the old ways, were voices of the past. The waves of change were all in the other direction.

The class meeting was in real trouble. The decline which had set in around mid-century continued its erosion. A spate of little books appeared which strove to analyze the trouble and prescribe remedies.[13] It seemed that nothing would work. Since people didn't attend regularly, attendance was made voluntary instead of compulsory. Probably, the decline of the class meeting and the decline of the itinerant form of ministry were related. When the circuit rider settled down in a "station" appointment, the class leader, along with the exhorter and the local preacher, frequently appeared to be unnecessary wheels. The minister was available for pastoral oversight. Why keep the old class and lay class leader, who had been most useful in the preacher's former extended absences, but now were superfluous?

In the same way the camp meeting was domesticated into the summer chautauqua, or, especially in the South, into protracted meetings in the church. The plaintive voices of those struggling under conviction and the glad cries of those rejoicing in salvation faded into the distance, while the chautauqua lecturer dispensed popular culture and the preacher preached what he had learned in the new liberal-minded seminaries.

As with the class meeting and the revival, notions about discipline also changed. In spite of the persistence of an agrarian-based Puritan ethic, the habitual Methodist attack on sinful amusements such as playing games, going to theaters, and reading novels—especially on Sunday—declined in both fervor and effectiveness. The only outstanding exception was the great crusade against alcoholic beverages, which became a focal point of Methodist social witness.

As the ordinary Methodist grew out of the old pattern, he took on new and lively characteristics. The age of decline for traditional discipline was also the time of his entry into the governing councils of his church. Even before the Civil War, voices were raised in behalf of the lay members. At last, however, the General Conference of 1868,

---

[12] MQRS, VII (1853), 279-95. Osmon C. Baker, *A Guidebook in the Administration of Discipline* (1855), with several revisions in the nineteenth century; Moses M. Henkle, *Primary Platform of Methodism* (1851).

[13] Among them John Atkinson, *The Class Leader, His Work and How to do it* (1875); Hilary T. Hudson, *The Methodist Armor* (1889); James H. Hutchins, *The Narrow Way, Experience Illustrated, Reminiscences, Sub-Pastoral Work* (1889).

Chapter 23
Westward West

History rarely comes well arranged in a neat package. In particular, the image of westward expansion advancing deliberately mile by mile and year by year breaks down west of the Mississippi River. Although the main themes remain valid, the details exhibit wild vagaries. Hence, expansion of Methodism beyond the Mississippi must be approached free of preconceptions based on experience east of the great river and must take due account of multiple complex variations at different times and in different places.

Distinctive Factors

As westward movement in the United States is always related to increased population, so is the spread of Methodism related to its size. We must beware, however, of unqualified reliance on statistics of church membership, especially before and after the Civil War.[1] The main point lies in standards for membership which were at first strict and increasingly relaxed later. In the early period attendance at worship ran three times larger than the membership, and the constituency was twice the attendance. After the Civil War these relationships tended to reverse. In this light, then, we must view the figures rising from a total of 580,000 in the Methodist Episcopal Church in 1840:[2]

	M. E.	M. E. S.	Total
1860	994,000	757,000	1,751,000
1880	1,743,000	848,000	2,591,000
1900	2,930,000	1,482,000	4,412,000
1920	4,394,000	2,267,000	6,661,000

During the same period the Methodist Protestant Church increased from 41,600 in 1840 to 184,000 in 1900. United Brethren had 47,000 in 1850 and 241,000 in 1900. At the turn of the century the Evangelical Association had about 166,000. All these figures may·be compared with the increase in total population, which in 1840 stood at 17,000,000:

[1] See the discussion of Winthrop Hudson in *Religion in America* (1965), 129-30.

[2] Figures have been rounded out to the nearest thousand

| 1860: | 31,000,000 | 1900: | 76,000,000 |
| 1880: | 50,000,000 | 1920: | 106,000,000 |

Methodists, who in 1850 had comprised 5.4 percent of the population, by 1900 had increased their slice to 6 percent. That was close to the high point.

General statistics, however, do not tell us much. The real story lies in the complex skein of influences which imposed themselves with infinite variety at different times and in different places. There was, first of all, the westward movement itself. Both natural and human factors interfered with an orderly progression. Frontiersmen faced entirely new challenges: treeless plains, formidable mountains, frightening deserts. They had to discover the hard way that invisible and indeterminate, but all-important boundary between high grass and short grass country which runs from north to south across the endless expanse of the Great Plains. Only by dint of persistent exploration did they find the few surmountable passes across the Rockies.[3] Then, there were the embarrassing presences of Indians of all kinds, Mexicans, and Englishmen. Even more than in the East, the frontier was confused by the succession of many varying and sometimes conflicting frontiers, those of explorers and furriers, traders, miners, cattlemen, farmers, and urban developers. Methodists were to be found almost everywhere among all groups.

These variant factors in the general scene were further complicated by specifically denominational influences. There were now two episcopal Methodisms separated by strong sectional pressures, as well as several sectarian and racial varieties. In the land west of the Mississippi, the northern and southern branches of the church did not always remain in their own bailiwicks. The M. E. Church was early and strong in southern California, and the M. E. Church, South, was well represented in Montana and the Pacific Northwest. The timing and manner of arrival was likely to vary considerably.

An additional complicating factor was the increasing activity of the Missionary Society in domestic missions. The pioneer circuit rider came more and more to look like a home missionary. Indeed, the Missionary Society had a clear purpose and policy of involvement, as stated in the annual report for 1850-51: "By sending them a pastor, and affording them an appropriation from the missionary funds, they lay the foundation of a Church, which, as it grows requires less missionary support, until in a few years, it becomes a self-supporting Church, and begins to contribute to the missionary cause. . . . So we

[3] The many natural and man-made forces are thoroughly discussed in Ray Allen Billington, *Westward Expansion* (1949). See especially Chaps. 20-21, 24-25, 27 and 34.

must endeavor to do in Illinois, Missouri, Iowa, Wisconsin, Minnesota, and on westward to the Rocky Mountains." [4] The report unintentionally reveals two important points: that the society was already caught in the stereotype of orderly progression westward, ignoring California, the most lively development of that very time; and that development was likely to be a slow process, covering many decades between exploration and urbanization. Illinois and Missouri, both of which had pioneer circuits dating from the early nineteenth century, were still regarded as missionary territory. The work was impressive. In 1874, the high point, the society was supporting in whole or in part three thousand missionaries in the United States, some of whom were back East on the urban frontier.

Furthermore, expansion was strongly supported and determined by the efforts of the Church Extension Society, which came into being just two years after the important Homestead Act of 1862. C. C. McCabe, the enthusiastic secretary of this society, was a major force in the westward expansion of Methodism.

The presence of Indians affected western growth in more significant ways than in the East, where they had constituted a nuisance and embarrassment and obstacle. In the West they were a challenge and opportunity as well. The story of Methodism in Oklahoma and the Southwest, to say nothing of Oregon, cannot be told apart from the mission to the Indians. The church had a long and exciting history in the Sooner state for decades before land was opened to white settlement in 1889. Although Jason Lee was instrumental in opening the Pacific Northwest to American settlement, his mission was to the Indians. Many pioneer churches in the West were composed of Indians with a scattering of whites.

Early and Indian

Notice has been taken in a previous chapter of the arrival of Methodist circuit riders on the shores of the Mississippi River early in the nineteenth century. Benjamin Young had received his appointment to "Illinois" in 1803! McKendree Chapel, first surviving Methodist building across the Mississippi, and now a carefully protected historic shrine with much of the original rough siding still in place, began its long history in 1819. Other chapels, such as Shiloh in Caledonia, were built earlier but no longer exist. In Iowa, which was organized into an annual conference in 1844 (two years before admission of the territory as a state), three Methodist circuits were or-

[4] Quoted in Wade C. Barclay, *History of Methodist Missions,* III, 195.

ganized between 1834 and 1836. About the same time early circuits appeared in Wisconsin. The history of the church in Arkansas also long antedates the Civil War. Thus, it is clear that Methodism had expanded on both sides of the great river in the first half of the nineteenth century. In fact, just before mid-century, it had frog-jumped all the way to California! The division of this westing experience into "Westward East" and "Westward West" is more a matter of convenience than chronology.

The Rock River Conference, which was organized in 1840 from the old Illinois Circuit and conference, still included all of Wisconsin, which became an annual conference in its own right only in 1848.[5] In 1844, the Iowa Conference came into being and the Minnesota in 1856. Many secular factors influenced these developments. For example, A. D. Field reported that the Rock River Conference of 1854 was the last one to which the preachers traveled "in old style"—that is, in private buggies. After that they attended annual conferences in towns served by the railroads.[6]

Perhaps the last frontier to arrive was that of theological education. John Dempster, who was a key figure in the rise of Methodist theological seminaries in both East and West, expatiated on the Midwest, "the future garden of the New World," and then made his point:

> The West—the generous, magnanimous West—rich in its resources, irrepressible in its energies, magnificent in its achievements—stretching one hand to the Atlantic on the east, and the other over the Pacific on the west—the future center of nations where the destiny of the species may yet be arbitrated—this grand, mysterious reservation of God for the home of his Church, is the place for our next *ministerial school*. There, near Chicago, the future London of the New World, will it stand on the salubrious banks of that inland sea.[7]

All of these developments, including the foundation of the second theological seminary, for long known as Garrett Biblical Institute, antedated the Civil War. In terms of the whole sweep, however, the substantial part of the movement west of the Mississippi belongs to the second half of the century.

There is one notable and sometimes overlooked exception: the Indian mission. For its beginnings in the West, we must return to the 1830s. This topic is treated in this book in several different ways; as part of the westward expansion of Methodism, as an aspect of ethnic variety, as part of the history of home or national missions, as one of

[5] I am deeply indebted to William Blake, author of *Cross and Flame in Wisconsin* which I have used in manuscript form, for data on that state.
[6] A. D. Field, *Memorials of Methodism in the Bounds of Rock River Conference* (1886), 396.
[7] John Dempster, *Lectures and Addresses* (1864), 197.

the major social problems in American history, and as a prime ethical issue facing Christians in the twentieth century. Here we look at it as a facet of westward expansion, the result of the tragic drama of Indian Removal, instituted by that American president who most vividly expressed the spirit of the pioneer west, Andrew Jackson. All too accurately the story of Methodism among the Indians belongs under the rubric of westward expansion. Most of the eastern tribes, including the Shawnees, the great "civilized tribes" (Cherokee, Chickasaw, Choctaw, Creek, and Seminole), and even the Christianized Wyandot, were driven west by land-hungry white Americans under the terms of the Removal Act of 1830. Later generations would apply the romantic name, "trail of tears," to this migration. Tragic it was and sordid, but not romantic. Although many Methodists, along with most other Americans, were unaware of what was going on or did not care; the Methodist Episcopal Church and its leaders, especially those who were most directly associated with Indian work, did not bring dishonor by approving the destructive policies of the Removal Act.[8] Most of the missionaries of every denomination opposed the plan for removal. Men like James B. Finley developed a real understanding of the Indian and sympathized with his problems in confronting white pressures. Commenting on the long history of oppression, he had this to say about the Gnaddenhutten massacre, in which nearly a hundred Indians had been killed in 1782: "God of humanity, what an act!" In explaining the construction of a house and school, he was at pains to state, "All this we did ourselves. We did not make the Indians our hewers of wood and drawers of water." When his beloved Wyandots were finally removed from their ancient Ohio lands, he sadly recorded the failure of his efforts to prevent the expulsion:

> They had comfortable homes and fertile lands, and were enjoying all the blessings of the Gospel in civilized life; but the white man coveted their possessions, and they must go to the far-off western wilds, again to be exposed to all the temptations and trials incident to savage life. May the God of missions be with them! [9]

Bishop O. C. Baker later commented in similar vein as he inspected the end result of the great migration in Kansas.[10]

[8] See Norwood, "The Invisible American—Methodism and the Indian," in *MH*, 8 (Jan., 1970): 3-24. This article was first prepared on the basis of findings in an advanced seminar at Garrett Theological Seminary, as the Stover Lecture at the St. Paul School of Theology in 1969.

[9] Finley, *Autobiography*, 206-9, 356-80; quotes from 209, 359, 379-80.

[10] Letter dated 29 Jan. 1857, quoted in Don W. Holter, *Fire of the Prairie, Methodism in the History of Kansas* (1969), 14, 16.

As it turned out, this forced removal of Indians to lands west of the Mississippi River was part of the westward movement of Methodism. The first fruit was the establishment of the Shawnee Methodist Mission and Indian Manual Training School near Kansas City in 1830.[11] Founded by Thomas and Sarah Johnson, it continued in service till 1862 and was the most successful of Christian missions among the Indians in Kansas. Younger brother William worked with the Kansas or Kaw Indians. The substantial log and brick buildings, now a state historical site, still stand as a monument to this significant endeavor. The work with the Kaw, who settled in Council Grove after 1847, was not successful.

Methodist missionaries accompanied the Cherokees and their fellow tribesmen in the migrations of the 1830s. Especially close to Methodist history in its westward movement was the resettlement of the Wyandot tribe from Ohio in 1842. For decades the Methodist mission at Upper Sandusky had served these civilized and peaceful Indians. All had to be uprooted and moved west. Elsewhere missions to the Indians were associated with Methodist expansion. A great deal of Alfred Brunson's early work along the upper Mississippi was directed to Indians.[12] The rest of the story belongs with ethnic Methodism, missions, and social issues.

Hops, Skips, and Jumps West

One cowboy wrote of life across the Mississippi River in the 1830s, "No Sunday west of St. Louis, no God west of Fort Smith." Under such circumstances Methodism began to feel its way. One spectacular leap took the church all the way to Oregon. Motivated by publicity arising from a visit to St. Louis by Flathead and Nez Percé Indians, the Missionary Society in 1833 appointed Jason Lee as missionary to the Indians in Oregon. The following year he arrived at Fort Vancouver, where he was well received by John McLoughlin, agent of the Hudson's Bay Company and almost sole white official in the vast territory which lay between the forty-second parallel and parallel 54° 40'. The boundary between British and American territory had not yet been settled ("Fifty-four-forty or fight!"). Although Lee and his fellow missionaries, of whom Presbyterians Marcus and Narcissa Whitman were most notable, were instrumental in opening this land to American settlement; their chief purpose was mission to the In-

---

[11] In addition to the treatment in Barclay, *History*, III, see Martha B. Caldwell, *Annals of Shawnee Methodist Mission* (1939).

[12] Brunson, *A Western Pioneer*, II, 68, 75, 81.

dians. The first endeavor was in the fruitful Willamette Valley, where a flourishing mission station soon rose, with schools and farming as well as preaching and camp meetings. From here many branch centers were established, and an ambitious Indian Manual Training School was begun. Unfortunately, a combination of adverse circumstances, including epidemics and conflict with newly arrived white settlers, compounded by misunderstanding and opposition in the Missionary Society itself, led Lee to return to New York to defend his cause. He sickened and died before he could return west. The mission declined and all but disappeared before William Roberts came in 1847 to develop the church in the Northwest.

Even before the Texan Revolution which brought independence from Mexico, attempts were made to enter the Southwest. Circuit rider William Stevenson, first Protestant preacher in Texas, began work in 1817 at Pecan Point along the Red River. In eastern Sabine County, work dating from 1815 centered in historic McMahan's Chapel. The real founder in Texas, however, was Martin Ruter, who came from the presidency of Allegheny College in 1837.[13] By 1840 an annual conference was organized with 1,853 members, 230 of them Negroes. Three years later, it was divided into East and West Texas conferences. Methodism profited from the heroic witness of the men of the Alamo, some of whom, like William B. Travis, earnestly wished for the planting of Methodism.[14] By 1861 the Texans, who of course had joined the M. E. Church, South, counted twenty-five thousand white and almost six thousand black members. A conflict developed between the dominant southern church and efforts of the northern Arkansas Conference to expand into Texas. One Anthony Bewley, appointed to the Texas mission, was hanged as an abolitionist without a trial in 1859.

As the spread of Methodism was encouraged by the Texan Revolution, so its introduction into California depended on two secular events: the Mexican War and the discovery of gold. Before either event, however, William Roberts had organized a class in San Francisco which was in 1847 a little village called Yerba Buena. Roberts was under appointment as superintendent of the Oregon Mission of

[13] Beyond general reference to Martin Rist's chapter in *HAM,* II and Barclay, the literature on westward Methodism is too large for specific listing. Some of it is older, but still important such as James W. Bashford, *The Oregon Missions* (1918) and Thomas Harwood, *History of New Mexico Spanish and English Missions of the Methodist Episcopal Church from 1850 to 1910* (1908–10). Many histories of annual conferences deal extensively with regional expansion; some of them are well done, but others must be used with care.

[14] See the illuminating discussion by Norman Spellman, "Leaders of Early Texas Methodism," in *Forever Beginning,* 199-233.

the M. E. Church. Aware of the significance of California as a new center for American growth in the Far West, Roberts brought about the formation of the Oregon and California Mission Conference in 1849, the same year William Taylor, who later won fame as missionary-wanderer extraordinary, and Isaac Owen arrived. No grass grew under their feet. In 1851 they had over five hundred members and twelve churches, had started a *California Christian Advocate,* and had obtained a charter for California Wesleyan College (University of the Pacific).

In southern California the prospects for Methodism of either branch were not good. The absence of gold and the presence of Spanish-speaking Roman Catholics inhibited new developments under Protestant auspices. After a few false starts, the real beginnings belong to the work of Adam Bland, who arrived in Los Angeles with his family under appointment from the California Conference in 1853, rented a two-room building called the El Dorado Saloon for church and parsonage, and proceeded to organize a society while his wife started a school for girls. The work faltered during the Civil War, and in 1868 only four charges with 128 members were reported. The completion of rail lines and development of land led to the organization of a Southern California Conference in 1876. From then on, growth was steady into the twentieth century.

The M. E. Church, South, also entered California, slightly after the northern church. Two years after arrival in San Francisco in 1850, Jesse Boring and his associates established a Pacific Conference. By 1860, there were 2,500 members, including 268 in Oregon. The same year the northern church reported 3,441 members. Considerable rivalry existed between the two branches, both of which claimed full rights to expand into the Pacific states; but a surprising degree of cooperation also developed, particularly between the two bishops, Levi Scott of the North and H. H. Kavanaugh. This era of good feeling came to an end with the Civil War. Generally the two branches ran parallel and overlapping courses. A Los Angeles Conference of the southern church preceded by six years the Southern California Conference of the M. E. Church. After the war the northern church grew more rapidly in northern California than the southern church.

When William Roberts organized a society in San Francisco in 1847, he was on his way to Oregon to begin work with white settlers. He arrived when the original Oregon mission of Jason Lee, which had been directed chiefly to Indians, was almost defunct. Not until 1853 was Methodism in Oregon given an annual conference of its own with 706 members. In 1858, southern Methodism came into this northwest region under the leadership of Orceneth Fisher, who ably laid foundations for a slowly growing church, which by 1866 was formed into a small Columbia Conference. Fisher in his memoirs recalled the strong opposition set up by northern Methodists to this extension of southern church work so far north.[15]

When Washington Territory was set apart from Oregon in 1853, David Blaine came by way of Panama with his wife to lay the foundations of the church around Puget Sound.[16] The church, started by Blaine in Seattle that year, was the first of any kind. The Blaines were struck by what appeared to them to be the heathen condition of the inhabitants, both Indian and white. Of the latter they wrote, "Separation from religious influences has rendered them quite indifferent to Gospel Truth . . . . They live with savages and as savages live . . . . Their piety and ardor have oozed out of their hearts during their journey hither." Of the Indians they could find nothing good to say. Apparently they never gave up a somewhat patronizing eastern outlook. Nevertheless, the decade of service rendered by Blaine laid the foundations for Methodism in the Northwest, which continued to grow, though very slowly.

The story of the movements into the Great Plains and Colorado is closely associated with the career of one of the key figures in Methodist history west of the Mississippi, William H. Goode.[17] Two years before political organization under the Kansas-Nebraska Bill of 1854, Nebraska Territory was added to the Missouri Annual Conference. Goode was appointed to scout the land in the interests of Methodism. The result was the formation of four mission circuits, over which he became presiding elder and which he helped develop into the Kansas-Nebraska Conference. He preached what was said to be the first sermon to white settlers in a log cabin near Baldwin. For the most part, early leaders had to do without even log cabins on the high plains, where the dearth of trees forced settlers to live in sod huts. The early church buildings were also of sod construction. These privations, combined with the uncertainties of recurrent drought and always current threat from unsubdued plains Indians, made life extremely hard in the first generation.

These conditions did not prevent lively competition between the

[15] In Sweet, *Religion on the American Frontier*, IV, 490-91.

[16] Reference should be made to the interesting collection of Blaine letters in the Huntingdon Library, San Marino, California, in typescript copy covering the years 1853–62. Page references are to this manuscript: 19, 56-57, 134-35. See also article by Richard A. Seiber in *MH*, 1 (Apr., 1963): 1-17.

[17] One of the important documents of westward expansion is his autobiography, *Outposts of Zion* (1864). An excellent source is Holter, *Fire on the Prairie* (1969).

two branches of Methodism, since the southern church began work about the same time as the northern. An ecclesiastical parallel grew to the political forces which set North and South in opposition. For these reasons, most of the work languished during the Civil War. The southern church was naturally more active in the Kansas portion than was the northern church.

The account of westward expansion moves naturally from Kansas-Nebraska to Colorado Territory, because of geographical contiguity and chronological sequence, and especially because of the career of William H. Goode, who was a central figure in the development of both regions. However, the process of settlement was different because of gold. Colorado was developed, not by orderly extension westward, but by the helter-skelter scurrying of miners to claim gold-bearing land. In the year of the first gold rush, 1858, George W. Fisher, a northern Methodist local preacher, held a service in a log-cabin gambling saloon in Denver. The next year William H. Goode was appointed, along with Jacob Adriance, to scout the land in the interests of the M. E. Church. As a result, Methodism was the first to organize formal church work in the territory. The churches at Central City, Golden City, and Denver were the first fruits. By 1864, the miners of Central City had built that sturdy stone structure which still adorns the steep hillside along the main street. The Rocky Mountain Conference was formed in 1863. Among the early circuit riders was "Father" John L. Dyer, nicknamed the "snowshoe itinerant" from his use of homemade skis in wintertime. He was instrumental in starting churches in South Park and elsewhere. Colorado's first magazine, the *Rocky Mountain Sunday School Casket*, was a product of early Methodism.[18]

The southern church was not slow to enter the territory. By 1860 a society was organized in Denver and the first church building erected in the city. Unfortunately, all was lost during the Civil War, and not until 1871 was effective work resumed. All these events took place several years before the territory gained statehood (1876).

One of the southern ministers who tried unsuccessfully to make a start in Colorado was L. B. Stateler, who went on to wild Montana with his wife in the summer of 1864, where there was a new gold rush to Grasshopper Creek (Bannack) and Alder Gulch (Virginia City). He preached, organized a small class, and even built a rustic brush chapel before he moved on to Oregon in 1866. Official beginnings belong to the northern church, which sent A. M. Hough with his wife to Vir-

[18] See John L. Dyer, *The Snow-Shoe Itinerant* (1890), and Walter J. Boigegrain, "A History of the Methodist Church in the Eagle-Colorado River Valley in Colorado from 1880 to 1906" (Diss., Univ. Denver, 1962).

ginia City in the fall of 1864, where he soon had put up a substantial log chapel. When miners began to flock to a new dig, Last Chance Gulch (Helena), a Methodist minister went along to organize a society and build another log chapel.[19] When L. B. Stateler returned to Montana in 1867, he found all southern work had disappeared. He made a new start, supported himself by farming, and by 1870 was able to form a Montana District of the new Western Conference of the M. E. Church, South.

A new day began in the "big sky country," however, with the arrival in 1872 of William Wesley Van Orsdel, the fabled "Brother Van" of Montana Methodism. Sailing up the Missouri River, he landed at Fort Benton on Sunday. Learning that a Roman Catholic priest was holding a service in the local saloon, he proceeded to hold a Protestant service in the same place that afternoon. From then on Methodism in Montana was cut to the design of this free-wheeling, independent-minded, wandering evangelist, friend of cowboys and Indians alike. During the 1870s he followed a circuit some six hundred miles around, contended with blizzards and road agents, and found his way into the hearts of all Montanans. One of his close friends was the cowboy artist, Charles M. Russell, who painted him—hat, flying coattails and all—on a buffalo hunt. He lived through the coming of the railroads and the hard winter of 1886–87, never married, never settled down, yet left his own distinctive mark on the church before he died in 1919.

Elsewhere in the mountainous regions, Methodism both South and North was established, either by expansion from contiguous areas or by missionary enterprise from the East. In Cheyenne and Laramie, which lay along the line of the Union Pacific Railroad, the church was introduced by local preachers who were also medical doctors. The work in Santa Fe goes back to 1850, when a northern missionary, Enoch G. Nicholson, organized a small society among English-speaking residents. With the help of a priest, who had left the Roman Catholic Church, work was begun among Spanish-speaking people. But the most significant development in New Mexico was the arrival of Thomas and Emily Harwood in 1869. Working from their head-quarters at La Junta (Tiptonville) in the northeast, they carried out a vigorous mission with both English and Hispanic Americans. They took the trouble to learn Spanish and began many educational enterprises, the best known of which, the Harwood School for Girls in Albuquerque, is still active. In the early 1870s, work was begun in

[19] Interesting, but poorly organized, material may be found in Edward L. Mills, *Plains, Peaks, and Pioneers* (1947). In a manuscript form is the diary of Van Orsdel and an excellent monograph, "How They Brought the Good News to North Montana," both by Roberta B. West. See also E. J. Stanley, *Life of Rev. L. B. Stateler* (1916).

Arizona as a missionary enterprise by G. A. Reeder of Ohio. It was strengthened by completion of the Southern Pacific Railroad and by the arrival of G. H. Adams from Colorado. An Arizona Mission Conference was organized in 1881. The southern church began work about the same time, but both branches experienced difficulties in a land unused to Protestant Christian witness, and growth was very slow.

Almost at the end of the complicated story, we return east to the Dakotas. Here, a two-pronged approach brought the church into the extreme southeast and the extreme southwest. Treaty settlement with the Yankton Indians made possible the organization of an early society in Vermilion in 1861. At the other end of the territory Henry Weston Smith, famous as "Preacher Smith," followed the gold rush into the Black Hills, arriving in May, 1876. After itinerant preaching in Deadwood and other roaring mining camps, he was killed—but not scalped—by Indians in August of the same year. Two years later formal work began with appointment of James Williams from the Northwest Iowa Conference.

At last, in 1889, Oklahoma territory, which had a long history as refuge for resettled eastern Indian tribes, was opened for white settlement in unassigned lands. In one day a hundred thousand people rushed in, and almost overnight Oklahoma became white man's country. The Cherokee Strip was opened in 1893, and in 1907, Oklahoma became a state. After some fifty years, the Indian Mission Annual Conference of the M. E. Church, South, reported in 1894 thirty-nine hundred Indian and fourteen thousand white members. More and more congregations tended to be racially segregated. Hence in 1906, one year before statehood, the old Indian Mission Conference was transformed into the Oklahoma Conference, thoroughly white in its character and leadership. Subsequently, the Indian Methodists were separated once again into an Indian Mission Conference, formed in 1919.

The northern church also entered Oklahoma, beginning with the relocation (from Kansas) of the Wyandot mission in 1874. After the organization of the Indian Mission, some work with Negroes was included. J. M. Iliff struggled against many difficulties, chief of which was the established presence of the M. E. Church, South. Most of the work remained with minority groups until the opening of the territory in 1889, when the Indian Mission Conference was organized. This soon became the Oklahoma Annual Conference. By 1901 there were 11,564 members.

Chapter 24
Black Churches

The Civil War had an overwhelming impact on black churches. For all its limitations, the Emancipation Proclamation opened a new era in the life of the American Negro. Three and a half million Blacks, most of whom had no experience of freedom and no education, had been proclaimed free men. The governmental agency, the Freedmen's Bureau, was briefly useful immediately after the end of hostilities, but the task went far beyond the power of government and involved long-range relationships. Although most of the denominations took part in efforts to serve the freedmen, the most extensive work was done by the American Missionary Association (largely Congregational) and those churches with a large black membership—Baptists, Methodists, and Presbyterians. Hence, the Methodist-sponsored Freedmen's Aid Society was not the only religious agency at work.

At the same time, movements of freedom into separate churches of their own cut across denominational lines. The Formation of the Christian (originally Colored) Methodist Episcopal Church had its parallels among Baptists and Presbyterians. This came about partly through the desire of black people to run their own lives, and partly as a result of the continuation of racial discrimination. In fact, new forms of discrimination rose quickly enough to take the place of the legal walls destroyed by emancipation. After the institution of slavery was gone, social barriers served to keep the races separate and the Negro "in his place." The end result was that relatively new thing in the South, Jim Crow laws. Gilbert Haven, editor of *Zion's Herald* and later to be elected bishop, put the matter succinctly in his paper in 1863: "The slave is gone, the negro remains. . . . The basis of slavery is caste. That feeling of caste yet prevails exceedingly over all the land. The blackness covers our heart deeper than it does the faces of our brethren. It must be removed." [1] Under these conflicting pressures, then, black Methodism grew and adapted in the last half of the nineteenth century.

[1] *ZH,* 10 June 1863.

271

Negroes in the Methodist Episcopal Church

Immediately after the war, a group of northern Methodists organized in Cincinnati the Freedmen's Aid Society, designed to bring the resources of the Methodist Episcopal Church to bear on the large challenge of service to the newly free black people in the South. It was approved by the General Conference of 1868 and became an official arm of the church in 1872. It started scores of elementary schools and six colleges, including Central Tennessee College (Nashville), Clark University (Atlanta), Rust College (Holly Springs, Mississippi), and Meharry Medical College. These grew in both number and strength over the years. Although the work first was restricted to black freedmen, a policy change later introduced work for Whites as well.[2] Theoretically, there was supposed to be no color line; in fact, there was. The work heavily emphasized educational opportunities; but the influence of the Freedmen's Aid Society reached directly or indirectly into many facets of southern life.

The end of the war saw the organization of separate annual conferences for Negroes in the M. E. Church. The first of these were the Delaware and Washington conferences, which occupied areas overlapping white conferences. In the South the initial organization of the Mississippi Conference reveals no objection to racially integrated conferences. By 1866 there were nine such conferences with 47,000 white and 88,000 black members. Ten years later, however, social pressures for segregation, together with some early expressions of what later would be called black nationalism, led the general conference to authorize segregated conferences in those areas in which a majority of both white and black members desired them. By 1895 there were no racially mixed conferences left in the M. E. Church.[3] Hiram Revels, black senator from Mississippi and Methodist presiding elder, stood vigorously in opposition to these segregationist practices.[4]

It becomes clear that emancipation did not solve many problems of race relations in the M. E. Church. Two Negroes were elected missionary bishop, which assured they would not serve in the United States. No black man was elected general superintendent until 1920. Prob-

---

[2] See discussion of the issue in episcopal addresses, *JGC*, 1880 and 1888. A useful account of black experience in the M. E. Church is Willis J. King, "The Negro Membership of the (Former) Methodist Church in the (New) United Methodist Church," *MH*, 7 (Apr., 1969): 32-43.

[3] An excellent case study is Warren M. Jenkins, *Steps Along the Way, the Origin and Development of the South Carolina Conference of the Central Jurisdiction of the Methodist Church (1967)*.

[4] See William B. Gravely, "Hiram Revels Protests Racial Separation in the Methodist Episcopal Church," *MH*, 8 (Apr., 1970): 13-20.

lems continued to plague leaders as they struggled to reconcile public prejudices with Christian ideals. Some leaders, like Gilbert Haven, editor of *Zion's Herald* and later bishop, were forthright, courageous, and on occasion politically naive. Haven was one of the few men of his day who unflinchingly favored social equality including the removal of all laws forbidding interracial marriage. Now and then the church in its high councils would hear from Negroes who sought changes, some of which had strong overtones of black nationalism. In 1860, for example, a group of black local preachers petitioned the general conference to make several changes, including boundaries, procedures for trial, power to elect their own deacons and elders, and full annual conference autonomy. The last two requests were not granted.[5]

The amazing part of the story is that in spite of everything many thousands remained faithful members of the Methodist Episcopal Church, patiently waiting the day when they would be fully recognized as members equal with all others. In the twentieth century this day would slowly dawn, but in the meantime black Methodists made their own unique contribution to a church always marked by wide diversity. Not the least of those contributions lay in the field of church music. Negro spirituals filled a need to which no other kind of religious music could speak. Even prejudice-bound whites melted as they heard the plaintive strains:

> Oh, brethren, will you meet me,
> Where sorrows never come?

> or

> My sister, you want to git religion,
> Go down in de Lonesome Valley;
> My brudder, you want to git religion,
> Go down in de Lonesome Valley.
> Go down in de Lonesome Valley,
> To meet my Jesus dere!

Sometimes a black evangelist like <u>Amanda Smith</u> would catch the attention of Methodists, black and white alike. In her day she became something of an institution.[6] In the long run the Negro constituents of Episcopal Methodism provided a much needed impetus by their very presence. Even when separated in black conferences and black

[5] *JGC* (1860), 308-09.
[6] Amanda Smith, *An Autobiography* (1893).

273

churches, they could not be ignored. Later, in the twentieth century, they would be able to contribute to almost every facet of the life of the denomination.

A Black Church in the South

When the Civil War ended, a part of the shambles that constituted the Methodist Episcopal Church, South was its Negro constituents. The years of conflict had witnessed a catastrophic diminution in their numbers, from about 208,000 in 1860 to 79,000 at the end of the war and 20,000 in 1869. For an entire generation the lot of slaves had been unhappy, ever since the risings of Denmark Vesey and Nat Turner. Their worship, as well as every other aspect of their lives, was carefully overseen by white people whose concern had prevented complete segregation in the old South. Now all that was changed, and the slave was a free man. One of his first acts was to get out of white-controlled churches. The African Methodist Episcopal and Zion churches, to say nothing of Methodist Episcopal leaders in the South, were not slow to take advantage of this situation. The result was a rapid draining away of black members from the M. E. Church, South.

At the all-important postwar General Conference of 1866 provision was made that, whenever Negro members who so desired formed two or more annual conferences of their own, these might be brought together in a separate general conference, all under the friendly auspices of the southern church. By spring, 1870, when the southern General Conference met again, five such annual conferences had been set up in Texas, Tennessee, Georgia, and Alabama. Three more came into being that summer. As a result, a separate general conference was authorized and plans were made for an organizing conference in Jackson, Tennessee in December, 1870. The name Colored Methodist Episcopal Church was chosen (leaving out the designation "South"). William H. Miles and Richard H. Vanderhorst were elected bishops and were consecrated by Bishops Robert Paine and Holland McTyeire of the M. E. Church, South. These two white bishops had been designated, along with other ministers, to help the new church get started. Unlike the older black churches, which in theory had no race barrier, white persons were specifically excluded from the C. M. E. Church. The plan assumed that a complete separation of races would take place in the South. It is interesting to note, therefore, that the general minutes of the southern church continued for many years to include reports of black members. As late as 1895 there were 389, but there were no white members of the C. M. E. Church. Although control of church property was complicated by tentative arrangements made after the war with the A. M. E. Church, the intention was to transfer to black control in the C. M. E. Church all churches and lands used by the black congregations. In this and many other ways the M. E. Church, South, acted as midwife in the birth of the new denomination.[7]

The close connection between these two churches continued over the years, and led other black churches to criticize the C. M. E. denomination as a creature of white origin. Relations with the A. M. E. and A. M. E. Z., as well as M. E. churches in the South, were embittered by much name-calling and unscrupulous competition. All the other black Methodist forces were doing all they could to expand into the South, and most of the loss of black southern Methodists could be attributed to their missionary work. C. M. E. leaders replied to these attacks with a vigorous defense. The new church, they explained, was organized out of "an almost universal desire" on the part of both black and white. Black Methodists had no wish to "rebel and secede," but rather chose freely "to be regular and orderly." The work was accomplished in an atmosphere of "fraternal sympathy, a mutual good will, a kindly interest that made the relation cordial and highly helpful." [8] Opponents, of course, brushed this off as Uncle Tomism. The "old slavery church" was in their judgment still under the domination of the former white masters. Many years would pass before the bitter feelings would subside.

In 1873, Isaac Lane was elected bishop. He had grown up under ✲ desperate conditions of slavery, but his master was relatively humane. He had to learn reading and writing secretly. His young wife was taken away when her master moved elsewhere, but his master was helpful in getting her back by purchase. These early struggles defined his attitude on race relations later on. He found it possible to work with white people in and out of the church without any sense of degradation.

Lane's autobiographical account unfolds an almost unbelievable series of struggles, both before and after his elevation to the episcopacy. His character was forged in the fiery furnaces of life. His first episcopal journey, which took him west into Texas, became a sort of pioneer saga overlaid with all the difficulties a black man might

[7] The most useful general history of the C. M. E. Church is C. H. Phillips, *A History of the Colored Methodist Episcopal Church in America* (1900). An important primary source is Isaac Lane, *Autobiography of Bishop Isaac Lane, LL.D.* (1916).

[8] See the discussion in Lane, *Autobiography*, 18, 21, 58. See also the historical statement in the introduction to the C.M.E. *Discipline*.

experience in the old South. Through it all he worked endlessly to serve his church, keep his family together by farming, and lay the foundations for Negro higher education, especially through the college which bears his name in Jackson, Tennessee.

The membership of the Colored Methodist Church in 1874 was about seventy-five thousand with five thousand more added the next year. In these terms it would be about one-third as large as each of the African churches and about one-half as large as the Negro constituency of the M. E. Church in the South. That the denomination was able to overcome the unfavorable criticism of its origins is proved by its continued growth to the end of the century. In the 1890s, the membership ran over one hundred twenty thousand, served by over a thousand traveling preachers, twice as many local preachers, and using over three thousand church buildings. It enjoyed from the beginning a church paper, the *Christian Index.*

Lane College, which had its beginnings as a brain child of Isaac Lane, the man who had struggled so hard to educate himself, opened the doors of its first building in 1882. Another institution, Paine College in Augusta, Georgia was the only college started by mutual support from the M. E. Church, South, and the C. M. E. Church.[9] During Reconstruction, the southern church had remained relatively inactive in the area of mission to Blacks, but after 1880 renewed concern led to more active relations. Isaac Lane lived to see his church grow into the twentieth century, retired in 1914, and lived until 1937! The denomination in 1954 changed its name to the Christian Methodist Episcopal Church.

The African Methodist Episcopal Church

The two African Methodist churches experienced slow growth down to the time of the Civil War, when they were still small and struggling. They had been effectively excluded from any development in the South. Then came a spectacular change which had almost revolutionary effects. Within twenty years, 1860–1880, they almost exploded in both size and geographical extent. The A. M. E. Church grew from about twenty thousand to nearly four hundred thousand, while the Zion Church rose from about six thousand to less than three hundred thousand. The largest growth developed in the South, which suddenly became open and attractive. Southern churches under white control were almost helpless for several years. The C. M. E. Church was formed while a veritable stream of black Methodists

[9] See George E. Clary, Jr., in *MH*, 9 (Jan., 1971): 24.

was flowing out of the M. E. Church, South. Much the same thing was happening in other denominations which were broadly represented across sectional lines.

Growth in numbers was also encouraged by the expansion of the church westward. From the early beginnings in Philadelphia and the East, African Methodism was caught up in the westward movement. The Allen Temple in Cincinnati traces its origin to difficulties all too familiar in old Wesley Chapel, where whites and blacks began worshiping separately. In 1824, the black members had withdrawn, joined the A. M. E. Church, and founded Allen Temple, the beginning of African Methodism in the Ohio Valley. After that, however, developments were motivated not so much by racial troubles as by natural expansion westward and by missionary endeavors. Black circuit riders were as active as white. Such men as William Quinn, George Bowler, and Moses Freeman built the work until the Ohio Conference was organized in 1830. In that year St. John's Church was founded in Cleveland. Shortly after the middle of the century, there were missions in Wisconsin and Minnesota. A Missouri Conference was established in 1852 to give support to work where possible in the Southwest. Early in the 1850s, A. M. E. congregations were started in California. Black men were as entranced by the glint of gold as white men! William Quinn, especially after he became bishop, was active in many parts of the country. Quinn Chapel in Chicago was founded in 1847. A church was started in Lawrence, Kansas in 1862.

While African Methodists were thus sharing in the westward movement, a major thrust was taking the church into the South, where it expanded into twelve states. The most interesting location was Charleston, South Carolina where African work, after an early start under the leadership of Morris Brown, was suppressed following the Vesey revolt. In 1865 Daniel Payne, who had been forced to leave town in 1835 on account of his educational work with Negroes, returned as a bishop to reestablish the A. M. E. Church in his hometown. It was a great day when the South Carolina Conference was organized in May.

The church produced many able leaders, among them Daniel Payne, William Paul Quinn, Henry McNeal Turner, Benjamin Tucker Tanner, Levi Jenkins Coppin, and Reverdy Cassius Ransom. Many of these men rose to the episcopal office via editorship of the church paper, the *Christian Recorder,* or its intellectual quarterly, the *A.M.E. Church Review.* To develop such leadership a major educational program was essential. Hence, much effort was put into schools and training centers of various kinds. John T. Jenifer calls his church "a graded training school for race leadership." "There was a period in her history, when African Methodism, like Negro Christianity generally, had no colleges nor schools. These were outlawed; the Negro church house was the school house, the preacher was the only instructor, the pulpit the teacher's desk, and the church services the sole instruction, hence . . . African Methodism has been an efficient training school for Negro leadership." [10] One of the principal results of this endeavor was the establishment of Wilberforce University, which began as a joint venture of the M. E. and A. M. E. Churches in 1856. Closed during the Civil War, it was reopened as an A. M. E. college under the leadership of Daniel A. Payne, who became its president and the first black college president. Allen University, Paul Quinn College, and Morris Brown College are other A. M. E. institutions.

An *A. M. E. Church Magazine,* started in 1841, became the *Christian Recorder* in 1852. An intellectual quarterly, the *A. M. E. Church Review,* was begun in 1884. Its first editor, one of a series of able literary leaders, was B. J. Tanner. From the beginning the publication took account of the many social problems which afflicted the black man. Beyond that, education and missions received strong support.

As Bishop Turner clearly set forth,[11] the polity of the church in all major respects was almost identical with that of the M. E. Church. The influence of Elijah Hedding's writings is evident in such matters as episcopal authority and class meetings. As time went on the denomination became a center for expression of black experience and provided not only a forum but also a laboratory. Unlike the C. M. E. Church, the African Methodists from the beginning asserted independence from white controls in rather strong language. Payne said the church was a "refuge for the hated race." Since the color line has not changed much since the time of Allen, said another, the Negro would be well advised to keep his own church, "but let them not do as the whites." This meant keeping the doors open for any Whites who desired fellowship. Some viewpoints foreshadowed twentieth century emphasis on the significance of blackness. "The Whites have their work to do, and in their own way. The Blacks likewise." [12]

The African Methodist Episcopal Zion Church

Owing to a number of factors, including complications of origin, problems of organization, and dearth of vigorous leadership, the A.

[10] *Centennial Retrospect History of the African Methodist Episcopal Church* (1916), 118-21, 146.

[11] Henry McNeal Turner, *The Genius and Theory of Methodist Polity; or, The Machinery of Methodism* (1885).

[12] See, for example, *A. M. E. Church Review,* 1 (1884): 1, 101; 2: 88; 3: 202.

M. E. Zion Church grew rather slowly and did not spread widely in the early years. The membership rose from a little over five hundred at the time of organization in 1821 to less than six thousand in 1860. As already noted both major African churches grew tremendously as a result of the Civil War and emancipation. The General Conference of 1864 reported a total of 13,700 members, over half of whom lived in the New York and Philadelphia annual conferences.[13] After the significant growth following the Civil War, the membership was 257,000 in 1916.

This increase did not mean, however, that the Zion Church spread with equal effectiveness into other parts of the country. For many years it remained firmly settled on the eastern seaboard, with expansion taking place north into New England and south into North Carolina. The North Carolina Conference was organized in 1864 with a membership reported of 2,654. Of course, within a few years several other southern conferences were organized. Efforts to spread into the Midwest, however, were not very successful. A schism, which distracted the denomination in the 1850s, was particularly damaging on work in the central part of the country. When the Ohio Conference was organized in 1891, there were still only four churches in the state. Elsewhere the situation was much the same. On the other hand, there were already three churches in California in 1852, only a few years after Methodist Episcopal beginnings there. A California Conference was organized in 1868.

One of the most significant aspects of the life of the Zion Church was its long-lasting witness against slavery. Although this has already been noted, it may be well to recall the outstanding work of clergymen like Thomas James and Jermain Loguen and laypersons like Catherine Harris, Frederick Douglass, and Harriet Tubman.

The structure of the A. M. E. Zion Church was in most respects the same as other branches of Methodism. Distinctive features have been a limited or term episcopacy and a strong tradition of lay participation. The former became an issue in 1852, when a debate over the nature of the episcopacy, especially whether a second bishop was "assistant" to the first bishop, led to a schism in which Bishop William H. Bishop withdrew to form the Wesleyan Methodist Church (not to be confused with the white church of the same name). This schism was healed before outbreak of the Civil War. It was decided that all bishops should enjoy equal status and authority, but should be subject

[13] Bradley, *A History of the A. M. E. Zion Church,* 146. Membership statistics for all groups are unreliable.

to the ultimate authority of the general conference. Lay delegates to the general conference were present in 1864, and by 1928 had achieved equal representation. New bishops were elected to replace Christopher Rush, who had given such effective leadership for so long in the early years. Among them were John J. Moore, Singleton T. Jones, and J. J. Clinton.

Many unsuccessful efforts were made to start a denominational magazine or paper before the *Star of Zion* was officially adopted by the General Conference of 1880 as an official paper. Four years later it became a weekly and has continued since then. In 1899 the *A. M. E. Zion Quarterly Review* was founded by Bishop Clinton. Much of the history of church publication is unwritten on account of the loss of many early records. In fact, Zion Church has suffered the loss of many important records for all aspects of church life. Little is known about the development of the hymnal and of Sunday school literature. Nevertheless, the publishing house, which began as the New York Conference Book Concern around 1841, has continued, in spite of recurrent financial difficulties, to produce materials for the churches.

As one might suppose, discussions took place from time to time on the possibilities for union and merger with other bodies. Both African Methodist groups were involved. Factors of competition and personalities prevented merger in the early years, as the two denominations went their separate ways. Splits took place, as for example, the secession of the African Union Church in Wilmington during the very process of founding the A. M. E. Church in 1816. On the other hand, repeated efforts were made to bring about union or reunion, both among the two black denominations and also with the M. E. Church.[14]

Most significant was the negotiation in the 1860s between the two main African churches. The A. M. E. Church began the movement for union. A vote in 1868 brought approval from the Zion church, but rejection by A. M. E. Among the central problems were definition of the episcopal office and role of the laity. A further complicating factor was the negotiation carried on between the Zion Church and the M. E. Church. Bishop Singleton Jones brought greetings to the M. E. General Conference of 1868 in Chicago. Later efforts between the two African churches, in 1885 and 1892, came to naught. Early in the twentieth century a series of discussions were carried on between the

[14] See Roy W. Trueblood, "Union Negotiations between Black Methodists in America," *MH*, 8 (July, 1970): 18-29.

two African Methodist Churches, and the C. M. E. Church. The "Birmingham Plan" failed of acceptance in 1918. Black Methodists have also participated regularly in the Methodist Ecumenical conferences. At the first in 1881, there were ten A. M. E., one C. M. E., and four Zion, representatives.

Chapter 25
Ethnic Varieties

One of the central themes of American history is immigration. The Indians of course were first, but even they in their arrivals and subsequent migrations pushed out still older Mound Builders, the Adena, Hopewell, and other cultures of mysterious origins. Next were the Spaniards. The conquest of Mexico by Hernando Cortes in 1519–22 was followed by the exploits of Francisco Coronado in the Southwest and Juan Cabrillo along the California coast. When the first permanent English settlement was founded at Jamestown in 1607, there were perhaps two hundred thousand Spaniards in the Americas, most of them south of the present United States. In 1598, Juan de Oñate made the first settlement in New Mexico, and around 1609, Santa Fe was founded. Immigration was strengthened by the activity of the friars, who not only pacified Indians but began to Christianize them.

The classic period of immigration, however, occupied the nineteenth century from about 1820 down to statutory restrictions imposed a hundred years later. Statistics for once tell the story straight: Germany, 6,249,000; Sweden, 1,228,000; Mexico, 839,000; Norway, 815,000; Denmark, 340,000; Japan, 297,000.[1] These figures include, of course, only those countries among whose people Methodism developed significantly in the United States. This chapter is organized according to the sequence of settlement by the various groups, rather than the beginnings of Methodist work.

American Indians

Part of the story of Methodism among the Indians belongs under the westward movement. Another part belongs under home missions. This part has to do chiefly with the development of an indigenous Indian Annual Conference, which although it retained subborn qualities of missionary enterprise, represents at its best an authentic ethnic form of Methodism.

After the tragic removal of eastern tribes to Indian territory,

[1] Taken from table in *HAM,* II, 470; figures rounded off to nearest thousand.

Methodist work continued among the relocated tribes especially in the area of eastern Oklahoma, where the five Indian nations were settled.[2] Just prior to the division of the church, there were twelve white and three Indian traveling preachers, all members of the Arkansas Conference, plus twenty-one Indian local preachers; about 1500 Cherokee members, 1000 Choctaw, 600 Creek, 150 Negro, and 100 white. These were formed into the Indian Mission Annual Conference in 1844. Bishop Thomas A. Morris held the first session in Tahlequah, a village cradled in the rolling hills of eastern Oklahoma. One of the local preachers was the famous chief of the Creek nation, Samuel Checote, who served as principal chief in 1869, 1872, and 1879. "If any one man was the bridge between the Creek Nation and the Christian Church, it was Chief Samuel Checote." [3] During the Civil War he served as an officer in the Confederate Army. He and his fellow Creek, James McHenry (Jim Henry) helped develop a most successful work with that tribe. Among the organizers who came together in small Riley's Chapel, located about two miles outside Tahlequah, was William H. Goode who was elected secretary. The first-year membership was reported as follows: 2,992 Indians, 133 Negroes, 85 Whites. Four deacons were ordained, two Indian and two white. At this time there were about seventy-five thousand Indians belonging to the five Indian nations in the territory. After five years, 3,226 Indian church members were reported, along with 376 Negroes and 156 Whites. Some of the black members were slaves of Whites or Indians. At the division of the church in 1845, this conference decided, after considerable difference of opinion, to align with the southern church. Goode and other Northerners transferred.

When Bishop George Pierce admitted James McHenry, who had become notorious as the hero of the Creek War in the East, to membership on trial in 1855, he was moved to comment:

The lion has become a lamb, the brave, a preacher. The war-whoop is hushed; the midnight foray is with the past; the Bible and the Hymn Book fill the hands that once grasped the torch and tomahawk. The bold, valiant savage, who spread consternation among the peaceful settlements on either side of the Chattahoochee, now travels a circuit, preaching peace on earth, good will to men. The Lord make him an apostle to his people." [4]

[2] See Sidney H. Babcock and J. Y. Bryce, *History of Methodism in Oklahoma: Story of the Indian Mission Annual Conference of the Methodist Episcopal Church, South* (1935), and Leland Clegg and William B. Oden, *Oklahoma Methodism in the Twentieth Century* (1968). A later volume of Barclay's *The History of Methodist Missions,* not available at this writing, should give full coverage. Walter Vernon is carrying on extended research in the area.

[3] Clegg and Oden, *Oklahoma Methodism,* 27.

[4] Babcock and Bryce, *History,* 119-20.

Men like McHenry and Checote brought a strong Indian influence to the leadership of the conference. Checote, especially, was vigorous in promoting the cause of Indian culture and language. His struggle for the use of Indian languages, although unsuccessful, symbolized the incentive for native self-expression.[5] When the Civil War broke out, the Indian tribes were divided in their loyalties, but inclined to the South on account of their fears of expulsion by the North, the abandonment of northern forts, their relation to the southern church, and their own ownership of black slaves. The conference survived the war and gradually expanded, helped through the difficult years by Bishop Enoch Marvin. Influential Indian leaders who were active in the Indian Conference were John Ross, a Cherokee Methodist layman who struggled for the rights of his people, and John Page, a Choctaw ministerial member.

Much of the work in the 1880s was educational, as illustrated by the Indian paper started in 1882, *Our Brother in Red,* whose motto ran, "Christian education the hope of the Indian." After 1887, the activity which had been restricted to the five Indian nations in such centers as Tahlequah, Muskogee, and Okmulgee, was extended to the Plains Indians with the appointment of J. J. Methvin, who worked among Arapaho, Ponca, Kiowa, Apache, Comanche, and others. After 1889, the rapid incursion of white settlers turned the Indian Conference into a more and more white-oriented organization, which in 1906 became the Oklahoma Conference.

An Indian Mission Conference of the M. E. Church was formed in 1889, rising from long-standing work among the Wyandots. In 1892 it became the M. E. Oklahoma Conference.

Hispanic Americans

If the history of Methodism among Hispanic Americans is referred to at all, it is usually subsumed under the heading of home missions. It belongs there, of course, in part and is dealt with, especially with regard to widespread urban missions, under that head. In a deeper sense it belongs more properly here as an aspect of ethnic variety. The history of Methodism among Spanish-speaking Americans, especially those whose history in the Southwest goes back to the very beginnings of the American nation, deserves treatment in and for itself. The roots of the work with Hispanic Americans in the Southwest go back to the middle of the nineteenth century, shortly after Texas and New Mexico became part of the territory of the United States. It was a classic confrontation of two cultures—expansive

[5] See discussion in *Ibid.,* 214-20.

Protestant-oriented English culture from east of the Mississippi moving west, and traditional Catholic-oriented Spanish culture from south of the Rio Grande moving north. They collided and mingled in Texas, New Mexico, Arizona, and the southern part of California.[6]

The first event did not take place in Texas at all, but in the territory of New Mexico in 1853, when the first Methodist sermon was delivered at the entrance to the governor's palace by a former priest. The first recorded conversions of persons with Mexican ancestry, however, took place in southern Texas between 1856 and 1860. This means that the earliest work among these Hispanic Americans came from both the M. E. Church (New Mexico) and the M. E. Church, South (Texas). Both experienced slow and difficult but continuous growth. Three names stand out in the development of structure along the Rio Grande: Alejo Hernandez, Alexander Sutherland, and Frank S. Onderdonk, all related to the southern church in Texas. The administrative genius of these men spanned the latter half of the nineteenth century and the first half of the twentieth century. Hernandez came from Mexico as a young man, was converted and joined the Methodist church in Brownsville, and was ordained deacon in 1871 and elder in 1874. The latter event, which took place in Mexico City under Bishop John C. Keener, was a truly ecumenical affair, since he was assisted by a former priest, a Congregational minister, and an Episcopalian rector.[7] Unfortunately, he suffered a stroke and died the next year.

In 1874, a Mexican Border Mission District was organized in the West Texas Conference under the leadership of Sutherland, who was assisted by three ministers and three supplies, all Spanish-speaking. A second district was formed after six years, the two reporting 732 members. By 1884, of the nine districts in the conference, four served Hispanic Americans. During these years men like Policarpo Rodriguez struggled against cultural and economic odds to plant Methodism among the people of the Rio Grande Valley. With his own hands he built the solid stone chapel near Bandera which stands today as "Polly's Chapel." Anglos simply could not master his colorful name. The attractive and well-kept building serves as a symbol of Hispanic American Methodist history. San Antonio, only about fifty miles

---

[6] Material on Hispanic American Methodism is scarce. Olin W. Nail, *The First One Hundred Years of the Southwest Texas Conference of the Methodist Church* (1958), has a little, 117-25. A little more is in *Spanish Doorways* (1964), ed. by Henry C. Sprinkle et al. The best source, in Spanish, is the "Sección Historica" by Alfredo Nañez in the minutes of the Rio Grande Conference, 1971, 115-30. See also José Espino, *Perfiles* (El Paso, 1963). 1963).

[7] Nañez, "Sección Historica," 121.

distant, was an early center for Spanish-speaking work. An annual conference was organized in 1885 to include all the Mexican work in southwestern United States and had a membership of 1,370 persons.

This structure, which testified to the growing importance of the Hispanic Americans, created serious problems of communication between Anglos and Mexicans. Important cultural forces were at work, sometimes leading to unfortunate contradictions. In the twentieth century efforts were made to bring the two forms of Methodism closer together. With the formation of the Methodist Church in 1939, the Rio Grande Conference came into being as a separate ethnic annual conference in which Methodists of Mexican ancestry could take positions of leadership. The membership in 1971 was 15,727.

Independent from these Texas developments, which were supervised by the M. E. Church, South, was the work in New Mexico which had begun in the 1850s with the preaching of the former priest, Benigno Cárdenas, under the supervision of the appointed missionary of the M. E. Church, Enoch G. Nicholson. This effort had languished in the 1850s. With the arrival of Thomas and Emily Harwood, however, in 1869, Methodist activity revived. They reestablished the earlier societies and began vigorous new work with both English and Spanish inhabitants. A New Mexico Mission was formed in 1872, later divided into an English Mission and a Spanish Mission. They led in setting up schools for Hispanic-American children and in publishing religious material in Spanish—especially a paper begun in 1879, *El Abogado Cristiano*. In 1892, the general conference established the Spanish Mission Conference. The most successful educational enterprise was the Harwood Girl's School in Albuquerque, which is still doing excellent work.

Among other institutions working with Hispanic Americans on both sides of the border are Holding Institute in Laredo, founded in 1882 with support of the Woman's Board of Foreign Missions, and Lydia Patterson Institute in El Paso, begun in 1913 as a project of the southern church's Board of Missions. Both have emphasized education for children and young people, and the latter has carried on a program for the training of young men for the minstry.[8]

German Methodism

Perhaps the first Methodist missionary to Americans of German ancestry, if we do not count the generation of Asbury and Henry

[8] I am indebted to Pres. Maurice Daily of Holding Institute and Pres. Noé Gonzalez of Lydia Patterson Institute for data and interpretation in conversations held in December, 1972.

Boehm, was Lawrence Everhard, appointed German missionary at the Baltimore Annual Conference in 1817.[9] All the continuing contacts with the United Brethren and Evangelical Association constitute an early chapter in German Methodism in a broader sense. Considered strictly within the Methodist Episcopal Church, however, the ✳ real beginnings are centered in the life of William Nast. For a long generation he was a dominant figure, not only in his ethnic circle, but also throughout the Methodist connection. The *Northwestern Christian Advocate* described him in 1860 at the general conference as of medium size with a florid face and strong accent, "one of the really great men, . . . a regular Teuton, and loves his pipe, as every Dutchman should." [10]

After Protestant theological training in Germany, he migrated to the United States in 1828 and was converted at a revival in Danville, Ohio. In 1835 at the Ohio Conference he was appointed missionary to the Germans and began work in Cincinnati. Working alternately in the city and on a large circuit, he succeeded in organizing a society of German Methodists in 1838. The next year he began editing a surprisingly successful German language "Advocate," *Der Christliche Apologete.* His career was advanced by the marriage of his daughter Fanny to William Gamble, son of an Irish soapmaker. This German-Irish alliance brought significant results in several Methodist service institutions.

Several other leaders were enlisted, especially the Nuelsen family and Ludwig S. Jacoby, who planted German Methodism in St. Louis. German-speaking districts dated from 1844 and a German Methodist Annual Conference from 1864. One of the important spin-offs of this work was the planting of Methodism in Germany by missionaries from America. Together with efforts which came from British Methodism, a vigorous free church developed on the Continent. Among the more influential enterprises in America were several educational institutions, particularly German Wallace College in Berea, Ohio, which was chartered in 1864 and merged with Baldwin University in 1913 to form Baldwin-Wallace College. *Der Christliche Apologete* continued publication for over a century. Although it generally took a moderately conservative position on the intellectual trends of the day, such as the higher criticism of the Bible, it brought to

[9] A note in a letter from Edwin Schell (20 May 1963) calls attention to this early endeavor. Everhard soon located; he had earlier supplied pulpits for the United Brethren in Pennsylvania.

[10] *NWCA*, 30 May 1860, 85. Carl Frederick Wittke, *William Nast, Patriarch of German Methodism* (1959) is an excellent biography. The standard source is Paul F. Douglass, *The Story of German Methodism* (1939).

German-speaking Methodists a broad spectrum of commentary and interpretation that helped bridge the cultural gap. The paper was consistently in favor of Americanization and patriotism. That did not spare it, however, from repeated attacks by superpatriots during World War I.

One of the continuing problems of German Methodism, common to all the language and ethnic groups, was that of cultural identity. To put it bluntly, were German Methodists really German, or were they American, or were they somehow a combination? Nast had definite convictions so far as his fellow churchmen were concerned. He strongly urged establishment of a German Annual Conference, but insisted vehemently that German Methodists were no less American than any others. This was not a valid issue, he thought. He doubted that the term "Americanization" applied, because German Methodists were already Americans except for their language.[11] Increasingly, in the latter half of the nineteenth century *Der Christliche Apologete* emphasized patriotic themes and identified Americans of German background with the American way of life. Debates on continued use of the German language spread over the whole period, as native-born generations replaced original immigrants. By the time of World War I, the German Methodists had committed themselves to full involvement as American citizens, even though many older persons clung to the German language and culture. They tried to remain neutral along with the rest of the country in World War I, but were unprepared for the intolerance which came with American involvement. That is a sad story which belongs to the uncertainties of the twentieth century. It was not easy for German Methodists, who had many meaningful relations with Methodism in Germany, to make the hard decision which was forced upon them.[12]

By 1915 there were ten German Annual Conferences with a membership of 60,271. A distinctive feature of German Methodism was the deaconess movement, which was introduced from German Protestantism. In Germany, Switzerland, and Austria, deaconesses were very active in Methodist service organizations such as hospitals and schools. In the latter part of the century this deaconess movement became strong in the United States, especially among Lutherans and German Methodists. In Cincinnati a whole group of benevolent in-

[11] See report of his speech at the General Conference of 1860 in *NWCA*, 20 June 1860, 97.

[12] A symbolic example is the close relation which continued between Baldwin-Wallace College in Berea, Ohio and the Methodist Seminary in Frankfurt-am-Main. See Norwood, "Frankfurt-am-Main and Baldwin-Wallace College," *The Ohio State Archeological and Historical Quarterly*, 60 (1951): 20-27.

stitutions, collectively known as Bethesda, resulted from early interest in utilizing the service of deaconesses. The work of the Bethany Society (East German Conference) in Brooklyn would be another example.

Scandinavian Methodism

In many ways, the history of ethnic Methodism ran parallel courses among Germans, Swedes, and Norwegian-Danes, but the origins of Swedish Methodism go back to a ship in New York harbor.[13] Responding to a need for religious ministry to visiting seamen, the New York Conference in 1845 appointed Olof G. Hedström to what is called the North River Mission, better known as Bethelship. An old brig (two masts) was acquired and renamed the *John Wesley*. Operating from this pier-bound, water-born chapel, Hedström carried out a unique ministry and brought many Scandinavian sailors to Christian commitment and Methodist membership. Out of it rose Immanuel Church in Brooklyn, the first Swedish Methodist Episcopal church. Hedström's brother Jonas organized the second society, Victoria, near Galesburg, Illinois, in 1846.

Swedish Methodism spread with the immigration of Swedish people, especially to the Midwest around Chicago and in Minnesota. In the one hundred years after 1830, about 1,300,000 came. By 1920 there were over 112,000 foreign-born Swedes in Minnesota and over 105,000 in Illinois. A Chicago Swedish mission resulted from revival meetings in the early 1850s. Other societies were organized as far away as Massachusetts and Texas. Efforts were made to bring these together in an annual conference, but this was not accomplished until 1877, when the Northwest Swedish Conference, covering work in Illinois and Minnesota, was organized. By the time of the first World War there were four annual and two mission conferences. They served almost 20,000 members.

As with the Germans, institutions of education, publication, and benevolence were established. Rather than starting new colleges, however, the Swedes concentrated on a theological seminary for training ministers, which was begun in 1870 and moved to Evanston, Illinois in 1875. In 1934 this school merged with a Norwegian-Danish seminary in the same town. A weekly church paper, the *Sändebudet*, began a long series in 1862. Later, it became a monthly and continued into the twentieth century. Among Swedish service institutions were

---

[13] The only monograph on Swedish Methodism is Nils M. Liljegren et al., *Svenske Metodismen i Amerika* (1895).

Bethany Home and Hospital in Chicago, Scandinavian Seamen's Missions in New York and Galveston, Texas, and many camp meetings to serve the revival spirit which ran strong.

Merging of these language conferences with the English-speaking conferences took place in the 1920s. Similar factors of history, society, and culture played a part in the rise and fall of Scandinavian Methodism as a separate channel of Methodist witness.

To everyone except Swedes, Danes, and Norwegians, Sweden, Denmark, and Norway add up to Scandinavia. The last two, however, even within the fellowship of the Methodist Episcopal Church, were acutely conscious of *not* being Swedes. That feeling was mutual. Hence Methodist work among Norwegians and Danes, although historically related to the Swedish development, followed more or less separate organization patterns.[14] In the early years Scandinavian work was treated as a unit, and Olof Hedström was appointed head of the mission. The founder of Norwegian Methodism in the United States was Ole Peter Petersen, who had been converted under Methodist auspices in Boston and New York. In 1850, licensed as local preacher, he was appointed to serve Norwegians in northern Iowa.

The roots of Norwegian Methodism are multiple—or at least dual, if we count as one several influences of the westward movement. In 1825, a Norwegian Quaker group had become Methodist and moved west, and there were several other movements along the frontier. This westward drive, combined with the leadership of Petersen, brought Methodism to the growing numbers of Norwegians and Danes who were settling in the Old Northwest and on the Great Plains. In Washington Prairie, Iowa, Petersen preached the first Norwegian sermon. Soon small societies were organized in southern Wisconsin and northern Illinois. Characteristically, the Chicago society for some time had a Swedish class and a Norwegian-Danish class. There was a Swedish minister and a Norwegian minister, both members of the Rock River Conference. Developing along the pattern of language districts, a Northwest Norwegian Conference (later Norwegian and Danish Conference) was organized in 1880. In much the same manner as the German and Swedish Methodists, a mission was sent to plant the church in the home countries. Petersen was leader of this mission to Norway.[15]

[14] Full treatment in Arlo W. Andersen, *Salt of the Earth, A History of Norwegian-Danish Methodism in America* (1962), based in part on Andrew Haagensen, *Den Norsk-Dansk Methodismes Historie paa begge Sider Havet* (1894).

[15] See Arne Hassing, "Methodism and Society in Norway, 1849-1918," (Diss., Northwestern, 1974).

Something of the cultural experience of the Norwegians and Danes is reflected in the publishing history of their chief magazine. It began in 1869 as the *Missionaren,* which became *Den Kristelig Talsmand* in 1887; this was succeeded by the *Evangelisk Tidende* in 1922. However, by 1940 people were reading the *Gospel Advocate,* which finally became *Fellowship News Bulletin* in 1943. The central issue of cultural nationalism is well illustrated by the long career of Andrew Haagensen, who came to the United States from Norway in 1857 and retired in 1908. He stalwartly maintained the conservative position: "The church stands as historical proof that it is possible even for a smaller denomination to retain its mother tongue. We must work to preserve our language."[16] All Haagensen's efforts failed to stem the tide of cultural assimilation. Both the Norwegian language and the Norwegian-Danish Conference merged into the American melting pot of the twentieth century.

Before that happened, however, the influence of the *Kristelig Talsmand* and the Norwegian-Danish seminary established in Evanston, Illinois had deeply dyed one more variety of American Methodism. Although the outward trappings of institutionalization are gone, much of the spirit remains alive among descendants who, far from forgetting, are seeking more and more to remember that which makes their heritage distinctive. Much the same can be said of the other ethnic varieties discussed in this chapter.

Among the several other ethnic varieties are the Japanese Methodists, who are largely concentrated on the West Coast. Their story in America began in 1887 with the baptism of Kanichi Miyama, the first Japanese immigrant Christian, who became a Methodist preacher. He was the founder of Japanese Methodist work in California and Hawaii. The official beginning of the Pacific Japanese Mission dates from 1900. As a result of the union of 1939, the Pacific Japanese Provisional Annual Conference came into existence. It lasted until 1964, when it merged with the California-Nevada Annual Conference.[17]

---

[16] In Andersen, *Salt of the Earth,* 167.
[17] Data from letter by Lester E. Suzuki, Berkeley, California.

Chapter 26
Sectarian Movements

At least four major factors played a part in the development of sectarian movements in Methodism in the second half of the nineteenth century: (1) ecclesiological concerns such as those earlier expressed by the Methodist Protestants, (2) the social and moral issues associated with the institution of slavery, (3) theological emphasis on what Wesley liked to call perfect love—sanctification or holiness, and (4) the influence of powerful and charismatic personalities. Besides these many secondary factors further complicated the question of motivation—secret societies, forms of worship, pewed churches, sabbatarianism, amusements, dress, to mention only a few. The first major factor was always present, although sometimes obscured by polemics focused on the others. For the Wesleyan Methodists and the Free Methodists, a close correlation existed between theological and social concerns. In fact, the two were inseparable. The Wesleyan Methodists sprang from the crisis over slavery in the M. E. Church in the quadrennium 1840–44, yet claimed to revive the original Wesleyan doctrine of Christian perfection which the church had abandoned. The Free Methodists in 1860 combined Christian perfection and antislavery with what they regarded as the ecclesiastical tyranny of the "Buffalo Regency" in the Genesee Conference. These same major factors played a part in the roiling vagaries of the Holiness movement of the 1880s and 1890s, although slavery itself was gone. Similar tensions, though not over slavery, brought schism to both Evangelicals and United Brethren.

Revivalism and Perfectionism

Consideration of the doctrine of perfect love as an aspect of Methodist theology is dealt with in another chapter. Our concern here is to clarify the importance of the renewed interest in holiness which became a central emphasis of early nineteenth-century revivalism. This was the nub of the theological motivation of men like Orange Scott and Benjamin Titus Roberts.[1] Briefly, Wesley's original

[1] In addition to the standard denominational histories two excellent monographs approach perfectionism from different angles: John Leland Peters, *Christian Perfection*

strong emphasis on going on to perfection was transplanted completely into American Methodism not only through his own writings, which were widely dispersed, but also through the influence of Fletcher's *Checks* and Watson's *Institutes.* On the frontier, however, and everywhere in the struggle to plant and build a new church, the niceties of Wesleyan theology were obscured. All preachers could do was convince men to "flee the wrath to come." There was precious little chance to lead them on to perfection.

During the revivals it became apparent to some that an important part of the Wesleyan heritage was being lost. Not only Methodists but other influential revivalists like Charles G. Finney began to preach ✳ "holiness" as a work of grace subsequent to conversion. In 1839 Methodist Timothy Merritt began publishing the *Guide to Christian Perfection* (later *Guide to Holiness*), which had great influence for several decades, and by 1873 had 40,000 subscribers. About the same time Phoebe (Mrs. W. C.) Palmer organized her "Tuesday Meeting for the Promotion of Holiness" in New York, which enjoyed the patronage of many leading Methodists including several bishops. Nathan Bangs and both of the bishops elected in 1844, Edmund S. Janes, and Leonidas L. Hamline, were strong supporters. Randolph S. Foster, later bishop, wrote in 1851 *The Nature and Blessedness of Christian Purity.* Until the 1850s, many articles on the subject appeared in the *Methodist Quarterly Review.*

In the Methodist Episcopal Church two lines of development may be discerned: the one combining revivalist-perfectionism with social concern for the Christianization of society, after the classic fashion of men like Finney and Asa Mahan; the other divorcing the two factors, as we see in the work of Phoebe Palmer. William Arthur, who wrote *The Tongue of Fire* (1854), represents the former: "Nothing short of the general renewal of society ought to satisfy any soldier of Christ. . . . To destroy all national holds of evil; to root sin out of institutions; to hold up to view the gospel ideal of a righteous nation . . . is one of the first duties of those whose position or mode of thought gives them any influence in general questions."[2] To some extent Matthew Simpson and others shared these views, but not Mrs. Palmer, who wielded immense influence through her Tuesday meeting. To her, the solution of social ills lay exclusively with the conversion of individuals. The tradition whereby committed Christians seeking perfection stayed out of politics and avoided entanglements with

---

and American Methodism (1956) and Timothy L. Smith, *Revivalism and Social Reform in Mid-Nineteenth-Century America* (1957).

[2] 1880 ed., 145-46; quoted in Smith, *Revivalism,* 154. On Palmer, see *ibid.,* 211.

worldly issues had one of its beginnings here. Hence, on the great issue of the day, slavery, her circle had little or nothing to say.

These, then, were some of the background theological factors which contributed to the sectarian movements discussed here.

Wesleyan Methodist Development

The Wesleyan Methodist Church, which had sprung from the controversies over slavery in the early 1840s, continued after the generation of Orange Scott and La Roy Sunderland with antislavery witness combined with Wesleyan perfectionism. That the latter came more and more to the front is illustrated by the important resolution adopted in 1883 by the general conference of the connection, which singled out entire sanctification for emphasis. A few years later entire sanctification was redefined as follows:

> That work of the Holy Spirit by which the child of God is cleansed from all sin through faith in Jesus Christ. It is a distinct, instantaneous and subsequent work to regeneration, and is wrought when the believer presents himself a living sacrifice, holy and acceptable unto God; and is thus enabled through grace to love God with all the heart and to walk in His holy commandments blameless.[3]

Along with this emphasis on holiness came a series of increasingly rigid regulations on daily activities and amusements. In the twentieth century tobacco was more stringently forbidden, in cultivation, sale, and use. An interesting accompaniment of this high standard of purity was recognition of "associate members," who were not so strictly bound. In 1927 the membership was 22,000. Not until 1947 was the denominational name changed from connection to church. The persistence of the old term is symbolic of the original opposition to institutionalized forms of church order associated with episcopal domination. The change to the new term is yet another illustration of the apparently inevitable process by which a charismatic movement eventually settles into institutional form.

The Free Methodist Church

The four major roots of sectarian movements were all present in the controversies which led to the organization of the Free Methodist Church. Institutional criticism, the Wesleyan doctrine of perfect love,

---

[3] Quoted in Ira F. McLeister, *History of the Wesleyan Methodist Church of America* (1959), 111-12.

the issue of slavery on the eve of war, and the charismatic presence of Benjamin Titus Roberts all conspired to raise a conflict within one annual conference into a major split which affected many parts of the church. In so many ways the history of the Free Methodists runs parallel with that of the Wesleyan Methodists that one always wonders why they should have remained separate movements. Even as late as the 1950s, negotiations between the two ended in failure.

Curiously, the trouble started, not only in a local situation, but also over a relatively minor issue.[4] However, minor issues in the Genesee Conference had a way of exploding. After all, this was the same area that had produced repeated fiery revivals that gave it the name "Burned-Over District." It spawned the likes of Joseph Smith, who strode out to form the Church of Jesus Christ of Latter Day Saints (Mormons). The issue among Genesee Methodists was their opposition to secret societies, especially the Masonic Order. The conflict quickly brought in other, more basic problems, such as forms of worship, episcopal authority, doctrinal emphasis, and the rest. On the one hand were the "Nazarites," a term originally used in derision by their opponents. They demanded reform and opposed innovations in worship and church life, secret societies and rented pews, moral compromise on slavery, and tyranny by bishops. Wesleyan perfection was their goal. On the other side was the "Regency," so-called by opponents as a sort of citadel of the *status quo,* the establishment. Behind these differences lay a deep sociological chasm between the relatively plain rural people who liked the old ways and the sophisticated city people who believed in progress. The Regency was strong in Buffalo, and the Nazarites found much of their support in the country.

Among the Nazarites was Benjamin Roberts, who graduated from Wesleyan University and joined the Genesee Conference the very year trouble broke into the open. He was already strongly antislavery from his New England associations. Appointed to the Niagara Street Church in Buffalo, he worked hard to revive its "dead" members and tried unsuccessfully to abolish its pew-rental system. One of the original meanings of the "Free" Methodist Church was freedom from private pews. There were social undertones to this issue, since private pews favored the prosperous middle class and discouraged the poor and farm folks long on land and short of cash. By 1855 the conflict had become wildly polemic, as may be seen in the "Documents of the Nazarite Union," which stated, along with much else, that Regency supporters were

[4] Leslie R. Marston, *From Age to Age, A Living Witness* (1960).

clerical professors in Odd-Fellow regalia, "shawled to the nose and bearded to the eyes," reading foolscap sermons one day, and praying to open secret Lodges the next;—pipelaying and managing in the Conference to oust out some, and hoist in others—and its lay professors rigged out in brass and feathers, and imitation posies, together with all its artifices to entice the world to love and support the Church; such as its sham donations, post-offices, lotteries, grab-bags, and oyster suppers for God. . . . They have other Masonic duties than building the walls of Jerusalem; other tents to pitch than the goodly tents of Jacob.[5]

The Regency used this document, which did not represent the responsible leadership of the reform party, as propaganda. Roberts defended the Nazarite movement in an article which thrust him forward as leader. His "New School Methodism," was published in the *Northern Independent,* a reform magazine started by William Hosmer, who had lost his position as editor of the official *Northern Christian Advocate.*[6] Roberts attacked the "New School" as followers of Theodore Parker and other liberals, equating Christianity with "beneficence." By this he meant works-righteousness and the merging of justification and sanctification. People who believe this, he added, join lodges.

The fight came into the open at the Annual Conference of 1857, as Roberts lost election as secretary by a vote of forty to his Regency opponent's forty-five. The sides were closely drawn and almost equal. Roberts was subjected to censure, but was given an appointment. By now rumor and slander exacerbated feelings. The next year he was brought to trial before the annual conference, convicted of contumacy, and expelled by a vote of fifty-four to thirty-four with many abstentions. He promptly appealed to the general conference, which was scheduled to meet in Buffalo in 1860.

Affairs were developing rapidly. In 1858 and again in 1859, "Laymen's Conventions" were held to protest the censures and expulsions. The result was more censures and more expulsions. Out of the laymen's movement came "bands" which gave support to Roberts and other expelled leaders. Two "Free" Methodist churches were organized in Buffalo. When the general conference did meet, Roberts and his cause were caught in a situation in which far larger concerns entered. His appeal from the first censure resulted in a tie vote which had the effect of supporting the Genesee Conference. Action on the expulsion was avoided by a technicality and thus left to stand.

As a result, almost immediately after the general conference, a

---

[5] Quoted in *HAM,* II, 344-45.
[6] See Marston, *From Age to Age,* 182-84. The article is given in an appendix, 573-78.

convention was held in Pekin, New York, called on the basis of adherence to Wesleyan doctrine, equality of ministers and lay persons, and opposition to slavery and secret societies.[7] A new church was formed, the Free Methodist Church. On the basis of the Call, there was a revision of the articles of religion, with clear emphasis on instantaneous sanctification and strict standards for church membership. The requirements for full membership, which followed a six-month probationary period, paint a clear picture of a sectarian church bound in strict discipline.

While this new church was forming in the Genesee Conference, a separate influence came from Illinois, where John Wesley Redfield, a holiness revival preacher, gave unrestrained expression to emotional displays in his camp meetings, especially in St. Charles. The Rock River Conference was roughly shaken by this independent and fiery personage. He was uncompromising in his demands for sanctification of an immediate and specific form. A. D. Field, one of the conference members who lived through the conflicts, spoke of "the wild scenes of Nazaritism . . . the wildest people history has known." Of Redfield himself: "Morbid, erratic, *brilliant,* but *grim,* . . . censorious, . . . abusive." [8] Redfield started a movement of his own, which joined in uneasy alliance with the New York movement. It brought an extremist element into the new church which was not characteristic of Roberts and his followers.

When the dust of battle settled, a new split had taken place and many persons had been hurt. Bitterness lingered long until finally an act of belated justice restored Roberts' papers and honors. By that time it was far too late for mending fences and healing wounds. Although the Free Methodist Church began on the high moral tone of antislavery, its increasingly rigid moralism forced it into opposition to the labor union movement and alienated many potential members. By 1878 it counted 10,862 members. The responsibility which lay with both sides in a schism which ought not to have happened is ably summarized in the *History of American Methodism.*

The Holiness Controversy

The schisms which occurred in Methodism before 1867 were the product of many forces, only one of which was the theological emphasis on sanctification. Beginning with the first "National Camp Meeting for the Promotion of Holiness," however, this theological

[7] *Ibid.,* 253, 260.

[8] A. D. Field, *Memorials of Methodism in the Bounds of the Rock River Conference* (1886), 491, 498.

concern came to center stage.[9] The chairman of the New York Methodist Preachers' Meeting, John S. Inskip, was the chief instigator of this new association, which met at Vineland, New Jersey. Intended to be interdenominational in character, but strongly Methodistic in support, it spread across the entire country within a few years and served as a rallying point for many diverse, independent interests. Presbyterians like William E. Boardman and Baptists like A. B. Earle contributed to the literature devoted to Christian perfection. The Civil War interposed an artificial intermission, although interest revived swiftly after its conclusion. Both the new president of Drew Theological Seminary (founded 1867), J. C. McClintock, and the man he appointed as professor of systematic theology, Randolph S. Foster, were committed to the idea of holiness. Many bishops in the two main branches of the church were personally interested and active. An influential layman, Washington C. DePauw, who gave much money and his name to Indiana Asbury University, was head of the National Publishing Association for the Promotion of Holiness. In 1885, the first General Holiness Assembly met in Park Avenue Methodist Episcopal Church in Chicago. Throughout the early years Methodism was deeply involved in the Holiness movement. One powerful factor in the election of William Taylor as missionary bishop in 1884 was support from advocates of holiness.

In the 1880s, however, voices of criticism were raised more and more frequently. Whereas, formerly, the Holiness movement was seen as a means for strengthening faith within the denomination, it seemed to some that a trend was growing toward what came to be called "come-outism." One of the leaders in the 1885 Chicago assembly tried to state the nondenominational character of the movement: "Come Methodists, come Baptists, come Presbyterians, and Mennonites, and U.B.'s, and Salvation Armyists." [10] He might well have added the Evangelical Association, which was actively involved. When the movement became antidenominational, voices of protest were raised. Sometimes come-outism was countered by "push-outism."

Increasingly, the issue centered on the meaning of entire sanctification. Although Wesley was regularly quoted, the controversy concentrated on the distinction between regeneration and sanctification as a "second blessing" and on the manner in which that blessing was manifested. *Entire* and *instantaneous* became battle cries, answered by

---

[9] In addition to the pertinent portions of the works already cited by Peters and T. Smith, see Robert E. Chiles, *Theological Transition in American Methodism: 1790–1935* (1965) and Timothy L. Smith, *Called Unto Holiness* (1963).

[10] Quoted in Smith, *Called Unto Holiness*, 33.

progressive and *gradual*. Miner Raymond, whose three-volume *Systematic Theology* was a first fruit of formal Methodist theological education in America, sought to retain the Wesleyan understanding while yet allowing for individual varieties of experience. As to the manner, he thought it was "generally by a gradual process, perhaps sometimes instantaneously." [11] The influential English Methodist, William Burt Pope, thought assurance of sanctification "more appropriate to his aspiration than his professed attainment," and insisted that, though the act of the Holy Spirit may be in one moment, it must be preceded and succeeded by development.[12] Other voices joined in. Southern Methodists like J. M. Boland *(The Problem of Methodism),* and George H. Hayes *(The Problem Solved),* and northern Methodists like James Mudge *(Growth in Holiness Toward Perfection; or, Progressive Sanctification),* filled their books between 1888 and 1895 with critical studies of the doctrine. John Miley in his *Systematic Theology* (1894) objected to the separation of sanctification from regeneration and rejected the notion of a "second blessing." He called for toleration of different views on the work of holiness.

Toleration was what the more extreme proponents were not prepared to exercise. On both sides intolerance was the order of the day. Defenders of holiness were quick to insist that there was only one definition and only one process, that which had received formulation at the General Holiness Assembly of 1885. It was to be understood as "entire," a "second definite work ... received instantaneously by faith, by which the heart is cleansed from all corruption and filled with the perfect love of God." [13] That did not leave much room for maneuvering or negotiating. The crisis is well illustrated by the forthright statement of the episcopal address to the general conference of the M.E. Church, South, in 1894. After affirming, as the Methodist churches had always affirmed, the validity of Wesleyan teaching on perfect love, the bishops went on: "But there has sprung up among us a party with holiness as a watchword; they have holiness associations, holiness meetings, holiness preachers, holiness evangelists, and holiness property. Religious experience is represented as if it consists of only two steps, the first step out of condemnation into peace, and the next step into Christian perfection." [14] The bishops deplored the tendency to claim monopoly over holiness as susceptible of only one definition and one process.

[11] Miner Raymond, *Systematic Theology* (1877), II, 350.
[12] Quoted in Peters, *Christian Perfection,* 159.
[13] As quoted in *Ibid.,* 162.
[14] *JGC,* MEC, South (1894), 25.

The result of this kind of confrontation was the separation of a large number of very small groups. In the 1880s, there had come into existence such sects as the Church of God (Anderson, Indiana), the Church of God (Holiness), and the Holiness Church. For a time, the distinction between independent denomination and independent-minded holiness association was blurred as everything went into flux. In the 1890s many completely separate sect groups came into existence. They carried such names as the New Testament Church of Christ, Burning Bush, First Church of the Nazarene (local in California), Association of the Pentecostal Churches of America, Apostolic Holiness Union, Missionary Church Association, Pentecostal Alliance, Pentecostal Bands of the World, and the Independent Holiness Church. All of these were heavily Methodist in leadership and membership. One of them became a prime source for the new denomination, the Church of the Nazarene, which was founded in the early twentieth century by Phineas F. Bresee. He is a classic example of a prominent Methodist leader (presiding elder in California) who at last, reluctantly, left the M. E. Church to become founder and first general superintendent of a new denomination. The last decade of the nineteenth century and the first decade of the twentieth were the high point of come-outism. The attitudes of those who saw them go varied from "what a pity!" to "good riddance!"

A movement related to, but different from, holiness is Pentecostalism.[15] Many advocates of holiness became Pentecostals as a further stage of their religious quest. In the case of Pentecostalism, however, the connection with Methodism is much less clear. Although some leaders and many members of various Pentecostal sects had been Methodists, the same could be said of others who had been Baptists, Presbyterians, and Episcopalians. The Pentecostal movement, in other words, was not particularly Methodist in origin.

Some direct relations may be identified. Charles Fox Parham, one of the original leaders, had been a Methodist minister, but withdrew to join the holiness movement. His Pentecostal work in Topeka, Kansas became one of the fountainheads of the movement. Willis C. Hoover had been a Methodist minister in Chile before he founded the Methodist Pentecostal Church. A. B. Crumpler, founder of the Holiness Church, which later joined with the Fire-Baptized Holiness Church to form the Pentecostal Holiness Church, had also been a Methodist minister. On the other hand, early developments like the Azusa Street Mission in Los Angeles and the Assemblies of God, the largest of Pentecostal churches, were not Methodist in origin. Many of

[15] Most recent and best study is John Thomas Nichol, *Pentecostalism* (1966).

the groups, like the Assemblies of God, had a Congregational or Presbyterian polity; but the Pentecostal Assemblies of God had a Methodist church order.

As the twentieth century dawned, American Protestantism was in the midst of an orgy of sectarian diversification. Methodists made a major contribution to the development of holiness churches, but had no special share in the rise of Pentecostalism. One main result was to drain from Methodism the more fervent advocates of the Wesleyan doctrine of perfect love. Interest in this part of the tradition would become the prerogative of historical theologians and a rather small coeterie of revivalistic or fundamentalistic laymen. Only with the mid-twentieth century would a more general interest in this part of the Wesleyan heritage revive.

Chapter 27
Education and the Printed Word

Among the many contributions of John Wesley to his American followers was a concern for nourishment of the whole person, in mind as well as in body and spirit. He bequeathed an interest in education which was not to be understood narrowly as religious education. This early development has many remarkable similarities to those perspectives of the later twentieth century which would be called secular gospel and global outlook.

From the beginning Methodism was interested in the Sunday school movement. This, too, came from England and was quickly imported into America. As early as 1790, efforts were made to provide Sunday schools for "poor children, white and black," as Asbury put it. Not until early in the next century, however, did the movement grow strongly. By that time it had taken on more of the aspects of religious education and had the support of literature provided by The Methodist Publishing House.

Among the United Brethren and Evangelicals, Sunday schools were started in the 1820s and 1830s. Both groups encountered opposition to the idea of Sunday schools; nevertheless, they grew. In 1835 the Evangelical General Conference encouraged ministers to organize "German Sunday Schools . . . wherever possible," a phraseology obviously open to restriction, delay, and even obstruction. Not until 1849 did the United Brethren General Conference give similar advice, although without the peculiar language stipulation. Firm organization on a denominational basis came in 1865 with the United Brethren Sabbath School Association.

Growth in the Methodist denominations was strong, especially after the Civil War. In 1868, John H. Vincent was elected secretary of the Methodist Sunday School Union and from that position greatly stimulated the work through a series of Sunday school institutes. All the churches provided a full plan of Sunday school literature.

Higher Education

The early abortive attempts to build colleges reveal an almost pathetic eagerness to enter the field of higher education. The story of the failure of Cokesbury College and Asbury College also suggests an element of inflated pride. So at least, thought Wesley; and so, ruefully concluded Asbury. The lesson was plain: God did not call the Methodists to create institutions of higher education.

The general conference, however, was not to be dissuaded by some pretended effects of divine displeasure. In 1820, this body recommended to the annual conferences the establishment of colleges, under Methodist auspices and conference control, designed to provide a broad liberal arts education in the context of Christian faith.

There followed a lively score of years in which many Methodist colleges came into being. Many colleges were founded in the decades before the Civil War: Ohio Wesleyan, Northwestern, Iowa Wesleyan, Baker (across the prairies and plains); Trinity (later Duke), Wofford, Central (across the South).[1] As time went by, these schools lost their frontier characteristics and became well-defined centers for higher education. After the Civil War, newly founded colleges often had special goals and interests. Drew, which began as a theological seminary in 1867, later expanded to university status. Boston University and Syracuse University, both of Methodist origin, opened soon after.

Although several collegiate institutions had been established in the South earlier, the first full university was Vanderbilt, which opened in 1875 in Nashville. This school began as a creature of annual conferences and its control passed presently to the general conference of the southern church. In 1905, however, a complicated legal struggle was instituted by the chancellor and a majority of the trustees to free the university from ecclesiastical control. After dragging almost ten years all the way to the U.S. Supreme Court, the case was finally settled in favor of the university, which, through substantial gifts, became one of the outstanding universities in the South. Largely as a result of this loss two new universities were established under direct church sponsorship and control: Southern Methodist and Emory.

The secularization of Vanderbilt illustrates a development common in the later nineteenth century: the abandonment of church affiliation by colleges which owed their origin to church support and leadership. A conflict of fundamental forces in American culture came to focus on religious control of higher education. Bishop J. C. Kilgo put it this way: "The issue is joined in the South. . . . We have got to answer for all time this supreme question, Shall Americans Chris-

---

[1] For general coverage see the educational sections of *HAM,* II. A convenient survey is John O. Gross, *Methodist Beginnings in Higher Education* (1959). Also Sweet, *Methodism in American History,* Chap. 11. There are a number of good histories of individual institutions.

tianize their Schools or shall the Schools paganize Americans? This is no mere dream; it is the awfullest reality we have ever confronted in this country." [2] An even more vehement protest about the secularization of Methodist colleges came from Heman Bangs in a letter addressed to Laban Clark, president of the Board of Trustees of Wesleyan University, way back in 1853. Charging that some members of the board wanted "to drive a religious predominance from the University," he resigned his membership on the board, saying, "If we cannot have a religious education I desire no education at all. An infidel education I consider as worse than no education." [3]

For all the immense efforts and funds that went into Methodist higher education, pockets of resistance maintained themselves throughout the century. As late as 1890, the southern general conference was warned by the Board of Education itself that, though the church could take just pride in its educational institutions, there remained a danger that too much reliance on human intellect might prove disastrous. One of the old school, southern Bishop George F. Pierce, put it this way: "Give me the evangelist and the revivalist rather than the erudite brother who goes into the pulpit to interpret modern science instead of preaching repentance and faith, or going so deep into geology as to show that Adam was not the first man and the Deluge a little local affair." [4] This passage raises another touchy point—the impact of modern science on traditional biblical and theological understanding. Some conservatives regarded the colleges as hotbeds of evolutionary teaching.

Nevertheless, Methodism gave generous and enthusiastic support to the educational institutions it had spawned so prolifically. In 1880, the M. E. Church alone had forty-four colleges and universities, as well as eleven theological seminaries and institutes and one hundred thirty secondary schools of various sorts. It had a board of education responsible for all the many aspects of the work.

The only leader among early United Brethren and Evangelicals who approximated the standard of learning and culture represented by John Wesley was Philip William Otterbein. The sequence of their development was much the same as all denominations: first Sunday schools, next a general conference course of study, then the founding of church-related colleges, and finally theological seminaries.

[2] Alfred M. Pierce, *Giant Against the Sky, The Life of Bishop Warren Akin Candler* (1948), 143.

[3] Printed in Frederick A. Norwood, "More Letters to Laban Clark," *MH*, 11 (Oct., 1972): 41.

[4] Quoted in Tigert, *Bishop Holland Nimmons McTyeire*, 178.

The United Brethren made the plunge at the General Conference of 1845, which opened the way for the establishment of Otterbein College, Westerville, Ohio, two years later. That year the general conference of the Evangelical Association heard John Dreisbach plead for "a seminary for general sciences." After various obstructions and delays, short-lived Albright Seminary opened in 1853. The first permanent school was Union Seminary, 1856, which became Albright College. Both of these were located in Pennsylvania. The history of another Evangelical college, North Central in Naperville, Illinois, goes back to Plainfield College, started in 1861. Shenandoah College, Winchester, Virginia, began as a United Brethren school in 1875.

A movement related to educational enterprises was the Epworth League, formed by young people and organized in 1889. Experiments had begun about two decades earlier with the appearance of several local young people's societies. Also in 1881, an interdenominational Christian Endeavor Society was founded in Portland, Maine. In Central Church (later Epworth-Euclid) of Cleveland, Ohio, these groups came together and took the name Epworth League. Under the able leadership of Jesse L. Hurlbut, it spread rapidly and was made official by the next general conference. At the same time, young people's societies developed in the M. E. Church, South, and similar developments occurred among the United Brethren and evangelicals. A Young People's Christian Union of the United Brethren Church, later the Young People's Christian Endeavor Union, was set up in 1890; and the Evangelical Young People's Alliance, later the Keystone League of Christian Endeavor, followed in a year. Both of the later organizations were closely related to the interdenominational Christian Endeavor program.

Ministerial Education

The theme of anti-intellectualism in the United States is well illustrated by the progress of theological education among Methodists, Evangelicals, and United Brethren. Fear of an intellectually top-heavy clergy was a prime source of opposition to the establishment of any kind of church-related school. Although many outstanding leaders took a more enlightened view, many others, and for long the rank and file generally, looked with distaste on a formally trained minister. For one thing, he looked and sounded too much like the Episcopal rector and Presbyterian clergyman, whom Methodists had long since learned to disdain for their fancy pretensions.

305

Nevertheless, for self-defense if nothing else, some form of preparation for the ministry was needed. As a result, in all the churches a program for a *course of study* was begun. The original Methodist plan in 1816 was for each annual conference to make up a list of books to be studied by candidates for conference membership. On these they would stand examination. A uniform program with formal listings was prepared for the M. E. Church in 1848 and for the M. E. Church, South, in 1878. Evangelicals began a course of study in 1843 and the United Brethren in 1845. These examinations were taken quite seriously. In 1860, for example, the *Discipline* of the M. E. Church stipulated at the end of the first year: "The examination on the above to be strictly Biblical, requiring the candidate to give the statement of the docrine and the Scripture proofs. To prepare for this he should read the Bible by course, and make a memorandum of the texts upon each of these [doctrinal] topics listed as he proceeds."

In addition to this theologically oriented study of the Bible, the first-year student was expected to read the first part of Watson's *Institutes,* Wesley's *Plain Account of Christian Perfection,* Fletcher's *Appeal,* and Clark's *Mental Discipline,* plus general reading of Wesley's *Notes on the New Testament,* Stevens' *History of Methodism,* and Willson's *General History.* In 1893, Bishop John H. Vincent reported in the *Methodist Review* that "our largest school of theology" was supervising the work of 3,545 students in a four-year course designed to follow the studies for admission on trial.[5] Similar progress was reported in the M. E. Church, South.[6]

While the course of study was rising to a dominant position in theological education in all the groups of Wesleyan relationship, voices began to be heard in favor of more formal training in special theological schools. John P. Durbin's last editorial in the *Christian Advocate* of July 18, 1834 dealt with "An Educated Ministry Among Us." The prevailing opinion was that this could best be accomplished in the general colleges supported by the church. There *all* young Christians should have the opportunity for Bible study and related disciplines. "As a Christian community, all our institutions of learning should be sanctuaries of theological science." [7] Here again is the ideal of the priesthood of all believers. The debate ran high well into the 1850s, with arguments both for and against seminaries. *The Northwestern Christian Advocate* in 1856, spoke in favor of theological schools, but the general conference of that same year heard arguments op-

[5] *MQR,* 53 (1893), 190-205.
[6] Cf. *JGC,* 1898, 121.
[7] Episcopal Address, (pamphlet) General Conference, 1840, 14-15.

posed. In fact, the term "biblical institute" was designed to avoid the polemical excitement aroused by the more formal term. What is now known as Boston University School of Theology began in Concord, New Hampshire, in 1847 as a Methodist Biblical Institute. What is now Garrett-Evangelical Theological Seminary began in 1855 in Evanston, Illinois, as Garrett Biblical Institute.

One man tied the history of these two schools together—in fact, symbolized in his life work the entire theological enterprise of Methodism. That man was John Dempster, who came to Evanston in ✳ 1854, fresh from seven years service to the school in Concord. He served as Garrett's first president until the end of 1863, when he embarked on another enterprise to found a theological school in the Far West. He died before he could finish that work. He set forth his understanding of the ministry in a series of addresses in which he never wearied of pointing out the central importance of spirituality:

> What one function belongs to the ministerial office not demanding the deepest spirituality? The whole character calls for a high controlling piety—a living, energetic, all-conquering piety—one that imbues the heart, the life, the studies, the habits, the whole man. This principle must sway the minister with the power of a passion. He can have no substitute for this living, glowing spirit—for a heart throbbing and flaming with restoring love. Nothing else within the compass of thought can disclose to him the soul's worth, or gird him with power to snatch it from the gulf; nor can any thing else invest him with that harmony of character which sheds the light of consistency over all the various events of his history.

His definition of the chief elements of effective ministry, if recast in contemporary expression, proves rather durable: "a high state of mental discipline, large acquaintance with science and literature, a mastery of pulpit elocution, a comprehensive acquaintance with theology and Biblical literature, a burning love for ransomed man, an intenser interest for the Redeemer's glory, fraternal affection and harmonious action among his anointed servants." [8]

The Centenary of 1866 took as its prime aim financial support for theological education. The Ladies Centenary Association, spurred on by Frances Willard, raised $50,000 for a new Garrett building, Heck Hall. The centenary effort, generously helped by a special gift from millionaire Daniel Drew, made possible the founding of Drew Theological Seminary in 1867. By the early twentieth century the M. E. Church enjoyed the services, not only of the schools mentioned, but also of Gammon Theological Seminary in Atlanta, Iliff School of Theology in Denver, and four other schools no longer in existence. In

[8] John Dempster, *Lectures and Addresses* (1864), 36-37, 67.

the M. E. Church, South, were Candler School of Theology in Atlanta and Southern Methodist University School of Theology in Dallas. The Methodist Protestants had one seminary, Westminster Theological Seminary in Westminster, Maryland.

Something of the same story, though on a smaller scale, goes for the Evangelicals and United Brethren. John Dreisbach was a perennial defender of a well-trained ministry in a day when that position was very unpopular among Evangelicals. As early as 1845, he had published an article "Teachers and Preachers Should Not Be Ignorant." [9] He argued that all ministers are under obligation to study theology, and that was what colleges were for. Evangelicals should not be opposed to educated ministers, but only to *unregenerate* ministers. These views were also expressed among United Brethren. Daniel Berger and Milton Wright, editors of the *Religious Telescope* during the period after the Civil War, strongly favored seminary training. As a result, Union Biblical Seminary opened in Dayton, Ohio in 1871. This school, which later was called Bonebrake, became the United Theological Seminary in 1954. It joined with the Evangelical School of Theology in Reading, Pennsylvania, which had emerged in 1928 as a development of educational changes dating back to the old Union Seminary in New Berlin. In 1877, the Evangelicals opened a seminary in connection with North-Western College (North Central College) in Naperville, Illinois. It was called the Union Biblical Institute and later the Evangelical Theological Seminary.

By the end of the century relatively few Methodists, Evangelicals, or United Brethren regarded theological schools as "mere tinsel." Some of them found it easier to say biblical institute and to take great pride in the general conference course of study, to which (in Methodism) seminary education had become an exception under the "seminary rule." According to the mysterious workings of God's providence, seminaries had come to stay. They were not yet completely welcome, and it would be long before the churches would accept full responsibility for their support. Nevertheless, they were rapidly becoming indispensable in an age which had moved from complacency toward catastrophe.

The Printed Word in Methodism

Important changes in the publishing activities of the three main Methodist denominations, the Evangelicals, and the United Brethren in the 1850s make that decade significant in many ways. Thomas

---

[9] Albright, *History of the Evangelical Church* (1942), 215. From the *Evangelical Messenger*, 26 Dec. 1855, 204.

Carlton took the helm as book agent of the publishing house of the northern church. In the South the "Book Agency" became a full-fledged publishing house. Methodist Protestant publishing was divided with the church. The United Brethren established their publishing headquarters in Dayton. The Evangelical Association moved its book interests to Cleveland. Except for the Methodist Protestant division, which was a setback, these changes marked substantial advances. The troubles and disasters of the 1860s marked not so much a period in publishing history as an extraneous disruption which forced retrenchment or reorganization. The promise displayed by the events of the 1850s were largely deferred till the postwar recovery.[10]

After the separation of 1844, the southern church was caught in the long legal struggle over control of the publishing house. The original idea of amicable division of property fell through and landed in the civil courts. The case was not settled until 1854 and then only in the United States Supreme Court. For ten years, publishing activity had to be carried on under an *ad hoc* arrangement as a book agency. In 1854 it received its share of interest in the property and was able to establish a publishing house of its own. One of the most active figures was John B. McFerrin, long-time editor of the Nashville *Christian Advocate*. He was instrumental in securing the location of southern publishing interests in Nashville and in establishing the publishing house in 1854. He either defended the Nashville center from its detractors or saved it from bankruptcy at least four times before his death in 1887.

On the eve of the Civil War, the periodicals of Southern Methodism posted an impressive record. The Nashville *Christian Advocate* led with a circulation of 12,000 followed closely by the *Southern Christian Advocate* (Charleston) with 11,000. Other *Advocates* were published in Richmond, St. Louis, and New Orleans, with about 7,000 each. The five southern papers reached a little less than half the readership of the five principal northern papers. The other southern periodicals were not doing so well, although McFerrin was working to strengthen them. The scholarly *Quarterly Review* had less than 1,500 circulation, and the *Sunday School Visitor* and the *Home Circle* were struggling along at a loss. No wonder that southern editors found paid advertising less distasteful than did their more finicky northern counterparts.

When war came, the southern publishing house identified itself

---

[10] The most recent as well as comprehensive books are James Penn Pilkington, *The Methodist Publishing House* (1968), I, and John H. Ness, Jr., *One Hundred Fifty Years, A History of Publishing in the Evangelical United Brethren Church* (1966). For later Methodist material see *HAM*, III, Chap. 28.

completely with Confederate interests, even proposing to publish Confederate school books. Editors were plagued with paper shortages and difficulties of transportation and communication. The end in Nashville came soon enough. In 1862 the city was captured by Union forces as a result of the fall of Fort Henry and Fort Donelson on the Tennessee and Cumberland rivers. Almost all the staff of the southern publishing house were forced to leave, and the plant was taken over by federal military authorities. For the rest of the war, until Sherman's march through the South, the M. E. Church, South, was served fitfully by the *Southern Christian Advocate* in Charleston and the *Richmond Christian Advocate,* both of which managed to stay alive —barely—until 1865.

At war's end the publishing house, like all southern Methodism, was in shambles. Indomitable John McFerrin stepped in to rescue the perishing. With amazing vigor he began putting affairs together, so successfully that by January, 1866 he was able to print an issue of the Nashville *Christian Advocate.* Owing to McFerrin's persistence, President Johnson, himself, ordered the return of the properties to the church. With recovery of the southern church came rebuilding of the publishing house. A. H. Redford became book agent and T. O. Summers became editor of the *Christian Advocate.*

There followed years of struggle on lean resources. Once again, in 1878, McFerrin was called back to rescue the business from a slump brought on by a combination of adverse circumstances. Once again this doughty editorial warrior saved the book concern from bankruptcy. When he died, the publishing house of the southern church was in firm control of its destiny. Periodicals recovered one by one. Near the end of the century the congress of the United States at last got around to settling the war damage claims with the M. E. Church, South, in the amount of $288,000. This provided funds for the expansion of the publishing house. Following World War I, the work expanded and moved into spacious new quarters in Nashville.

After the division of the church, publishing interests in the northern church continued to grow. By the early 1850s, however, affairs had reached a low ebb. At this time appeared Thomas Carlton, who served as book agent for twenty years until 1872. He was a minister with a flair for business administration. He did not step in, as McFerrin in the South did repeatedly, to save a failing business. On the contrary, the publishing house was in good financial and editorial condition, even though it had a bad press in the church. In 1852, the total sales for the quadrennium were reported at over $853,000 with promise of passing the one million mark. As Carlton became book agent, the general conference authorized two new official *Advocates:* the *North-Western* in Chicago and the *California.*

The periodicals were thriving. Just before the Civil War the *Western Christian Advocate* briefly outran the *Christian Advocate and Journal* in New York with a circulation of 31,000 to the latter's 29,000. The new *North-Western Christian Advocate* had 13,000, while the Pittsburgh and St. Louis *Advocates* had each about 8,000. All of these, however, bowed to the immensely successful *Sunday School Advocate* with a circulation of 208,000 in 1860. The *Ladies' Repository* had a very respectable clientele of 33,400. Very successful in a relative way was *Der Christliche Apologete,* which had 9,166 subscribers and paid its own way. The intellectual journal, *Methodist Quarterly Review* (so called at this time), managed to reach 4,250 subscribers, which was rather good in comparison with other learned journals. This influential magazine was dominated throughout the third quarter of the century by Daniel D. Whedon, editor from 1857 to 1884. During this entire time it was a fat quarterly which carried long articles on theological trends and took some account of cultural changes in American life. Through its pages, Methodists were kept well aware of the powerful theological influences which emanated from Europe. Although generally regarded with suspicion, the articles were courageously struggled with, both sides of the issue being carried.[11]

Northern editors could enjoy the pleasure of debate over the admission of advertising copy. Under the canny guidance of Thomas Carlton and James S. Porter advertising eventually was accepted, and Methodists were urged to buy everything from church bells and cemetery markers to hoop skirts and patent medicines.

A new era for the Methodist Episcopal Tract Society began with its restitution in 1852. The old society, formed in 1817, had lost out in 1836 as interest turned to the American Bible Society and the Sunday School Union. But Methodists refurbished their own organization and gave it enough financial muscle to compete with the American Tract Society, one of the many voluntary interdenominational agencies which characterized American Protestantism in the nineteenth century. Huge numbers of cheap paper tracts were distributed everywhere,[12] along with these tracts the offerings for children expanded, with such titles as *Clara, The Motherless Young Housekeeper; or, the Life of Faith; Little Mabel, and Her Sunlit Home; Daisy Downs; or, What the Sabbath-School Can Do; What Catherine Did, and What Came of It.*

---

[11] See analysis of theological and cultural content in Norwood, "Theological and Cultural Concerns of the Methodist Quarterly Review," *Forever Beginning,* 138-50.

[12] Examples of titles are given in Pilkington, *The Methodist Publishing House,* I, 384.

Much of this treacle was replaced after 1870 with the more substantial *Berean* series of Sunday school papers. But children's literature of all kinds, with a few noble exceptions, would stay at a low level of literary pablum for several decades.

With the start of a new *Advocate* in Chicago, the burgeoning emporium of the West became a new center for Methodist publishing activities. It became a major depository in 1856 and grew strongly in the later nineteenth century. It almost, but not quite, became a publishing center equal with New York and Cincinnati.

The decade dominated by the Civil War allowed publishing activities without break and some notable growth. During the war, William P. Strickland, assistant editor of the New York *Christian Advocate and Journal,* filed a tremendously stimulating and valuable series of reports from the field along the coastal regions of South Carolina, where he was serving as military chaplain with occupying Union forces. The tensions of the issue of slavery are evident in the appearance in 1860 in New York of a dissident paper, *The Methodist,* edited by conservatives like Abel Stevens, who opposed the strong abolitionist sentiments of Edward Thomson, new editor of the *Christian Advocate and Journal.*

After the war the publishing house grew apace, but came on evil days when John Lanahan, junior book agent, alleged fraud. For several years this scandal reverberated through northern Methodism and subsided only with the removal of Lanahan (without real refutation of his charges). In the 1870s the *Ladies' Repository,* which for a while was very popular as the church's answer to *Godey's Ladies Book,* was changed in format to the *National Repository.* This was a mistake, for the publication declined and went out of existence in 1880.

Early in the twentieth century (1904), the general conference brought together the operations in New York and Cincinnati under the form of the Methodist Book Concern, which had responsibility for the total publishing enterprise. Under these auspices the production of new kinds of church school literature, especially the graded lesson series, became a major part of the work. Dividends from the earnings, which were regularly paid to the annual conferences for the benefit of retirement programs, rose to very respectable proportions. In the quadrennium 1908–12, they amounted to $370,000.

The rest of the story, including the gradual demise of ethnic publications for Germans and Scandinavians as well as the tremendous growth of The Methodist Publishing House after unification in 1939, belongs to a later period.

EDUCATION AND THE PRINTED WORD

Among United Brethren and Evangelical Association

In the earlier period we saw the appearance of the *Religious Telescope* (1834), *Der Christliche Botschafter* (1836), *Der Deutsche Telescop* (1846), and the *Evangelical Messenger* (1848). Shortly after the start of these magazines, the United Brethren moved their publishing headquarters from Circleville, Ohio to Dayton (1853); and the Evangelical Association moved from New Berlin, Pennsylvania to Cleveland (1854). Thus, the decade of the 1850s marks a turning point for them as well as for Methodists.

After the war Milton Wright, father of airmen Orville and Wilbur Wright, was elected editor of the *Religious Telescope,* the influential magazine of the United Brethren, in a closely contested battle bet-✳ ween conservatives and liberals. Wright, the champion of the former, identified himself with those strictly opposed to secret societies. This specific issue became a symbol in the controversies which led after some years to schism in the denomination. Now conservative Wright was in the saddle, and the so-called radicals controlled the press. As a result the liberal forces undertook publication of an independent journal of their own, the *United Brethren Tribune,* which began in 1873 and continued through the decade.

When the editorship of the *Telescope* became more moderate, the conservatives (radicals) had their turn at independent journalism with the *United Brethren in Christ,* which appeared from 1879 to 1885. All these publishing ventures foreshadowed the conflict which came to a head in 1889. Other independent papers appeared from time to time.

The walkout of Bishop Wright and his followers from the General Conference of 1889 (see next chapter) led to a struggle for control of the publishing house. In general, the liberals, who considered themselves the legal continuation of the denomination as representing the majority and the overwhelming vote of the general conference, won in the courts. The mainline church grew and expanded its publishing efforts. In the early 1890s, the *Religious Telescope* had 15,000 subscribers, while cash sales of the publishing house ran over $100,000 annually. In 1890 a *Quarterly Review* was launched on a stormy and uncertain course.

The replacement in 1897 of William Shuey, who had served for thirty-three years as publishing agent, marked the changing of the guard looking toward the new day of the twentieth century. Shuey had filled a position which carried even more influence than that of bishops. He had personified the spirit of the United Brethren for a generation. His departure marked a profound change in direction, as his successor, William R. Funk, brought so many new and stimulating ideas that he almost bankrupted the institution. A disaster hit the Dayton plant in 1913 when a huge flood spread destruction all over town and left the plant in eleven feet of water. It caught the publishing house in an unfortunate bind of capital investment for a new building. Out of it, however, came a new plant which was dedicated in 1915.

In the case of the Evangelical Association, the big change came in 1854 with the shift of headquarters to Cleveland. One of the first new endeavors was publication of a children's paper in German, the *Christliche Kinderfreund*, which began in 1856. The business weathered the depression of 1857 handily and in that year published William Orwig's history of the association (German 1857, English 1858). Just before the Civil War, the magazines had a circulation as follows: *Christliche Botschafter*, 7,416; *Evangelical Messenger*, 3,116. The new *Christliche Kinderfreund* for children had 6,528. In 1864 the *Sunday School Messenger* began publication with a circulation of 9,000; Reuben Yeakel, editor.

The years after the Civil War saw the rise of the controversies which led eventually to schism. The editor of the *Evangelical Messenger*, H. B. Hartzler, engaged in public conflict with the editor of the *Christliche Botschafter*, William Horn, over the conduct of Bishop J. J. Esher. As a result, Hartzler was brought to trial at the General Conference of 1887 and deposed from his editorial office.

Almost immediately there appeared an independent journal, *The Evangelical*, edited by the same H. B. Hartzler. By 1891 two general conferences met, each claiming to be the true voice of the Evangelical Association, and out of that situation came the schism of 1894. The effects of these disputes, which were violent and personal, wrought deep injury on the publishing interests. The United Evangelical Church began its own publishing house in Harrisburg, Pennsylvania in 1888. The Cleveland business survived, but with heavy losses. By 1906, however, the total sales for the first time passed the one million dollar mark. During the First World War, the problem of continued use of the German language afflicted the denomination, since the Evangelicals, more than the United Brethren, had clung to the German cultural heritage longer. Although the *Christliche Botschafter* continued in publication until 1946, several German-language items were dropped.

The United Evangelicals' Evangelical Publishing Company grew, after difficult early years, in Harrisburg. A large new building was dedicated in 1918. When the two groups were reunited in 1922, the

Harrisburg organization was given responsibility for English-language publications (which were growing), while the Cleveland plant took over the German publications (which were declining). Both of the predecessors of the Evangelical United Brethren Church entered the twentieth century sadly divided. World War I with its nationalistic and cultural tensions loomed darkly. Before the dread war exploded, these folk had ample reason to view the new century, not with the optimistic glow so characteristic of the times, but with considerable forebodings about the future. It is probably just as well they didn't know how right they were.

Through all the troubles, a succession of vigorous editors provided leadership. Men like the United Brethren I. L. Kephart and J. M. Philippi of the *Religious Telescope*, the Evangelical S. P. Spreng of the *Evangelical Messenger*, and H. B. Hartzler of the *Evangelical* exerted more influence than most bishops.

Chapter 28
New Theology

On the surface much of the nineteenth century in America, culturally and intellectually speaking, was orderly and progressive. Underneath, a new world was seething, struggling to be born. If one begins where one must begin—with the eighteenth-century tension between Edwardian Calvinism and rationalistic Enlightenment—the steps through Timothy Dwight to Samuel Hopkins and Nathaniel Taylor follow. The culmination for New England Puritanism arrived in the 1820s with Taylor's address *Concio ad Clerum* at Yale Divinity School. Hopkins' "disinterested benevolence," which had dealt a blow to old-line Calvinism from within, was developed by Taylor to change the focus of theology from God to people. If it might be an exaggeration to say that the chief end of man was no longer "to glorify God and enjoy him forever" but rather *to be man,* the trend was unmistakable. The result could be a barren rationalism or agnosticism, or it could be a warm emotionalism expressed through the revivalism of a Charles G. Finney. We have seen how Wilbur Fisk was a Methodist spokesman in the Calvinistic controversy.

Most typical was that cultural manifestation known as transcendentalism, which describes not so much a position as a process of change. Western man was caught between the firm old standards of belief and value and the heady new doctrines and values which had yet to be formulated. Some writers and thinkers, like Hawthorne and Melville, would continue to struggle with the Puritan understanding of the ways of God with people. Others, like Walt Whitman and Theodore Parker, would strike out along new paths marked by freedom and emotional release. Emerson at least had an idea of what was going on: a world was passing and a new one coming in. What worried him was that, though the old world was passing obviously enough, the new world was not so visible in its birth. "Our torment is Unbelief, the uncertainty as to what we ought to do; the distrust of the value of what we do." Oliver Wendell Holmes lived through that transition, although he thought he had a vision of the new world coming —science. "The truth is that the whole system of beliefs which came in with the story of the 'fall of man' . . . is gently fading out of enlightened intelligence."

Within the Protestant churches the impact of these intellectual forces created by philosophy and science was felt in many ways. In some, hardening of the shell provided isolation and seeming safety. In others, the new vision appeared to be the culmination of faith. For most Christian thinkers there was no way but a long painful adjustment which offered ways of understanding divine creativity, Providence, and salvation in a world from which many of the old landmarks had disappeared. Finney and the revivalists offered one popular way. Liberals like Newman Smyth, William Newton Clarke, George A. Gordon, Borden Parker Bowne, and William Adams Brown offered another. Theological liberalism—a catchall for many different views—was the result.

Theological Development

Intellectual leaders in the Methodist churches were not unaware of what was going on. Although there were denominational variants, Protestant theology generally cut right across church lines. Methodist thinking did not take place in a vacuum.[1] The publication in 1864 of Daniel Whedon's *Freedom of the Will* was something of an event. The author was the influential editor of the *Methodist Quarterly Review.* He began where everyone must begin, with Jonathan Edwards. Edwards, he wrote, accomplished superbly what he set out to do, and his ultimate failure was not his fault. Grimly Whedon set forth the issue, took full account of the "necessitarian arguments," and then proceeded to present the case for freedom of the will in a Christian context. In the process he referred to Wesley, but more to Fletcher.

> The simple question is, Is he so limited in power in *the given case* to the one solely possible choice or volition as not to be free to volitionate otherwise instead, or does he possess a power of disjunctive volition, so that he is *free* to choose either one of several ways? Choosing thus our own ISSUE, as is our right, we affirm under requirement of the moral sense, as against necessity which denies, that there does exist in the agent a freedom of just this kind.

[1] One of the best general treatments, which follows a sort of case-study method, is Robert E. Chiles, *Theological Transition In American Methodism: 1790–1935* (1965). He takes Watson, Miley, and Knudsen as his "cases." Two excellent surveys, though unpublished, are Leland Scott, "Methodist Theology in America in the Nineteenth Century" (Dissertation, Yale, 1954), and William J. McCutcheon, "Theology of the Methodist Episcopal Church During the Interwar Period, 1919–1939" (Dissertation, Yale, 1960). For special aspects see John Peters, *Christian Perfection and American Methodism* (1956), and S. Paul Schilling, *Methodism and Society In Theological Perspective* (1960). Several theological articles are in *Forever Beginning.*

Two hundred pages later he has refuted the arguments of necessity and demonstrated that human freedom of will is not inconsistent with the foreknowledge of God, which he understands, not as a rigid knowledge of events, but rather as a knowledge of "*a* PECULIAR QUALITY *existent* IN THE FREE AGENT" which indicates that, though he might have made another choice, he will in fact make this choice. At last he is ready to set forth his own interpretation, which he bases on the moral ground that a man cannot be blamed for what he cannot help.

> We inaugurate, then, this, what we will call the AXIOM OF FREEDOM AND RESPONSIBILITY, and hold it as valid as any axiom of geometry. POWER MUST UNDERLIE OBLIGATION. *There can be no full moral obligation to an act, volitional or non-volitional, for which there is not in the required agent full and adequate power.* Or otherwise, *there can be no guilt or responsibility for act or volition, for avoidance of which there is not complete and adequate power;* that is, for which there is not *a power adequate to counter act or volition.* If guilt, or responsibility, or obligation be a reality, then the power of counter choice is a reality. *Responsibility, therefore, demonstrates free-will.*[2]

This work helped to crack open the doors for the theological winds of following decades.

When Miner Raymond, professor of theology at Garrett Biblical Institute, published his *magnum opus* in 1877–79 in three substantial volumes, he began by paying tribute to Richard Watson as a faithful interpreter of Wesleyan theology whom he did not wish to deny. "But fifty years is a long time" for any book to endure. The time had come, he averred, to update theology with due attention to the influences at work in the later years of the century. He tried diligently to avoid a break with the past. In much that he wrote he was traditional and cautious. He retained a high regard for miracles and prophecy as evidences of Christian truth, and held to a sort of inerrancy of the Scriptures; but he was more concerned with human participation. At the very outset he indicated his new lines of investigation:

> The topics discussed are viewed from modern stand-points. This has necessitated a more extended discussion than is usual of the Origin, Antiquity, and Unity of the race, the distinction between natural and revealed religion, and the possibility of the former; the doctrine of Intuition as applied in matters of religion; the Positive Philosophy, the doctrine of Evolution, and other phases of modern materialism; the distinction between the Augustinian and Arminian theories of Federal Headship, and specially the wide difference between the Anselmic and Arminian Soteriologies.[3]

[2] Whedon, *Freedom of the Will* (1864), 39, 271, 398.
[3] Raymond, *Systematic Theology,* I, 3. On Wesleyan background, 11-12.

This work by Raymond opened the way for a more thoroughgoing revision by John Miley, who taught at Drew from 1873 to 1895. His *Atonement in Christ* (1879) took off from the same theme as Whedon, but even more forthrightly emphasized the elements of reason and moral responsibility in man. His two-volume *Systematic Theology* (1892–94) was a major point of theological transition.[4] At Boston William F. Warren interpreted German theology and introduced comparative religion.

In contrast, Thomas O. Summers, writing from the southern bastion of Nashville, stood for more traditional Methodist doctrine consciously rooted in Wesleyan authority.[5] The title of his basic work is indicative: *Systematic Theology, A Complete Body of Wesleyan Arminian Divinity* (1888). As one-man editor and author, Cannon observes, "he seems to have accepted for publication practically everything that he wrote." As editor of the *Sunday School Visitor* and the southern *Methodist Quarterly Review*, as senior book editor of the publishing house, and, after 1874, as dean of the faculty and professor of systematic theology at Vanderbilt, he exerted tremendous influence in the intellectual world of southern Methodism. Wilbur F. Tillett, also of Vanderbilt, represents a later, more liberal viewpoint.

But another day was dawning, to which these early thinkers were but gleams on the horizon. Borden Parker Bowne at Boston University caught the attention of the philosophical world for a generation with his "personalism," as his emphasis on the central importance of personality came to be called. He attempted to retain a connection between science and religion without rejecting either and to provide a ground for "warranted belief." The theological development of these ideas was carried out by Albert Knudsen, whose work at Boston began in 1906 and continued till his death in 1953. Along with Harris Franklin Rall and Edwin Lewis, he represents a new generation whose work belongs more properly to the twentieth century.

One of the more significant figures in biblical theology was Milton S. Terry, longtime professor at Garrett. His *Biblical Dogmatics* (1907) was a major effort to adjust Methodist reliance on the authority of Holy Scripture to modern trends in scientific and historical study of the Bible. He courageously affirmed that Christians must adjust their views to "newly discovered facts." Truth can never be hurt by new light. In accordance with the theological approach of the day, he began his study with man, the visible entity, and went on to God, the

---

[4] See careful discussion in Chiles, *Theological Transition*, where he serves as one of three main transitional points of reference.

[5] See William R. Cannon's article in *Forever Beginning*.

invisible ground. He spoke in favor of scientific study, historical method, comparative religion, and against theories of inerrancy, unjustified reliance on miracles, and blind authority. He proved himself well acquainted with European theologians. As a source book for theology, he viewed the Bible as a product of growth (evolution) which allowed for various stages of revelation and understanding. He carried through what Whedon had started on the freedom of the will. Any literal view of Adamic sin is untenable. "The real cause of the first sin as of every other subsequent act of sin, is to be sought in the sinner himself." [6]

The most typical Methodist theological affirmation of the time, however, was probably not made by any of these systematic theologians in theological seminaries, but by an articulate practicing minister in New England, Daniel Dorchester, who gave a contemporary twist to "doing theology." "The most triumphant way of proving any doctrine involved in human duty is to *use* it. Persuade men to act it out by *doing* their duty. Make it thus prove itself as fact, and time will take care of it as dogma. This Methodism has done for the doctrine of human freedom through the whole of her romantic history." [7]

Many Methodists, including the bishops, were very much concerned about some of these trends. Episcopal addresses at general conferences in the 1880s repeatedly worried about "a spirit of latitudinarian speculation" which had led some ministers to preach "sentiments contrary to the faith of the Church." They deplored, more broadly, "a manifest loosening of the traditional bonds of popular respect for the Sabbath, the Bible, and the Church." When they tied these concerns with "the ominous mutterings of discontent from multitudes of the poor," great power in the hands of the rich, huge immigration, and westward expansion; they had good cause, they believed, to view the future with foreboding. Indeed, they perceived real shadows of coming events, already cast in the eighties and nineties, for those to see who had eyes.

The pressures and tensions engendered in such times of rapid change brought two side effects. First, attempts were made to redefine and revise the traditional doctrinal standards of Methodism. This, of course, raised the question of what those standards were. Obvious but not particularly Methodistic, were the twenty-five articles of religion. Several attempts, none successful, were made in the late nineteenth and early twentieth century to bring about changes in the

[6] Terry, *Biblical Dogmatics*, 97. See also 39-40, 58, 84, 97, 122-23, 340.

[7] Quoted in Daniel Dorchester, *The Why of Methodism* (1887), 74.

interests of clarification or updating. The main effect was further confusion as to what the standards were, and how they were to be received.[8] Apparently, the less certainty about the definition and application of doctrinal standards, the more insistence on their inalterable nature. This led naturally to the other effect, heresy trials, from which Methodism has usually been remarkably free. At the turn of the century two notorious heresy trials, both of them involving New England Methodists, stirred the church with unwonted excitement. Hinckley G. Mitchell, professor of Old Testament at Boston University School of Theology, and Borden Parker Bowne, professor of philosophy in that university, were charged with heresy on complaints which rose chiefly from students. Both cases ended without conviction, but Mitchell decided to leave his position. In the overall situation, however, Methodism survived the conflicts of the time without either change of doctrinal standards—whatever those were—or heresy hunts.

Science and Religion

In the first part of the nineteenth century, the metamorphosed science of geology presented a challenge to traditional Christianity. Lyell's *Principles of Geology* stimulated angry responses, followed by serious attempts to reconcile Genesis with geology. Books like *Footprints of the Creator,* which sought to show God's creative hand in the geological development of the earth, were widely acclaimed. Methodists shared in this effort at mutual understanding. In fact many geologists were vigorous in affirming that the record of the rocks could be understood as explaining how God operates in the work of creation.[9] On the other hand, opposing voices were also heard. They insisted that Genesis be taken literally and that God not be allowed a longer time for creation. In 1849 the southern *Methodist Quarterly Review* ran a series which denied Lyell's principles. A few years later, however, a review of *Footprints of the Creator* gave a favorable report.

When Charles Darwin dropped his bombshell, *The Origin of Species* (1859), the United States was preoccupied. Reaction was in general delayed until after the war. But then it came fast. Owing to lack of information and general lack of education, much misunderstanding

[8] *E.g.,* in 1872 Brunson proposed new articles designed to make clear the distinctive teachings of Methodism; in 1906 Tillett tried to secure changes in the M.E. Church, South on the ground that "we live in an age of transition." No one, however, wanted to handle so touchy a subject in view of the restrictive rule against change.

[9] See especially the long series which began in the *NWCA,* 4 Jan. 1860, and continued over several issues. The issue was also discussed frequently by the New York Preachers' Meeting, and in the *MQR* and *MQRS. MQRS,* 3: 270-1; 5: 489-516.

led to much prejudice. In Methodism, over the long run, the voices of men like William North Rice, professor at Wesleyan University, were heard to the effect that, although Darwinism might be suspect on scientific grounds, yet it did offer a reasonable explanation of available data on the processes of life. At the same time it did not deny the creative activity of God nor the Christian view of humanity. In the great debate over evolution, Methodist higher education played a major role in throwing more light than heat. E. O. Haven, president of Northwestern University, took the position that the Bible was concerned with religion, not matter. "So far, then, as the Darwinian hypothesis pertains to the origin of vegetables and animals or even man's physical structure, it is a matter of supreme indifference to Christianity." [10] Incidentally, no one apparently thought to call Wesley to the defense of evolution as one way of understanding the process of divine creation.[11]

Inevitably, a few persons became victims of prejudice. The most famous case was that of Alexander Winchell, professor of geology at Vanderbilt in 1875. He was a renowned scholar, having served many years at Syracuse University. He took the position that evolution was the best proof of theism because it gave clear evidence of design, but he was critical of the apparently chance elements in Darwin's ideas about natural selection. He got into trouble as a result of a series in the *Northern Christian Advocate* on "Adamites and Pre-Adamites," which set forth the theory that Adam was not the first man, but the first Caucasian. By this means he was able to preserve traditional chronology with reference to Adam, while allowing for far more remote origins of the human species. He stirred up vigorous opposition, especially from T. O. Summers, whose influence was tremendous. When Bishop McTyeire, the president, failed to reconcile the opposing forces, he reluctantly asked for Winchell's resignation. When the latter refused, his position was abolished (1878). Methodist papers were divided into opposite sides on the episode.[12]

In general, Methodism escaped the more violent expressions of the Darwinian debate. Typical sectional attitudes were reflected in the widespread denomination. But for the most part the controversy, though bitter at times, was kept at a relatively high level in the religious press. The extremes of scientism and fundamentalism were avoided.

[10] *NWCA,* 20 (27 Mar 1872): 102.

[11] See Robert E. Bystrom, "The Earliest Methodist Response to Evolution" (M.A. thesis, Northwestern, 1966).

[12] The Nashville *Advocate* and the *Methodist* were against Winchell; the *NWCA* and *NYCA* supported him.

Sanctification

A special strand of Methodist theology centered on the Wesleyan doctrine of perfect love, widely referred to in the United States as "holiness." This issue has already been discussed in an earlier chapter in so far as it affected the sectarian movements of the late nineteenth century.

Any pretension on the part of Methodists that Christian perfection is exclusively Wesleyan would be absurd. Wesley, in emphasizing this teaching, conceived himself to be standing in an ancient Christian tradition. If anything is really distinctive in his emphasis, it is the conviction that perfect love is a viable way of life, available to ordinary mortals in the daily round. Even though he brought together "select, societies," he wanted everyone to be pressing toward the goal. Although he was second to none in his recognition of the depth of human sinfulness, he firmly believed that with God all things are possible. The doctrine of perfect love is, in the end, simply a doctrine of grace. It is the love of God, overflowing, which makes perfect.

In America, after a period of relative neglect owing to the stresses of migration and the difficulties of frontier life, this Wesleyan emphasis was revived and preached. When it revived, however, it was subject to some modifications. Revivalism in the spirit of Charles G. Finney tended to bring out the elements which underlined divine intervention as an instantaneous act, breaking through human resistance to cleanse the soul, as it were, in a trice. The "second blessing" was set apart from the first more and more. The idea of process, the going on to perfection, was more and more understood as a state which could be achieved. In the heady American atmosphere of freedom, it was relatively easy to mistake man's achievement for God's grace.

The result was a polarization in Methodist thinking which gave undue influence to the opposite extremes. On the one hand, theological liberals who had lost the conviction of original sin also lost interest in the possibilities of sanctification through God's grace. On the other hand, proponents of holiness tended to view it in increasingly rigid and narrow categories which left no place for those whose way to perfection did not fit the definition of a separate and instantaneous second blessing. We have seen the results in the activities of the come-outers and the push-outers of the 1880s and 1890s. Later history in the twentieth century would make clear that neither extreme had the last word to say on so fundamental and durable an emphasis as Wesley's on perfect love. In the meantime, most Methodists would have agreed with a comment made by Bishop J. F. Berry in 1896:

> I read your book with very great interest and thoroughly admired its clear, strong chapters. The fact is, however, I do not believe in controversies over the "Holiness" question. To me it looks like rather an unholy business. We have had in the Methodist Episcopal Church within the last twenty-five years so much debate on the subject that a good many people have in that way grown tired of and prejudiced against the doctrine. Don't you think we ought to stop debating about it now and begin to be holy? [13]

United Brethren and Evangelicals

Theology in both these relatively small denominations tended to maintain a conservative stance through most of the storms of the later nineteenth century. At times it looked as if they were so isolated from main currents that they were unaware of challenges. In fact, they were painfully aware of the challenges to faith, but unwilling to change ground for more favorable battle. Evangelical S. P. Spreng spoke for many in the *Evangelical Messenger* as he attacked the pliable adaptability of Henry Ward Beecher: "The old faith is the safest, the best. . . . Why will it not do for us?" Bishop J. J. Esher, who published at the turn of the century a major three-volume *Christliche Theologie,* was advising the General Conference of 1875 not

> to lay down doctrines, rules of faith and practice for the communicants of the kingdom of God, or to establish new dogmas; this was done long since. God himself has given us the doctrines, the rules of faith and practice to secure happiness, and others long before us developed all needful doctrine into dogma. It remains for us simply to hold fast to the actually existing laws and ordinances of the kingdom of God.[14]

One result of this rigidity was the increase of charges of heresy laid against those who tried to adjust doctrine to the many new scientific and philosophical currents. The climate for theological liberalism was definitely not friendly.

This is not to say that liberal ideas and new expressions were absent. Anton Huelster, an Evangelical scholar with a German doctorate, published a work on the psychology of religion, *Die Seelenlehre,* in 1875, a remarkably early date for such a work. He was more open than some to the idea of evolution. He also advocated greater free-

[13] Quoted in Peters, *Christian Perfection,* 176.

[14] The unpublished dissertation by William Henry Naumann, "Theology in the Evangelical United Brethren Church" (Yale, 1966), is a principal source for study of the subject. The quotes, to which he gives reference, are from the *Evangelical Messenger,* 1 Aug. 1882, 241; and *JGC,* 1875, 4.

dom in the use of scholarly tools in interpretation of the Bible. Another young scholar, Solomon J. Gamertsfelder, then assistant editor of the *Evangelical Messenger,* was bold enough to speak favorably of the biblical work of William Rainey Harper at a time when J. W. Mendenhall of the *Methodist Quarterly Review* was denouncing him as an emissary of the devil. Later, as professor of systematic theology at the Evangelical Theological Seminary, Gamertsfelder would write the standard work setting the theological stance of the Evangelicals and also United Brethren (1921).

The United Brethren displayed a similar conservatism, although it was generally not so rigidly stated, and a liberal movement was allowed to develop. Neither United Brethren nor Evangelicals, in spite of their German cultural background, had ready access to the new theology coming from Germany ever since the days of Schleiermacher. There was nothing in their literature that would compare with the exposure to—and sometimes confrontation with—the Continental theology that the *Methodist Quarterly Review* maintained for decades.

One unhappy result of theological controversy among the United Brethren was the schism of 1889. Other factors were involved, but theology was a major concern. For many years revision of the constitution and confession of faith had been discussed, but nothing had been done on account of the restrictions imposed on the general conference. It was forbidden to make any changes in those standards "unless by request of two-thirds of the members of the whole society." In the 1880s the cumbersome machinery was used, and a very large majority of the members voted in favor of a proposed revision prepared by a special committee.[15] When the General Conference of 1889 voted 110 to 20 in favor, a small minority then walked out to continue, as they interpreted their action, the true Church of the United Brethren in Christ. These became known as the Old Constitution United Brethren.

The theological issue had to do with the development of doctrine. J. W. Holt, editor of the *Religious Telescope,* was of the opinion that confessional statements should be subject to alteration or revision to fit new times. Philip Schaff was called to witness that creeds, being of human origin, were imperfect and subject to improvement. Opponents saw religious truth as given for all time and hence immutable.

---

[15] New confession of faith: 51,070 yes, 3,310 no; revision of constitution: 50,685 yes, 3,659 no. Curiously, the form of the ballot provided in print for a yes vote, but required erasure and writing in *no* for a no vote. It is doubtful if this method, which would be denounced today, had much effect on the outcome.

Reaction to Darwinian theories was much the same as in Methodism, although fewer voices were heard in attempts at reconciliation. Spreng, the Evangelical conservative, would not revise the Bible to fit science, although he was willing to revise science to fit the Bible. Others were more open, and Henry Drummond's thought and work were well received by some. A curious aspect is the tremendous popularity of the powerful lecturer, Joseph Cook (Flavius Josephus Cook). His dominating style of oratory, which he used to assure Christians that science was either wrong or in accord with revelation, was widely sought and followed by Evangelicals and United Brethren—along with many other Americans. It brought world-wide fame to Cook. Without really facing the crucial issues, he blandly proclaimed that there is no real conflict between science and religion and that Christians have nothing to fear from the higher criticism of the Bible. He sounded very authoritative in an age when the old authorities were shaking.

The debate over holiness involved the United Brethren and Evangelicals.[16] The influence of Phoebe Palmer's circle spread to these groups. In the mid-1850s, an article in *Der Christliche Botschafter* and the *Evangelical Messenger* argued that only those who are entirely sanctified are saved. It raised a storm. The earlier position of the Evangelicals was very close to Wesley's teaching. In the 1860s there was much controversy and even a heresy trial over sanctification. An Evangelical publication authorized by the church's board of publication, *The Living Epistle,* was spokesman for the holiness movement as defined by the National Association for the Promotion of Holiness, meaning entire sanctification as a separate second blessing. By this time the advocates of holiness in the Evangelical Association were more influenced by Phoebe Palmer and John Inskip than by Wesley and Albright. To a lesser extent the United Brethren reflected a similar development. David Edwards, editor of the *Religious Telescope,* was a strong advocate of sanctification.

Changing Patterns of Worship

As the country became more settled, so did worship. Symbolic of the change is the erection in Pittsburgh in 1855 of the first Methodist Gothic church building in the United States—Christ Church. Thought was given to provision for choir and organ. Participation by the congregation was encouraged, but increasingly channeled along lines which discouraged the spontaneous shouting and free testimony

[16] On the latter see the article by J. Wesley Corbin in *MH,* 7 (Jan., 1969): 28-44.

of former years. The order of worship was not prescribed in detail, except for the formal ritual; but it was expected that the following would be included in any proper Methodist service: singing, prayer, readings from Old and New Testaments, preaching, and benediction. Also, ministers were instructed to lead the people in the Lord's Prayer and a doxology (northern church). The editions of the *Discipline* reflect increasing attention to the ordering of worship in the interests of uniformity. Orders and rituals for special occasions, particularly the sacraments of baptism and the Lord's Supper, were provided and their use required or at least urgently recommended. By the 1880s, regular orders for Sunday service were generally in use both North and South. The rise of seminaries brought in a new influence, drawn from the wider fields of liturgical expression with valuable cross-fertilization. Methodists began to pay attention to how other Christians were worshiping.

From the beginning, hymns were regarded as a device for the systematic teaching of Christian truth. Wesley himself arranged his hymnals according to their theological content, and described the result as "a little body of experimental and practical divinity." Throughout the nineteenth century, these well-ordered hymnals published by the church competed with the unofficial songbooks which tended to lay stress on the conversion of sinners and individual salvation. Both types played an important part in the development of forms of worship.

In almost every case the trend was away from unstructured freedom to orderly structure. The *Discipline* of 1896 provided a more elaborate form of worship than did that of 1888. Around the turn of the century everyone became conscious that Methodism was passing through a period of significant change. The *Methodist Quarterly Review* ran article after article either hailing the changes or bewailing them. Thomas B. Neely generally supported the formulations, although he was careful to point out that an earnest recommendation is not a command. C. M. Giffin thought everything was going in the wrong direction, namely, back to Rome: "We are aware that those who call for 'the enrichment of worship' do not propose to introduce ritualism or go to Rome at once. We simply pause before we start toward these inherited forms to view the drift in other ages and ask, If we face toward a certain point, may we not get there?" [17] At the very turn of the century, R. J. Cooke wrote *History of the Ritual of the Methodist Episcopal Church* (1900). He took a long running start from the time of

[17] Giffin, "More Liturgy or More Life," *MQR,* Jan.-Feb., 1902: 74; Neely, "The Order of Public Worship," *MQR,* Jan.-Feb., 1900: 82.

the Reformation in setting the background for Methodist worship.

A turning point which marks the decline of free spontaneity (or anarchic disorder depending on how you look at it) and the delineation of forms for worship was the publication of the *Methodist Hymnal* of 1905, accomplished jointly by the northern and southern branches for their common use. This was the first hymnal to include a psalter in the form of responsive readings. It marked a return to Wesley's recommendations, although his psalter was not responsive. A whole year's plan for readings was included, together with readings for special occasions. Earlier, in 1885, the *Epworth Hymnal* had been distributed for use in the Epworth League and other informal settings in which popular songs were desired. The M. E. Church, South, put out a *Young People's Hymnal* in 1897.

The center of worship remained the sermon. Whatever else the Methodist minister had been or became, he remained the preacher. Methods varied as widely as the personalities involved. Relatively little guidance was offered in the preparation and delivery of sermons, but every man knew that his chief calling was the proclamation of the Word of God from the pulpit. Ministers were judged and services measured according to the excellence of the sermon. In the early days, a very small fund of sermons would do on a broad circuit frequently changed. In the later half of the nineteenth century, the minister was under obligation to spend much more time in preparation of sermons simply because he was a stationed pastor who preached to the same congregation for two or more years. It was possible to develop a series of biblical or doctrinal sermons, to engage in extended educational effort in the pulpit, and to initiate change in many different aspects of the Christian life. This meant extensive study and preparation. Seminaries began to offer courses in sermon preparation and preaching technique.

This was a time for the outstanding princes of the pulpit. Matthew Simpson was one of the bishops who excelled in swaying multitudes with the power of his preaching. Endless examples of great preaching could be given. Southern Methodism produced, beginning with George Pierce and Holland McTyeire, whole generations of famous preachers. One man in the North must suffice as example: William A. Quayle, master orator. "He marshaled words as Napoleon marshaled troops," wrote Merton S. Rice, himself a famous preacher of another generation.

> His eloquence at times flamed with all the real impressiveness of genuine eloquence. I count some of the periods of his preaching the most thrilling

bits of eloquence I have ever listened to. There was a glow on his impressive face, and a song in his fine intonation, and a rhythm in his phraseology, and an avalanche in his vocabulary, and a pathos in his voice, and a conviction in his manner, and a compulsion in his thought, that were irresistible. He had mind, and heart, and passion.[18]

By the early years of the twentieth century it was clear that Methodists had opted for ordered worship and standard hymns. Nevertheless, the spirit of freedom and spontaneity which had characterized the church in the previous century continued. The difference between the hymnal used in Sunday worship and the songbook used in Sunday school is illustrative of the continued tension between both trends. Both are almost equally characteristic, for John Wesley was at once devoted to the *Book of Common Prayer* and insistent on free expression. Once again it must be said of the Methodist heritage that it was inclusive. "Holy, Holy, Holy" belongs. So does "Amazing Grace." Both of these fit easily the "little body of experimental and practical divinity" which Wesley provided for the edification and education of his followers. While the class meeting, the local preacher, and the time limit were passing, all bewailed by those who loved the old ways, the church school, the educated minister, and the durable pastorate were coming in. Both trends, the old going and the new coming, were representative of something indigenous to Methodism; societies in the process of becoming a church.

[18] Merton S. Rice, *William Alfred Quayle, The Skylark of Methodism* (1928), 140, 133.

Chapter 29
Missionary Enterprise

At the outset Methodism was altogether a missionary movement. Its very being lay in mission. There wasn't anything else to it. Gradually, however, a distinction arose between established societies and new enterprise, between ground well-traveled and virgin territory. In the United States the missionary movement took two directions: westward within the nation and overseas to serve the world. These two main directions came to be known as home and foreign missions. In the former, further lines developed: frontier missions, church extension, missions to minorities, urban ministries, rural ministries, deaconess work, other special ministries. The story is long, complex, and exciting.[1] For reasons of space and unity this history deals with the admittedly huge subject in a most cursory fashion, with more attention given to national than to world missions.

Sparked by the activities of John Stewart, the first Methodist missionary to the American Indians, the Missionary Society was founded in 1819 under the leadership of Nathan Bangs. In the early decades it had little money and incidental leadership, and its activities were limited largely to modest promotion and correlation of the work of a few dedicated persons like James B. Finley among the Indians of Ohio, Martin Ruter in Texas, and Jason Lee in Oregon. At the time of division in 1844, there were 360 missionaries of one kind or another in the United States, and one lone struggling foreign mission —Liberia. Organization for the work went through several changes before the organization of the Board of Foreign Missions and the Board of Home Missions and Church Extension of the M. E. Church in 1906 and 1907. In the southern church the Missionary Society was formalized and divided in 1866 into separate boards of home missions and foreign missions, but reunited in 1870. After 1910, a Department of Home Missions was set up in the Board of Missions.

In both North and South this machinery was strongly supplemented (and sometimes challenged) by missionary societies formed by women. The Woman's Foreign Missionary Society of the

---

[1] A masterpiece of compaction in Chap. 27, "The Missions of American Methodism," by W. Richey Hogg, in *HAM*, III, 59-128. At the other extreme is the diffuse, but highly documented, *History of Methodist Missions* by Wade C. Barclay (3 vols., 1949–57). Still incomplete, Volume III covers the M. E. Church only from 1845 to 1895.

M. E. Church came into existence in 1869 as a result of a small meeting of interested women in Boston, Massachusetts. A Woman's Home Missionary Society was organized in 1880. In the M. E. Church, South, the Women's Board of Foreign Missions dated from 1878 and served as administrative agency for the Woman's Foreign Missionary Society (composed of memberships in local societies). After 1890 a comparable home missions organization was provided.

The Methodist Protestants developed similar agencies. The United Brethren had a Women's Association from 1877, and the Evangelicals a Woman's Missionary Society from 1890.

Missions in the United States

Much of the westward expansion of Methodism was "mission." That story in general outline has already been told. Both Hispanic American and American Indian history have been dealt with as part of that larger story. Much of the work with Negroes has been related in connection with the Civil War, Reconstruction, and development of black churches. A chapter has told the story of ethnic varieties. It remains in this place only to summarize these and other facets as part of an organized missionary movement.

Many early circuit riders received modest assistance from the Missionary Society as they struck into new territory. As time went on, this activity took on the aspects of "church extension." After 1864, when the Church Extension Society was organized in the North (and 1882 the southern Board of Church Extension), much of the funds went in loans to start new churches.

After the Civil War, the old assumption that America was white, Protestant, and Anglo-Saxon was gradually modified in recognition of other facets of American life which, expressed in minorities, were not white, Protestant, or Anglo-Saxon. American Indians were a major concern. Tocqueville was probably right in his analysis of the plight of the native Americans: they had only two options if they wanted to survive, war or civilization. "They must either destroy the Europeans or become their equals." The philosophy of missions held by Nathan Bangs fitted perfectly: *"Christianity must precede* ✳ *civilization."* [2] Inevitably, the two got mixed up together. John Pitezel, who could not be accused of ignorance of Indian culture, commented about his relations with the Chippewas of Michigan's upper peninsula:

[2] Tocqueville, *Democracy in America*, I, 342; Bangs, *A History of the Methodist Episcopal Church*, IV, 293.

> As to our charity, I told him that we endeavored to do what we were sent to do—that we were not sent to feed them, but to preach the Gospel to them, to teach their children, and point out the way for them to be happy—that if they would only abandon their heathenism and go to work as the white people do, they would not be hungry and go begging about for some one to feed them.[3]

And he was quite right, of course, except that he was not preaching the gospel, but advancing Western Civilization. The issue came to a critical focus in the matter of language. Only a minority of missionaries to the Indians thought it was worthwhile to learn the native languages and help preserve Indian culture. E. R. Ames claimed that William Johnson, who served the Shawnee and Kansas missions for many years, was the only missionary among those tribes in twenty-five years who learned to preach in the Indian tongues—both Shawnee and Kansan. It was, once again, a case of only two options for the Indians, and one of them was to join the white man's civilization. No Indian language, even major groups of languages like Algonquin or Sioux, could hope to overcome the cultural diversity—almost anarchy—of tribal patterns. A third option would become possible only after the mid-twentieth century.

Both branches of Methodism conducted missions to the Indians. Outstanding in the South was the mission to the Oklahoma tribes, including, after 1887, missions to the plains Indians started by J. J. Methvin. The M. E. Church had missions scattered all the way from New York state to the Pacific. Now and then, but all too infrequently, an Indian preacher like Peter Marksman in Michigan would rise to leadership. By 1921, the northern church had forty-one missions in operation, but many of these were weak or intermittent. As a matter of fact, Methodism, along with other religious bodies, had little to brag about. There were just too many difficulties in the way: lack of central program, geographical separation, lack of trained personnel, the cultural chasm, governmental policy, and a disregard for the Indians' own religious sensitivity. The best, perhaps, that can be said is that if the missionaries smuggled in Western Civilization, they at least presented some of its better aspects, in contrast to the contributions of fur traders, mountain men, and pioneers generally. It was not missionaries who invented removal, repudiation, reservation, and rum.

Missions to black Americans have already been treated. The Freedmen's Aid Society became a powerful and successful expression of missionary commitment in the northern church. After the shock

---

[3] Pitezel, *Lights and Shades of Missionary Life* (1883), 206-7.

waves of Civil War and Reconstruction, during which the southern church directed most of its limited energy to support of the fledgling C. M. E. Church; the M. E. Church, South, strove to broaden its work with Negroes in the spirit of Atticus Haygood's *Our Brother in Black.*

Likewise, the development of special work with Hispanic, German, Scandinavian, and Oriental peoples is an aspect of home missions, although the first three are better seen as ethnic varieties of the main-, stream and have been dealt with accordingly. Nevertheless, especially in their beginnings, they belong to the story of missions. Bethelship, Harwood Girls' School in Albuquerque, Holding Institute in Laredo, Lydia Patterson Institute in El Paso, the Chinese Mission House in San Francisco and other works of Otis Gibson, the Japanese Mission House in the same city and other works of Merriman C. Harris—all these and many others illustrate the widespread effort to provide Christian witness and service to Americans of minority groups. Attempts to reach Chinese and Japanese immigrants met with only moderate success. In 1895 the Chinese missions counted only 138 members. The Japanese missions in that year had 665 members and were on the way to eventual formation of a Japanese Annual Conference. One of the outstanding leaders was Kanichi Miyama, who had become a Methodist Christian in 1877 under Otis Gibson.

As the century wore on, various sorts of missions were begun among people seriously affected by the Industrial and Agricultural revolutions. City and rural missions sprang up to help fill the huge gaps left by the increasing identification of Methodism with middle-class white society. In the North the great factory cities needed special ministries which were provided by such institutions as the Five Points Mission in New York, the Chicago City Missionary Society, and Goodwill Industries. In many of these activities, women were among the most active leaders and promoters. This was especially true of most of the mission enterprises in Chicago and also of the work with seamen in southern gulf ports. By 1912 the M. E. Church had a Department of City Work.

As population fled the country to crowd the cities, rural life began to suffer. In response, the missionary societies began a series of missions to run-down rural areas such as the Appalachians. In 1916 a Department of Rural Work was set up in the northern Board of Home Missions and Church Extension. This in 1936 became the Department of Town and Country Work. The greatest development in these areas of need, however, came after World War I.

Mention has been made of the activity of women in various aspects of home mission work. In fact, this was a major source of support, participation, and leadership. Almost from the beginning of the Missionary Society a New York Female Society aided its work; and by mid-century the New York Ladies' Home Missionary Society, led by Phoebe Palmer, was at work in the Five Points Mission. The work of the Woman's Home Missionary Society, started in 1880 under the vigorous leadership of Jennie Culver (Mrs. Joseph C.) Hartzell, who had worked among black women in New Orleans, is well known. This organization received a tremendous acceleration through the active participation of Lucy Webb (Mrs. Rutherford B.) Hayes, who served as president.[4] Building on the pioneer work of women like Laura Haygood in Atlanta (who later had an amazing career as missionary in China), the women of the Methodist Episcopal Church, South, organized a Home Missionary Society in 1890, led by Lucinda Helm. Involvement of women is symbolized also by the development of the deaconess movement. Methodism was one of the few American denominations to take up this movement, which began among German Lutherans and Methodists. Proceeding on her own, Lucy Rider Meyer, who founded the Chicago Training School in 1885, began in 1887 in Chicago to enlist girls to visit the poor and sick in ghetto communities. Soon she had going what became a deaconess home and hospital. When the deaconess movement was approved by the General Conference of 1888, she became one of the prime figures in the growth of all kinds of institutions served by deaconesses. Bishop Thoburn and his sister, Isabella Thoburn, were also enthusiastic supporters, not only in the United States, but on the foreign mission field. Among the more influential developments were the Chicago Deaconess Training School and the Elizabeth Gamble Deaconess Home and Training School in Cincinnati. By 1920, the northern church had about nine hundred deaconesses in the field and the southern church a smaller number. A deaconess was distinguished by her membership on the Deaconess Board of an annual conference, which gave her a quasi-ministerial status. In the early days she adopted the European fashion of a distinctive uniform.

Missions Around the World

After a few small endeavors outside the United States the missionary societies entered upon the two great programs which remained dominant throughout the nineteenth century; China and India, the two most populous nations on earth. They were not, of course, the first

[4] See Mrs. John Davis, *Lucy Webb Hayes, A Memorial Sketch* (1892).

Christians there. Methodists arrived, however, during the favorable eras succeeding the Opium Wars in China and the Sepoy Mutiny in India.

Both branches entered China in 1847–48. Whereas the northern church spread eventually into southern, northern, and western regions, the southern church stayed mainly in the coastal regions around Shanghai and Soochow. Methodist Protestants came after 1909 in the north. Northern missionaries Judson Collins and Moses White began their work in Foochow in 1847, while Southerners Young J. Allen and J. W. Lambuth began the next year in Shanghai. Clinging stubbornly to the new mission during the Civil War, Lambuth and Allen laid the foundations for a vigorous southern Methodist enterprise in east-central China. J. W. Lambuth was succeeded by his son, Walter R. Lambuth, who not only built the first medical mission of the southern church, but went on to carry the gospel to Japan, and, eventually elected bishop, to start a mission in the African Congo. Laura Haygood went from Atlanta to found the McTyeire School for girls in Shanghai.

The northern church took its mission into the interior under the leadership of Virgil C. Hart. James W. Bashford, by this time bishop, brought his tremendous energy and administrative ability to serve the China mission between 1904 and 1910. Lucinda Combs, the first female medical missionary in China, came to Peking under appointment from the Woman's Foreign Missionary Society in 1873. She was only one of many such missionary doctors, not the least of whose services was the training of native Christian women as physicians.

After the shock of the anti-Western Boxer Rebellion of 1900, many new enterprises were begun, especially outstanding educational institutions. Some of these resulted from cooperation with other denominations. Almost unique was the participation of the family of Charles J. Soong, who, in spite of discrimination, remained a loyal Methodist. One daughter married Sun Yat-sen; another married H. H. Kung; another married Chiang Kai-shek. The son, T. V. Soong, became a high official in the Nationalist government. Later on Chinese Christians entered fully as leaders in the development of their church.

In India, northern Methodism expended great energy, but the southern church did not enter into competition. William Butler came in 1856 and remained a leading figure till 1864. During this period the work was concentrated in a limited area around Bareilly and Lucknow. Not until the arrival in 1859 and 1870, respectively of James M. Thoburn and William Taylor, for both of whom the entire immense Indian subcontinent was too small, did the work spread almost irresistibly. Comity arrangements were wrecked along with all other limitations. Whatever their other differences, these two agreed that Methodism had a calling to spread all over India. Taylor flashed by like a comet, but Thoburn stayed until his retirement in 1908. He saw the Indian mission grow in membership from a mere score to over two hundred thousand, most of whom joined the church during his last twenty years. A major policy shift directed attention to the lower castes and outcasts, who proved receptive of a gospel which promised freedom. Now and then, whole villages would be converted in what amounted, locally speaking, to a mass movement to Christianity.

In India as in China, women, both American and native, performed outstandingly. The two first missionaries of the newly formed Woman's Foreign Missionary Society were Isabella Thoburn and Clara Swain; the one, sister of James Thoburn, the other, first of a long line of medical missionaries, indeed the first woman physician of any sort in India. Isabella spent her life in Lucknow in educational work that resulted, in 1895, in a college that now bears her name. In 1878 a little orphan girl, Lilivati Singh, entered Isabella's school and began a career that would lead her to world-wide fame as a Christian witness. Then, there was Mary Reed, whose monument is the Leper Colony at Chandag.

The Methodist mission in India was one of the most successful. Next to the Syrian Christians, the Roman Catholics, and the Anglicans, all of whom enjoyed special advantages of antiquity or political favor, the Methodist church was the largest in the land. In the twentieth century, India would produce many powerful spokesmen for Christianity, among them not only Lilivati Singh, but Jashwant Rao Chitambar. Later, even more famous leaders would arise.

In what many American Methodists would regard as the home country, Europe, missionary activity was carried on throughout the period. Most of this was supported by the M. E. Church; but after World War I, the M. E. Church, South, entered Belgium, Czechoslovakia, and Poland. In many cases the missions were started in the first place by ethnic groups in the American church, such as Germans, Swedes, and Norwegians. Among such leaders were Ludwig S. Jacoby, an immigrant converted under Nast; Ehrhart Wunderlich and Heinrich Nuelsen, both representatives of influential German Methodist families; Olof Gustav Hedström, famous for his work on Bethelship in New York; and Ole Peter Petersen, active among Norwegians on both sides of the Atlantic. A variety of missions were carried on in Finland, Denmark, Russia, the Baltic, the Balkans, Austria, Switzerland, France, Hungary, and Italy.

A tremendous surge of vitality entered the missionary enterprise in 1869 with the formation of the Woman's Foreign Missionary Society. It began in a very small way in Boston when Lois S. (Mrs. Edwin W.) Parker and Clementina Rowe (Mrs. William) Butler brought together a few women who braved a driving storm on March 23, 1869 in Tremont Street Church. There they formed a society for the purpose of "engaging and uniting the efforts of the women of the Methodist Episcopal Church, in sending out and supporting female missionaries, native Christian teachers, and Bible readers, in foreign lands." Within a few weeks they had started the *Heathen Woman's Friend,* later the *Woman's Missionary Friend.* They also stirred up a hornet's nest among male supporters of the missionary society, who feared competition injurious to the work. The corresponding secretary of the missionary society, Dr. John P. Durbin, thought it would be best if the ladies would turn over to the parent organization responsibility for administration of their funds. Little did he know of these women who were determined to maintain full control of all they did. There was even an unsuccessful effort made at the General Conference of 1884 to abolish the new enterprise.

As it turned out, not only did the women provide much needed support and personnel, but the entire missionary program was strengthened. Those who followed Clara Swain and Isabella Thoburn together comprised one of the most important involvements of women in the life of American Methodism. In 1895, the society reported 151 missionaries, 750 Bible readers and teachers, 390 day schools, 50 boarding schools, 11 orphanages, 10 training schools, and 13 hospitals. The men who worried in 1869 would have been surprised at the income of $3,740,910.27 between 1869 and 1895. Other women's organizations followed: the United Brethren Woman's Missionary Association (1875), the Southern Methodist Woman's Foreign Missionary Society (1878), and the Evangelical Woman's Foreign Missionary Society (1884). In 1906 the Southern Methodist women experienced a similar challenge from uncooperative men as the general conference of that year threatened to take control of the organization.

In the last quarter of the nineteenth century the world missionary program of Methodism attained its full stride and spread into almost every land on earth. Most projects had their start in this period rather than earlier. Richey Hogg in the *History of American Methodism* gives a concise summary of these works, and Wade Barclay in his massive *History of Methodist Missions* offers a detailed and thoroughly documented panorama.[5] It would be unprofitable here to attempt the impossible, namely, to give anything like adequate coverage of so large, varied, exciting, and significant a theme.

Japan saw its first Methodist missionaries after the "opening" by Commodore Perry in 1853. Not until 1873–74 did Robert S. Maclay, under the missionary society, and missionaries from the W.F.M.S. arrive. In 1886, the Lambuths of the southern church, with O. A. Dukes and his family, began their work in Japan. Before long, outstanding Christian leaders among the Japanese appeared, including Yoitsu Honda, one of the prime founders of the Japan Methodist Church, 1907.

In Korea the Presbyterians and the Methodists were most active. Maclay, the missionary to Japan, came in 1884. From the efforts of the Henry G. Appenzellers and the William B. Scrantons came a number of highly successful medical and educational institutions, among them Ewha Woman's University. In several cases the two major denominations joined forces in united enterprises. By the end of World War I, the members of the Methodist church in Korea numbered about 25,000. From then on growth was phenomenal.

In Southeast Asia, Methodist work was started in Burma, Malaya, Singapore, Sarawak, West Borneo, Sumatra, Java, and the Philippines. One of many high points was the work of William G. Shellabear in Singapore especially among the Malay population, with the establishment of an important periodical, *The Malaysia Message*. The late arrival of Protestant work in the Philippines, not open until 1898, did not prevent active work in the early twentieth century. By 1820 there were around sixty thousand Methodists.

Missionary effort in Latin America was a special case, partly because of the long domination by Roman Catholicism, partly because of the extremely diverse political situations, and partly because of the peculiar racial makeup of the population. Northern Methodists began work in Bolivia, Chile, Peru, Panama, and Costa Rica (largely on account of the early work of William Taylor). Southern Methodists had work in northern Mexico, Brazil, and Cuba. Mexico reminds us of the development of Methodism among the Hispanic Americans of Texas. Alejo Hernandez, who looms large in that story, also carried on work in his native land. Northern Methodists, including the W.F.M.S., also had work in that country. Argentina early became a

---

[5] At this writing the only volumes of Barclay available are the first two, which go only to 1844, and Volume III, which covers the M. E. Church missions to 1895. Later volumes are planned to deal with the period after 1895 and the work of the M. E. Church, South.

center for theological education and publication, with the Methodist Publishing House in that nation producing Spanish literature for use throughout the continent. Southern Methodism came to Brazil through the migration of Southerners after the Civil War. The first regular missionary, John J. Ransom, came to Rio de Janeiro in 1876. Between 1877 and 1883, William Taylor left his mark on the great continent, stirring up missions in Peru, Chile, and Brazil, always pushing his special plan for English-based outreach to start self-supporting missions among the natives. The results were extremely varied, all the way from total failure to outstanding success.

When Methodists approached Africa, the only portions not under European domination were Liberia and Ethiopia. The former, which had begun as a mission, was revived later in the century, again largely through the efforts of Taylor, newly elected missionary bishop. But Taylor was not the man to stay in that little corner. His vision, like Livingstone's, covered the whole continent. During the 1880s his activity, which always kept the missionary society on edge, took him to many of the great colonial areas, including the Congo. Great enthusiasm did not always make up for inadequate planning. Probably Taylor's greatest limitation was failure to understand the cultural environment in which he worked, sometimes like an American bull in an exotic china shop. The man who did most to keep together what Taylor had so abundantly planted was Bishop Joseph C. Hartzell, appointed to succeed Taylor in 1896.

By the end of the century, Methodism shared with Protestantism generally an almost euphoric excitement over the potentialities of global missionary opportunities. It was high time for the stirring challenge of Methodist layman John R. Mott, "The Obligation of This Generation to Evangelize the World," an address given at the Ecumenical Missionary Conference in New York in 1900. For the first time in history, he cried, all factors and opportunities were wide open. "The hand of God, in opening door after door among the nations, and in bringing to light invention after invention, is beckoning the Church of our day to larger achievements." [6] Mott's clarion call was echoed around the world, especially among young people, whose idealism and enthusiasm were aroused as never before. Doughty old James M. Thoburn saw a sort of millennium in India: "The old may rejoice that they have lived to see this day, but the young may rejoice still more in the hope of seeing a day when a million souls will be found inquiring the way to Zion in North India, a million in West India, a million more in Burma, and still a million more in South

[6] *Addresses and Papers of John R. Mott* (1946), I, 315.

India. A million? Why not ten millions? Why not the Christian Conquest of India?" [7]

Without doubt Christianity was on the march, occasionally with an almost arrogant stride. William F. McDowell, one of the peerless preachers of northern Methodism, proclaimed to the "militant Methodists" of the first National Convention of Methodist Men in 1913: "I will take my stand in New York or Chicago or Calcutta or Bombay or Foochow or Shanghai or Pekin or Tokio or anywhere in the world beside Jesus Christ, not simply that He is better than anybody else, but that He alone is adequate to world redemption. There is no salvation apart from Him." [8] The line between complete personal commitment and evangelistic imperialism is sometimes very narrow. One year later Western Christendom was embroiled in the first of its global wars.

[7] James M. Thoburn, *The Christian Conquest of India* (1906), 245.
[8] David G. Downey, E. W. Halford, and Ralph W. Keeler, *Militant Methodism* (1913), 37.

Chapter 30
Methodism and Society

One of the axioms of the religious history of the United States is that important issues cut across denominational lines and involve many church bodies. It certainly applies to the challenge of the new urban and industrial society and the response of the churches in the Social Gospel. As we relate the participation of the Methodist churches in this major theme, we must understand that we are presenting a denominational facet of a larger story. Because of its Wesleyan heritage, its great size and spread, and especially its pragmatic approach to new problems, Methodism offers a valuable case study.[1]

When the Methodist Episcopal Church was founded, about one-thirtieth of the American people lived in towns of eight thousand or more people. By 1860 about one-eighth of them lived there, by 1880 one-fourth. In 1860 there were nine cities with over one hundred thousand people. At the turn of the century there were five times as many. The central reason for this was the Industrial Revolution, whose roots lay in the eighteenth century. After the Civil War, the United States entered upon a period of rapid and revolutionary change in the economic and social basis of society. Among the many tremendous new developments was the factory—by definition an instrument for manufacture located at a source of power for operation of machines. The corollary was concentration of workers to operate the machines. This was the factory: power, machines, workers. Beyond the factory lay a new form of economic organization by which large capital funds could be directed to creation of expensive factories. This meant new forms of transportation for conveyance of raw materials to the place of manufacture and of products to market. Industrial, commercial, and financial capitalism rose by leaps and bounds. This new order left out the workers and the consumers. One

[1] The best resource is Richard M. Cameron, *Methodism and Society in Historical Perspective* (1961). This is continued for the later period in Walter G. Muelder, *Methodism and Society in the Twentieth Century* (1961). Both these volumes belong to the series published by the Board of Social and Economic Relations of the Methodist Church under the title, *Methodism and Society*. General background is provided by A. I. Abell, *The Urban Impact on American Protestantism, 1865–1900* (1943); Henry F. May, *Protestant Churches and Industrial America* (1949); and C. H. Hopkins, *The Rise of the Social Gospel in American Protestantism* (1940).

of the great struggles of the 1880s and 1890s was the attempt to organize unions for cooperative participation by workers in the manufacturing process. Consumers were generally left to the attention of still another new business, advertising.

This all added up to a new world. How should the Christian church respond to this new society? For centuries it had been oriented largely to relatively simple agrarian norms. What place did the church have in the factory, in the bank, in the workers' ghetto? At the same time new political forces were at work to change society. The United States, fresh from the holocaust of the Civil War, was flexing its growing muscles in the affairs of the world. What would a "new nation, conceived in liberty and dedicated to the proposition that all men are created equal," have to say among nations long dominant by right of antiquity? In addition, there were problems of race and human relations that went beyond even these tremendous issues. What about the other half of the human race, the female of the species? Along with all Americans, Methodists were forced to respond to these matters, which in the words of Henry May were social "earthquakes."

At first the churches' response took the familiar lines of the older rural-individualistic concern for personal morality, identified by Martin Marty as the "private" or "evangelical" approach.[2] If there were social problems, the job of the church was to set up rescue missions for hapless individuals. Social evils were recognized as those which tempted Christians: liquor, gambling, "improper diversions," ungodly literature, desecration of the Sabbath. Methodists had long fretted over what the *Discipline* of 1872 called "imprudent conduct": dancing, going to theater, and "such other amusements as are obviously of misleading or questionable moral tendency." These concerns were simply a residue from one of the more narrow bequests of Puritanism recast in prudish Victorian mold. As time went on it became clear that such individual-centered social witness was not sufficient. Recurrent financial crises which threw many good people to disaster, the labor battles of the 1880s and 1890s, the overawing power of organized corporate business, the stresses of imperialistic adventures, the new and sometimes strident voices of women—these forces required something more than a lifesaving boat.

Economic Problems

Eighteen seventy-three was a year of financial crisis. So was 1893. Many persons learned the hard way that there was more to financial

[2] *Righteous Empire* (1970), 179.

affairs than individual work, thrift, and probity. In the late 1870s a series of labor troubles began and reached a crisis in 1886 with the great railroad strike against Jay Gould by the Knights of Labor. On May 4 came the violent Haymarket riot in Chicago with its overtones of anarchistic conspiracy. Then came the strike against the Carnegie Steel Company, and the climax, the Pullman strike which resulted ultimately in a fundamental change of attitude regarding the labor movement.

During this period most Methodist leaders and editors of church papers were opposed to organization of workingmen and especially to the strike technique. They were standing in the old position of early capitalism and free enterprise for free farmers and free small businessmen. They did not yet grasp the significance of big business and the complexity of corporate finance and production.

But, already during the 1880s and even more in the next decade, some ministers and some writers were beginning to see the importance of a Christian understanding of economic life in the new industrial age. They got their ideas from two sources: the beginnings of the Social Gospel and direct experience of social problems. In 1876, Washington Gladden, a Congregational minister in Columbus, Ohio, published a series of lectures he had given on *Working People and Their Employers*. In 1889, Richard T. Ely brought out *The Social Aspects of Christianity*. Walter Rauschenbusch, Baptist theological professor, became the leading spokesman and theological interpreter at the turn of the century. Much of their understanding came from personal experiences in New York's Hell's Kitchen and Columbus' slums.

Most Methodists were untouched by this movement and unaware of the revolutionary changes in society. During the labor troubles and recurrent panics, the *Advocates* frequently urged relief for the unemployed, but they had little to say about the causes of labor unrest or the policies of employers. The churches, including the Methodist, either ignored or were unaware of poor safety conditions, exploitive wages, sudden layoffs, and waste of natural resources. One student surveyed Methodist literature for the years when lumbering operations were despoiling the Michigan and Wisconsin virgin forests and found not a single word of protest. In fairness it should be noted that almost nobody else was protesting either.

One of those apparently isolated incidents which signal a basic change of history occurred in Chicago in 1894, when the workers in Pullman went on strike. Pullman was a true company town, owned by George Pullman, president of the Pullman Palace Car Company. Like a proverbial Horatio Alger, he had built a great manufacturing empire on Chicago's south side. He had built the town in an attempt to provide an ideal environment for the workers, but the idea hadn't worked out. Gradually a subtle social control dominated the workers' lives. Pullman's enterprise was not philanthropic; he made an annual profit on rents and other income of 6 percent. He built a green stone church which he leased at a profit to the Presbyterians. In addition there were two Methodist churches (one Swedish), one Roman Catholic, one Episcopal, and one Baptist.

In May, 1894, the workers went out on strike on account of cuts in employment and wages. No cuts were made in rents paid by the workers. The Sunday after the strike began, William H. Carwardine, minister of the Methodist church, delivered a sermon which made the front pages of the Chicago papers and subsequently was reprinted or reported throughout the country. In it he denounced the policies of the company and came to the defense of the rights of the workers. The whole idea of a company town, not the workers, was wrong. For seven weeks the strike went on without violence until federal troops were called in to protect the mails, over the protest of Governor John P. Altgeld. Carwardine continued to support the strikers and helped the Strikers' Relief Fund. All the other ministers, except the Swedish Methodist, opposed Carwardine's open support of the workers, and for a few months he was almost alone. Yet, within a year he had gained the support of the Chicago Preachers' Meeting and the *Northwestern Christian Advocate*, which was published in Chicago.[3]

One result of the strike was the formation of the United States Strike Commission, 1894, which began the painful process of facing up to the unanticipated, but unavoidable, problems of the Industrial Revolution. The idea began to dawn that uncontrolled free enterprise would not automatically bring social peace and prosperity to all. Carwardine was one of those who testified before the commission, which finally reported that responsibility for conditions which brought on the strike lay with the American people, not the strikers. Attitudes were already changing from the vicious ones expressed by the press, which included the Methodist as well as the entire religious press, on the occasion of the Haymarket explosion of 1886. This incident was exacerbated by the much feared anarchist propaganda of the times and the native suspicion of all foreigners—that is, non–Anglo-Saxon Americans. In little more than a decade the Methodists would officially adopt in the general conference a Social

---

[3] *NWCA*, 42 (19 Sept. 1894): 8. The basic reference is the book by Carwardine, *The Pullman Strike* (1894). The whole episode is carefully analyzed by Stephen G. Cobb, "William H. Carwardine and the Pullman Strike," (Diss., Northwestern, 1970).

Creed which incorporated all the principles the workers of 1894 were fighting for.

Getting into Politics

Inevitably, the entry of the churches into the area of economic morality brought them also into politics. Many voices were raised in opposition to this course, for the emphasis of evangelistic spirit in the later nineteenth century (in contrast to prewar revivalism) lay with the individual, not with society in general. Some people were unaware that Christianity had a message to the nations as well as to persons. There was some inconsistency, however, depending on what the particular political issue was. Some Christians who took strong political stands in the name of the church regarding international affairs in the McKinley era and the temperance crusade were horrified at the thought of the church taking a stand on matters of finance and manufacture, to say nothing of race relations.

Americans, Methodists among them, were divided on the proper solution to the Indian problem. This was something quite different from the promotion of missions among the Indians and the encouragement of an Indian Mission Conference. It had to do rather with the question of the place of the Indian in American society and thus entered the realm of public policy. The first great issue, Indian removal from east to west of the Mississippi, has been dealt with elsewhere. That was but one stage in the long story of dealing with the native Americans. There remained the Indian wars and allotment. The twentieth century would see still more problems arising from difficulties in the reservation system and the flow of Indians to the cities.

Beginning in the 1860s and continuing till 1890 were a series of skirmishes lumped together as Indian Wars. These involved chiefly the plains Indians, whose way of life based on horse and buffalo was seriously threatened by the encroachment of miners, cattlemen, and pioneer farmers. Some political and military leaders thought the only way to deal with warlike Indians was to suppress or exterminate them. Others believed evenhanded justice might work wonders. A test case was the tremendous uproar over the defeat of Custer at the Little Big Horn on June 25, 1876.[4] One writer in the *Northwestern Christian Advocate* urged military reprisal, arguing for the defense of the help-less farmer and the right of all to natural resources—including gold. On the other hand, the *Western Christian Advocate* urged restraint

[4] See Norwood, "The Invisible American—Methodism and the Indian," *MH*, 8 (Jan., 1970): 3-24.

because there were two sides to the issue. The editorial made the following points: the land had been confirmed to the Indians in a formal treaty; Sitting Bull was the only hostile leader; the government had sent an exploring expedition into the gold country (South Dakota); rumors of gold resulted; the Indians had asked for protection; the government did not provide it. "The blood of these brave men will not have been shed in vain, if the shock of defeat shall serve to induce the country to think upon the character of this warfare against the Indian. Before we give wild shouts of encouragement to war of extermination, let us calmly look at its justice and necessity." [5]

The tragic figure of Chief Joseph, leader of the Nez Percé in their long search for sanctuary in 1877, affected even the bellicose *Northwestern Christian Advocate*. But it was once again the Cincinnati paper which frankly advised: "It would be wiser and cheaper to deal honestly and fairly with the Indian, and prevent the cost in money and human lives, as well as the crime of hunting and killing him." [6] The whole country was shocked at the final episode of the Indian wars, which took place at Wounded Knee in southwestern South Dakota, December 29, 1890. With that massacre, the whole sordid war policy collapsed.

A new day dawned with the Dawes Act of 1887, which provided for an "allotment plan" for dividing the reservations among Indian families. With the best of intentions the government proposed to get rid of the whole difficult reservation system and allow Indians to own and till their own farms like everybody else. Unfortunately, there was a hidden agenda; obliteration of Indian tribal society. As the federal Board of Indian Commissioners frankly stated: "This law is a mighty pulverizing engine for breaking up the tribal mass. . . . Undivided tribal funds perpetuate the Indian problem—break them up!" [7] In general, the missionaries serving Indians favored the allotment plan, because it would hasten the acculturation of the Indians who resisted the work ethic of individual initiative and because it would permit continuation of church-related educational endeavors. Several other denominations, however, were more active than Methodists in support of the allotment plan. One continuing problem was the uncomfortable alliance of government and churches in maintaining a school system for Indians. Reforms which reversed the allotment plan did not come until the early 1930s, by which time some ninety million acres had been lost.

Another area of public policy in which Methodists became actively

---

[5] *Ibid.*, 14. [7] *Ibid.*, 18.
[6] *Ibid.*, 15.

engaged was the Spanish-American War. In the White House lived an active Methodist layman, William McKinley. In those days the president could still go to church like anyone else, although he could not guarantee the event would go unnoticed. A crowd of five thousand gathered around Metropolitan Methodist Church in Washington the first Sunday to greet him and his mother. His pastor, Hugh Johnston, could still drop into the White House on "pastoral calls." [8] McKinley won election in part through the direct efforts of Bishop Charles Fowler, who unabashedly stumped for him in the campaign of 1900. He made many campaign speeches in behalf of the Republican candidate and was quoted in the *New York Sun* as saying: "Shall we have Bryan elected? No; a thousand times, No! I'd rather go to sea in a boat of stone, with sails of lead, with oars of iron, with the wrath of God as a gale, and hell for a port." [9] The Third Ecumenical Methodist Conference, which was meeting in London, was thrown into mourning by the news of the president's assassination.

Methodist papers generally had been sympathetic with the Cubans in their struggle against Spanish colonial control. Original neutrality changed as Spanish cruelty came to light. When McKinley asked for authority to use force on April 11, 1898, Methodists gave him their support through the religious papers. The *Western Christian Advocate,* however, was the only paper that joined the emotional uproar over the *Maine.* The northern College of Bishops passed a resolution of support for what they regarded as McKinley's wise policy of avoiding war until absolutely necessary. So did the general conference of the southern church. The favorable outcome of the war was widely acclaimed as a providential act of God. Adna B. Leonard, the missionary secretary, called for a massive response to the new opportunities. As early as September, 1898, an article in the *Methodist Review* frankly identified missionary with colonial interest: "There is no chance to shut one's eyes to the relation of missions to the success of governmental colonizing schemes." Expansion of the national interest was seen as a political expression of the missionary interest. When Bishop Thoburn visited the Philippines in February, 1899, he concluded that the best disposition of the newly emancipated islands would be annexation to the United States. The other options were unacceptable: the Philippine people were unable to govern themselves; the archipelago could not be returned to Spain; and no other European

[8] See article by H. Alden Welch, "A President and His Pastor," *MH,* 1 (Apr., 1963): 29-37. On the Methodists and imperialism see Kenneth M. MacKenzie, *The Robe and the Sword, the Methodist Church and the Rise of American Imperialism* (1961).

[9] MS letter and clipping from a friend, 10 Nov. 1900, in Fowler papers, Drew Theological Seminary.

power was entitled to possession. The United States, therefore, had a responsibility to "Christianize" them and "elevate them in the scale of civilization." [10] Perhaps, at the time an American wardship was necessary, but Methodist leaders tended to have little understanding of or sympathy with Aguinaldo's independence movement.

The most important involvement of Methodists in public affairs arose from the temperance movement and the drive to outlaw alcoholic beverages.[11] In this area Methodists, many of whom remained otherwise stalwartly opposed to the church in politics, were willing, even eager, to use any political means to achieve prohibition. Here was a clear-cut moral issue which could be seen in individual terms and at the same time could be solved by political methods, or so many supporters of the temperance movement thought.

As time went on this became the paramount issue of Methodist social witness. For a while it almost excluded any other social problems. It no doubt played an unintended part in delaying or submerging the concern felt by a small but increasing minority over some of the broader implications of industrial society and urban life. The saloon became a symbol of all that was wrong in American life. It was easy for some to jump to the conclusion that, if only demon rum could be exorcized, the problems of society would all fade away. The *Advocates* reflected this one-track social concern. Whereas one must search diligently to find material dealing with the problems of society generally, it is difficult to avoid the great bulk of editorial and article devoted, sometimes in extended fashion, to the issue of temperance. This was especially true in the years which culminated in the eighteenth amendment of the Constitution. The only rival, and that late, was the catastrophe of World War I.

This is not to suggest that the traffic in hard drink was an imaginary bogeyman. It worked its evils from the Indian reservation and lumbering camp down to the most degraded urban slum. Nor is it to suggest that Methodists had to fight the battle all alone. The most powerful organizations for temperance and prohibition were interdenominational in support. Methodists, however, were never far from frontline center. The war was long drawn out and covered at least three stages. Earlier in the century most of the effort was directed at development of a social conscience on liquor with appeals

[10] *CCA*, 23 Aug 1899, quoted in MacKenzie, *The Robe and the Sword*, 88. The *NWCA* also supported Thoburn's judgment, 25 May 1898, p. 8.

[11] The literature, both historical and polemic, is too vast to cite here. Very good summaries are in Cameron, 244-62 and *HAM*, III, 329-43. Illustrative of the intensive study is the 656-page work by Methodist minister Daniel Dorchester, *The Liquor Problem in All Ages* (1884).

for temperance in individuals and for ecclesiastical legislation to promote discipline within the church. A second stage came with the drive for local and state option laws. The third stage was the campaign for national prohibition.

Even before the Civil War, state legislation had appeared. Maine was the first in 1851. The General Conference of 1852 took cognizance of this and other current legislation and urged ministers to give support. Three great agencies claimed and received Methodist support in the later nineteenth century: the National Prohibition Party, organized in 1869; the Women's Christian Temperance Union, 1874; and the National Anti-saloon League, 1895. Methodists were very active and prominent in all three.

Emotional appeals for abstinence tended to give way to direct political action. In girding for the struggle the main Methodist churches cleared the decks with legislation setting standards for church members. Official Temperance Sunday (last Sunday in June) dates from 1868. By the time of the General Conference of 1884, the official position was full support of national prohibition by law as "the platform on which we stand as a denomination, and upon which we will battle until [it] is secured in every State and territory in the Union, and finally embodied in the Constitution of the United States." In 1890 the southern general conference proclaimed: "Voluntary total abstinence from all intoxicants is the sole and true ground of personal temperance, and complete legal prohibition of the traffic is the duty of the government." Methodist Protestants took similar action. Another little tidying-up operation was the replacement of wine with grape juice. Traditionally, Methodists with other Christians had cherished the symbolism of bread and wine. Adam Clarke insisted that wine was the only proper symbol, and articles in Methodist publications before the Civil War agreed. By 1864, however, a recommendation favoring grape juice was placed in an appendix to the *Discipline* of the M. E. Church. The other churches followed suit. The final step in preparation was the establishment of the Board of Temperance in 1904. Its beginnings go back to 1892 when a temperance committee was authorized. Continued opposition to a board came not from disagreement with its goal, but from opposition to bureaucratic multiplication of agencies.

Thus girded for battle, American Methodism embarked on its greatest crusade. Continual pressure was kept up via local and state option which possibly might turn the country dry piecemeal. So many difficulties were encountered that the dry forces decided on a concerted national drive. Dry option could just as easily be wet option.

The emergence of a Prohibition Party caused much controversy, not so much over the goal as the method. Some thought it politically hopeless. The only factor that kept the third party alive was the continued reluctance of the two major parties to take a strong temperance stand.

Of special significance was Frances Willard, who succeeded in the 1870s in bringing together the two main focal points of her career, temperance and women's rights. The first became both an end in itself and a means for achieving the second. She was engaged in a long struggle to promote temperance, beginning with local option in Evanston and Illinois and going on to national leadership in the Women's Christian Temperance Union and political involvement through the Prohibition Party, Republican Party, and labor unions.

In the end the crusade was crowned with complete victory by the passage of the Volstead Act and the eighteenth amendment to the Constitution. The bitter disillusionment did not come until later.

The Rights of Women

It usually goes without saying (but ought not) that women have always participated in the life of the church. To demonstrate that they have been effective behind-the-scenes workers and that now and then a woman would approach center stage would not be difficult. Women indeed, as Mary Beard strongly argues, have always been a force in history.[12] So have Methodist women, beginning with some of John Wesley's contemporaries in England. In America, we recall the participation of such women as Catherine Garrettson, Mary White, Prudence Gough, Mary Tiffin, and Mary Withey. The concentration of history upon the male, however, is illustrated by the need to identify some of these women in connection with their husbands. The male prerogative is obvious and sometimes insidious. Take the ladies' own magazine, for instance, *The Ladies' Repository,* edited by a man. The Book Committee (all men) instructed the editor to point out the religious duty of females, help them perform these duties, give examples by means of biographies of fine women, discuss appropriate biblical teaching, and encourage domestic economy. One gets the impression from reading accounts in the *Advocates* that women's roles were generally seen as serving well as helpmates and dying pious deaths. These attitudes, of course, were no Methodist monopoly.

Understandably then, the history of the struggle of women for equal rights has had to be fought inside as well as outside the church.

[12] Mary R. Beard, *Woman as Force in History* (1946).

One of the high points was admission of women as lay delegates to the general conference. In 1861 the *Western Christian Advocate* carried a two-column proposal for admission of lay delegates in both annual and general conferences.[13] Critics objected to the exclusion of persons under twenty-one and women. When the general conference of the M. E. Church met in 1888, it faced an immediate problem. No less than five women, one of them the famous Frances Willard, had been elected as lay delegates. Even the idea of lay delegates was new; but women! The bishops noted the presence of some "elect ladies," but warned the conference that a decision on their seating must be made solely on the law of the church. Chivalry of men and merits of the women should be rigorously excluded. They were not seated, but the reaction was powerful. Many influential men believed the time had come to give women their full rights as members, if not yet as ministers. Conservative voices, including the powerful James M. Buckley, succeeded in putting off the evil day with parliamentary debates over the meaning of the word *layman*. Although four women were accepted by the General Conference of 1896, not until approval of a new constitution in 1900 were women's rights as lay participants fully established. In the M. E. Church, South, the process followed similar lines with approval in 1922. Methodist Protestants, who had started so well with equality of women in the formative stages, specifically excluded them from lay representation in the constitution of the new church. Not until 1892 were they admitted as lay delegates in the general conference. Some of the smaller sects of Methodism included women in government from the beginning.

A very touchy subject was the ordination of women. The issue was not new, in fact, had been argued from the early church on. At mid-century the United Brethren had already made tentative first moves by granting to Charity Opheral a quarterly conference preacher's license and recommending, in its General Conference of 1851, Lydia Sexton as a "pulpit speaker." The first Methodist woman to get a preacher's license was Maggie (Margaret) Van Cott, who for thirty years after 1866 maintained a prodigious itinerant ministry of many thousands of miles, from New York's Five Points Mission where she began to the largest churches of the denomination. Her large figure, stylish dress, acting ability, and strong voice all contributed to an effective dramatic presence. Quite in contrast was the plain black washerwoman, Amanda Smith, who rose from slavery and poverty to become world famous as an evangelist.

The memorials which came before the General Conference of 1880

[13] *WCA*, 4 Dec. 1861, 386.

regarding Anna Oliver occasioned more than passing attention. The conference had received petitions from the church she was serving in Brooklyn, the Alumni of Boston School of Theology, and the New England Annual Conference, all requesting removal from the *Discipline* of all restrictions of sex in ordination. Moreover, a resolution signed by a number of prominent women, including Frances Willard, asked that "masculine nouns and pronouns" pertaining to trustees, stewards, Sunday school superintendents, class-leaders, exhorters, and both local and traveling preachers be removed and that "the word 'male' be expunged entirely" from the *Discipline*. These proposals were too much for the nineteenth-century ecclesiastical mind in every major denomination, and Methodist leaders did not propose to be an exception. Ordination of women would come in mainline Methodism, but not until well into the next century.

One partial exception was the Methodist Protestant Church. Anna H. Shaw had also sought ordination from the New England Conference. Being rebuffed, she joined the M. P. Church and, in 1880, received ordination at the New York Conference. Although the general Judiciary Committee declared the action unlawful, she continued to enjoy recognition in her annual conference. The issue of ordination remained in a sort of constitutional limbo. The same General Conference of 1880 forced Amanda Way, women's rights and temperance worker in Indiana, who had a license to preach, to go back to her ancestral Society of Friends for the freedom to preach she demanded.

A young United Brethren school teacher named Sarah Dickey was caught up in social issues during the Civil War and went to Vicksburg to work among the hordes of freed slaves. Subsequently, after completing her education at Mt. Holyoke, she returned to Mississippi to found Mt. Hermon School for black children in 1873, where she spent the rest of her life, sometimes suffering persecution at the hands of bigoted Southern whites. In 1894 she was fully ordained by the United Brethren.

Not until 1924 were women in Methodism given limited clergy rights, and only in 1956 could they be fully ordained.

In interesting contrast was the action of the general conference of the African Methodist Episcopal Zion Church in 1868 to remove the term "male" from regulations on ordination. A woman deacon was ordained in 1896 and an elder in 1898.

The important roles of women as missionaries and as deaconesses have been discussed elsewhere.

Behind all these moves to open opportunities for women in the structure of Methodism lay the campaign for women's rights generally. At this point we encounter one of the liveliest women of the nineteenth century, Frances Willard, whom we have already met as a leader of the temperance movement. In a speech she made to a mixed audience in 1888 she candidly admitted: "I don't know that it will make me stand any better with the ladies of the audience, and certainly it won't with the gentlemen, but honestly, I always thought that, next to a wish I had to be a saint some day, I really would like to be a politician." In her day of restricting clothes and regulations and mores, she was like a caged lioness. Being national president of the W.C.T.U. was fine and provided a natural field of action, but it was far less than what she wanted. The *Women's Journal* commented in 1892, "Miss Willard did not come to woman suffrage through temperance, but was a suffragist first, last, and all the time." Whereas Elizabeth Stanton and Susan Anthony seized more headlines, Frances Willard worked steadily at the business of being a free woman and helping her sisters do likewise. She was the key figure in bringing the interests of temperance and women's rights together. However much she might encounter opposition from the male world and from within the women's temperance movement, she persevered with the main goal always clearly in sight: equal rights for women in society. Her copy of John Stuart Mills's *Subjection of Women* contains the note, "Read by me at eighteen and never forgotten." From 1871 on, she was openly committed to woman suffrage. Using every avenue she could find, she was active in the Home Protection Party and its successor the Prohibition Party. She knew personally and worked with labor leaders. She even flirted with a mild form of socialism. She did not live to see the victory of the Woman Suffrage Amendment in 1920, but she inspired a whole generation of women to strive for it.

Toward the Social Creed

By the end of the nineteenth century, the M. E. Church and, more slowly, the M. E. Church, South, were ready for a fundamental change of perspective on social issues. It took the form of the Social Creed. The General Conference of 1900 heard Frank Mason North and others call for a new awareness and a new commitment to social Christianity. In 1907 Frank North, Worth M. Tippy, Harry F. Ward, Herbert Welch, and Elbert R. Zaring formed the Methodist Federation for Social Service, which under the leadership of Ward would have an influential and eventually a stormy life. The stage was set for official commitment of the church.

At the General Conference of 1908 the Social Creed of Methodism was adopted. It became the basis for the similar statement of the new Federal Council of Churches. It has remained, with updating revisions, a guiding document for Methodists to this day. It stands as one of the great symbols of the Social Gospel. It sought to rebuild the close connection the Wesleyan movement once had with the laboring man. It called for broad social reforms, some of them very extensive for that day, in a new century world full of optimistic expectation of great things coming. So resplendent was the potential sunrise that only a few noted with misgiving the gathering clouds of war and all the disasters that might come in its train.

One who was caught up in this heady conviction of progress was Daniel Dorchester, who wrote, in his revised edition of 1895, over 800 pages on *The Problem of Religious Progress.* Although he frankly acknowledged difficulties in the way, he adroitly turned adverse evidence to advantage—increase of lynchings reminds us of more barbaric slavery now gone, more divorces indicate decline in "runaways" and "French infidelity." He thus comes to "the comforting conviction that a very great and substantial improvement has taken place in the average moral purity of American society and of the American Churches." [14]

But recent progress is nothing compared to the promise of the future. After charting the progress of Christianity from its lowly beginnings, he concluded: "But, at the present time, no intelligent person, standing in the light of the last four centuries, and beholding the great religious movements of this age, can doubt whether Protestant Christianity is a setting or a rising sun. Every year it is robing itself in fuller effulgence, and pouring its blessed illumination upon new millions of earth's benighted children." [15]

[14] Dorchester, *The Problem of Religious Progress,* 229-31, 210.
[15] *Ibid.,* 671.

IV. Ecumenical Transformation 1914-1970

Chapter 31
Ecumenical Beginnings

Many Methodists would have agreed with William Rainey Harper, famous biblical scholar and president of the University of Chicago, in his judgment that: "We all realize that the world is growing better; that its ideals of life are gradually rising higher and higher. And this is so because the life of the individual is moving on a higher plane. Herein, perhaps, lies the most conspicuous evidence of God's presence." [1] Methodist publications and conferences of the turn of the century were full of this buoyant optimism. Churchmen were comforted by the enumeration of past successes and by the still powerful forces at the command of the church: the itinerant system, "the grand old Arminian theology," the reform spirit of Wesley, and the Word of God.[2] And yet, as though Methodists sensed the presence of invisible wraiths throwing shadows on what should be a sunny horizon, uneasiness pervaded the church. In commenting on the high promise of the new century a writer in the *Western Christian Advocate* worried, "And yet, and yet, there is such a newness, such a largeness in the thought of Nineteen Hundred, that a sort of mysterious dread seizes us, and we shrink from it." [3] Ah, yes: "and yet." A cursory survey of the issues and problems discussed in that paper during the first year of those "Nineteen Hundreds" offers a tiny inkling of what lay in store: women's rights, a black bishop, the Boer War, the Boxer Uprising, the H. G. Mitchell case, fiction and culture, the Social Gospel, the Negro in South and North. Many were the signs of change. The bishops in the episcopal address to the General Conference of 1900, expressing their belief that the theological foundations have remained unchanged and even venturing to state what those foundations were, went on to speak of the many changes:

> Which do they indicate, growth or decay? The class meeting, for instance, is considerably disused: have fellowship and spiritual helpfulness among believers abated, or do they find, in part, other expressions and

[1] *Religion and the Higher Life* (1904), 72.
[2] President James Bashford in *WCA*, 66 (27 June 1900): 809.
[3] *WCA*, 66 (3 Jan. 1900): 1. For issues and problems of early twentieth century see *WCA*, 66 (1900): 196, 354, 577, 610-11, 642, 772, 775, 782, 784, 837, 1058, 1060, 1347-49, 1443-44.

THE STORY OF AMERICAN METHODISM

other instruments? The rigid and minute Church discipline of former years is relaxed: is this a sign of pastoral unfaithfulness, or is it a sign of growing respect for individual liberty and of a better conception of the function of the Church? The plainness of the early Methodist congregations has disappeared: is this simply vanity and worldliness, or is it, in part, the natural and justifiable development of the aesthetic faculty under more prosperous external conditions? The strenuous contention for this or that particular doctrine or usage of Methodism, once common, is now rarely heard: is this indifferentism, or is it, in part, a better discernment of that which is vital to the Christian faith, and, in part, the result of an acceptance by others of the once disputed opinion?[4]

Seventeen bishops signed this document, which was equivocal in every respect except in an abiding faith that the Lord would shed more light and lead his people through.

Some were more outspoken in their opinions of the right and wrong of affairs. This was the age of James M. Buckley, longtime editor of the New York *Christian Advocate*. In fact, reported the *Western Christian Advocate*, "It is Dr. Buckley's General Conference." Recognizing the power of an idea whose time had come, he led the conference to approve equal representation for lay persons in the general conference. But, when a proposal was made that they also be given equal representation in annual conferences, the motion was roundly defeated, because Buckley was against it. He practically dominated general conferences between 1876 and 1916, and he knew how to stop change in its tracks when it suited him.

As the next general conference of northern Methodism drew around, the bishops were clearly determined to avoid loss of "the old paths." Noting the difference between essentials and nonessentials, they called for a return to the Wesleyan standards. "We deeply deplore the hasty, callow, dogmatic declarations of destructive critics." They finally were aware that the "manifest destiny" of the nations was not necessarily the same direction as the King's Highway. It has been "a snare to us." Instead, society suffers from many evils: political corruption, economic warfare, crime, "the pitiable condition of the negro race," intemperance, marital infidelity, destructive amusements, and many "isms of evil omen."

Thus the century which rolled in with paeans to progress and great expectations also brought in its train uneasy doubts and disillusionments. These were generally submerged in the heady optimism of the times; but they were there. At the turn of the century a tension existed between the new and the old, between advance and retrenchment. Not everyone was ready to dump the old wagon for a giddy

[4] *JGC*, 1900, 60.

ride in the new flying machine. (An irony here, since the father of Orville and Wilbur was archconservative Bishop Milton Wright of the United Brethren Old Constitution).

Ecumenical Directions

One of the signs of change was the decline of denominational rivalry in the interest of interdenominational cooperation. All the episcopal addresses from 1892 on through the turn of the century spoke of it with favor. This interest found expression on four levels: worldwide ecumenism, functional cooperation, ecumenical Methodism, and Methodist merger. The first is best illustrated by the World Missionary Conference of 1910 and the International Missionary Council. The second is exemplified by the Federal Council of Churches, the Men and Religion Forward Movement, and various educational projects and organizations. The third came to expression in the series of Ecumenical Methodist conferences which began in London in 1881. Almost all of the sundry Methodist bodies were brought together in these meetings. The fourth is seen in the extended discussions which proceeded right through World War I between the two Episcopal Methodist churches. They laid foundations for the reunion finally achieved in 1939. During these same years, representatives of the two sundered parts of the Evangelical Association were hammering out the basis for the reunion of 1922 in the Evangelical Church. No wonder that an article in the southern *Methodist Quarterly Review* reminded its readers of "the catholicity of Methodism." [5]

All these trends could claim deep roots in the Wesleyan heritage. Wesley, writer of "The Catholic Spirit," whose own roots lay deep in many traditions, Catholic as well as Protestant, Reformed as well as Pietist, who insisted that all men could be saved and urged all Christians on to perfect love, would rejoice at the extended hands of mutual acceptance. In this context John R. Mott was the typical—or perhaps better archetypal—Methodist. He was also unique. When Charles W. Ranson, secretary of the International Missionary Council, asked the delegates to the Ecumenical Methodist Conference of 1951, "What is Methodism's chief contribution to the Ecumenical Movement?" his answer was, "Dr. John R. Mott." The dawn of the twentieth century was Mott's day (although he lived to 1955). His career summarizes Methodist involvement in the most expansive ecumenical movement of the century, that which led to the formation of the World Council

[5] By W. J. Conoly, *MQRS*, 65 (1916): 716-28.

of Churches. From his participation in the World's Student Christian Federation through the formation of the International Missionary Council to his presidency of the WCC, he was in the middle of the most significant developments of the twentieth century. He was followed by other Methodist participants, each of whom personified the church's eagerness to support the Ecumenical movement: Bishop James C. Baker, Ralph E. Diffendorfer, Eugene L. Smith, and Glora Wysner (first woman staff member on the IMC).

In the formative years of the other two major channels toward the WCC, the Faith and Order Movement (theology) and the Life and Work Movement (social witness), Methodists were less active, partly because of the isolationist spirit of the country and partly because of lack of enthusiasm for theological discussion, characteristic of Methodism in the twenties and early thirties. But some individuals, like Paul B. Kern, Ivan Lee Holt, Georgia Harkness, and Francis J. McConnell, were active.

Both Evangelicals and United Brethren participated in the major steps toward the World Council of Churches. The Evangelical Church was the first American denomination to join the body. Both groups were represented in the Missionary Conference of 1910, in the International Missionary Council, and in the various ecumenical conferences of the time. They were also active in the formation of both the Federal Council of Churches and the National Council. Furthermore, the African Methodist Episcopal Church, the African Methodist Episcopal Zion Church, and the Christian Methodist Episcopal Church were charter members of the WCC.

This involvement meant a fundamental change of direction for the Methodist family. For decades the tone of denominationalism in America had been rivalry and competition, sometimes bitter. Now there was a reconciliation, a mutual acceptance; but this change, as always, brought its own tensions. However, in the midst of ecumenical ventures, the various Methodist and related churches were still separate entities. What about ecumenical relations within the family? In some ways the efforts toward Methodist union seemed to run counter to ecumenical unity. The gathering together of the Methodist clan, nationally and internationally, conflicted at points with the broader concept of ecumenicity which broke down denominational barriers. To be specific, the unification of Methodism into a still larger denomination could be seen as reinforcing those very elements of pride and self-identity which threatened Christian unity. Especially equivocal was the role of the World Methodist Conference and the World Methodist Council. The decennial series of Ecumenical

Methodist conferences had begun in 1881, and the World Methodist Council became the permanent structure for the movement.[6] The question then became one of choice of direction: unity through global Methodist unification or unity through ecumenical blending of different traditions. Up to a point the two could move harmoniously in parallel channels. Beyond that point, were the two channels contradictory?

Family Mergers

In 1900 the Methodist family looked like this:

Methodist Episcopal	2,754,000
Methodist Episcopal, South	1,469,000
African Methodist Episcopal	688,000
African Methodist Episcopal Zion	536,000
Methodist Protestant	209,000
Colored Methodist Episcopal	205,000
Free Methodist	29,000
Congregational Methodist	21,000
Union American Methodist Episcopal	16,000
Wesleyan Methodist	15,000

At the turn of the century there were over 241,000 United Brethren and 166,000 Evangelicals. Their story is told in a later chapter.

After the unhappy schisms of 1830 and 1844, the story of efforts for reunion goes back to the conference at Cape May, New Jersey, August, 1876. After the coldness of separation had gone on for a score of years following the division of Episcopal Methodism, a few tentative contacts bore fruit as the general conferences authorized a formal meeting to discuss the possibility of reunion. At the outset the issue of status had to be clarified. The southern delegates immediately raised the principles on which Lovick Pierce had based his approach in 1848, "there is but one Episcopal Methodism in the United States" and both branches are integral parts of that original church. The northern delegates found it possible to agree in principle. The result was a clarification of status as follows: "Each of said Churches is a legitimate Branch of Episcopal Methodism in the United States, having a common origin in the Methodist Episcopal Church organized in 1784." [7]

[6] See Ivan Lee Holt and Elmer T. Clark, *The World Methodist Movement* (1956).
[7] Quoted in *HAM*, II, 667.

After the successful achievement of a basis for negotiation, the conference embarked upon a preliminary discussion of some very difficult problems, especially the question of church property. It certainly could not be said that all parts of both churches were at once caught up in a euphoria of brotherly love. Some influential Northerners insisted that the M.E. Church wasn't a branch of anything, but remained the main trunk. Some Southerners insisted that errors and insults of the past could not be wiped out by expressions of good will. Actually, nothing came of the conference immediately, but the foundations had been laid for more intensive negotiations later on.

Just before the end of the century, both churches constituted commissions on federation which, meeting together in Foundry Methodist Church in Washington 1898, became a joint commission. Some valuable areas of cooperation were developed, such as publication of a joint hymnal (1904), but federation was acknowledged to be an inadequate goal. In 1916 the Joint Commission on Federation was replaced by a Joint Commission on Unification. This time the gloves were off and issues were faced head-on. In four years a plan for unification was hammered out. Matters fought over were the powers and relations of the general conference and bishops, various plans for "jurisdictions," and, first and last both under and above the surface, race. There were northern radicals, liberals, moderates, and mediators, and southern moderates and conservatives. There were two Negro voices; Robert E. Jones, editor of the *Southwestern Advocate*, and I. (for Irvine) Garland Penn, field secretary of the Board of Education for Negroes. They were not left to speak alone. However, northern radicals and southern conservatives held such divergent views that possibilities for reunion seemed remote indeed. Yet, the negotiations brought out extremely complex relations and attitudes, leading ultimately to a plan of union which involved compromises on the three central issues: Powers of the general conference, plan for jurisdictions, and status of black members.[8]

The plan called for six white regional (jurisdictional) conferences and one regional conference for the black members. Each would elect its own bishops who would be confirmed by the general conference. Negroes were to be represented in the general conference by delegates making up to 5 percent of the total conference. Whenever the black regional conference (or foreign regional conferences) reached 400,000 membership, it could request the general conference to es-

---

[8] A tremendous source for history of Methodist reunion is the three-volume record of debates, *Joint Commission on Unification of the Methodist Episcopal Church, South, and the Methodist Episcopal Church* (1918). The plan is in III, 261-72.

tablish an associate general conference. There was a Judicial Council and provision for continued support of the Colored M.E. Church. The plan met with equivocal response by both North and South, neither of which was willing to buy the package. Continued work resulted in another plan which provided for one general conference and two regional conferences (M.E. and M.E.S.), each enjoying the powers of the general conference with the exception of those powers vested in it. The general conferences of both churches, meeting in 1924, strongly approved the plan. Although a majority of southern annual conferences approved, the vote failed to reach the necessary three-fourths. Both sides, for the time being, heaved a sigh of relief and marked time.

Two results of the effort were increased awareness and participation of lay people and youth. The latter kept the idea of union alive even though they lacked direct political power. The former were growing in strength. The heart of uncompromising opposition lay in the Southeast, together with the Northwest and Central Texas conferences. Another result was the experience of working together which involved the best leaders of both churches—men like Bishops Earl Cranston, William F. McDowell, Edgar Blake, and Edwin Holt Hughes for the North and Bishops Warren A. Candler, Edwin D. Mouzon, John N. Moore, Collins Denny, and many very able laymen.

One more attempt was necessary, carried through in the 1930s, before union was a reality. By that time the Methodist Protestant Church, which had abstained from the long series of discussions which concentrated on issues between the two Episcopal branches, returned to the conference table. In 1908 the general conferences of the M.E. Church and the Methodist Protestant Church were meeting at the same time. As a result of earlier discussions between laymen of the two churches in Baltimore, a delegation was sent from the M.E. general conference to express interest in negotiations for union with the Methodist Protestants. The positive response raised a challenge and a problem. Thomas H. Lewis, the Methodist Protestant spokesman, in appealing for union, begged that the two branches of Episcopal Methodism might merge in order that his people would not face a painful decision: "Do not force us to separate from each other in order that we may rejoin the family. We want to unite with a united home." Hence, in 1910 there was held in Baltimore a meeting of the Joint Commission on Federation with the Commission of Nine of the Methodist Protestant Church. Out of these meetings came the Chattanooga Report, which laid a basis for future union plans for the three churches. But, since the immediate problem concerned chiefly

Chapter 32
Denominational Development

That impalpable unease expressed by an *Advocate* editor at the turn of the century was echoed in the episcopal address of 1912: "Ancient institutions are crumbling, parties and policies are in chaotic strife, and to many people all creeds seem to be dissolving in the crucible of this iconoclastic age." The shock of World War I brought the nineteenth century to a firm and irrevocable close. It was indeed a new world, distressed by war, depression, and what appeared to be a moral chaos; but it was also a heady world, blessed with radios, automobiles, movies, and that pearl of great price, the mimeograph machine. It was the age of the mechanized factory and the production line. It was the age of rural electrification (1935). It would become the age of television and of atomic power.

Inevitably, the churches were affected by these diverse influences. We turn to deal briefly with the various strands of Methodism in the twentieth century, carrying the story of the three contributory roots of the Methodist Church down to 1939 and the rest to the present.

The Methodist Episcopal Church

Since much that is said about the M. E. Church applies as well to the other two denominations involved in the merger of 1939, this section is longer and more inclusive. Edwin Holt Hughes, one of the prime figures of the time, mentioned in his autobiography some of his colorful contemporaries: Stephen Merrill and Charles W. Smith, "best ecclesiastical lawyers"; Robert McIntyre, "ornate and melodious"; William A. Quayle, "most scintillating"; "the largest in size, Bishop Peck, his name should have stood for a larger measure"; Naphtali Luccock, "wittiest"; and William F. McDowell, "most distinctive in manner and speech."

Some of these men were outstanding among the northern bishops. Much of their stature, however, derived from their personal qualities of leadership rather than from the power of the office. The episcopal address of 1912 recognized two prime characteristics of the office: it was "non-prelatical," by which was meant not hierarchical, not a third

363

order, and not in any formal succession; and it was "Church-wide . . . connectionally itinerant." [1] A crucial issue was resolved in 1884 when James M. Buckley succeeded in obtaining a rule which, although it permitted the general conference to invite a bishop to speak in its sessions, provided that the bishops had no right to demand the floor. A further diminution of the office came with the establishment of missionary bishops, whose authority was geographically limited. The assignment of episcopal residences in 1916 led to the delineation of the area over which each bishop would exercise his office as president of annual conferences. He would still retain many activities as general superintendent in the whole church. Episcopacy in the southern church followed somewhat different lines.

As to the traveling ministry, the history of the time limit is instructive. In brief, it went through successive extensions (M.E.: three years in 1864, five years in 1888, finally removed; M.E.S.: four years in 1866, plus numerous exceptions). District superintendents (presiding elders in the South) were limited to six-year terms. The bishops in their address of 1912 spoke nostalgically about the old itinerant ideal, which was likened to the eagle and a military company. "A militant company compactly organized will win a dozen victories while a town-meeting is wrangling about the choice of a leader." Sensitive to criticism, the bishops made a point of showing that the itineracy was "essentially democratic." But the times were changing. James A. Hensey wrote *The Itinerancy, Its Power and Peril*, published in 1918. The ideal is still valid, he argued, even though more settled pastorates have their advantages. Inevitably, the old ideal declined as the new century brought more complex responsibilities for the minister. Too frequent changes of appointment could disrupt long-range planning.

At the General Conference of 1872 a constitutional change was made which permitted lay membership in the general conference. As to their role in the annual conference, the southern church again led, beginning in 1866 and completing equal representation in 1926. This was not done in the North until 1932. On the other hand, the northern church extended lay rights to women in 1900, a move not made in the South until 1922.

Church architecture and forms of worship reflected the changing times. The trend everywhere was toward more formal structures. More substantial Victorian and Gothic buildings made possible a more complex order of worship. An order of public worship was adopted in the M. E. Church in 1896 which was printed in the front of the hymnal. Some ordering of worship had been printed in the

[1] *JGC*, 1912, 184.

southern hymnal since 1880. When the two branches brought out a joint hymnal in 1905, the carefully designed order of worship had a greater impact and called forth considerable criticism by defenders of the free style. The church has never lacked members who fret over the suppression of spontaneity. Nevertheless, the trend was heavily in the direction of dignified order, both in liturgy and music. The episcopal address at the General Conference of 1928, which acted to set up a commission on the revision of the hymnal and psalter, hoped that Methodist forms of worship would avoid equally bad extremes: "that perversion of liberty which makes of God's house a common meeting place," and "that soulless formality which exalts ritual at the expense of life." [2] Here, as elsewhere, Methodists were following the middle way. The final step before unification was the publication of a new joint hymnal by the three branches in 1935. The most obvious shift was the replacement of "O for a Thousand Tongues to Sing" by "Holy, Holy, Holy" as the first hymn. Only Methodists who knew the Wesleyan tradition and the long history of the former tune would grasp the significance. The main importance of the new hymnal was as an advance symbol of the coming union of the three branches and the continuation of the principle of order in worship. During the same years in all three churches standards of preaching changed, moving away from the style of the free evangelists, who were now frowned on, toward better-structured sermons which were supposed to reflect the higher standards set by seminary homiletics. There was still plenty of room, however, for the long-acclaimed scintillating sermonizing by nationally famous Methodist preachers. In the North the names of Albert E. Day, Lynn Harold Hough, Halford Luccock, Merton S. Rice, Roy L. Smith, and Ernest Fremont Tittle are illustrative.

In all three churches, work with youth proceeded at various levels. After the formation of the Epworth League in 1889, young people had an organization of their own in which to express their concerns. The Methodist Youth Fellowship in high school groups and Wesley Foundations at the college level were outgrowths in the twentieth century. The first Wesley Foundation was organized at the University of Illinois in 1913 under leadership of James C. Baker. One indication of increasing activity by youth was the action of the Methodist Young People's Convention in Memphis in 1926, when four thousand young delegates demanded the continuation of efforts for unification of Methodist denominations. A National Council of Methodist Youth was set up in 1934.

[2] *JGC,* 1928, 167.

In the twentieth century the various missionary organizations founded and carried on by women in the three branches of Methodism continued to grow. Many enterprises in the fields of foreign missions were developed by the woman's foreign missionary societies of the three churches. In the United States the woman's home missionary societies carried on extensive projects in education among black people and other minorities including poor Appalachian whites, in settlement houses in cities, and in hospitals. An outstanding black educator was Mary McLeond Bethune, for thirty years president of Bethune-Cookman College.

During World War I in the Midwest, several local groups of Methodist women engaged in business were organized. Encouraged by leaders in the W.F.M.S. and the W.H.M.S., a small group met in the First Methodist Church, Evanston, Illinois, in 1921 to form the Wesleyan Service Guild.[3] It was designed from the beginning to bring together working women who could not easily fit into the patterns of the missionary societies. Among the early leaders were Marion Lela Norris and Helen Wesp. Unwilling to identify exclusively with either foreign or home organizations, the Wesleyan Service Guild grew apace as a separate but related agency and by 1924 was recognized as a department in each of the other two societies. It thus foreshadowed the union achieved in the Woman's Society of Christian Service after 1939. In 1925 there were guilds in seventeen states supporting a variety of foreign and home projects. By 1940 there were 417 guilds with 6,520 members. Lela Norris continued as volunteer secretary until 1929. Only in 1935 was there provision for a paid secretary, a position first held by Marian Thayer.

Most of the story of Methodist activity during the postwar period can best be described in connection with programs for social reform, but three episodes belong in this general account. The 1920s have been described variously as "golden," "an age of normalcy," and "the flapper era." It was a time of disinterest in the issues which had clamored so loudly earlier—war, international government, missionary service. It was also the time of the Ku Klux Klan, a disreputable organization which arose from nativist sources. For a few years its success among various levels of society was so great that some Methodists were among the many who adhered. It was especially strong in Indiana, which was Methodist country. There is no justification, however, to see any relationship, let alone any cause and effect

---

[3] Sources on the Guild are scarce. See Ruth E. Meeker, *Six Decades of Service, 1880–1940, A History of the Woman's Home Missionary Society* (1969), and Florence L. Norwood, "Wesleyan Service Guild," mimeo privately distributed (1972).

connection. All of the church papers denounced the organization and its methods. National Methodist bodies condemned it. Many outstanding leaders spoke out against it, sometimes at personal peril. One bishop called it "Nordic Nonsense." Ministers in difficult local situations fought it as best they could, although some joined.

The election of 1928 was one of those rare political events which directly involved the church. Through the active campaigning of Bishop James Cannon of the M. E. Church, South, the Methodist forces were lined up openly against the "wet" candidacy of Alfred E. Smith. This was part of the struggle over prohibition.

Soon the country was plunged into the deepest economic depression it had experienced. The Great Depression of the 1930s seared the lives of millions of Americans, and threw most of the churches into severe financial crises. Membership in the three Methodist denominations went down over 15 percent in 1936 from that of a decade earlier. General funds were depleted, missions suffered, and ministers lost salaries—along with everyone else. The experience set churchmen thinking about the social implications of economic disaster and the contradictions of wealth and poverty. But that is another story for a later chapter. By the later 1930s, in time for unification, the churches and most of their members were on the way to recovery.

It would be wearisome to recount over again the many lines of development of the various arms and agencies of the church. Most of them continued to serve effectively and to change (as much as institutions may reasonably be expected to change) with the times. Take the *Advocates,* for instance. The liveliest description of their condition came with the introduction to readers of a "new dress" for the *Northwestern Christian Advocate* in 1925:

> The *Advocate* of New York will continue to be genial but official; it will never by any chance be frivolous, except in "Wise and Otherwise," and, even there, "where origin is known, credit will be given."
>
> Our brother of Cincinnati will still be oracularly Websterian; he of Kansas City will keep on showing, by the patient midnight oil, that every question has two sides; Portland will not desist from puncturing outsize bubbles; San Francisco will be grave and sensible; and all the others will perform as aforetime, "each in his separate star." Even THE NORTHWESTERN will be distinguishable, to the wary eye, from its fellows in the squad.
>
> As for the "semi-officials," some will wear all the uniform, and some will dress to suit themselves. But, in any guise, nobody would long confuse Detroit with Washington, or Pittsburgh with Boston.[4]

[4] *NWCA,* 73 (1925): 28.

The Methodist Episcopal Church, South

In 1918 a southern Methodist warned his fellows, "Hands off, brethren! Don't touch the ark, or try to turn over the cart." This was a call to keep the old ways secure and to resist change. Many southern Methodists heeded that warning; but increasingly, the forces of change were growing through the 1920s and 1930s. At last the M. E. Church, South, joined the twentieth century.[5] After World War I the southern branch, like the other churches, had to catch its breath and begin to adjust to a new world. The General Conference of 1918 elected no less than six new bishops, most of whom stood closer to the progressive side than their older fellow bishops. More open to change was Bishop John M. Moore, who would play so crucial a role in the negotiations for union with the other two branches of mainline Methodism. Edwin Holt Hughes of the northern church remembered some of the old southern bishops in his autobiography. There were Elijah E. Hoss, "sparkling" especially when angry; John J. Tigert III, "massive" (one of the younger leaders who died suddenly in 1906); Walter R. Lambuth, "glorious gentle soul"; Eugene R. Hendrix, "courtly gentleman"; Warren A. Candler, "drawling wit"; and Charles B. Galloway, "unassuming majesty."

Generally speaking, the issues were connected either directly or indirectly to the authority of the bishops. Conservatives tended to support the episcopal interests, whether the change proposed had to do with the control of the Board of Missions, the Vanderbilt affair, unification, lay representation in the annual conference, assignment of bishops, a judicial council, or even episcopal retirement age. On some matters the southern church could not quite make up its mind. It was unwilling to go very far in developing an organization for social concerns, yet it gave adherence to the Social Creed of the Federal Council of Churches. The general conference once voted to change "holy catholic church" in the Apostles' Creed to "Christ's holy church," but the bishops vetoed it.

The conservative trend is illustrated by the General Conference of 1922. The bishops found several objections to a proposal to assign a bishop to an area for four years. Moreover, they did not like the idea of continuing ministers in the same appointment more than four years. "It is a fact altogether worthy of note that we are still an itinerant Church. . . . There is in these perturbed and restless times

[5] Such in essence is the thesis of Robert Watson Sledge in his dissertation, entitled in revised form, "Hands off the Ark: The Struggle for Change in the Methodist Episcopal Church, South, 1914–1939" (Univ. of Texas, 1972). It is an excellent source for the period and received the Jesse Lee Prize for 1972.

much talk about making the Church more democratic. We are constrained to believe that this talk does not come primarily from our own people, but that it is of alien origin." [6] Except for the itinerant structure, the bishops said defensively, the church "is at other points vastly more democratic" than the government. The bishops did speak out for justice under law for the black man and against lynchings.

The issue of revision of episcopacy went on until 1927, when the progressive bishops, against the opposition of Candler, won a plan for the rotation of the chairmanship and, against the opposition of Denny, a four-year secretarial term. They also elected a new secretary, John M. Moore.

Southern Methodism also was caught up in the furor over the K.K.K. Because the prevailing social system affected churches and society alike, numbers of Methodists joined the organization. On the other hand, the leadership of southern Methodism took a stand against it. Many ministers of all denominations, especially those serving isolated rural places, were active in the Klan. This was not true of Virginia and North Carolina, but it was certainly true of Oklahoma, where both ministers and laymen were heavily involved. The argument in favor of such an alignment was that both church and Klan were trying to make society moral, and, since the church was supposed to stay out of politics, the Klan could act more directly. The bishops and the *Advocates* stood strongly against this involvement.

The Great Depression did not spare any section of the country. The bellwether of missionary giving is revealing: 1927 was a high point with contributions of $1,618,000; 1932 was a low point with $438,000. After 1932 giving increased, but it was long before the 1927 record was matched. The church could support in 1935 just half the number of missionaries ten years earlier.

Perhaps the trials of the Depression helped loosen things. The general conferences of 1930 and 1934 approved several changes in the direction of reform. Term episcopacy was proposed, but without success, both years. A Judicial Council was set up to remove some constitutional authority from the bishops, and they lost the responsibility for choosing the books for the course of study. These changes were symptomatic of the new influence of the progressives. Some of the church papers had been urging such reforms more strongly.[7] In the 1930s, then, the M. E. Church, South, went through a period of adjustment which made the process of unification considerably easier.

During the decades of the twentieth century before unification, the

[6] *JGC*, MEC,S (1922), 349, 350.
[7] See editorial in *MQRS*, 78 (1929): 296-306.

Methodist Protestant Church continued a process of slow growth which made it increasingly difficult for the denomination to continue as a separate church. Although it had remained faithful to the princi- ✳ ples which had led to separation in 1830, many of the issues were no longer very important simply because the larger Methodist Episcopal organizations had come around in one way or another to the position of the smaller body. This was especially true in the matter of lay representation. On the one hand, bishops had turned out not so tyrannical as once feared; and on the other, the Methodist Protestants had made their presidential office a full-time one in 1920. J. C. Broomfield, a leading minister and later bishop in the united church, put it succinctly: "Because of the way in which Episcopal Methodism is democratizing its episcopacy, and because of the way in which our folks are autocratizing the presidency, and the executive committee of its General Conference, the question of the episcopacy is increasingly ceasing to be an issue with us." [8] Thus, this little church was in position to pick up the pieces of the movement for unification which had been sidetracked by the failure of the two larger bodies in the 1920s. In 1930 Methodist Protestants made the first move toward the final and successful drive.

Black Methodism

Booker T. Washington wrote *Up From Slavery* in 1895. William E. B. Du Bois wrote *Souls of Black Folk* in 1903. The National Association for the Advancement of Colored People was founded in 1910. The National Urban League was founded in 1911. The cultural renais- sance of black people in America belongs to the time of Langston Hughes and Countee Cullen in the 1920s. This was followed by the rediscovery of black history in the 1940s (Richard Wright, Gunnar Myrdal, John Hope Franklin). At the same time came the Congress of Racial Equality and Student Nonviolent Coordinating Committee. Then came the definitive decision of the Supreme Court on educa- tional segregation. This sequence of events is a capsule of the de- velopment of an important racial minority in the United States. This is the latest chapter of a story that had begun with two hundred years of slavery. It is the backdrop for everything that happened in the Negro churches in modern times. [9]

[8] Quoted in *HAM*, III, 442.
[9] Among the many excellent sources on the experience of black people in the twentieth century are E. Franklin Frazier, *The Negro in the United States* (1957); Charles Flint Kellogg, *NAACP, A History of the National Association for the Advancement of Colored People* (1967); John Hope Franklin and Isidore Starr, *The Negro in Twentieth Century America* (1967); and C. Vann Woodward, *The Strange Career of Jim Crow* (1955).

The fundamental conflict between Booker T. Washington and W. E. B. Du Bois is part of another story, but it affected the development of black religion and the role of the black churches. When in 1895 Washington delivered an address in Atlanta in which he said, "No race can prosper till it learns that there is as much dignity in tilling a field as in writing a poem," and spoke of social equality of the races as "the extremest folly"; Du Bois denounced such an approach as "the Atlanta Compromise." Nevertheless, both men stood ultimately on the same ground. Their differences were matters of timing and tactics.[10] While these stirrings were going on in the black communities, the social processes in the country at large were moving from the older racial relations rooted in Reconstruction and the recovery of the South to a new level, popularly described as Jim Crow. The usable but precarious racial set-up of the old South where white and black had worked out a day-to-day basis of common life gave way to increasingly rigid segregation, spelled out in terms of Jim Crow laws which formerly had not been necessary. It is significant that South Carolina, the sturdiest citadel of the old ways, was the last state to go for Jim Crow segregation.[11]

Among the founders of the NAACP were two black Methodist ministers, Bishop Alexander Walters of the A. M. E. Z. Church and William H. Brooks of the M. E. Church. Throughout the era the churches were involved in the changes coursing through the black communities. Sometimes the voices were those of the past, as we hear from Bishop Evans Tyree of the A. M. E. Church: "We belong to a class of people that have been singing a long time: 'You may have all the world, give me Jesus Christ.'" [12] He did think that sometimes Negroes had gone too far in that direction! Among the black denominations the Baptists were already largest and growing fast. Methodists came next as a large family in which the African Methodist Episcopal Church was the largest, followed by the A. M. E. Z. and the C. M. E. Churches. The A. M. E. were strong in both the South and North. The A. M. E. Z. were proportionately stronger in the South. The C. M. E. had almost all of their membership in the South. Many people were members of the M. E. Church, organized into annual conferences which, although originally mixed, had become almost entirely black. These churches in the twentieth century can be defined almost as a fifth—or sixth—form of religion, along with Judaism, Roman Catholicism, Eastern Orthodoxy, "secularism" of

[10] Franklin and Starr, *The Negro*, 86, 90-91.
[11] Woodward, *The Strange Career*, 67.
[12] *Third Ecumenical Methodist Conference* (1901), 230.

various kinds, and white Protestantism. In many ways Negro churches constituted a thoroughly different type of religious expression.[13]

The black church and the black minister played a unique role in the life of the black communities.

> The church was the first community or public organization that the Negro actually owned and completely controlled. And it is possibly true to this day that the Negro church is the most thoroughly owned and controlled public institution of the race. Nothing can compare with this ownership and control except ownership of the home and possibly control of the Negro Lodge. It is to be doubted whether Negro control is as complete in any other area of Negro life, except these two, as it is in the church.[14]

Their church was "home" to the black person in a very special sense. They have found a larger and more significant share of their lives in their churches; hence, the minister has filled a larger place in their communities. One need only mention two prominent Baptists, Adam Clayton Powell and Martin Luther King, personally quite different but both writ large in the experience of their race.

The Methodist churches with predominantly (or totally) black membership reflect this function of black Christianity. To a great extent it is also true of the membership in the M. E. Church. We have already seen how they were involved in the negotiations which eventually led to merger in 1939. The two black delegates, I. Garland Penn and Robert E. Jones, were a very small minority in these discussions; but they had sympathetic support from the liberal northern delegates, and at least a neutral willingness to listen from the moderate southern delegates. Both these men were political realists and accepted, though under protest in principle, the various compromises which opened the way to a plan for unification. They symbolize the continuing willingness of black members of the M. E. Church to stay in even at considerable cost to themselves.

Although two Liberians had been elected bishop for Liberia and an American Negro elected missionary bishop earlier, the first full bishops of black race were Matthew W. Clair, Sr. and Robert E. Jones, both elected in 1920, the one from a pastorate in Washington, D. C. and the other from the editorship of the *Southwestern Christian Advocate*. In 1936 Alexander Preston Shaw, another *Southwestern* editor, became bishop. Although these bishops usually presided over

---

[13] See Joseph R. Washington, Jr., *Black Religion* (1964), and Robert Handy in Jerald C. Brauer, ed., *Reinterpretation in American Church History* (1968), 96-97 (quoting Gerhard Lenski, *The Religious Factor* (1961), 20, 36).

[14] Benjamin E. Mays and Joseph Nicholson, *The Negro's Church* (1933), 279.

the black annual conferences, they were traveling general superintendents in the full sense and participated in the total activity of the church. That these men were quite capable of speaking out on race relations is shown in an address by Bishop Jones before the General Conference of 1924 (in the middle of the Ku Klux Klan fury):

> Your cry of white supremacy gives us no concern. I want to point out to you that the Negro has waked up. It is a matter of impossibility to keep us where we once were. You white men would never stand for a moment what we go through. We get along remarkably well. Thank God for the sweet brotherly communion we have had during this Conference. . . . You talk about Anglo-Saxon supremacy over the black man. To make the race worth while we must have the same show to make the thing a race.[15]

There were nineteen black conferences in the M. E. Church before 1939. They generally followed the pattern of the church at large in procedures and concerns. For example, they, like the white conferences, were more concerned about temperance and sabbath observance than about fundamental problems of race relations and the industrial order. They did devote some effort to fighting social abuses like lynching. These were the conferences, ministers, and people who constituted the Central Jurisdiction in the union of 1939.

The African and C. M. E. Churches

When Booker T. Washington addressed the A. M. E. General Conference in 1912, he emphasized the rural character of black Americans, 82 percent of whom lived in the country and small villages. He revealed his rural bias in warning against migration to the cities.[16] In this he was trying to stand against yet another irresistible tide of history. Within a generation the black man would migrate in huge numbers from the rural South to the industrial North. His churches went with him.

By mid-century this largest of the black Methodist bodies had about 1,166,000 members. The office of class leader continued long after it had disappeared from the white churches, and the leader continued to carry financial responsibilities for contributions from his class. There were thirteen episcopal districts to which the bishops were assigned. They met in a Bishops' Council which administered the affairs of the church between general conferences. There was a Judi-

[15] *NWCA*, 72 (1924): 543.
[16] John T. Jenifer, *Centennial Retrospect History* (1916), 245.

cial Council composed of three bishops, three elders, and three laymen. Overseas work was extensive enough to be organized into five districts. There was a Woman's Missionary Society with head-quarters in Washington, D.C.

Something like the conflict in southern Methodism over the author-ity of the bishops led to a series of struggles in the 1920s and 1930s, some of which reached the secular courts. There was considerable opposition to the continuation of the same bishop in the same district over a long period of time. Some of the bishops were brought to trial before the general conference and expelled from office.

The A. M. E. Church has strongly supported higher education for Negroes and has maintained several colleges and universities of excel-lent quality. Its Turner School of Theology has been one of the participants (along with C. M. E., Methodist, and Baptist schools) in the Interdenominational Theological Center in Atlanta. The church's periodicals include the *Christian Recorder, Voice of Missions, Woman's Missionary Recorder,* and the *A. M. E. Review.*

The African Methodist Episcopal Zion Church is smaller, but still impressive with 780,000 members in 1960. The figure for 1970 was 940,000. In most respects the structure and activity of Zion is identical with that of Bethel (A. M. E.). The strongest school is Livingstone College in Salisbury, North Carolina. The church has been especially involved in missionary work in Liberia and Ghana (Gold Coast, inde-pendent since 1957). A major contribution to the development of the latter was made by James E. K. Aggrey, who early in the twentieth century was educated in the United States and later returned to Africa. The Woman's Home and Foreign Missionary Society has been especially effective in support of the overseas program. The periodicals include the weekly *Star of Zion, Missionary Seer,* and *Quarterly Review.*

In 1954 the Colored Methodist Episcopal Church changed its name to Christian Methodist Episcopal Church. From the beginning in 1870 this denomination has differed in several respects from the African churches, although polity is in general the same. At mid-century there were almost 400,000 members. Its work has been outstanding in the field of higher education, beginning with Lane College, founded in 1882 in Jackson, Tennessee. Others are Paine College in Augusta, Georgia (supported in part by the M. E. Church, South, and its successors), Miles College, Mississippi Industrial, and Texas College. The main church paper is the *Christian Index,* begun in 1868, two years before the formation of the denomination. The friendly relations with the southern white church which attended the organization of the C. M. E. Church have continued to the present.

Several attempts have been made to bring the three main black Methodist bodies together.[17] Three plans for union between the two African churches, in 1864, 1885, and 1892, failed largely over differences in the office of bishop and the role of lay persons. A tri-council of bishops, representing the three denominations, met in the early twentieth century and proposed the "Birmingham Plan" for union, which also failed, partly because it left so many features to be worked out after union. In April, 1965, the bishops of the three churches met in St. Louis to seek paths for union. The hope was expressed that a plan might be implemented in the early 1970s. Commissions got to work soon thereafter, but results have been slow in coming. At the same time discussions were continuing with a view to union of these churches with The United Methodist Church, and all three have been actively engaged in the Consultation on Church Union.

Other Methodist Bodies

In 1910 the Genesee Conference of the M. E. Church, which had expelled Benjamin Titus Roberts fifty years before and thus set in motion the events which resulted in organization of the Free Methodist Church, reversed its action and validated and returned the canceled credentials of all those who had been expelled. The principles which had been defined at the beginning—free pews, freedom from ecclesiastical control, freedom from sin, and free worship—were maintained in principle and largely in fact. Opposition to choirs and musical instruments weakened around mid-century, but the church has maintained a very conservative stance on science, morals, and the Bible. It has continued the emphasis on tithing by members with much success. Episcopal authority is limited by four-year terms. The membership in 1960 was a total of fifty-seven thousand, including eight thousand preparatory members and four thousand youth members. The figure for 1970 was sixty-five thousand. Church papers include the *Free Methodist, Missionary Tidings,* and *Sunday School Journal.* A noteworthy radio program entitled "Light and Life Hour" was started in 1943. The Light and Life Press puts out religious literature from Winona Lake, Indiana. Although this denomination has many characteristics of the small sect and has been reluctant to engage in many ecumenical activities, it has also sought not to isolate itself from activities in which common Christian witness would be appropriate. Hence, it has been a participant in the National Associa-

[17] See Roy W. Trueblood, "Union Negotiations Between Black Methodists in America," *MH,* 8 (July, 1970): 18-29.

tion of Evangelicals and the World (formerly Ecumenical) Methodist conferences.

Another small group which continued into the twentieth century is the Wesleyan Methodist Church of America. Until 1891 it had symbolized its opposition to typical denominational structure by retaining the name Wesleyan Methodist Connection. One of the central principles has been loyalty to the standards of John Wesley, especially to the doctrine of Christian perfection. It was a holiness church long before the holiness movement, and has continued to emphasize the doctrine. In 1960 there were forty-four thousand members including four thousand "associate" and four thousand youth. Periodicals were the *Wesleyan Methodist, Wesleyan Missionary,* and *Wesleyan Youth.* An attempt to unite with the Free Methodists was strongly rejected in 1955. In 1959 a move to unite with the Pilgrim Holiness Church barely failed to receive the necessary two-thirds majority; but in 1968 the union was achieved under the name Wesleyan Church, with eighty-four thousand members in 1970.

Methodism has continued to spawn a number of very small sects whose concerns over authority or doctrine or style of ministry have led them to separate from the parent bodies. Frequently these small groups have themselves experienced further divisions. Some persist, but others are quite ephemeral.

The Centenary and World Missions

The crowning achievement (and as it turned out the swan song) of the missionary movement of nineteenth-century Methodism was the Centenary Campaign of 1919 in recognition of one hundred years of the Missionary Society.[18] The idea came from the northern church; before long the plan was being developed by a joint centenary commission which included representatives of the southern church. A central feature was a highly organized financial campaign for an ambitious postwar expansion on all fronts. Some of the promotional techniques of the Liberty Loan campaigns of World War I were employed, and for the first time modern advertising was freely used. The culmination was the great centenary celebration held in Columbus, Ohio in the summer of 1919. The whole operation was inevitably tied in with the forces unleashed in World War I. It was at once a sort of religious expression of democratic devotion and a celebration of the end of the war. Dan Brummitt wrote of it: "This *is* part of the

[18] See John Lankford, "Methodism 'Over the Top': The Joint Centenary Movement, 1917–1925," *MH,* 2 (Oct., 1963): 27-37. An official account in typescript with many photographs is in Garrett Theological Seminary.

main business of the hour. It is linked up with the whole defense of democracy and the lifting up of democracy." [19] There was a great deal of talk about "open doors" and "overwhelming needs." With 100,000 "Minute Men" enthusiastically engaged in building up support, both northern and southern churches exceeded their goals: $113,741,455 and $35,787,338 respectively, in the form largely of subscriptions or pledges.

There was cause, then, for a victory party—the centenary celebration held in Columbus in June and July. Oh, what a grand display it was! The day of "world's fairs" had arrived. Some persons drove their newfangled autos all the way from New England, Florida, and Oklahoma—no mean achievement in those days. Attendance totaled over one million.

Other denominations were involved in postwar campaigns similar to the Methodist centenary. When they were all over, the churches discovered that the euphoria of peace and democracy, to say nothing of missionary zeal, had somehow evaporated. Just as idealistic Woodrow Wilson was succeeded by earthy Warren G. Harding, so wartime excitement was followed by the era of normalcy and isolation, the years of the flapper and the K. K. K. Already by the fall of 1919 financial receipts were in arrears. The Nashville *Christian Advocate* ran a full-page ad which insisted that "Methodism will not fall short of her appointed task. The Church that promised more than she was asked will pay more than she promised." Wishful thinking. A year later the northern Board of Foreign Missions and the Board of Home Missions and Church Extension stated baldly that, unless the decline were reversed, appropriations for 1922 would have to be reduced from 10 to 25 percent. An "I Will Maintain" drive accomplished little. By the mid-twenties both churches were ready to wind up the remnants with what they could save in partial payment of pledges. When it was over, about 70 percent of the pledges were paid, an outcome not at all bad considering the postwar slump and cultural myopia of the times. One useful result was the creation of the World Service Commission in 1924. Undeniably, however, there were unhappy psychological effects when such high hopes of a brave new world were dashed. The Great Depression was still to come. No wonder there was a religious depression in the 1920s and 1930s!

Robert T. Handy has spoken of the religious depression which afflicted American life between the two world wars. The failure of the centenary campaign was symptomatic of generalized illness. The Depression of the 1930s was a worldwide economic affliction of which it

[19] *CA*, 93 (1918): 433.

might be said only the poorest nations escaped because they didn't know the difference. It was a sad time for everyone, including those who placed high hopes in the vow of the churches to evangelize the world in a generation. Retreat was general on all fronts. In the face of open doors and unexcelled opportunities, the missionary forces seemed to be moving backward rather than forward. Methodism, along with other denominational families, was in the grip of forces beyond its power to measure, let alone control. Only in the later thirties did signs of recovery from the financial debacle appear.

At the same time some of the open doors eased—or slammed —shut. China was already in turmoil. Europe was caught in the forces of a new kind of power—totalitarianism, in all its malign variations in Russia, Italy, and Germany. The huge Russian Orthodox Church suffered major catastrophe in the Russian Revolution. The homeland of Roman Catholicism was captured by Mussolini's Fascism. In 1933 the National Socialists under Adolf Hitler succeeded in grasping control of the German government. In the Far East, a militant Japanese imperialism grew apace. The age of the goose step and hard heel had arrived. As authoritarian systems appeared to gain strength, Western democracies seemed to decline. Certainly the day of expansionist colonialism by the great powers of the West was over. Henceforth, if the cross were to advance, it would have to do without the sword.

As Christendom perceptibly lost its grasp on world culture, non-Christian religions, especially Islam and Buddhism, experienced a resurgence. In many parts of the world Christianity would have to deal with adherents of other faiths on a basis of equality. This did not mean that all religions were necessarily of equal worth, but that each could claim an equal right to maintain itself and offer its own interpretation of the meaning of life. This religious resurgence was part of a general cultural revival, as new nations strove to discover their own identity in terms of their own history and tradition. No longer would Western norms be accepted unquestioningly as suitable for all people everywhere. It now became a question of how the Christian faith might be presented in a way appropriate to persons of non-Western culture. What is the *essence* of the Gospel? This meant that native leadership would become more and more important. If a missionary enterprise was not developing leaders among the people it sought to bring into the Christian fold, it was failing in its first obligation. India is a case in point. Africa is another.

On top of these many challenges came the fearful test of World War II. For eight years (the war began in China in 1937), the world was caught in another of those demonic conflicts typical of the century of stress and change. In many areas Christian work had to be deferred or abandoned. Once again, religious forces were lined up politically and militarily on opposite sides.

The response of Methodism to these diverse challenges was manifold. The variety and multiplicity of postwar needs brought the Advance for Christ Program of 1948 and following years. This program sought to make possible more direct action in specific areas of need as it arose and changed. "Advance Specials" were designated over and beyond the standard continuing programs under World Service. By 1960 these Advance Specials amounted to more than half of the total income for world missions. In 1952 the Division of Foreign Missions was renamed the Division of World Missions—a first step in recognition that mission is always a two-way affair. The Board of Missions was set up under three major divisions: World, National, and Woman's Division of Christian Service. The last represented the autonomous work of the former Woman's Foreign and Woman's Home Missionary societies, which had come into being partly in response to the tendency of the Missionary Society to follow male domination. Stalwartly, the women insisted that any reorganization of the board should preserve the integrity of the program administered through women's organizations. Top-level consultation provided for gearing in of the three more or less autonomous programs of the three main divisions.

During the 1950s the work of all three divisions grew strongly. A progress report in *World Outlook* in 1959 was able to post significant growth almost everywhere.[20] Since the three Methodist denominations had united their mission work, the figures were all impressive:

	Missionaries	National Preachers	Members
Africa	354	590	83,703
Europe & N. Africa	47	642	116,667
Latin America	354	514	92,001
East Asia	234	3,574	214,004
Southern Asia	279	896	193,464
Southeast Asia & China	209	704*	186,713**

*Excluding mainland China's 500.
**Including mainland China, about half the total.

The report for national missions reflected the adjustments to ever-

[20] *World Outlook*, 49 (Apr., 1959): 169-74.

changing needs and challenges, especially in the burgeoning cities. Among the special fields were activities with minorities, especially Negroes, Spanish-speaking communities, and Indians. Mountain missions, town and country projects, and urban work all were expanding. Through all activity, both world and national, the Women's Division played a major, almost crucial role. The Section of Home Missions was divided into three departments, Town and Country, Urban, and Goodwill Industries (which in 1960 had centers in 141 cities). There was also a new Department of Research and Survey to coordinate study projects for the missions.

Chapter 33
New Liberalism and New Reformation

The intellectual battles of the nineteenth century, although they had already been well gnawed over, continued to agitate the Christian world well into the next century. Rationalism of the earlier times had become the scepticism and materialism of modern times, eating away at the traditional foundations of faith. Roaring along like tidal waves came philosophical scepticism, scientism, Marxism, Darwinism, one after the other, until even the firmest roots bade fair to lose their hold. Only the most resilient faith and the most lively theology could hope to survive and thrive in such seas. At the end of the nineteenth century, two major forms of response took shape: theological liberalism and biblical fundamentalism. The early decades of the twentieth century, at least in Protestant circles, were dominated by this developing controversy between the two responses. Although many issues were involved, the central problem was that of religious authority. How, in this day and age, can one *know* the truth?

One issue was the age of the earth, raised by the new science of geology, which appeared to contradict the biblical record of Genesis. Another issue was the process of creation, raised by the new science of biology, especially by Charles Darwin. How can the biological process of the origin of life be reconciled with the biblical account of creation, of humanity made in the image of God? Another issue was raised by the new history which discounted the design of divine Providence. History, some said, is the product of universal laws which are anything but providential. Perennial class struggle is leading inevitably to the great revolution, the dictatorship of the proletariat, and the classless society—here on a materialistic earth, not in a nonexistent spiritual heaven. Still others concluded that nothing whatever has any meaning; all is vanity or is of a purely personal, "existential" significance. In the face of these buffetings, the great question remained: What is the proper Christian response? The theological liberals took one path, the fundamentalists another. Both were seeking a viable form of Christian witness, but they were going in opposite directions.

Liberalism versus Fundamentalism

John A. Faulkner, a northern Methodist historian, looking back in his book, *Modernism and the Christian Faith* (1921), found the theological pot boiling in "that seething decade 1883–93, when all the doctrines of Christianity were put in the crucible." After a long list of controversies, he expressed the judgment that a central issue was the inspiration of the Bible. Is it, or is it not, the Word of God? And what does that mean? He suggested his own answer in the title of chapter ten: "Ritschl or Wesley?" As between the modernist stance represented by liberal German theology and the traditional position of the past, he would opt for Wesley. "It was Schleiermacher who saved Germany from infidelity, but in doing that he threw overboard so much that what was left was hardly worth saving." [1] He considered Ritschl chiefly responsible for drawing Methodism away from Wesley in an enormous "sea-change," common to all Protestantism.

John J. Tigert III, a southern Methodist spokesman, was not afraid of the effects of historical study of the Bible—the higher criticism. It was indeed a helpful tool to be welcomed in intelligent hands like those of S. R. Driver. "All history worthy of the name begins with documentary criticism." [2] The threefold anchors of tradition, the Word, and Christian experience, would hold fast and be strengthened. Bishop E. E. Hoss agreed. "To go indefinitely accepting and repeating the formulae of the fathers, as if they possessed some magical virtue, and were too sacred to be touched or modified in any way, is to commit an act of supreme folly." [3] Here were two spokesmen from the conservative South trying to remain open to the new influences which so disconcerted Faulkner, a conservative Northerner.

About 1910 there appeared a relatively new thing called fundamentalism, a name taken from a series of pamphlets published by a variety of conservatives under the title *The Fundamentals.* This movement brought together diverse forces, all the way from Moodyite premillenialists to professorial conservatives like Princeton Seminary's J. Gresham Machen. Most of these early leaders were not Methodists, but a reactionary Methodist maverick, L. W. Munhall, exploded with *Breakers! Methodism Adrift* (1913), in which he attacked just about everything within reach. The Sunday school literature was "unmethodistic, erroneous, and destructive." The church papers and the Missionary Society had gone over to the enemy. Boston and Ohio

[1] John A. Faulkner, *Modernism and the Christian Faith* (1921), 28, 215.
[2] Speaking at the Third Ecumenical Methodist Conference (1901), 146.
[3] *Ibid.*, 286.

Wesleyan had packed the college of bishops with liberals. As to Charles J. Little, president of Garrett Biblical Institute, he concluded: "The uniform teaching of this school is admittedly in harmony with these antibiblical and un-Methodistic utterances of its president, as can be easily proven by the published writings of members of the faculty, notably those of Professors Milton S. Terry and Charles F. Eiselen." [4] He lumped together for denunciation Henry Smith, Lyman Abbott, M. S. Terry, George Adam Smith, Charles F. Kent, William North Rice, John E. McFayden, S. R. Driver, William R. Harper, and Washington Gladden—all as authors of dangerous books. Most educated Methodists, even those of a conservative temperament, would have been honored by inclusion in that list.

Liberal-minded leaders were quick to defend modern trends in biblical study and theology, not so much against people like Munhall as against those who were apparently determined to reject the twentieth century. Frederick Carl Eiselen of Garrett spoke for biblical scholars in *The Christian View of the Old Testament* (1912). Writing from a moderately conservative position, he insisted that God reveals his power and will in different ways. "The Bible makes not the slightest claim of being a scientific treatise." [5] There are many positive values of the higher criticism, from which we learn clearly that Moses did not write the Pentateuch. That information, however, has nothing to do with the authority of the Bible, he averred. The seminaries were indeed citadels of liberalism, while tight corners of fundamentalism held out in rural strongholds.

Unfortunately, the conflict sometimes descended to personal attacks. To conservatives, as Edwin Holt Hughes remembered, liberals "lacked piety," while to liberals, conservatives "lacked scholarship." [6] Both sides exacerbated emotions by vindictive reprisals. Some other denominations were more afflicted than were Methodists, who escaped much of the violence because of the long-standing nonconfessional stance of the churches. With Presbyterians and Baptists it was another story. The stage was set in these early forays for the crucial struggle of the 1920s, when the liberals, represented by such men as Edgar Sheffield Brightman and Harris Franklin Rall, had it out with conservatives like Harold Paul Sloan. Brightman was one of a galaxy at Boston University School of Theology who took his stand on what he called rational empiricism, that is, meaningful interpretation of experience. "The cause of religion, as well as the cause of philosophy,

---

[4] Munhall, *Breakers!*, 9, 70. See also 41, 119, 150.
[5] F. C. Eiselen, *Christian View*, 56. See 46-48, 53, 75-76, 85-90.
[6] Hughes, *I Was Made a Minister* (1943), 166.

stands or falls with the cause of reason." On this basis he defined the nature of God as limited or finite—"powerful enough to lead the world toward higher and higher levels, yet, if we are to believe the evidence of experience, not powerful enough to do it without great difficulty." [7]

Rall, who began a long career as professor of systematic theology at Garrett in 1915 (to 1945), personified in many ways the liberal Methodist position. He was deeply influenced by a strong background in both the Wesleyan tradition and modern German theology. He was in tune with a modern scientific view, and understood the Christian mission as concerned with the redemption of the individual and the reconstruction of society—the building of the kingdom of God.[8] Against the worldly pessimism of many fundamentalists, especially premillenialists, Rall presented the Christian faith as a challenge to establish the kingdom of God in society, "the kingdom as a new and free humanity." Conflict and crisis result from the ingrained evil in individuals and institutions, but change is inevitable, and "revolution is an opportunity, not a solution." [9] By virtue of his long-term role as secretary of the commission on the course of study he was in a key position to influence the theological education of a whole generation of Methodist preachers. That same role threw his diminutive person into the maelstrom of the struggle over the course of study, a key issue in the liberal-fundamentalist battle. He had a potent influence on Ernest Fremont Tittle, famous prophetic preacher of First Methodist Church, Evanston, Illinois.

Until his remarkable theological shift in the 1930s, Edwin Lewis of Drew Theological Seminary was also on the side of liberalism. He stood firmly with the theological positions taken by Brightman, Rall, and others, and recommended archliberal William Newton Clarke's *Outline of Christian Theology* as the best of all. The nearest approach to liberalism in the M. E. Church, South, is seen in the career of Wilbur Fisk Tillett as professor of theology at Vanderbilt University.

Against this formidable array of liberal leadership, aided by a number of outstanding bishops like Francis J. McConnell, stood the stalwart fundamentalists. Harold Paul Sloan, a leading member of the New Jersey Annual Conference, was deeply disturbed by the current trends and determined to do something about them. Taking up where Faulkner left off, he assailed what he regarded as the debilitat-

---

[7] Quoted in *HAM*, III, 274-75.

[8] *HAM*, III, 283.

[9] One of Rall's most influential books was *Modern Pre-Millenialism and the Christian Hope* (1920), 110, 208, 223. See 110-15, 200-14, 222-23.

ing doctrines of modernism. He headed up a campaign which brought some thirty memorials to the General Conference of 1920, all directed against the course of study, which was alleged to contain many dangerous and modernist books. A regulation was passed which tightened control over the choice of books, required that all books should be in "full and hearty accord with those doctrines and that outline of faith established in the constitution of the church," and specified the inclusion of the *Discipline*, especially the Articles of Religion and the fifty-two standard sermons of John Wesley.

Sloan continued his pressure with a book on *Historic Christianity and the New Theology* (1922). It was a detailed critique of the course of study. He insisted that he was not against higher criticism as such, but against what so frequently went with it, Darwinism and humanism.[10] He was especially critical of Rall's books. He would have preferred to see on the list such titles as Faulkner's *Modernism and the Christian Faith,* Olin Curtis' *The Christian Faith,* the works of Wesley and Finney, and George Frederick Wright's *Scientific Confirmation of Old Testament History.*

There were plenty of fundamentalists in the southern church, influenced by powerful Baptist voices. John A. Rice, liberal professor at Southern Methodist University, got into trouble with his *The Old Testament in the Light of Today* (1920). A fundamentalist paper, *The Southern Methodist,* was started in Memphis in 1921. Bishop Edwin D. Mouzon answered the conservative attacks with his *Fundamentals of Methodism,* in which he charged that the Methodist fundamentalists had gone over to Calvinism. After the middle of the decade, however, excitement lagged and fundamentalism was largely a dead issue by 1930, at least in the leadership of the church.

In the North the crisis came at the General Conference of 1928. Harold Sloan and Clarence True Wilson had organized in 1925 a Methodist League for Faith and Life, which published a paper called *The Call to Colors* (later *The Essentialist*). When the general conference assembled, the bishops felt obligated to warn Methodists against heresy-hunting. Taking their stand on moderate freedom of thought, the bishops stated that no minister should be chained to either "arrogant mechanistic philosophy" or "despotic traditionalism." Little success attended attempts to define precisely what the standards and limits of Methodist belief were. A series of recommendations brought in by the Committee on the State of the Church spelled out the decision of the general conference, which adopted them. All attempts to suppress books from the course of study and to control teaching in

[10] See Sloan, *Historic Christianity,* 9, 15, 30-31, 34, 89-98, 172 ff.

Methodist institutions were rejected. It was the end of major fundamentalist attacks within Methodism, although it was not the end of regional and local conflict. In local churches, even those with liberal ministerial leadership, the Sunday school might remain a redoubt of fundamentalism.

Rise of New Reformation Theology

In spite of the obsession of Americans in the 1930s with social problems arising from the Great Depression, intellectual life was quite lively, particularly in the seminaries. All fields were affected, especially biblical interpretation, ethics, and theology. It became clear to some that a social understanding of Christianity was inadequate. In some quarters the Social Gospel was practically abandoned.

Methodist biblical scholars were aware of new forms of biblical study associated with such eminent European scholars as Rudolf Bultmann, Martin Dibelius, and C. H. Dodd; but not many of them fully accepted the new emphases. John Newton Davies at Drew denounced form criticism as underrating the teachings of Jesus and overemphasizing "the eschatological, super-historical, transcendental, and future aspects of the Kingdom." [11] Paul Minear was the only major figure in Methodist seminaries to accept most of the new trends. His reviews of Dibelius, Bultmann, Dodd, and others reflect both understanding and enthusiasm. Another Methodist biblical scholar, Clarence Tucker Craig, likewise served to emphasize Continental trends.

It was the field of theology, however, which caused the greatest stirrings and alarms in the 1930s. These came as a delayed reaction to movements in Europe which date from the end of World War I, when Karl Barth published his famous commentary on Romans. In the early 1930s the already voluminous writings of the German-Swiss theologian were only beginning to appear in English translation. It required more incentive than most Methodists possessed to plow through his turgid German prose. Intellectual leaders like Ernest Fremont Tittle were aware of the thought of Barth and others and considered it a proper balance to a superficial social humanism, but were unwilling to accept what appeared to them unjustified dogmatism and even anti-intellectualism. At Boston both Brightman and Knudsen were critical of Barth. The latter took the trouble to analyze thoroughly the development of Barthian theology, to recognize its

[11] See the helpful article by William J. McCutcheon, "Praxis: 'America Must Listen'," *CH,* 32 (1963), offprint 23 p.

strong points, and to indicate its weaknesses and contradictions. He dealt effectively with both Karl Barth and Emil Brunner and was influential in clarifying the issues involved. He complained of dogmatism and extremism, especially in the dichotomy set between God and man, revelation and reason. At Garrett, Rall also took account of Continental theology and recognized its value as a reaffirmation of Reformation teachings. He believed that Barth failed to acknowledge the central significance of the saving act of God in Christ. A leap of faith is not a sufficient definition of Christian commitment.

> His teaching is more calculated to emphasize our need than to meet it. It is not a theology that Wesley could have taken to his colliers, or that we can use with common folk in our churches, or that will meet these pressing questions of the modern mind. It is well to lift up God, especially in this day when man has been so satisfied with himself. But the Christian evangel proclaims not only the God high and lifted up, but the God who draws near. In his effort to stress the first, Barth has set such a gulf between man and God that he cannot give place to the second.[12]

The theologian most caught up in the rise of New Reformation theology was Edwin Lewis of Drew. While he was deeply engaged in editing the *Abingdon Bible Commentary*, he changed his own understanding of the Christian faith. He moved from modern liberalism to strongly expressed New Reformation theology, and in doing so acknowledged the tremendous influence of Barth. "What therefore Barth chiefly did for me—and it was a great deal—was to help me find the courage, at an important period of my life, to throw off the shackles of mere contemporaneity and keep my mind 'exposed' to the Bible in the effort to determine the nature and the significance of the Christian faith." [13] He put this new message into *A Christian Manifesto* (1934), in which he rejected his own former liberalism and accepted the New Reformation theology, with emphasis on the sovereign God, the wholly other, the absolute uniqueness of God's revelation in Christ. The church, he insisted, and especially his own Methodist Episcopal Church, had abandoned the center of the Gospel and gone over to the world.

Some of the emphases of "neo-orthodoxy" might appear to mark a sort of victory for fundamentalism. Harold Paul Sloan rejoiced in the new vision of Lewis. It certainly was a victory in the sense that the New Reformation theology repudiated the shallow liberalism which also troubled the fundamentalists. But neither Lewis nor other spokesmen

[12] H. F. Rall, quoted in *HAM*, III, 303.
[13] "How Barth Has Influenced Me," *Theology Today*, 13 (1956): 358; quoted in McCutcheon, "Praxis," 20, and *HAM*, III, 314.

intended to reject the Social Gospel as a facet of Christian witness in the world, nor did they turn away from modern science (as distinguished from the pseudoreligion of scientism) and serious biblical interpretation. On both sides of the Atlantic neo-orthodox scholars effectively used the tools of modern biblical research. Nevertheless, at times Lewis and others sounded very much like the old fundamentalists with their unified structure of the truth—take it all or leave it. On the other hand, most American theologians, including Lewis, were capable of criticizing Barth and others regarding emphases and directions.

Along with Reformation themes came a revival of Wesleyan studies, a veritable *Rediscovery of John Wesley,* as George Croft Cell entitled a book in 1935. For decades, interest in the original Wesleyan Revival had languished in American Methodism as the claims of modernism and the Social Gospel pushed forward. Since Methodists generally had never taken structured theology very seriously, or rather had never taken a confessional stance very seriously, the decline of Wesley study in the later nineteenth century was not surprising. In the heady theological atmosphere of the 1930s, with the shades of great reformers lurking everywhere, John Wesley returned to center stage as spokesman for Methodism. At least part of Wesley returned, the theological part. He reappeared as an interpreter of the Reformation to eighteenth-century England whose message was exceedingly important for the present day. Cell made the most of those elements in Wesley's writings which indicated a rootage in Calvinist theology, especially doctrines of God and sin—but not predestination! Other Wesley scholars made other approaches. Maximin Piette, writing from a Roman Catholic perspective, claimed Wesley as a saint rather than a theologian and certainly not a Calvinist. Umphrey Lee agreed, placed Wesley more directly in the environment of eighteenth-century Enlightenment, and emphasized the importance of Christian experience as a source of religious knowledge.[14] Others both in England and America, notably Ernest Rattenbury and Francis J. McConnell, contributed to the growing body of Wesley studies. This interest continued with the formation in 1955 of a Wesley Society by Franz Hildebrandt of Drew, David Shipley of Garrett, and Richard Cameron of Boston. One major result of the continued interest is the projected new edition of the complete works of Wesley. Recent interpretations of Wesley's theology by William R. Cannon, John Deschner, Colin Williams, Philip Watson, and Albert Outler,

[14] See my bibliographical articles in *CH,* 28 (1959): 391-417; 29 (1960): 74-88; 40 (1971): 182-99.

together with a major new biography by Martin Schmidt, indicate that the status of Wesley as a significant theological spokesman is not ephemeral.

United Brethren and Evangelicals

Both United Brethren and Evangelicals were affected by the conflicting forces of liberalism and fundamentalism, and the varied responses were in many ways similar to those of Methodism. Both denominations, if only because of their relatively small size, had tended in the nineteenth century to take a conservative stand, but at the turn of the century more liberal influences were discernible. The courses of study all had some moderately liberal books on the list, especially after 1910. Partly because of the original German rootage, the churches were aware of and in a measure friendly toward liberal theological forces in Germany. This would be more accurately applied to the seminaries in Naperville and Dayton. Evangelical S. J. Gamertsfelder began his long career in 1906 with a period of study in Germany, where he learned to admire both conservative and liberal scholars. He became a professor of theology in the Naperville Seminary and in 1913 published his influential *Systematic Theology,* in which he paid tribute by reference to the German theologians. The Evangelical Press published this work in 1921, and for many years it was the standard work for the denomination. Professor J. P. Landis represented the force of liberalism in the United Brethren seminary in Dayton. Gamertsfelder and Landis brought a spirit of tolerance, humanitarianism, and openness to twentieth-century culture.

Nevertheless, until at least the mid-twenties, conservatives remained quite strong. The old guard—men like Jacob Hartzler, H. B. Hartzler, and Bishop Rudolph Dubs of the United Evangelicals; Bishop Thomas Bowman, S. P. Spreng, and W. H. Bucks of the Evangelical Association; and J. M. Philippi and Bishop W. M. Weekley of the United Brethren—were deeply involved in the fundamentalist movement that grew out of the Niagara Bible Conference of 1895, with the classic definition of fundamentals that marked the movement. The spirit of these men was that although tolerance is appropriate in human relations, it is inappropriate in matters of faith. Hence, Spreng approved of the heresy trial of Bowne in Boston. Like their conservative fellow Methodists, they were chiefly concerned about protecting the vigor of evangelical witness. Theology was of interest only insofar as it contributed to the proclamation of the true gospel. Both United Brethren and Evangelicals were divided when

Harry Emerson Fosdick became an issue with his sermon in 1922, "Shall the Fundamentalists Win?" The *Evangelical* and *Evangelical Messenger* carried warnings against liberal colleges, Methodist Sunday school materials and seminaries. As usual, Harris Franklin Rall was in the center of the hurricane. In 1919, H. B. Hartzler quoted in the *Evangelical* this item from the *Eastern Methodist:*

> Prof. H. F. Rall, of Garrett Biblical Institute, was president of Iliff School of Theology before going to Garrett. He is a German and was educated in Germany. He unloaded his German U-boat theology upon Iliff and is now doing the same at Garrett. He is the supremely moving spirit in the Commission on the Course of Study for our young preachers, and is more than any one responsible for the unMethodistic, anti-Biblical, faith-wrecking infidel character of this course.[15]

These attacks on Methodist seminaries were not characteristic of the attitudes of United Brethren and the *Religious Telescope,* but William Jennings Bryan was quite popular among many United Brethren members. In fact, it was not until his death (1925), along with those of Weekley and Philippi, that fundamentalist pressures began to subside.

Some of the conservative leaders, especially among the United Evangelicals, became involved in premillenarian movements. H. B. Hartzler of the *Evangelical* was a supporter of C. I. Scofield, the promoter of dispensationalism, a view which would organize Scripture according to "dispensations" culminating in the the return of Christ. The Evangelical Association and the United Brethren were not much involved in these premillenarian movements.

Although these denominations had roots in German language and culture, their Pietist leanings obstructed any significant influence by twentieth century biblical and theological developments associated with the names of Dibelius, Bultmann, Barth, and Brunner. Theologians, of course, were aware of the development of New Reformation theology, but the churches were not widely affected.

---

[15] 5 Mar., 1919, 7. Quoted in dissertation by William Henry Naumann, "Theology in the Evangelical United Brethren Church," draft ms. p. 430. Principal source for this section.

Chapter 34
The Social Gospel

The term *social gospel,* if used specifically of a historical movement, applies to only one of several facets of the broad theme of Christianity and society. Since it was the most important characteristic of Christian social relations in the early twentieth century, it can be broadened to describe the outlook of the times. This broad approach is applicable to Methodism. By the time of the Social Creed, most mainline denominations had come to a new understanding of the bearing of the Christian faith on the whole of society and not merely on the personal lives of its members. The established concerns for personal morality and relief of suffering continued; but they were strengthened, indeed were transformed, by the new awareness of social issues which could not be reduced to simple terms of individual morality. One must remember that these decades witnessed the metamorphosis—no other term is strong enough—of American society from a predominantly agrarian collection of regional and local communities to a highly interrelated community founded on the industrial city. Throughout the period both patterns continued to influence the quality of life in the United States; but the long-term trend was strongly away from the old toward the new. These trends were strongest in the Northeast and weakest in the South. The Midwest is epitomized by the sight of Chicago, brawny and bumptious between eastern farms and western ranches.

The Social Creed

Although Methodists presently became famous for engagement in social action, they were at the outset relatively slow in response.[1] Episcopalians and Congregationalists were early on the field. With the General Conference of 1908 and the establishment of the Social Creed, Methodism forthrightly embarked upon a career of social witness from which it never retreated. It was not always equally effective or perceptive in all social problems, but it tried.

[1] Henry F. May, *Protestant Churches and Industrial America* (1949), 182; *HAM,* III, 373-78, 389. An excellent survey is the chapter in *HAM* by Robert Moats Miller. The best monograph is Walter G. Muelder, *Methodism and Society in the Twentieth Century* (1961). More general is R. M. Miller, *American Protestantism and Social Issues* (1958).

In the Social Creed the church took a stand in favor of "equal rights and complete justice for all men [women?] in all stations of life"; for industrial arbitration, factory safety, abolition of child labor and protection of women workers, reduction of hours of labor and guarantee of a living wage, an "equitable division of the products of industry," and finally, "for the recognition of the Golden Rule and the mind of Christ as the supreme law of society and the sure remedy for all social ills." These principles served as a foundation for much social legislation of later years directed to the eight-hour day and six (five, four) day week, workingmen's safety and compensation, social security, unionization, insurance and retirement. This Social Creed was adopted by the M. E. Church, South, in 1914 and by the Methodist Protestant Church in 1916. After they once got started, Methodists would take second place to no one in social witness. It might be assumed with so large a denominational family that tensions and disagreements on specific issues would develop.

General conferences of the new century regularly gave much attention to social problems. The whole church was brought to face the challenges of industrialization and large corporate structure, the need for increasing public responsibility for control, and the regulation of the economic system in the interests of justice for all. Along with these economic issues many others pressed for response—political action, militarism, temperance, race relations, population, and the status of women. Men who attended the First Convention of Methodism Men, held in Indianapolis, Indiana, October 28-31, 1913, got a full dose of the Social Gospel.[2] The corresponding secretary of the Freedmen's Aid Society reminded the churchmen of their responsibility to "these black men in the cellars of our civilization." A bishop urged the continued presence of Methodism in the growing cities, especially by means of "institutional churches," a term used for city churches with a social program for their communities. Francis J. McConnell pointed out the connection between the cherished Wesleyan doctrine of sanctification of individuals and the sanctification of society. Harry F. Ward appealed for a trained industrial ministry. Herbert Welch in "The New Day in Social Reform" pointed out that welfare and settlement work is not enough, for men who have a decent wage don't need or want welfare.

This is a fair sample of the continuing emphasis throughout the twenties and thirties. The most active agency for proclaiming the Social Creed in Methodism was the Methodist Federation for Social Service (later Social Action). It was organized in 1907 by five minis-

[2] Downey, et al., Militant Methodism, 150, 169, 178, 185, 238-41, 256-61.

ters: Frank Mason North, Worth Tippy, Harry F. Ward, Herbert Welch, and Elbert R. Zaring. Ward, who became the leading figure, was in the center of the organization which engaged in increasingly controversial activity. As Bishop McConnell, who served as president, put it, the federation's purpose was to raise disturbing questions —ahead of time. The general direction of thought in the organization under Ward's leadership was from social reform toward more fundamental social change. Ward's theological stance was liberal along the lines of the "Chicago School," and hence he was very critical of Barthianism and other expressions of New Reformation theology, which he regarded as abandoning the ideal of Christian socialism. This position brought him into conflict with another social-minded professor at Union, the seminary where he taught in New York —Reinhold Niebuhr.[3]

In the 1930s many prominent Methodist leaders were active in the federation, among them Bishops Welch, Blake, and McConnell; editors Dan Brummitt, Halford Luccock, L. O. Hartman, and George Elliott; professors like Harris Franklin Rall and Georgia Harkness; and preachers like Ernest Fremont Tittle and G. Bromley Oxnam. The stormy, triumphant career of Tittle at First Church, Evanston, Illinois, is illustrative of the violent tensions. Partly because of the more radical sentiments of Ward, the church became more and more polarized on the federation, which began to carry the motto, "An organization which seeks to abolish the profit system in order to develop a classless society based upon the obligation of mutual service." At the General Conference of 1936 (which the *Christian Century* called the "Battle of Columbus"), an attack was mounted against it, which, although it failed, gave rise to continuing protests by such conservative movements as the Methodist League Against Communism, Fascism, and Unpatriotic Pacifism and the Chicago Conference of Methodist Laymen. Finally, during the heyday of anticommunist campaigns associated with the name of Senator Joseph R. McCarthy, after both McConnell and Ward had retired and many other prominent participants had resigned on account of the controversial leadership of the federation, two measures were taken at the General Conference of 1952: the term "Methodist" was to be removed from the name, and a new official Board of Social and Economic Relations was established.

In spite of the ups and downs of the Methodist Federation for Social Service, the mainline churches continued the emphasis on the Social Gospel. Many leaders like Ralph Sockman and other ministers

---

[3] McCutcheon, "Praxis: 'America Must Listen'," *CH* 32 (1963): 11 (pamphlet reprint).

in New York protested the excesses of the Red Scare of 1919 and the oppressive Lusk Laws: "A common resolve to abide by our time-honored principles of free discussion and the regular processes of constitutional government is the need of the hour. Unhappily, violence, recently employed in the name of patriotism, has been allowed to go unpunished by the authorities, and has even been praised by leaders in government and in the press." [4] The church papers, from *Zion's Herald* to the *Nashville Christian Advocate*, denounced the irrational witch-hunting of the times. As the Great Depression settled like a pall over the land, a mission study conference brought 350 delegates to Delaware, Ohio to study areas of concern in the modern world which involved race, family, nationalism, and business. The conference called for collective bargaining in The Methodist Publishing House and ethical investment practices for church agencies. The Social Gospel changed and developed different emphases, but it never was abandoned.

World War I and Pacifism

Before the First World War the popular ideal for peace was arbitration in such an agency as the Hague Tribunal. The outbreak of fighting ended all that for the time being. Although a few Methodists had joined others in adherence to pacifist ideals, the coming of war brought an abrupt change. The church papers were critical of Quakers and others who had conscientious scruples. Some Methodists who had been pacifists changed their mind with regard to a war fought to achieve peace. There were almost no outspoken pacifists.[5]

The churches, both North and South, engaged in a patriotic program which was the same as that found everywhere in the country. If the religious journals sound superpatriotic, they were at least more restrained than the secular journals. Saving the world for democracy was viewed as a Christian duty. Liberty bonds were sold in churches, and patriotic sermons were delivered. For a season Christian faith and patriotism were almost indistinguishable. Methodists were no more and no less involved than the members of other churches. All of this was simply an illustration of the predominant culture of the era, especially of the overwhelming belief in progress and the advance of civilization.[6] Even in the face of an obvious disaster, progress must

---

[4] Quoted in Muelder, *Methodism and Society*, 91-92.

[5] For one exception see *Ibid.*, 81-82.

[6] See John Hayek "The Attitudes Expressed in Eight Methodist Periodicals Toward the First World War," (M.A. thesis, Northwestern, 1972).

somehow be substantiated. Apparent setback must lead to a leap forward. Hence, world peace from war. The peacemakers spent four cruel years killing one another for the vindication of progress.

Inevitably, a strong prejudice against the Germans and all things German found expression. One of the benefits of the war was seen in release from the "baneful influences" of German theology. *Zion's Herald* ran headings like "Theology Without Germany" and "A Holiday from German Theology." [7] Especially hard hit were the German Methodists, caught between the two powerful forces of cultural heritage and patriotic fervor. In 1915, not counting the European membership, there were over 63,000 German Methodists. Throughout the war, Methodism in Germany and German Methodism in the United States managed to maintain relationships, but it was difficult and left the Americans open to criticism as something less than wholehearted patriots. The editors of the *Christliche Apologete* were required to file translations of articles with the postal authorities. Toward the end of the war an investigating committee set up by the M. E. Church reported that the magazine "was not in full harmony with the spirit of the church and the country" because the church at large was "unequivocally" opposed to the Central Powers and "wholeheartedly" for the Allies.[8] When the publishing agents forced the editors to sign a loyalty oath, Albert Nast, who had served as editor for twenty-six years, resigned. Suggestions were made that all German language publications should be dropped. The president of Baldwin-Wallace College (product of merger of German Wallace College and Baldwin University in 1913) was fired. These actions must be seen in the context of patriotic fervor in the country generally, which decreed the abolition of teaching German in schools and demanded the change of German place names and even personal names.

The Methodist churches did not quite lose all reason. Their people and papers remained somewhat more moderate than the secular forces. Expressions of affection and trust were not lacking for German Methodists personally. The Methodist Federation for Social Service and the Rock River Annual Conference both called for the release of political prisoners, such as Thomas J. Mooney and Warren K. Billings. In the course of the war the doctrine of progress suffered severe buffeting, but was not abandoned. Granted, the war was lasting too long; but out of it eventually would come world peace. Granted, even worse than war was the Russian Revolution; but that

---

[7] *ZH*, 95 (1917): 1126-27; 93 (1915): 1351-52. Cf. *MQR*, Sept.-Oct., 1917, 798-99.
[8] This was reported in all the *Advocates*. See *NWCA*, 66 (1918): 122; *CA*, 93 (1918): 132; *WCA*, 84 (1918): 98.

was hopefully a temporary setback. The February Revolution fitted the general plan, but it was difficult to see how the October Revolution advanced civilization.[9] One is constrained to ask, could this by any stretch of the imagination be seen as the best of all possible worlds?

Inevitably, the end of war brought reaction. The jag of patriotism left in its wake normalcy, isolation, and the flapper era. Revulsion against this new thing—*world* war—gave rise to a wave of pacifism. In the twenties and thirties, large numbers of Christians in mainline denominations joined their fellows in the traditional minority peace churches in identifying their faith with pacifist commitment. An incident which took place in the First Methodist Church, Evanston, Illinois, in 1924 is illustrative.[10] At a meeting of the Epworth League the invited speaker was a conscientious objector who had served a term in prison in World War I. The Evanston American Legion was opposed to the appearance of this speaker. Ernest Fremont Tittle, minister of the church, permitted the American Legion to state its case, then took a vote of the young people as to whether the speaker should speak. The outcome heavily favored his speaking. He did, and then answered questions. After the formal meeting, a speech on Americanism was hissed by the students. Unfounded charges were made that a riot ensued and that it was the flag which was hissed. The *Advocate* had trouble exonerating the students. This pacifist spirit increased in the early thirties. A poll taken in 1931 of Protestant ministers and theological students revealed that almost two-thirds of the former and four-fifths of the latter believed the church should not lend its support to any war. Almost as many declared their personal opposition to any war. Both northern and southern Methodist churches repeatedly declared their support for conscientious objectors. Many Methodists were active in the Fellowship of Reconciliation and other peace groups.

These sentiments continued down through the thirties and ran head on into the new challenges to freedom coming from Europe —Communist Russia, Fascist Italy, Nazi Germany. Those who agreed with leaders like Reinhold Niebuhr rejected the absolutist claims of pacifism as abdication of Christian responsibility for service in a world beset with sin. By the time World War II broke out, three major branches of Methodism had finally come together in The Methodist Church.

[9] See "The Mills of God Grind Slowly," *WCA*, 84 (1918): 1374-75.

[10] *NWCA*, 72 (1924): 341, 386. See also Robert M. Miller, *How Shall They Hear Without a Preacher? The Life of Ernest Fremont Tittle* (1971), 213-21.

Temperance

The relations between the temperance movement and the Social Gospel were equivocal. Assuredly, the effort to combat the insidious effects of alcoholism was a major part of the social witness of the churches. On the other hand, so dominant and so highly organized was the temperance movement that it appeared to exist in isolation from the social environment of which it was only a part. Many antisaloon people had no interest in the Social Gospel; and many social reformers considered abstinence a leftover from Puritanism. Nevertheless, before and after prohibition temperance was an important part of the involvement of Christians in social problems. From a larger perspective, the triumph of prohibition in the eighteenth amendment was the last great victory of agrarian America against the growing power of the cities. In this campaign the Methodist churches played a crucial role; the General Conference of 1908 heard stated flatly without demur: "The Methodist Episcopal Church is a temperance society." A perceptive paragraph in the *History of American Methodism* points out this larger significance:

> No other single issue provides such illumination of Methodism's involvement in, estrangement from, and accommodation to American culture. In a very real sense and in its larger outlines, the prohibition movement reflects and reveals Methodism's hopes and fears, powers and limitations, victories and failures. Inextricably enmeshed in the prohibition struggle were issues of rural-urban strain, ethnic tension, Protestant-Catholic controversy, church-state relationship, adjustment of means to ends, individual redemption and social reform, the elation of success and the frustration of failure, and finally reconciliation to living with an intolerable situation without succumbing to despair.[11]

The establishment of national prohibition occurred in a narrow space of time when Protestantism in America was still the dominant religious force, but when the trends of the future were already going the other way. Political achievement of a constitutional statute was still possible. Its subsequent enforcement became increasingly impossible. Prohibition was a victory doomed to failure. The role of Methodism in this process was amply stated by H. L. Mencken, whom Halford Luccock called "the Peck's 'Bad Boy' of American letters and master of the Grand Lodge of the *Intelligentsia*." Mencken gave full credit to Methodism for what he regarded as a disaster to civilization.

> It was among country Methodists, practitioners of a theology degraded almost to the level of voodooism, that prohibition was invented, and it

[11] Robert M. Miller in *HAM*, III, 330.

was by country Methodists, nine tenths of them actual followers of the plow, that prohibition was fastened upon the rest of us, to the damage of our bank accounts, our dignity, and our ease. On the steppes Methodism has got itself all the estate and dignity of a state religion; it becomes a criminal offense to teach any doctrine in contempt of it.[12]

Whatever else Mencken proved, he proved that urban bias could be as powerful and blinding as rural bias and that in the war of words surrounding prohibition, neither side knew the meaning of restraint.

All through the twenties the controversy over prohibition raged with excesses committed on both sides. Mencken's diatribes were matched by attacks on the liquor traffic, legal or illegal, as responsible for all the ills of society. The Social Gospel was shoved aside as subsidiary to the great crusade. On the other hand, those who opposed prohibition and favored legalization of alcoholic drinks seemed to claim that, once the restrictions which brought in corruption and gangsterism were gone, social ills would disappear. Whatever the causes, it was increasingly clear that prohibition by constitutional statute was not working well. Temperance forces were sadly divided between those who pinned all their hopes on absolute prohibition and teetotal abstinence and those who favored a more moderate approach which would acknowledge the pluralistic character of American society.

The presidential election of 1928 brought all these matters to a political focus, although the campaign was confused by the presence of a Roman Catholic candidate. The prime reason for Methodist opposition to Alfred E. Smith was not that he was a Roman Catholic, but that he was a wet. An address to the General Conference of 1928 by the Methodist bishop most fully involved in the political arena makes the point clear: "Shall America elect a wet cocktail president?" So utterly committed were the forces behind prohibition that they allowed themselves to get into politics, something they would never have considered doing on any other issue. Unfortunately, the latent nativism always present in Protestant circles surfaced in this campaign against a liquor-drinking grandson of Irish immigrants.

As it turned out, of course, the battle was lost with repeal in 1933. Liquor was back; but corruption, crime, urban decay, and gangsterism did not fade away. As for the temperance movement, though the battle was lost and sobriety by law appeared to be a thing of the past, the war was far from over. Methodists have continued the struggle against alcoholism and against its evil train of consequences.

[12] Halford Luccock, "Meditations in the Methodist Desert," *NWCA,* 72 (1924): 1233.

Economic Life and Labor

The common working day at the beginning of the twentieth century was ten hours for six days a week. Hours of labor went *up* from this. When the International Ladies' Garment Workers Union was organized in 1900, women and girls were working seventy hours a week. Children were employed without controls in exhausting and dangerous occupations. All forms of unionization and collective bargaining were strenuously opposed by manufacturing and government leaders. Workers could be fired on short notice for no reason. The wage paid for work performed was subjected to the inexorable laws of supply and demand, the labor supply being totally unorganized, the demand highly structured. Some of the results we have already seen in the crises of the late nineteenth century.

The mainline churches, including the Methodist, were deeply associated with what has come to be called the middle class. By and large both leaders and members shared the outlook of the class of citizens who had achieved some measure of success in the business world. They tended to associate religious virtue with economic success, and economic failure with immorality. The lay delegates to the General Conference of 1904 consisted of 55 merchants, 39 lawyers, 34 educators, 27 physicians, 20 bankers, 15 manufacturers, 12 judges, and a scattering of other professional and business types.[13] Ministers like William Carwardine, who understood and sympathized with the workingmen in his Pullman congregation, were few and far between. Most of the ministerial delegates would have been quite at home with the lay delegates. Alienation of the churches from the working population became so extreme that the Industrial Workers of the World (IWW) could make a popular point with their marching song about long-haired preachers offering "pie in the sky when you die."

Several revealing sociological studies illustrate the degree to which Methodist churches became entwined in the social structure of their communities.[14] In every case the leadership of the local church has been dominated by the managerial class and the membership has had little or no contact with the workingmen. Sometimes the churches have been practically owned by the dominant industrial power. Occasionally, one Methodist church would be understood as the one for middle class supporters and another the center for working people. This alienation proceeded too far before the dangers were recognized.

[13] *HAM*, III, 375.
[14] Liston Pope, *Millhands and Preachers* (1942); Arthur Edwin Shelton, "The Methodist Church and Industrial Workers in the Southern Soft Coal Fields "(Diss., Boston, 1950).

The other side of the story is the account, already made in its early stages, of the response of the church to these problems. The Social Creed marks a sort of watershed. Another crucial point of contact was the report on the steel strike of 1919.[15] Three weeks after the strike began in Pittsburgh and Gary, a commission of inquiry was set up by the Interchurch World Movement, along with the Federal Council of Churches. Chairman of the executive committee of the former was that indefatigable ecumenical Methodist, John R. Mott. Of the two bishops on the investigating commission, Francis J. McConnell and James M. Cannon, the first was a key figure. The commission carried out a professional analytical study which had tremendous influence both in course of the study and after publication when it was submitted to President Wilson. The commission documented such labor practices as the twelve-hour day, long shifts at special times, low pay, seven-day weeks, and the absence of consultation with workers. The study received full publicity in the religious and secular press. As a result, most of the evils exposed were corrected in the early twenties. More important, attitudes of churchmen changed perceptibly in the face of incontrovertible evidence.[16]

Although the twenties were not particularly favorable to the Social Gospel, ministers began to see that problems of social organization of society could not be left to the decision of industrial management and conniving politicians. Bishop McConnell, who became something of a hero during the investigation, paid tribute to the manner in which the Pittsburgh Annual Conference stood by him under pressure. The strike and the investigation were eye-openers for the Gary clergy. First Methodist Church in that steel city was transformed as a result.

Then came the Great Depression, which left a permanent mark on the religious establishment in America. Its effect was not only negative in the area of lost funds and tightened budgets, ministers without salaries and churches without coal. It also forced ministers and people alike to face basic questions about the economic system. As the Methodist bishops put it in 1930, there was something deeply wrong "with a social system that, in the midst of plenteous abundance, dooms untold numbers of our people to unbearable poverty and distress through no apparent fault of their own." [17] Two years later the general conference heard about

[15] See Muelder, *Methodism and Society*, 96-115. It was published as *Report of the Steel Strike of 1919* (1920).

[16] See R. M. Miller, *American Protestantism and Social Issues*, 212-13. McConnell, *By the Way*, 219-20.

[17] Quoted in Muelder, *Methodism and Society*, 131.

granaries bursting and thousands starving; cotton piled high in warehouses, millions insufficiently clad and prices so low as to be the despair of the planter; banks bulging with money and widespread poverty; machinery equipment standing idle with multitudes in need of the things the machines could produce; mountains of coal and people freezing; able-bodied men and women, eager to work and not too particular about the amount of their wage, forced to take the necessities of life for themselves and their children from charity. It can not be denied that the industrial practices of past decades have given us the deplorable conditions of to-day.[18]

In that year also was founded the Religion in Labor Foundation which, though interdenominational, had much Methodist participation and support. There were also the Christian Social Action Movement, the Fellowship for Reconciliation, and the League for Industrial Democracy; all of which included Methodists. Though much of the talk of the day was anticapitalistic and socialistic, action programs usually took the form of specific reforms. The spirit of the New Deal closely paralleled many of the principles of the Social Creed.

In response to all these stimuli of the Depression and the movements which grew out of it the Social Creed was expanded and defined more inclusively. The General Conference of 1932 undertook to spell out some of the implications for industry, for agriculture, and especially for race relations which had unaccountably been a sort of blind spot with earlier social reformers. By this time the principle that the Christian faith had a gospel for social as well as individual redemption had become a commonplace. It remained to develop a usable theological foundation beyond easy liberal formulations and compromises.

Race Relations

The Dawes Act of 1887 had brought yet another new day to the troubled area of Indian relations. Under this plan, which was being implemented in the early twentieth century, the reservations were to be divided among the individuals and families of the various tribes and the remainder opened for public use. Most of the churches, from ignorance of the actual circumstances, from concern for education and welfare, and from habits of long association with governmental policy, went along with the plan. Western customs of family life and long-standing emphasis on the virtues of diligence and hard work contributed to the favorable attitude toward allotment. Unfortunately, this close relationship with government did not contribute to a

[18] *JGC,* 1932, 173.

full understanding of the plight of the American Indian. The Commissioner of Indian Affairs, addressing the General Conference of 1928, was uncommonly frank: "It is quite safe to venture the assertion that the Church and State are more closely associated in the Indian country than is the case elsewhere."

Now and then a voice would be raised in protest against the trend of allotment. In 1924 the *Northwestern Christian Advocate* reported a resolution to protect the lands of the Pueblo Indians against allotment. The fact that the resolution passed without opposition may indicate that it also passed without understanding. Generally speaking, however, until Commissioner of Indian Affairs John Collier set up a "New Deal" for the Indians in 1934, Methodist periodicals and spokesmen simply ignored the whole thing.

Under the Roosevelt-inspired reforms of John Collier the Indians were to be given a say in their own affairs and destiny. They were to be offered the benefits of civilization, but allowed to remain Indians. Disposition of tribal reservations was to be subject to decision by the Indian tribes who possessed them. In many ways it was an admirable change of direction, but some implications worried church leaders, who saw the missionary and educational programs imperiled. Only a few Methodist leaders, notably Mark A. Dawber of the Board of Missions, were able and willing to give full support to the Collier reforms. Although Dan Brummitt, editor of the *Northwestern Christian Advocate,* strongly denounced the white man's treatment of the Indians, he also feared that Collier's program would inevitably bring the Indian to a blind alley, a "Stone Age" binding him to a dead past rather than to a promising future. Two facts were abundantly clear as Methodist unification came near: (1) Methodists, along with other Americans, were finally becoming aware of the enormity of the Indian problem; (2) no one in authority had yet come up with a practicable government policy because no one was listening to the Indians themselves.

The story of the participation of black people in the history of Methodism has already been told, both within and outside the mainline Episcopal Methodisms. Here we take up the theme in relation to the Social Gospel. By curious coincidence, the very era which witnessed the development and acceptance of the Social Creed also saw the resurgence of race prejudice, especially in the South. A new kind of virulent racism, which had been almost unknown in the 1870s and 1880s, appeared in the wake of Reconstruction as the South sought to build some kind of society to replace that destroyed by war. It took the form of various Jim Crow laws which segregated the Negro as he had never been segregated before, even under slavery. This is not to suggest that slavery would have been better. Although voices were raised, from individuals to the general conference, against violence, especially lynchings, little was either said or done about Jim Crow segregation. It seemed to slip in unnoticed.[19]

There were, of course, general statements of good will based on the universality of Christian love. These are not to be taken cynically, but they simply did not do much good. There was for long no concerted attack on racial segregation. When it finally came, it derived as much from secular pressures as from religious. There were some notable exceptions. Frank Mason North, for example, followed and supported the NAACP from its foundation in 1910. He understood that the problems of the Negro were not only those of the rural dweller in the Jim Crow South, but also those of the more and more numerous black city dwellers. The southern church was largely sidetracked into encouraging its stepchild, the C. M. E. Church, which was showing surprising vigor. If there was any difference in the attitudes of the two Episcopal Methodisms as unification approached, it was that, whereas both agreed with the ideal of separate but equal treatment, the South was more interested in the separate and the North was more interested in the equal. The M. E. Church, South, was quite clear that however much its members might be involved in the peculiar social system of the South, it stood for justice in all human relations. The Episcopal Address of 1938 called the church to account:

> Whatever may be the sins of others and whatever may be pleaded in extenuation of our own shortcomings, a large bulk of omission needs to be rectified in the course of our future relations with our brother in black. The Negro wants good wages, good schools, better housing, wholesome recreation, police protection, justice in and out of the courts, a larger share of civic improvements, and a chance to make the most of himself and the same things for his children. This is nothing more than, as a human being and an American citizen, he has the right to expect. For the most part, however, he has lived since the manifest of his freedom under an economic and political system that has not always fostered his best development.[20]

Well and good! But who would communicate these principles through the churches in the length and breadth of the deep South? Who would implement them in local situations? And how? Another world war, a Supreme Court decision, and numerous episodes of violence and mayhem would have to be lived through before some start could be made. In the meantime, Methodism would hear the

---

[19] See C. Vann Woodward, *The Strange Career of Jim Crow* (1955).
[20] *JGC*, MEC, South (1938), 245-46.

racist nativist conservatism of Bishop Warren A. Candler as well as the enlightened moderation of Bishop John M. Moore and the insistent radicalism of the Methodist Federation for Social Service. Methodism, no more than any other such widespread form of American life and culture in the first half of the twentieth century, had found a united voice on racial equality.

Other Aspects

In 1920 the population of the United States was 105,711,000, of whom over 34 percent were foreign born. Among them in order of size were English, German, Italian, Polish, Yiddish, Swedish, French, Czech, and Norwegian groups. Methodist activity was strongest among the Germans and Scandinavians. During the period under consideration all these ethnic groups abandoned their separate annual conferences and merged with the English-speaking structure. Under pressures which grew in World War I, the separate ethnic cultures were suppressed as everyone tried to dissolve in the melting pot. Whereas in 1924 there had been ten German, six Swedish, and two Norwegian-Danish conferences; by the time of unification, most of these had merged. The same happened more slowly to the Oriental work in the West. Only the Spanish-speaking Methodists preserved and strengthened their cultural autonomy. They were therefore in a good position to greet the resurgence of ethnic culture in the later decades of the century.

Methodism has never had outstanding success in dealing with recent immigrants. During the great days of immigration the church tended to remain aloof from the masses pouring into the industrial cities with various cultures and habits out of tune with American norms defined in Puritan terms. Hence, it was difficult for Methodists to find ground for understanding. The church had responded with some success to the challenge of the older immigrants—Germans and Scandinavians, but it had little to say to the more recent hordes coming from Europe and elsewhere. Only gradually did the church realize that people of other than traditional Western cultures and English language had a right to their own forms of expression. For these reasons Methodism was vulnerable to the appeals of nativism so commonly heard in the 1920s, to the insidious propaganda of the Ku Klux Klan, and to the fears generated by the election of 1928. A specific case in point was the Sacco-Vanzetti case. A murder in 1920 resulted in their conviction in 1921 and execution in 1927. The *Northwestern* hit home: "It is this suspicion that they were condemned, not for the murder, but for being foreigners, radicals, and pacifists, which has raised such a tremendous wave against their execution without a new study of the evidence." [21]

In view of Methodism's rich, though equivocal, heritage in ethnic variety, it is a matter of some interest that recent trends indicate a revival of ethnic pride and an emphasis on the diversity rather than the melting-pot unity of American life.

One more issue of paramount importance should be mentioned, the rights of women, a topic already treated in the context of the nineteenth century. Since the day of women's liberation did not arrive until a later period, however, discussion may properly be deferred. Women, the only oppressed minority comprising a majority of the human race, continued to experience ups and downs during the period under review. It was well after World War II before they made their presence known with a new voice and vigor.

[21] *NWCA,* 19 May 1927.

Chapter 35
The Methodist Church, 1939-1968

Even under a monotheistic dispensation the mills of the gods grind slowly. This characteristic of Christian history is amply illustrated in the reunification in 1939 of three major branches of American Methodism. The first division had come in 1830, the second in 1844. A hundred years elapsed before these wounds were patched up—not necessarily completely healed. We have traced some of the negotiations through the hopeful beginning at the Cape May Conference, the dogged wrestling of the joint commission, and the frustrating setbacks in the early twenties. Throughout, the prime issues were the same: the office of bishop, the authority of the general conference, the status of black members, and the idea of jurisdictions. Regional attitudes tended to remain the same, because the widespread Methodist system had been inextricably caught in the web of sectionalism, which has been one of the central forces in American history. As we have seen, for better or worse Methodism had been Americanized. Only the personnel changed. There came a day finally when new leaders were able to throw off the shackles of past prejudices and failures and accept the promise of a new era. At the same time the members generally were willing to move.

The failure of the plan of 1924 in only one of four necessary votes (in the annual conferences of the M.E. Church, South, 4,528 to 4,108, a majority in favor, but not the constitutional majority) was frustrating but not disastrous. Bishop Edwin H. Hughes believed the outcome was a moral victory. "I recall my elation over this result." [1]

Reunification

The long process of working toward reunification was revived in a significant manner by the Methodist Protestants.[2] In 1929, representatives of that denomination approached Bishop Herbert Welch with a proposal for renewed discussions with the Methodist Episcopal

---

[1] *I Was Made A Minister,* 276. For his later views below see 281.

[2] The overall story is told by Frederick E. Maser in *HAM,* III, Chap. 32. The best book is John M. Moore, *The Long Road to Methodist Union* (1943). Essential for the Methodist Protestant interpretation is James H. Straughn, *Inside Methodist Union* (1958). More broadly conceived is Paul N. Garber, *The Methodists Are One People* (1939).

Church. This proposal led to the constitution of a new body, including the M.E. Church, South, to carry on three-sided negotiations. Three commissions were formally established by the next general conferences (1932 for M.E. and M.P., 1934 for M.E.C.S.).

The joint commission began work at once and rapidly devised a plan. It was able to proceed with such dispatch because of the tremendous work previously accomplished by earlier commissions. And the time was ripe. Ecumenism was in the air with the various activities associated with the formation of the World Council of Churches. The new plan called for the formation of "The Methodist Church." It would have one general conference and six jurisdictional conferences, five of them geographical, the sixth for the Negro annual conferences. Equal representation was provided for ministers and lay persons in all conference levels. The office of bishop would continue to be organized in a Council of Bishops, Methodist Protestants being entitled to elect two of their own bishops. A Judicial Council would act as supreme arbiter of the law of the church. The Articles of Religion would be retained. The crucial problem for the Methodist Protestants was acceptance of the office of bishop. It was practically solved, however, by the passage of time: what the Methodist bishop had become was no longer so dire a threat, and Methodist Protestants had not only retained, but strengthened their own Methodistic structure. The crucial issue for Episcopal Methodism in relation to Protestant Methodism was equal lay representation in the annual conference. The knottiest issue remained the one which plagued American Protestantism and had frustrated North-South union: the place of the black Methodists in the Methodist Episcopal Church. There were over 300,000 of them, mostly in segregated annual conferences.[3] The arrangement by means of which this problem was settled, the creation of a racially oriented Central Jurisdiction, is a measure of the status of the black man in the church at unification, of his place in the American society before World War II, and of the involvement of church and world in the twentieth century. It was also a usable compromise which was made to work for the time being. It could never be, nor was it ever intended to be, a permanent solution of the problem of race relations.

The joint commission which was given responsibility for preparing a plan decided that the task of reuniting the church was quite enough to handle without embroilment in the larger task of reforming the church. "Our commission," wrote Bishop Hughes, "was not set to

[3] See Willis J. King, "The Negro Membership of the (Former) Methodist Church in the (New) United Methodist Church," *MH,* 7 (Apr., 1969): 32-43.

remake the Church, but to reunite the Church." The historic position of the southern church was honestly and moderately stated by Bishop John M. Moore:

> The South and the Southern Commissioners were all but unanimous in the opinion that a united Negro Methodist Church in the United States, embracing the Negro constituency in the Methodist Episcopal Church, the Colored Methodist Episcopal Church, and the two African Methodist Episcopal Churches, should be the goal in the union movement. To that end they held that the Negro membership of 315,000 in the Methodist Episcopal Church could best be served, and could best serve the cause of union, through an independent organization of their own. The Northern Commissioners held that their Negro constituents could not be set up into an independent organization except by their own will and action and that they were unwilling to inaugurate such a movement. . . . Separation of the races in the South had become a well-established custom. The Southern people were fully convinced that this state of things was best for both races, and best for Southern civilization, and that it should continue. Any movement or trend that might change this condition was disturbing and was regarded with suspicion and opposition. This philosophy of race relations was deep-seated and stronger even than any church affiliations.[4]

On the other hand the M.E. Church, although it was firmly unwilling to abandon or exclude its Negro members, had developed a system of separate black churches, annual conferences, areas, *Advocate,* and two bishops elected by separate ballot. Black Methodists were very uneasy over the Central Jurisdiction, but were divided on its acceptability, because although it contained the insidious poison of racial prejudice and segregation, it also promised a guaranteed larger voice for a self-conscious minority. Therefore, the plan, including jurisdictions and equal lay representation as unanimously approved at the meeting of the joint commission in Louisville in 1935, was submitted to the churches for ratification.

Inevitably there was criticism. A fifth of the annual conferences of the Methodist Protestant Church voted against the plan, chiefly because these theologically conservative conferences feared liberalism. But the vote in the general conference was 142 to 39, and that of members of annual conferences, 1,265 to 389. The votes in the M.E. Church were overwhelmingly favorable, in spite of strong criticism from influential spokesmen like Ernest Fremont Tittle and Lewis O. Hartman, who resented the ethical implications of the Central Jurisdiction. Bishop McConnell spoke to the situation as he recalled that the whole matter had been worried over for twenty years and

---

[4] *The Long Road to Methodist Union,* 137.

everyone concerned was "very devoted, very able, very well informed, very tired, and a trifle bored." [5] He recommended it as the best possible for that time, hoping that it would become the basis for a more nearly Christian relationship in the future.

In the M.E. Church, South, vigorous and determined opposition was mounted by those who had opposed the idea of union all along, led by retired Bishops Candler and Collins Denny and the latter's son, Collins Denny, Jr. Candler was the epitome of loyalty to the old South, which he loved. He had frankly opposed union on any basis all along simply because he believed regional differences were good, not bad. He believed the variety and competition of denominations was wholesome and that Methodism had profited from its divisions which permitted "special access to peoples" of different cultures. In 1939 he resignedly bowed to the will of the church, commenting, "I'll be in heaven anyway before Unification gets to working good." [6] At last, however, even in the South the idea's time had come: the votes were 434 to 26 in the general conference and 7650 to 1247 in annual conferences, only one of which actually voted narrowly against the plan (North Mississippi).

Final success came as result of a fortunate combination of favorable circumstances: decline of differences in organization and doctrine, global situation (one world, plus totalitarian challenge), insistence of youth, generational changes in personalities, experience from the Depression, and general ecumenical spirit. A great Uniting Conference was held in Kansas City, April 26–May 10, 1939. The chairmen of the three commissions, Bishop Edwin H. Hughes of the northern Church, Bishop John M. Moore of the southern, and James H. Straughn of the Methodist Protestant, presented the declaration of the plan of union, which was approved. The Methodist Church came into being, and the carefully done commingling, reforming, and editing of the new *Discipline* provided a fundamental constitution. The Methodist Church was a reality, so real in fact that it bore birthmarks and scars, none of them, however, debilitating. Even black Methodists, who had reason to feel they had the short end of the deal, made the most of their very real new opportunities for leadership in episcopacy, general conference, jurisdictional conference, and general boards and agencies of the church. At the very least they were provided with a base for future advance. In the new church bishops were elected by jurisdictional conferences to service in the jurisdictions which elected them, a new form of something quite old

---

[5] Letter to *ZH*, 4 Mar. 1936, quoted in *HAM*, III, 456.
[6] Pierce, *Giant Against the Sky*, 205, 209. Cf. Sweet, *Virginia Methodism* (1955), 395-99.

—regionalism. Some feared that the jurisdictions would become so provincial that they would become autonomous little Methodisms. This tendency was balanced by the strong central structure exemplified by the general conference, the Council of Bishops, and the series of powerful national administrative agencies. Others feared that the latter would take over direction of the church. In most respects the new *Discipline* continued, although with revisions, the principles and policies which represented the consensus of the three former denominations.[7]

Dissatisfaction continued to find expression in mutterings from northern liberals, in unhappiness of black Methodists with the idea of a Central Jurisdiction (in contrast to obvious advantages in practice), and in overt opposition by a small minority of the former M.E. Church, South. The latter forced a long and complicated test in court which reached the Supreme Court. Although the outcome confirmed the legal status of the new church and its control of its property, an irreconcilable minority proceeded to form a small denomination which was called the Southern Methodist Church. It grew out of the unbending opposition of a few leaders, particularly Bishop Denny and Collins Denny, Jr., together with an organization called "The Laymen's Organization for the Preservation of the Southern Methodist Church," formed in 1937. A meeting in Columbia, South Carolina in 1939 brought the Southern Methodist Church into being.

At unification the three churches reported members as follows: Methodist Episcopal, 4,684,444; M.E. South, 2,847,351; Methodist Protestant, 197,996.

Into Another Maelstrom

The Methodist Church had scarcely achieved unity when the world was caught up in another of those global earthquakes, World War II. In fact the conflict had already been going on for two years in the Orient when the Occident was engulfed with the invasion of Poland by German Nazi armies in August. An international youth conference in Amsterdam was almost inundated. The World Council of Churches was paralyzed in act of birth. The years between 1939 and 1945 were exceedingly difficult for human beings everywhere. In an excruciatingly painful fashion, the ancient issue of Christian attitude toward war was raised. For two decades since the First World War the Christian conscience had recoiled against modern warfare, and many Christians had taken a firm stand for pacifism. Among them were

[7] For resume of chief elements see *HAM,* III, 460-76.

outstanding Methodists like Albert Edward Day and Ernest Fremont Tittle, who had a sizable following. Others, like Bishop McConnell, believed the ethical situation of the Christian prevented any simple stand against any and all wars, but favored the neutrality of the United States unless attacked. Still others, influenced by such theologians as Reinhold Niebuhr, believed that in a world of no absolute choices the lesser evil of the moment would be resistance to Nazi tyranny. The no-war stand prevailed in the General Conference of 1940, which met before the United States was involved. Shortly after American involvement, the Council of Bishops issued a statement which concluded: "We roundly condemn the processes of war even while accepting the awful alternative, not of our making, forced upon us by the selfishness and the perversity of men. From a measure of the guilt of this, none of us is free." A crucial battle was fought at the General Conference of 1944, in which Tittle sought to obtain reaffirmation of the position taken in the previous general conference. His committee's majority report, however, was rejected in favor of a minority report which emphasized the responsibility to resist aggression as opposed to pacifism. It should be pointed out that neither side in the debate rejected the conscientious right of the other side. It was rather an issue of what stand the church should take as an institution. Services of the church were offered both to men in military service and to conscientious objectors. Relatively little of the emotional patriotism so noticeable in World War I found expression this second time around.

Instead, the energies of the church were gathered around a crusade undertaken by the bishops, particularly by G. Bromley Oxnam, in 1943 and early 1944, the "crusade for a new world order." The main thrust was toward effective expression of Methodist will and energy for international collaboration after the end of hostilities to guard against a return to isolation.[8] Calling on the church's long heritage of missionary spirit and world vision ("The World is our Parish"), ministers and members participated in an effective program of education and action designed to give support to the idea of world government before the critical decisions were made. An ecumenical perspective led the crusade to take up and support the "Six Pillars of Peace" as stated by the Federal Council of Churches. Almost all the agencies of the church were recruited for promotion of the crusade, including the Woman's Division of Christian Service. In this concerted effort, the connectional structure and centralized leadership of

[8] See G. Bromley Oxnam, *The Crusade For A New World Order: A Report By The Chairman* (1944).

The Methodist Church was at its most efficient. The net result was a tremendous surge of concern and support for a United Nations.

Some of the byproducts of total war were pernicious. One was the forced relocation of Japanese, most of whom lived on the West Coast, to interior camps where they were interned for the duration of the war. A Pacific Japanese Provisional Annual Conference was formed in 1940 (to 1964). The Southern California-Arizona Conference, which was directly involved in the wartime resettlement program, took a strong stand in behalf of those fellow citizens who were of Japanese ancestry, many of whom indeed were members of Methodist churches.

> The all-inclusive fellowship of the Church embraces with profound sympathy the Japanese who have been uprooted by the evacuation orders. We are not unmindful that powerful interests, popular war hysteria, provincialism, and vigilantism, as well as military precaution enter into the situation. We do not join in a wholesale suspicion of disloyalty on the part of the Japanese of any generation. We deeply regret that the citizenship rights of many of them have been violated. We urge our church people to join in a positive movement to protect these people from threats of permanent loss of civil and economic rights. We seek with them for a new birth of freedom.[9]

Another byproduct of the war, not necessarily bad in itself, was population displacement, at first necessitated by exigencies of war, later voluntary, which introduced an unprecedented mobility into the social structure. Regional differences were blurred and long-standing viewpoints challenged. The church was hard put to keep up with its peripatetic members, who outran the now settled circuit riders. This social mobility would expand rather than contract after the war.

Postwar Development

After the end of World War II, the enormous size of growing Methodism became apparent in the complexity of administrative provisions devised for its connectional system. That unloved compromise, the jurisdiction, had a checkered history. It served to protect regional interests and was for that reason especially favored in the South. The two southern jurisdictions, in fact, were much more highly organized than their counterparts elsewhere. The Central Jurisdiction served the purpose for which it was intended, elected twelve bishops in its first twenty years, provided a framework within which 320,000 black Methodists could express their interests, and

---

[9] *Journal, Southern California-Arizona Conference,* 1942, quoted in Mueder, *Methodism and Society,* 198.

gave opportunities for leadership. It also offered a sounding board for continued protest against segregation in the structure of Methodism. Bishops like Marquis L. Harris, Edgar A. Love, Charles F. Golden, Noah W. Moore, Jr., Matthew W. Clair, Jr., and Prince A. Taylor, Jr., who were effective in 1960, ably continued the work of bishops like Alexander P. Shaw, Willis J. King, J. W. E. Bowen, and Robert E. Jones. These, together with many black leaders who served on national church boards and agencies, gained invaluable experience in administration, and produced leadership which would be much needed in the church in the future. The *Central Christian Advocate* (before unification the *Southwestern Christian Advocate*) gave journalistic coverage for the work of the Central Jurisdiction. A constitutional amendment which became effective in 1958 began the process of replacement of the Central Jurisdiction by permitting individual churches or annual conferences to identify themselves with a regional annual conference or jurisdiction if the respective conferences approved. The General Conference of 1964 determined that the Central Jurisdiction should be ended by 1968.

Altogether The Methodist Church in 1940 counted 7,360,187 members, plus 672,011 "nonresident" members. The figure for 1960, which is not precisely comparable either to the full member figure or the total of 1940, was 9,910,741. That is to say, Methodists were in a ten-million-member church—far cry from the insignificant beginnings of 1784! Probably more significant was the influence of social mobility: rapid and repeated transfers of membership in and out, with inevitable losses along the way; large numbers of new congregations formed in areas of burgeoning population, with consequent losses in depressed areas. According to one study, over a thousand new congregations were formed in the eight years 1950–1958. As the physical structure of the church expanded in the United States, so its outreach stretched financially. General World Service giving increased, but annual conference benevolences and "Advance Specials" increased phenomenally.

Structural changes were many and diverse, although none was revolutionary. The Council of Bishops and the Judicial Council both established impressive records for leadership. In various ways the bishops escaped a purely regional role by service on national boards, through the Council of Bishops, and by participation in episcopal visitation of mission areas. An attempt to facilitate transfer of bishops from one jurisdiction to another, however, failed. Increasingly, the bishops' lieutenants, the district superintendents as they were now designated, continued inexorably to depart from the old pastoral idea of presiding elder to become willy-nilly administrative associates of the bishop.[10]

A force of increasing influence was the collective power of the administrative secretaries of the national boards and commissions. The bishops became aware—unhappily—that much of the leadership in developing quadrennial programs rested in the hands of the Council of Secretaries and the Coordinating Council. More and more it looked as if programs and crusades and emphases were designed to advance the interests of this or that major agency. In order to keep from treading too frequently on one another's toes, the executive secretaries were brought together in a Council of Secretaries in 1940. The intention was to avoid waste and duplication of effort and to coordinate the disparate activities. A Commission on Promotion and Cultivation was set up in 1952 to oversee publicity for all the agencies.

The bishops' crusade for a new world order provided precedent for the development of special quadrennial emphases for concerted action by the whole church. Thus, the General Conference of 1944 approved a program for the "Crusade for Christ," which included the wartime effort for world government. A drive for funds to help the millions of refugees made homeless by war and its aftermath was the second emphasis. It recognized the terrible truth that the twentieth century had become not so much the century of the common man as that of the homeless man. Other emphases were directed to spirituality, stewardship, and Christian education. Success of this quadrennial program encouraged the agencies to develop another for the quadrennium 1948–1952, called "Advance for Christ and His Church." With a view to making these quadrennial programs permanent, a Coordinating Council was established in 1952 to consult with the Council of Bishops and the Council of Secretaries to "formulate and present to the General Conference . . . plans for a unified, ongoing program for the church, including long-range objectives." Such were the fruits of connectional amplitude. By 1960, complaints were heard that since everything was being emphasized in a quadrennial emphasis, nothing was—except perhaps the Commission on Promotion and Cultivation.

One of the most valuable improvements following unification was the coordination and expansion of educational and publishing activities. Although various forms of cooperation already existed, these were now brought under central management with a great increase in efficiency. The Board of Education, located in Nashville, included a

[10] See Murray H. Leiffer, *Role of the District Superintendent in the Methodist Church* (1960), esp. 113-15.

number of large departments which worked out programs and published materials for Methodists from nursery through old age. In response to the surge of new births following the war, leadership training classes and laboratory schools were held. In 1944 the Methodist Youth Fellowship took up the old work of the Epworth League and Christian Endeavor, while the National Conference of Methodist Youth became a recognized part of the structure of the church. It overcame an earlier misunderstanding in which college youth had their own autonomous organization and kept the establishment at a distance. By 1952 this breach had been healed. In 1960, a Methodist Student Movement replaced the National Conference.

Two activities in the united church reflect the trends of the times: the Television, Radio, and Film Commission (TRAFCO, 1956) and the General Board of Lay Activities. The former came in response to the demands of the startling new means of communication which were revolutionizing general culture. The latter exemplified the new relationships brought into The Methodist Church from the former Methodist Protestant Church, which from the beginning had made full provision for the equal participation of laymen. Although the M.E. Church, South, already had a Board of Lay Activities, the new emphasis derived principally from the Methodist Protestants. Even more than formerly, the Woman's Division of Christian Service, structured within the Board of Missions, made plain the importance of women as lay participants.

One of the more spectacular results of unification was the development of The Methodist Publishing House and its book division, Abingdon Press. For the first time a religious publishing organization entered the circle of major publishing enterprises. It was capable of undertaking expensive ventures such as the twelve-volume *Interpreter's Bible,* published between 1951 and 1957, and the new journalistic product *Together,* which began in 1956 and within four years reached a circulation of a million. The presses in Nashville were modernized to take care of the demands for church-school literature, books, and professional and popular religious magazines.

As in the church at large, so in the ministry unification brought growth and complexity. The Board of Education made provision for a new Department of Ministerial Education to coordinate the old course of study program with the increasingly important role of theological seminaries, which began to receive more formal recognition and more direct support from the general funds of the church. Two new seminaries—St. Paul School of Theology in Kansas City and the Methodist Theological School of Ohio—were built, partly to pro-

Chapter 36
The Evangelical United Brethren

One of the oddities of denominational history is that the story of the union of the United Brethren and the Evangelical Church begins with an account of schism in both. Furthermore, before they could finally achieve the merger, they had both to drop out of another project for church union, one which might have taken them permanently out of their Methodist heritage had it come to fruition. Some difference of opinion may exist as to whether this sequence of failures and successes represents the peculiar providence of God.

The United Brethren Before Merger

During the course of the nineteenth century both groups, although relatively small, took on the features of institutional religion. The United Brethren had a hymnal since 1808 and a *Discipline* since 1816, the *Religious Telescope* since 1834, a missionary society since 1841, a college since 1847, a seminary since 1871, and a Women's Missionary Association since 1875. Then, in 1889 they achieved the ecclesiastical distinction of schism. It happened this way.[1]

Long simmering debates over the prohibition of membership in secret societies, lay representation, and proportional delegation in the general conference came to a head in the debate over the alteration of the constitution. The problem was the unclear language of the constitution of 1841 about amendment. By the 1880s a majority of ministers and people were in favor of revising the *Discipline* on these matters, but that meant changing the constitution—and could it be changed? The General Conference of 1885 set up a commission with power to prepare amendments and submit them to the entire membership for ratification. This was done, and the referendum was taken in 1888. Every proposal for change—confession of faith,

[1] Among the sources for this chapter is the brief history by Paul H. Eller, *These Evangelical United Brethren* (1950); Raymond W. Albright, *A History of the Evangelical Church* (1956); A. W. Drury, *History of the Church of the United Brethren in Christ* (1924); John H. Ness, Jr., *One Hundred Fifty Years, A History of Publishing in the Evangelical United Brethren Church* (1966).

amendment of the constitution, lay delegation in general conference, and the rule on secret societies—passed by a very large majority. On the basis of this referendum the next general conference (1889) adopted the whole plan, 111 to 20. When the new constitution was proclaimed in effect, Bishop Milton Wright and fourteen other delegates withdrew in protest against what they regarded as an illegal act. They proceeded to meet separately under the old constitution as the true Church of the United Brethren in Christ. After failure in court to substantiate their claim, they took the name United Brethren Church (Old Constitution). Curiously, the dissidents, who took their conservative stand on the old ways, were called the "radicals"—that is, people committed to the *root*. The majority who voted for change were the "liberals."

Out of this bitter dissension came a small church which had to start from scratch because it lost its claim to church property. The membership was estimated at about 15,000, compared with about 190,000 who accepted the revised constitution. The bitterness engendered by this schism was never healed.

By 1920 the United Brethren were no longer small: they numbered almost 343,000, a third of a million. A number of changes continued to be made in the interests of modernization. For example, the traditional warning about nonconformity to the world was dropped, the ritual was improved and expanded in 1921, and a new hymnal was published in 1935 which included more elaborate aids to worship. As befitted its larger size, the church began to multiply agencies. In the 1920s an inclusive Board of Christian Education developed departments for every level of the educational work of the church. At the same time, a new Bureau of Evangelism replaced the older Department of Evangelism. In 1905, separate foreign and home missionary societies were organized, and four years later the Women's Missionary Association, which dated from 1875, was given official status with the other agencies. As World War I ground toward an end, the United Brethren joined with other churches in the ambitious Interchurch World Movement, the same that gave rise to the Methodist Centenary Campaign. They called their form of participation the United Enlistment Movement, which was crowned with moderate success. The special home missions projects in Kentucky and New Mexico were maintained and expanded. The former area had four centers equipped with schools and later hospitals or clinics. The Women's Missionary Association promoted their work through the "Woman's Day," which became "World Mission Advance Day."

The Depression hit both small denominations very hard. They had less financial strength for prolonged resistance and served a membership that did not control high finance. The missions programs suffered most, but adjustments were made, sometimes painfully, and the church weathered the economic storm. In 1937 an agency which had real meaning for the United Brethren was formed: the Rural Life Commission. It helped the many rural churches and pastors to find effective means for ministry among farming folk.

The ministry was strengthened, particularly in standards of preparation. A proposal to allow ministers who possessed only a license to preach to administer the sacraments was rejected, even though some protested that the prohibition worked hardship. Instead, the church moved toward a well-trained and fully ordained ministry with increasing emphasis on seminary education. In 1929 a survey showed that of over a thousand ministers only one hundred fifty had a seminary degree. During the 1930s college preparation became standard, and in 1941 both college and seminary were required, except for those admitted to the course of study. Bonebrake Theological Seminary in Dayton acquired a new campus in the early 1920s.

Two trends are noticeable in the social outlook of the United Brethren. First, some of the old and outmoded concerns, which had once been important issues, were either dropped out or neglected, the rule against secret societies, for example. Emphasis on temperance continued without abatement as United Brethren experienced the bitter disillusionment of the repeal of the eighteenth amendment in the early 1930s. Somewhat like the Methodists, there was a surge of antiwar and pacifist agitation after World War I, and a decided difference of opinion among members and ministers as World War II loomed in 1941. The social position of the church as reflected in the *Discipline* was strengthened by additions in 1933 on international relations and race relations—these for the first time. The general conference of that year also approved a fifteen-point Social Creed, which was a revision of that of 1913. A new Social Service Commission was set up to replace the former pietist-evangelistic Commission on Social Advance.

The Evangelical Church Before Merger

Evangelicals, too, had to suffer the ordeal of schism. It was especially bitter because personalities were involved in a most distressing way. For many years rivalry had simmered between the German and

English church papers, *Der Christliche Botschafter* and the *Evangelical-Messenger*. It resulted in the trial and conviction of the editor of the *Evangelical-Messenger,* H. B. Hartzler. This incident merely set the stage for the donnybrook of 1891, in which two rival general conferences met, one in Indianapolis and the other in Philadelphia, each claiming to be the true body. Bishops J. J. Esher and Thomas Bowman were with the majority group in Indianapolis, and Bishop Rudolph Dubs with the minority in Philadelphia. Behind the personal quarrels lay issues of the use of German, episcopal authority, theological conservatism, sectionalism (remember the original subordination of the Western Conference to the Eastern), and old versus new immigrants—the majority in Indianapolis being in favor of German, bishops, the West, and the new immigrants. There were also disputes over mission policy and sanctification. Add to these the personal quarrels that centered in publication—unbridled emotion, battle and counter-attack, controversy in open court—and you have a recipe for schism.

When the East Pennsylvania Annual Conference, which was heavily identified with the minority group, claimed the right to locate the general conference in Philadelphia, schism was already a fact since the majority accepted the Indiana location. For a quadrennium, until the courts settled the matter, there were two Evangelical associations, each claiming to be the whole. In 1894, however, the minority (Philadelphia) organized the United Evangelical Church in Naperville, Illinois, while the majority (Indianapolis) continued as the Evangelical Association. The former had about 61,000 members, the latter 110,000.

This unhappy division, although bitter in its inception, was eventually healed in 1922 with formation of the Evangelical Church. New leaders were not personally scarred by the old battles, and a new day had dawned. From 1911 on, a joint commission worked hard to perfect a plan, which was accepted eleven years later by both branches. Almost all the traditional Evangelical principles were continued. What was new was the word "church," which for the first time came into the title. The confession of faith, the additional doctrinal articles, principles and forms of membership including the class meeting, conferences, two orders of ministry, bishops—all were retained. In spite of the successful reunion, however, the Evangelicals were less well prepared to greet the twentieth century than the United Brethren, who remained in schism. The break had taken out a small minority, but had permitted the opening and updating of the church with a new constitution and confession of faith. The Evangelicals on the other hand had been caught in a three-to-two ratio of division in which neither side was able to establish its commanding control of the tradition. As a result, both tended to remain on dead center.

Like the Methodists and United Brethren, Evangelicals were involved in the Interchurch World Movement, promoting a campaign called the "Forward Movement." This effort was not aborted as a result of the reunion of 1922. Also, the church was deeply caught in the fundamentalist drive. This developed partly because of the long-standing emphasis on the central authority of the Bible, partly because of the emphasis on sanctification. As the *Evangelical Messenger* put it in 1926: "We want no abbreviated nor expurgated Bible, for the reason that no man has intelligence enough to perform such a delicate task . . . and for the further reason that we believe the Bible to be a unit requiring every part of it to make it a perfect whole." [2] On the other hand, a sizeable minority of moderate liberals were to be found, leaders who laid the basis for a resolution of the conflict after the most difficult days had passed.

Many of the administrative developments were in line with other denominations including the United Brethren. The new church of 1922 had a missionary society and a woman's missionary society, both inherited from nineteenth-century beginnings. The strongest area of work overseas was Germany. In the United States an outstanding project was the Red Bird Mission in eastern Kentucky, which continued to receive special support. A distinctive feature was the Deaconess Society, which reflected German influence throughout. It expanded enthusiastically in the 1920s, with hospitals and a new headquarters in Chicago and a deaconess home. Unfortunately, the Depression caught the work overextended, and a financial debacle resulted in the loss of much of it. In one way or another, however, the Deaconess Society continued until the new merger of 1946. Overseas, deaconesses remained active throughout the Depression.

The ministry went through much the same process of development as we have seen in the United Brethren. The course of study continued, but increasingly the seminary set the standard for training. There were two seminaries, one in Reading, Pennsylvania, the other in Naperville, Illinois. A necessary compromise was the diploma offered for students who entered without a college degree. Attempts to require a college education in the 1930s failed. Not until union in 1946 did the college standard become normative for admission to theological study. Albright College continued to serve as one of the church-related colleges and kept the seminary under its legal wing

[2] *Evangelical Messenger* (23 Oct. 1926): 2.

until it merged with the former United Brethren Seminary in Dayton in 1954. No radical changes were made in the forms of worship, which had a minimum of ritual and set form. A new Evangelical hymnal was prepared in 1921.

Evangelicals were relatively slow to respond to the challenge of the Social Gospel, and for long retained an individual-oriented moral stance. By 1934, however, the general conference declared that "men must be converted not simply to a personal faith in Jesus Christ, but to the program of Jesus as a method of social reconstruction as well." A nine-point Social Creed fortified this stand, and in 1938 a Board of Christian Social Action was established.

Both denominations were active in the ecumenical movements, the Federal Council, and the various activities which led to the World Council of Churches.

The Evangelical United Brethren Church

The Evangelical United Brethren Church was formed November 16, 1946 in Johnstown, Pennsylvania. It was the fruit of extended negotiations between the Evangelical Church and the United Brethren Church which had begun in 1926. These relationships had been delayed because in the 1920s both were involved in another, larger project for church merger with the Reformed Church in the United States (German Reformed) and the Evangelical Synod of North America. The Evangelicals were never actively engaged; but the other three went on to devise a plan of union for "The United Church of America," on a doctrinal basis drawn from the confessions of the three denominations correlated with the Heidelberg Confession. Prospects looked good in 1929, but the next year the project fell apart and the United Brethren withdrew. Subsequently, the remaining two formed the Evangelical and Reformed Church.

Then, in 1934 Evangelicals and United Brethren came together in an official joint commission, which began work on a plan for union. This was submitted in 1942 to the general conference of the Evangelical Church and in 1945 to the general conference of the United Brethren. The votes were 226 to 6 and 224 to 2 respectively. According to constitutional requirements, it then was submitted to the annual conferences. The vote of Evangelicals was 2,173 to 51, that of United Brethren 2,291 to 134. In addition, the United Brethren carried through a referendum among the members with a resulting vote of 80,777 to 13,033.

Both churches held final general conferences in Johnstown prior to the meeting of the constituent convention and the first general conference of the new church. It was held in the First United Brethren Church, which was tightly crowded as Evangelical Bishop John S. Stamm and United Brethren Bishop A. R. Clippinger presented the Declaration of Union. It was a service of profound impressiveness and great joy, similar to the threefold celebration of Methodists in Kansas City in 1939. The Lord's Supper provided a spiritual symbol of the union of over 705,000 members. This merger was accomplished without the loss of any individual congregations.

The new denomination took over the former articles of faith, together with the Evangelical's additional statements on regeneration, sanctification, and Christian perfection. The combination was not smooth because the United Brethren had revised and modernized theirs previously, but in 1962 a new confession of faith was prepared which greatly improved the doctrinal stance of the church. In addition to the ordinary forms of Methodistic organization, a general council was established to provide continual oversight and guidance for the various agencies. An impressive example of the strength of the new organization was the United Crusade, carried on from 1954 to 1958, which brought in over five million dollars. In every area the merger improved the efficiency and energy of activity. Architectural symbols are the new plant for the Evangelical Press, 1955, and the headquarters and Board of Education buildings in Dayton in the 1960s.

Several adjustments had to be made in the form of ministry. The former United Brethren quarterly conference preachers, who were not ordained and had no vote in the new conference structure, were phased out as the church moved toward a better-prepared ministry. A minimum of two years of college was required for entering men, and they were urged to go on to a seminary. The course of study remained as an alternate route. A new Commission on Ministerial Training was set up. Gradually, the standards were stiffened with the result that the three seminaries became more important as training centers. When a recommendation was made that they be consolidated, the small school in Reading was willing and in 1954 merged with Bonebrake in Dayton as the United Theological Seminary. The Evangelical Theological Seminary in Naperville, Illinois remained active and grew, thus giving the church a school from each of the former traditions. At the college level there was an embarrassment of riches as many small schools, some of them struggling for finances and standards, continued to provide a church-related liberal education. Among the stronger were Albright College in Reading, Pennsylvania, which until 1954 was mother hen to the seminary; Otterbein College in Westerville, Ohio, near Columbus; Lebanon Valley College, Annville, Pennsylvania; Indiana Central College, Indianapolis; North Central College, Naperville; and Westmar College, Le Mars, Iowa. Most of the funds from the United Crusade went to the colleges and seminaries.

When the Evangelical United Brethren Church was formed, the world was gasping from the conclusion of World War II. All missionary programs had been disrupted to greater or lesser extent. A single Board of Missions assumed responsibility for the total program with three departments similar to the Methodist structure: World Missions, Home Missions and Church Extension, Women's Service. The Women's Society for World Service maintained its semiautonomous relationships and provided education through the Girls' Missionary Guild, the Mission Band, and the Little Heralds. Overseas missions were developed in Japan, Hong Kong, the Philippines, Puerto Rico, Santo Domingo, Sierra Leone, Nigeria, East and West Germany, Switzerland, France, Brazil, and Ecuador.

In the United States much effort was devoted to service in the rural church, an environment in which both former churches had deep roots. The Department of Home Missions and Church Extension continued an emphasis on rural farming communities, especially in depressed areas. There was a full-time director of Rural Life and a Rural Life Christian Fellowship. The Appalachian projects at Barnetts Creek and Red Bird Center were brought together in a Kentucky Missionary Conference. New schools and a medical program were established. In New Mexico the mission among Hispanic Americans also grew, with erection of new schools, chapels, and hospitals. At the same time a new concern was expressed for the problems of urban life with organization of an Urban Church Commission, which among other activities sought to encourage ministry to "people of other races," a phrase which would be self-evident in meaning for most Evangelical United Brethren, as well as for most American Protestants. Throughout American Protestantism after World War II, a deep, sometimes agonizing reassessment of the meaning of mission in the world was made. Evangelical United Brethren were caught up in some of the basic questions arising from a less favorable global political climate, a resurgence of other world religions, a new nationalism in new nations, the sometimes bitter harvest of Christianity planted as a byproduct of Western expansion, and all the rest. Especially important was the relevance of denominationalism to world mission. The new church with its broad ecumenical background could readily understand these trends and better accommodate itself to them.

From the merger of 1946 also came a Commission on Christian Social Action. That the church was not unequivocally in support of this commission, however, is indicated by the fact that not until 1966 was a full-time executive secretary provided. There remained a durable residue of traditional concern for personal morality, which the commission combined with a new emphasis on the need for social justice in institutions as well as individuals. It urged support for the United Nations and world order, supported movements for economic justice through collective bargaining, and sought a Christian basis for race relations. The Evangelical United Brethren, in part because the church had not had much contact with black people or numbered many in its membership, reflected a weakness of the early Social Gospel in neglecting race relations. In the 1950s the commission sought to make up for that weakness and took action to gain support throughout the church for racial justice.

As the 1960s arrived, the Evangelical United Brethren were engaged in a congenial task: ecumenical conversations with several other denominations with a view to union, as well as continued participation in the broader expressions of the ecumenical movement as represented by the National Council of Churches and the World Council of Churches. As discussions with the Methodists were getting under way, conversations were continuing with the Church of the Brethren, the Church of God in North America, and the United Presbyterian Church. When the prospects for union with the Methodist Church strongly improved, these other relations were dropped by friendly mutual agreement. There remained one more great event for this denomination with long roots but brief history, the merger to form The United Methodist Church.

Chapter 37
United Methodism in American Culture

Toward the end of April 1968, The United Methodist Church came into being as a result of the union of the Evangelical United Brethren Church and The Methodist Church. It marked the penultimate gathering of the strands of the different movements which in one way or another represented the major expressions of the Evangelical Revival in American religion. With the exception of the large black Methodist denominations and a number of smaller churches which continued to go their own way, the heirs of Wesley were more than ever one people. In an imperfect world in which very few goals are fully achieved, this outcome can properly be greeted with joy, even in the simultaneous acknowledgment that Methodism is in fact not yet united, and that even the incomplete union achieved in 1968 has left over many strings untied and many frays unmended. In this, United Methodists have guidance from Charles Wesley, who urged us to give thanks for the blessings we have "and humbly ask for more."

A New Union

Before giving an account of the process of unification in the United States, some attention should be given to an event immediately prior to formation of The United Methodist Church—church union in Canada. Early in the twentieth century United Brethren in Ontario had united with Congregationalists, and in 1925 Methodists and Congregationalists were among the groups forming the United Church of Canada. The rest remained separate down to the formation of the Evangelical United Brethren Church. When prospects for a merger with American Methodists became lively, Canadian Evangelical United Brethren had to choose between a Canadian or American oriented union. They chose the former, and in January, 1968, the Canada Conference became part of the United Church of Canada.

In the United States, formal discussions between The Methodist Church and the Evangelical United Brethren Church began in 1956. They were certainly not the first. Besides the repeated contacts of Francis Asbury with William Otterbein, Martin Boehm, and others, there had been negotiations or discussions in 1809–14, 1829,

1867–71, 1903–17, 1946, and 1949.[1] The first meeting of the joint commission, however, took place in Cincinnati, March 6-7, 1958. It opened the way to active planning for merger. When this recommendation was reported to the EUB General Conference in 1958 and the Methodist General Conference of 1960, two decisions were made: first, both churches formally agreed to proceed with a plan of union; and second, Methodists dropped discussions with the Episcopalians. This decision was one of the most significant because it meant that, for the time being at least, Methodism at a fork in the road chose the way more congenial to its Pietist than to its Anglican heritage.

As discussion continued through the 1960s, it became clear that even the best of intentions and good will could not ignore several very difficult problems. One was size. Eight hundred thousand Evangelical United Brethren could easily be lost in ten million Methodists. The logistics of mutual adjustment of 4,331 EUB churches, 7 colleges, 2 seminaries, 2 publishing houses, and 10 homes with the much larger number of Methodist institutions was sufficient to give even the most efficient administrator a headache. Another problem, of legal and psychological if not substantial significance, was a name for the new church. In practical terms this meant getting rid of adjectives. A third problem was the nature of the episcopacy. All the components had bishops, but the definition of the office varied. Among the Evangelical United Brethren, bishops had less actual power and were elected for four-year terms, compared with the Asburian tradition and life tenure of Methodist bishops. All agreed that the episcopacy was an office, not a third order, and that doctrines of formal apostolic succession were more or less irrelevant. A fourth problem was the place of the district superintendent—whether he is the appointee of the bishop or the representative of the annual conference. Charles Parlin, a leading layman, described this as "the most troublesome item which confronted the Joint Commission." In Methodism the district superintendent was appointed by the bishop for a six-year term. He was elected by the EUB Annual Conference for a four-year term with the possibility of reelection. A fifth problem was the number of orders in the ministry. The unitary concept of the United Brethren had carried over into the Evangelical United Brethren, but the Methodists had inherited a twofold order, deacon and elder.

There was a further problem which, unlike the others, was not even faced in the negotiating sessions: theology. That became an immediate problem only after unification, when The United Methodist

[1] See Paul F. Blankenship, "The History of Negotiations for Union between Methodists and Non-Methodists in the United States," (Diss., Northwestern, 1965).

Church belatedly began to ask itself what were its doctrinal standards. All American religious institutions exhibited what has been called a cultural lag in theology, but some more than others. For various reasons the Methodist Episcopal Church had been able to assimilate the new influences which dated from the work of Friedrich Schleiermacher in the early nineteenth century. In spite of their German cultural background, the pietistically inclined United Brethren and Evangelicals were less successful. The relative isolation and caution characteristic of small groups affected them. Hence, they were subject to a greater cultural shock from the impact of twentieth century thought, including the Barthian movement. On the other hand, whereas the Methodists had persisted in the anomaly of adhering to Wesleyan doctrinal standards without knowing what those standards were and had in the Articles of Religion a very much dated statement which was not even particularly Wesleyan, the Evangelical United Brethren had updated their confession of faith in 1962. One of the most significant theological variants was the background in Lutheran and Reformed theology. There was nothing like the Heidelberg Confession in the immediate Wesleyan tradition, although all of the strands, of course, sprang from the fountain of the Reformation. Although all groups affirmed the biblical standard, Evangelicals especially tended toward a more literalistic approach. They were also more emphatic in their adherence to that form of sanctification characteristic of the holiness movement. This item of faith was substantially modified in the new confession of faith accepted by the Evangelical United Brethren. It brought into United Methodism a special Wesleyan emphasis which the Articles of Religion lacked.

During the discussions of the 1960s the Evangelical United Brethren participated with good will, but considerable uneasiness. In the Northwest, especially, opposition developed. There was understandable grumbling about Methodist bandwagons. Relations to union churches in Africa, Asia, and Latin America were out of alignment, as were university campus ministries. In recognition of the heavy imbalance of numbers, plans were made for the temporary continuation of certain EUB forms and double representation for a period of years. In 1963, for the first time the issue of the Methodist Central Jurisdiction was raised openly, by a group of EUB ministers and the faculty of Evangelical Theological Seminary. In the final plan the Central Jurisdiction was not to be a part of the merged church, and a time limit was to be set for its dissolution.

Before union could take place, several problems, some of them only indirectly related to the specific plan of union, had to be dealt with.

That was part of the responsibility of the parallel meetings of the general conferences in Chicago in early November, 1966. The General Conference of the Evangelical United Brethren met in one room of the Conrad Hilton Hotel, while a special adjourned session of the Methodist General Conference met in a nearby room. A complex series of moves and responses took place, in the course of which the two bodies, meeting separately but in close contact, reacted to one another's pressures. A vigorous minority of Evangelical United Brethren opposed the project for union as a betrayal of the old tradition, as unacceptable compromise with secular and social radicalism, as hopeless absorption of a small church by a very large one, or as a combination of all these. Another group was acutely concerned about crucial issues of episcopacy, district superintendency, and black segregation. The majority believed that the ideal of unity and the advantages of union were worth fighting for in the expectation that a new church could more effectively work for Christian ideals. Methodist ideas on episcopacy and district superintendency prevailed. At the same time, powerful pressures were brought to secure a firmer commitment on racial desegregation. As it turned out in political maneuvering between extremes, the setting of a target date of 1972 for elimination of segregated structures was an acceptable compromise. Four black annual conferences had already been integrated into white conferences, and the expectation was that those remaining (twelve in the Southeastern and South Central Jurisdictions) would be wound up by the target date. As the final votes were taken, Methodists approved 749 to 40 and Evangelical United Brethren, 325 to 88. With two-thirds needed the EUB annual conferences gave 70 percent and the Methodists, 87 percent.

At the constituting general conference in Dallas, April 23, 1968, The United Methodist Church came into being. Bishops Reuben H. Miller and Lloyd C. Wicke joined hands; and after them, representatives of the entire people, 10,289,000 Methodists and 738,000 Evangelical United Brethren.

That general conference, after high moments of spiritual exaltation, set itself to struggle with an accumulation of problems, each of which created tensions which threatened to become divisive. In addition to a huge appropriation of 25 million dollars for World Service, the conference approved a quadrennial emphasis for relief and renewal amounting to another 20 million dollars. It accepted churchwide responsibility for ministerial education in the seminaries. It authorized autonomous status for twenty-eight overseas annual conferences in fourteen countries. It decided to investigate the operation of The United Methodist Publishing House in matters of employment and race relations. It supported the Board of Missions in withdrawing investment funds from a New York bank in protest against involvement in racial prejudice in South Africa. It established a new Commission on Religion and Race. It passed a resolution in limited support of nonviolent civil disobedience. All this added up to a promise of lively times for the new United Methodist Church, embarked on stormy seas over which it had very little control.

The United Methodist Church

The issues which occasioned debate in the process of merger were the relatively small residue of historic differences between the denominations, which all along had much in common. The new church represented this massive common heritage, which was able to overcome most of the lingering differences. Nevertheless, a price is almost always exacted for a major advance. In this case a regionally centered minority of Evangelical United Brethren in the Pacific Northwest was adamant in opposition and broke off. On both sides some who approved of merger did so with uneasy minds, acutely aware of the imperfections characteristic of human inventions. Evidences of incomplete union would persist in many areas, and differences in ethical and theological outlook would become more visible; but The United Methodist Church went to work.

By the end of the 1960s it had become a heavily urbanized institution, like most other forms of American society. The episcopal address to the General Conference of 1968 cried, "The city, the place so many shun or curse. The city, the place over which He wept. The place where He died! The city, the testing plot for the Gospel." By 1960, 70 percent of the membership of The Methodist Church lived in urban areas.[2] Ten years later the percentage was considerably higher. At the same time the startling increase in population brought ever larger numbers of people together in the cities which were bursting their seams. The results in terms of social problems and violence belong to the history of the most tumultuous decade in the history of the nation. Because it was large, even more because it was spread everywhere, The United Methodist Church was caught in the maelstrom. Union with the Evangelical United Brethren only underlined the involvement; for however great was the urban expression, Methodists could never forget or abandon that decreasing minority, the rural dwellers, among whom Evangelical United Brethren as well

[2] Robert L. Wilson and Alan K. Waltz, *The Methodist Church in Urban America, A Fact Book* (1962), 8. *JGC*, 1968, 227.

as Methodists had long and effectively ministered. Town and country commissions were needed, as well as commissions on urban life. During the national and global conflicts which rose in crescendo toward the end of the 1960s, the church tried, sometimes with an air of desperation, to devise ways of dealing with the problems of society which inevitably became problems of Christians in the churches. The decade became an era of social activism as the more intellectual concerns of theology were shunted, for the time being, off to the side. Leaders of the church were made aware, sometimes rudely, of the diversity which existed within the huge entity of The United Methodist Church. At last minority groups of all sorts, some racial, some national, some social, found a voice and made their presence and influence known. Old assumptions about the unity of Protestant expression had to be revised. Pluralism became a fact of United Methodist life as well as of the nation.

This development became evident in the second general conference held in 1972 in Atlanta, which undertook a major realignment of direction and structure. One of the important matters left unresolved from the union was that of doctrinal standards. For four years a special commission had worked on a new formulation of doctrinal standards and had come to two basic conclusions: (1) that the times were not favorable to a new formal confession of faith, (2) that guidelines for theological interpretation were very important in an age of theological transition. Following sections reviewing the history of the development of doctrine among Methodists and Evangelical United Brethren and analyzing the Methodist articles of religion and general rules and the EUB confession of faith, a substantial statement offered four guidelines within which Methodist theology might properly develop: Scripture, tradition, experience, and reason—all four firmly rooted in the Wesleyan teaching. Not one approach but several would be encouraged, providing "theological pluralism" and allowing expression of minority and other viewpoints. "Since these aspirations are inherent elements in God's original design for his creation, we cannot resent or deny the positive objectives these theologies espouse nor withhold support from their practical implementation."

A moderate but extensive restructuring of the agencies of the church was also approved. At the center was established a Council on Ministries composed of 118 representatives of different elements of the membership of the church, including lay men, lay women, clergy, and recognized minority groups. It was designed to provide continuing authoritative leadership, along with the Council of Bishops, in the intervals between general conferences. Major agencies in the new

structure were Global Ministries (former Missions, Health and Welfare, Ecumenical Affairs), Discipleship (former Evangelism, Laity,
part of Education, and Worship), Higher Education and Ministry,
Council on Finance and Administration, and a new Board of Church
and Society. Other agencies remained without great change. A new
Commission on the Status and Role of Women was established, which
set up headquarters in Evanston, Illinois. It grew out of the work of a
study commission on the role of women in the church recommended
by the Woman's Division of The Methodist Church and established by
the General Conference of 1968, through the efforts of the Methodist
Women's Caucus established a little earlier, and with the support of
the Board of Christian Social Relations.

Other actions included the much-debated new statement of social
principles designed to update and correlate previous social creeds. It
gave vigorous support for birth control and limitation of population
growth, as well as cautious approval to abortion and remarriage of
divorced persons under certain circumstances. The support for conscientious objectors was extended to include opposition to particular
wars. More explicit approval was given to the struggle for racial and
social justice, as expressed by the efforts of minority groups.

Other specific measures taken by the general conference included
setting a mandatory date (July 1, 1973) for the dissolution of remaining segregated annual conferences (four black and seven white conferences in the South). For the first time American Indian delegates
from the provisional Oklahoma Indian Conference were seated with
voice, but without vote, as were a few youth representatives. Looking
to the future, the conference designated the Bishops' call for peace
and the self-development of peoples as the quadrennial emphasis. It
also approved an immense budget totaling 47,800,000 dollars each
year for general programs of the church. Consent was given for
continued self-determination of minority groups which receive support through the Commission on Religion and Race. Hard realities of
current financial stringency were recognized in tighter budgets for
some activities, although the total exceeded the amounts received
yearly in the previous quadrennium. During the general conference,
organized caucuses of Hispanic Americans and Asian Americans
joined the Black Caucus in advancing their special interests.

Diversity in United Methodism

One of the most significant features of the recent history of United
Methodism was the rise of self-conscious caucuses designed to prom-

ote the interests of minority groups within the church. There were the black Methodists, Hispanic American Methodists, Asian Methodists, and women Methodists. Waiting in the wings were American Indians and a number of ethnic groups who had decided long ago that their best interests would be served by merger with the predominant structures of the church. In addition, one might mention various age groupings, especially youth.

By far the most influential caucus group has been the Black Methodists for Church Renewal, which was formally organized in 1968 at the First National Conference of Negro Methodists in Cincinnati.[3] It came into being as a consequence of the national upheaval over civil rights for black citizens, often associated with the Supreme Court decision of May 17, 1954 against segregation in education. The first Methodist agency to hail the landmark decision was the Women's Division of Christian Service, which has a long record of social awareness. Although in some local situations Methodists were involved in projects designed to obstruct implementation of the decision, the main efforts were in support. Methodists were active in Montgomery in 1955, in 1957 in Little Rock, and in 1963 in Birmingham. In the latter case, however, Martin Luther King's famous "Letter from Birmingham Jail" was elicited by a criticism of his tactics signed by eight Alabama ministers including two Methodist bishops. He expressed disappointment at the slowness of the churches—all churches—in responding to the social crises of the day. "So here we are moving toward the exit of the twentieth century with a religious community largely adjusted to the status quo, standing as a tail light behind other community agencies rather than a headlight leading men to higher levels of justice." He still retained his hope in the responsibility of his fellow Christians to work for social justice, the contemporary equivalent of a cup of water for a thirsty man. The public campaign for desegregation had its ramifications for The Methodist Church, as pressures rose for abolition of the Central Jurisdiction. In 1955 the South Carolina Annual Conference of the Central Jurisdiction passed a resolution which included: "We believe that the Central Jurisdiction is a moral sin on the part of The Methodist Church and an insult to its 350,000 Negro members." [4] As we have seen, it was abolished.

Black Methodists for Church Renewal held its second conference in

---

[3] I have had the use of numerous documents pertaining to the history of BMCR through the courtesy of Julius Del Pino, a student at Garrett Theological Seminary who has been active in the organization.

[4] Warren M. Jenkins, *Steps Along the Way* (1967), 38.

Atlanta in 1969 after the formation of The United Methodist Church. Three of the six black bishops were in attendance. Strong support was expressed for the Fund for Reconciliation which had been authorized by the general conference, for the Black Community Developers program, and for the strengthening of black colleges. At the same time, more militant leaders agitated for separation from white churches and expulsion of all nonblack ministers from black churches. In general, however, BMCR was remarkable in its intention to work within the structure for the reform and cleansing of United Methodism. At first black church renewalists made uncritical common cause with white renewalists, but later both realized that in some ways their interests diverged. By 1970 chapters were organized in each of the jurisdictions and in many annual conferences. Already BMCR was being plagued with a multiplication of competing agencies, each seeking to serve the interests of black church renewal.[5] Some participants were concerned lest the organization fall into the pattern of all institutional agencies. The fifth conference, held in Philadelphia in 1972, demonstrated that the movement of BMCR had matured into something more durable. It was giving continuing support to a number of substantial projects.

Indications of change were evident in the emerging tensions within the black renewal movement caused by youth and women, and outside it by the appearance of other minority caucuses whose interests did not always coincide with the black cause. Blacks had to share the minority stage with Asians, Hispanic Americans, American Indians, other ethnic groups, and—not least—women. At the general conference in Atlanta several minority caucuses claimed attention. Probably the most potent of all the new voices was that representing women in Methodism, the only minority group which was actually a majority. Along with the women's service agencies, which for a long time had given women an independent voice in the affairs of the church, a new caucus movement embodied the current crusade for women's rights in society generally and sought to bring this to the attention of the church. It looked as if the day of the Methodist woman as a sort of second-class church member was almost gone. Establishment of a new Commission on the Status and Role of Women acknowledged this force. At long last the proposal made in 1880 to cleanse the *Discipline* of the traditional language of sex discrimination was adopted. More and more women began to enter all levels of church life, including the ordained ministry. These specific victories, however, did not mean the end of the struggle for women's rights in and out of the church.

[5] See Cain Felder's Progress Report for 1971.

The little company of people like Mrs. Porter Brown, Georgia Hark-ness, Theressa Hoover, and Glora Wysner was increasing.

At the same time Hispanic Americans, who had a long history as an autonomous group within Methodism, found a new voice and de-manded representation befitting their status as a full annual confer-ence (Rio Grande) in the South Central Jurisdiction. There are, of course, other concentrations of Hispanic Americans in large cities. Illustrative of the new vigor in south Texas is the statement of pur-pose for the Good Neighbor Settlement House in Brownsville, Texas:

> The Good Neighbor Settlement is an agency of social concern committed to the development of its neighborhood. It operates on the belief that a neighborhood organized around its own interest can do much to en-hance personal dignity of the individual and restore the democratic principle of self-determination.
>   Our philosophy is that this type of agency represents one of the important efforts of the church to witness to its love and concern for the people of our community. The center by its very commitment can help the church-at-large to maintain a sensitivity to, an awareness of, and an involvement in processes of social change.[6]

In implementation of this program, some leaders in the Rio Grande Conference have been personally active in the new political move-ment, La Rasa Unida, which seeks to give Hispanic Americans a political voice. As stated by Arturo Mariscal, director of the settlement house, this means action in two directions: "direct service" and "social action," the latter designed "to change cruelty systems." Roy D. Bar-ton, director of the Rio Grande Program Council, explained in an interview in 1972 that although the Hispanic-American Methodists of south Texas and New Mexico desire more open relations with their "Anglo" associates, they have no desire to abandon their ethnic con-ference and lose their cultural identity. This trend is clearly evident in the recent organization of *Metodistas Asociados Representando la Causa de los Hispano Americanos* (MARCHA, "Methodists Associated Repres-enting the Cause of the Hispanic Americans"), which held a national consultation in El Paso, Texas, April 30–May 2, 1971. Related to the Commission on Religion and Race, it addressed itself to social issues which bring persons of various Latin American backgrounds to-gether. It represents a resurgence of the ethnic and cultural diversity of American life in the later twentieth century.

Asians and American Indians have also been heard from within the

[6] "Su Buen Amigo, Good Neighbor Settlement House, Fiesta 72," prepared by Arturo Mariscal. This publication puts into the hands of the people the policy of the Board of Missions which is quoted here.

structure of United Methodism. Both were present in organized caucuses and in less structured form at the General Conference of 1972. Japanese Methodists formerly had a provisional annual conference of their own on the Pacific Coast, but decided recently to merge with the geographical conferences where they resided. They are increasingly aware, however, of their cultural history as a minority expression within Methodism. Thus the story which began with Kanichi Miyama in 1887 may become more important in the future as Japanese Methodists seek to recover their heritage. Both northern and southern churches had Japanese missions, which with union became the Pacific Japanese Provisional Annual Conference until it merged with the California-Nevada Conference in 1964. For the last fifteen years Taro Goto was superintendent, the first Japanese to serve in that capacity.[7]

Indian Methodists continue as a special annual conference in Oklahoma (and nearby areas), which has the second largest Indian population of any state in the Union. With about twelve thousand members and over seventy ministers, all of whom are Indians as are the district superintendents and most of the staff, it is one of the most influential Indian church organizations in the country. Its support comes from local United Methodist churches, Oklahoma Annual Conference specials, other conferences of the South Central Jurisdiction, the Board of Global Ministries, and private organizations. Elsewhere, work with Indians is carried on on a smaller scale, as in North Carolina, where eleven churches serve the Lumbees and two others serve the remnants of the once great Cherokee Nation in the western part of the state; in Michigan; and in New Mexico, where the Navaho Methodist Mission School in Farmington operates with a substantial budget from the national division.

As to the place of Indians in American life and culture, the church has taken a more direct interest in recent years, including research by the Department of Research and Survey of the National Division of the Board of Missions. United Methodist leaders have joined other Americans, including Indians themselves, in seeking a way of providing tribes on the reservation as well as individuals living independently in city and country the advantages of modern culture without depriving them of their own cultural heritage.

With this acknowledgment of diversity The United Methodist Church takes its place as one of the many aspects of ecumenical Christianity.

[7] Data through courtesy of Lester E. Suzuki, Berkeley, California.

Chapter 38
Denominationalism and Christian Unity

At the end of this history we return to one of the main themes set by John Wesley: the catholicity of Methodism. "Methodism, so called," he wrote in Sermon fifty-five, "is the old religion, the religion of the Bible, the religion of the primitive Church, the religion of the Church of England, . . . of the whole Church in the purest ages." Even though he believed the Anglican church to possess the best and the richest Christian tradition, he admitted in the sermon "On the Church," "I cannot exclude from the church catholic, all those congregations in which any unscriptural doctrines . . . are sometimes, yea, frequently preached; neither all those congregations in which the sacraments are not 'duly administered.'" In a similar vein William Otterbein and Jacob Albright strove to avoid identification of their movements with a new church or sect. Wesley more consciously associated his views with the precedent of the early church Fathers, whereas the founders of the Evangelical Association and the United Brethren took their inspiration from pietist antecedents. They all came together, however, in a truly catholic concept of the church. The theme to be elucidated in this concluding essay, then, is the bearing of the Wesleyan view on denominationalism on the one hand and ecumenicity on the other. The destiny of United Methodism in the next hundred years is bound up in that theme.

Latent Potentialities

In addition to The United Methodist Church, one list of denominations whose name includes the word *Methodist* contains twenty bodies, ranging from the large African Methodist Episcopal Church to exceedingly small sects. This does not take account of the many others, like the Church of the Nazarene, which are derived in whole or in part from the Methodist movement, but have given up the designation. The point is that Methodism is not yet united, in spite of the title of the largest body. In fact, the *United* comes in acknowledgment of the Evangelical *United* Brethren tradition. Even at the level of denominational merger within the family there are still many possibilities. Some conversations are continuing.

437

Beyond that, however, over the years several other lines of discussion have been carried on outside the immediate family, particularly with the Presbyterians and the Episcopalians. These negotiations are certainly latent at present, but they are not necessarily moribund. In the years 1928 to 1932, conversations were carried on between the Methodist Episcopal Church and the Presbyterian Church. Although the conclusion was that organic union was not yet feasible, the discussions proceeded amicably and helped facilitate the development of the Consultation on Church Union many years later. Then, in the 1940s, earlier occasional discussions with the Protestant Episcopal Church gathered steam as efforts were made to find a means of intercommunion acceptable to both churches. Bishop Ivan Lee Holt was especially active in the several conferences held between 1948 and 1960. Interest in this line of experiment faltered partly as a result of the failure of Lambuth Conference in 1958 to ratify a plan and partly because of the revival of conversations between the Methodists and the Evangelical United Brethren. Methodists, as it were, turned from one conversation with one friend to another with another friend, who did not really know one another except through the Methodists. It was clearly not a case of "the friend of my friend is my friend."

Since 1960, the ecumenical interests of several large American churches, including all of those involved in the earlier discussions, have been caught up in the Consultation on Church Union, an effort toward larger church union in the United States. At this writing the plan is certainly latent, and at least in major aspects probably moribund.

World Methodism

All the time that these specific negotiations were proceeding with other denominations, The United Methodist Church and its antecedents were moving toward a global concept of family life. This was especially true of the Methodist Church. Two characteristic expressions of global relationships in the latter part of the twentieth century were the World Methodist Council and the Commission on Structure of Methodism Outside the United States (COSMOS). The former derives from the series of Ecumenical Methodist conferences which began in London in 1881 and continued every ten years thereafter until World War II, which disrupted the sequence. A conference was held in 1947 and again in 1951, and then every five years thereafter. At the eighth conference in 1951 the name World Methodist Council was chosen, with a permanent organization of an executive committee and executive headquarters in Lake Junaluska, North Carolina. Recently, another headquarters has been established in Geneva, Switzerland.

Over the years various types of Methodist organizations have affiliated with the council, the members differing in the degree of independence or autonomy from parent organizations. In 1972 there were fifty-four member groups, of which The United Methodist Church was one. In addition to the quinquennial conferences, activities have included publication of *World Parish*, several books, and a series of Oxford Theological Institutes. It was instrumental in choosing observers for the Second Vatican Council. Some of the members are central conferences with ties to The United Methodist Church. Others are autonomous churches, and still others have grown into full independence. Some are fully Methodist and others are products of various union movements. Some are derived directly from the Wesleyan movement of the eighteenth century, such as the Methodist Church in Great Britain, The United Methodist Church in the United States, and the Methodist Church in Australia. The black Methodist churches of the United States, the Free Methodist Church, and the Wesleyan Church are all members.

COSMOS, an agency of The United Methodist Church, has had responsibility for planning the changes in structure of overseas Methodism which originated from missionary work. Development of central conferences, autonomous churches, and independent or union churches came under its advisory jurisdiction. It was formed by the General Conference of 1948 to study the problems of overseas structure and make recommendations. After 1964 its work accelerated to a rapid pace as more and more regional entities sought autonomy or independence. That COSMOS was favorably disposed to the process is clear from the statement of 1963:

> We recommend that each annual conference and, where applicable, the Central Conferences of the Methodist Churches in Asia, which are not already autonomous or in United Church structures, undertake immediately to study the desirability of the Methodist Church in the area becoming autonomous. . . . Annual Conferences are urged to study the form of autonomy best suited to the Church in the area, including the formation of United Churches.[1]

The implications of this statement are enormous as a judgment on the direction of the Christian world mission. Behind it is the entire massive alteration of global history which is bringing new life and power to the non-Western portions of earth. A world conference, held by

[1] Data in typescript from the Commission, Asia Consultation, 1963.

COSMOS in 1966 in Green Lake, Wisconsin, reaffirmed the intention to decentralize controls over the widespread harvest of Methodist missionary enterprise. Another was held in 1970.

Finally, the General Conference of 1972 approved a recommendation submitted jointly by COSMOS and the World Methodist Council, which would vest in the restructured council chief responsibility for liaison with the many autonomous Methodist and United churches, along with all of the older Methodist bodies which did not derive from United Methodist missions. With that action COSMOS as such ceased.

Ecumenical Methodism

Although the plan of uniting all the Methodists of the world (paralleled by several other global confessional bodies like the Lutherans and the Baptists) was one kind of ecumenical venture, it appeared sometimes to run competition with another approach which sought to break down denominational barriers. Methodists, Evangelicals, and United Brethren had long cooperated in the many projects for interdenominational cooperation which stopped short of organic union: the Federal Council of Churches and its successor the National Council of Churches, the International Missionary Council, and several specialized agencies such as the Commission on Chaplains, Religion in American Life, and professional organizations like the International Council on Religious Education. They were involved in almost all of the cooperative efforts to bring relief to the many forms of suffering in the world, whether of natural or man-made causes.

Beyond that, United Methodism has been active from the start in the processes that led to the formation of the World Council of Churches in 1948. Bishop G. Bromley Oxnam was one of the presidents of the council, as were Charles C. Parlin and D. T. Niles of Ceylon, fitting successors to that perennial ecumenical Methodist, John R. Mott. The election in 1972 of Philip A. Potter, of Dominica in the Caribbean, as general secretary of the WCC continues Methodist presence. Methodists were more influential in the International Missionary Council than they were in the Life and Work movement and the Faith and Order movement. As to the latter, until recently Methodists might be described, to use Bishop William R. Cannon's phrase, as "the great proletariat of ecumenicity." They had not yet found a clear *Wesleyan* voice. The revival of Wesleyan theology, however, has helped to correct the deficiency. The understanding of theology as primarily a definition of the royal road of salvation; of synergistic cooperation of man and God in the process, "Working Out

Your Own Salvation" by prevenient grace; of the fruits of faith in holy living carried on to Christian perfection through the perfect love of God; and of assurance of forgiveness welling up in the joy of the gospel—these are some of the emphases which may take on livelier significance in an ecumenical context than they sometimes have within Methodism. When the World Council of Churches came into being, not only the Methodist Church, but also Evangelical United Brethren, the African Methodist Episcopal Church, the A.M.E. Zion Church, the Christian Methodist Episcopal Church, and several other Methodist-related bodies were among the founders.

Closer to home is the work of the recently established Commission on Ecumenical Affairs, which has helped guide the church in its negotiations in the Consultation on Church Union and which is given responsibility for coordinating all of the ecumenical ventures of The United Methodist Church. The commission was established by the General Conference of 1964 with representatives from the Council of Bishops, the seminaries, and several church agencies; with a general secretary, Robert W. Huston and headquarters in Evanston, Illinois. The commission was active in negotiations leading to merger with the Evangelical United Brethren in 1968, in preparation of a policy statement on Christian unity adopted by the General Conference of 1968, and in formulation of a statement on Jewish Christian relations adopted by the General Conference of 1972. Huston has participated regularly in the discussions of the Consultation on Church Union. In the 1972 General Conference the commission became the Division on Ecumenical and Interreligious Concerns of the Board of Global Ministries with headquarters in New York. Recently new emphases have included development of dialogue with other world religions and realignment of financial participation by The United Methodist Church in ecumenical activities.

As we come in this history to what can be no more than a conclusion for the time being, we may seek once more for the main channels, the directions which give significance to all the details. Those channels mentioned at the beginning have been sufficiently illustrated: revival, westward movement, social process, metamorphosed theology, Americanization, and the many diversities caused by the tensions between authority and freedom, between isolated independence and involvement in the Atlantic community, and between racial and ethnic and social variants. The result has been a rich pluralism which earlier interpreters tended to overlook as they concentrated on one aspect regarded as the mainstream.

That pluralism has brought out defects and failures which could be ignored or covered up in the mainstream approach. The story we have had to tell includes failures as well as victories, conflict as well as reconciliation, pain as well as pleasure. In theological terms it includes sin as well as saintliness. Both belong in an honest history of Christianity. Perhaps the hurts and wounds, which are a part of the history of Wesley's heirs, fall into perspective along one of the principal channels: the tension between discipline and democracy, between magistrates and mavericks. Yes, American Methodism has had its share of troublemakers, sometimes reckless rebels who have done far more harm than good. But it also has had its authoritarian powers, who drove the rebels into their excesses. William Gladstone understood this when he wrote: "There are civil cases when, though we may not be able to say the rebel is in the right, yet we can clearly see that the possessor of power, who drove him to be a rebel, is far more profoundly in the wrong." [2] A more theological way of saying it comes from the pen of John Cotton, one of the Puritan forefathers who instilled in John Adams and even Thomas Jefferson a healthy respect for the power of sin in human affairs: "There is a straine in a mans heart that will sometime or other runne out to excesse, unlesse the Lord restraine it, but it is not good to venture it: It is necessary therefore, that all power that is on earth be limited, Church-power or other: If there be power given to speak great things, then look for great blasphemies, look for a licentious abuse of it." [3]

American Methodism and its relatives have all exhibited excess from time to time. Perhaps blasphemies have been uttered. In all this, however, if the church has not always been Christian, it has always been human. And it is a human tale we have to tell. Here you have it, in the flesh, warts and all. When something more breaks through, as it frequently does, some current derived beyond the channels of history, some powerful wind irresistible even though unseen, then those who are called to ride these channels may be grateful.

The endurance of the Methodist heritage does not depend, at last, on the perseverance of any particular denominational form. If a generation should come to whom is given the high privilege of witnessing the reunion of all of Jesus' followers in one church, then their children can be counted on to seek out the sources and springs that made that ecumenical sea and claim them for their own. And Wesley *redivivus* would rejoice.

[2] Quoted (significantly) in Drinkhouse, *History of Methodist Reform*, I, 463, from Gladstone's article, "The Place of Heresy and Schism in the Modern Christian Church."

[3] John Cotton, "An Exposition Upon the Thirteenth Chapter of the Revelation (1656)," excerpted in Perry Miller and Thomas H. Johnson, *The Puritans* (rev. ed. 1963), I, 213.

INDEX

INDEX